To Chuck
for his birthday
Dec 31st, 1979

Anne and John

THE CONCISE DICTIONARY OF

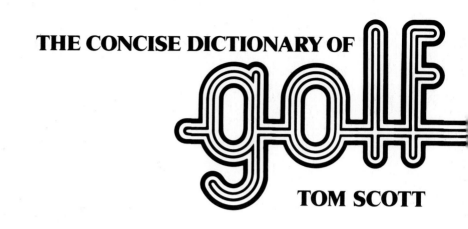

golf

TOM SCOTT

MAYFLOWER BOOKS

MAYFLOWER BOOKS, INC.,
575 LEXINGTON AVENUE,
NEW YORK CITY 10022.

 A Bison Book

THE CONCISE DICTIONARY OF
golf

TOM SCOTT

MAYFLOWER BOOKS

MAYFLOWER BOOKS, INC.,
575 LEXINGTON AVENUE,
NEW YORK CITY 10022.

A Bison Book

First published 1978 by
Mayflower Books Inc
575 Lexington Avenue
New York NY 10022

Copyright © 1978 by Bison Books, London

Produced in cooperation with Colourviews Ltd.

ISBN 0-8317-1750-5
Printed in Hong Kong

contents

players

AARON, Tommy – *born Gainesville, Georgia, USA, 22 February 1937*
This bespectacled Southerner's outstanding achievement was his US Masters victory in 1973, until which he was chiefly renowned for consistency, which saw him finish among the top 50 money winners in all but one year after he turned professional in 1960. His other victories were in the 1969 Canadian Open, after a play-off against Sam Snead, and 1970 Atlanta Classic. Aaron played in 1959 Walker Cup side as an amateur and 1969 and 1973 Ryder Cup teams.

ABREU, Francisco – *born Santa Cruz, Tenerife, 30 August 1943*
Once a Greco-Roman wrestling champion, this burly Canary Islander played a significant part in Spain's rise to the top of European golf. Abreu first showed his international class when he took 1973 German Open title. In 1976 he returned a 13 below par total over Puerta de Hierro course to win Madrid Open. That year he earned over £5000 prize-money and despite restricting his appearances outside Spain, Abreu increased that to £13,000 in 1977 after five top ten finishes to finish ninth in the European Order of Merit.

ACOSTA, Ernesto – *born Mexico*
Surprise winner of World Cup individual title in the US in 1976, Acosta crossed to Europe to score top 15 finishes in Penfold PGA Championship and French Open in 1977 and was capped for the Rest of the World in Double Diamond Internationals. He finished 57th in the Order of Merit with £3200 prize-money.

ADAMS, James – *born Troon, Scotland, 21 October 1910*
Runner-up in 1936 and 1938 British Open Championships. Won many British, Irish and overseas events in late '30s, '40s and early '50s, including Irish and Ulster Professional titles and Dutch, Belgian and Italian Opens. Played in four Ryder Cups.

AHERN, Kathy – *born Pittsburgh, Pennsylvania, USA, 7 May 1949*
She turned professional at 17 and joined LPGA Tour in 1967, winning her first tournament in 1970 and two more in 1972 and pushing her official prize winnings past $100,000 by end of 1974.

ALCOTT, Amy – *born Kansas City, Missouri, USA, 22 February 1956*
This 1973 US Junior Girls' Champion, runner-up in Canadian Championship in 1974, won

over $70,000 in 1976, her second year on the proette circuit, after being voted Rookie of the Year in 1975, and looked destined for the top.

ALEXANDER, Stewart – *born Philadelphia, Pennsylvania, USA, 1918*
'Skip' Alexander's pro career was jolted when he was seriously injured in a plane crash, but he came back to add a second Ryder Cup cap in 1951. He won several events and in 1959 was awarded Ben Hogan Trophy in recognition of his triumph over injury.

ALLEN, Donald – *born USA, 1938*
New York State Amateur Champion four times, insurance salesman Allen gained first of two Walker Cup caps in 1965 after tying third in US Amateur Championship and second in North and South Championship that year.

ALLIN, Bud – *born Bremerton, Washington, USA, 13 October 1944*
A quiet, unassuming product of Brigham Young University where he played regularly with fellow student Johnny Miller, Allin, in his first full year as a pro in 1971, won Greater Greensboro Open. He added Florida Citrus title in 1973, Doral and Byron Nelson in 1974 and

Far left: The best known of the early professionals, Tom Morris Senior and Tom Morris Junior.
Below: Tommy Aaron's best performance was the winning of the 1973 Masters at Atlanta.

8

Above: Scots-born Willie Anderson was the first man to win four United States' Opens.

Pleasant Valley Classic in 1976. Prior to his golf career, Allin spent a year in Vietnam, earning four decorations as an officer. His best year was 1974 when he was ninth in the money list.

ALLISS, Percy – *born 1897*
Twice British PGA Match Play Champion in the '30s. Made three Ryder Cup appearances. Won German Open five times in eight years, Italian Open twice. Runner-up in 1931 Canadian and French Opens. Son Peter followed him to Ryder Cup honours.

ALLISS, Peter – *born Berlin, Germany, 28 February 1931*
Winner of more than 20 major events before retiring from the tournament circuit. Missed only one Ryder Cup match between 1953 and 1969 and played ten times for England in World Cup. Victories included Spanish, Italian, Portuguese and Brazilian Opens, three British PGA Close Championships and British Assistants' Championship. Was British PGA Captain in 1962 and won Vardon Trophy in 1964 and 1966.

Right: Peter Alliss, former British professional, is now a successful TV commentator.

Far right: Tommy Armour had the unique experience of playing for both Great Britain and the United States in international matches. Photo taken in 1931.

ANDERSON, Jamie – *born St Andrews, Scotland, 1842. Died 1912*
Won British Open Championships of 1877, 1878 and 1879 at Musselburgh, Prestwick and St Andrews. Worked most of his life in his native St Andrews. A notable clubmaker.

ANDERSON, Jean – *born North Berwick, Scotland, 2 May 1921*
The former Jean Donald was three times Scottish Champion and runner-up in 1948 for the British title. Won 1947 French Championship and made three Curtis Cup appearances. Represented Britain against Canada, France, Belgium and New Zealand and played for Scotland for seven straight seasons from 1947 before turning professional in 1953.

ANDERSON, Willie – *born Scotland, 1878. Died 1910*
Took the game to the USA and won US Opens of 1901, 1903, 1904 and 1905 – the first man to win championship four times. Also won Western Open, then second in importance to Open, on four occasions. Died of arteriosclerosis at the age of 32.

ANDREWS, Gene – *born USA, 1913*
Took US Public Links title in 1954 and was beaten by Jack Nicklaus in the semi-finals of 1959 US Amateur Championship and final of North and South Championship. He gained a Walker Cup cap in 1961.

ARCHER, George – *born San Francisco, California, USA, 1 October 1939*
Until 1974 the 6ft 5in tall Archer had only once finished out of the top 50 in the money list – in 1964, his first year on tour, when he was 51st. Was among the top five performers three times in the five years from 1968 and in that period only once failed to end the year with more than $100,000 earnings. Has won a dozen major titles, following an outstanding amateur career, most important being 1969 US Masters. Like many big men possesses a delicate putting touch. Slumped to total winnings of under $10,000 after a wrist operation in 1975 but bounced back to his best in 1977.

ARDA, Ben – *born Cebu City, Philippines, 1929*
Best golfer the Philippines have produced. Became a World Cup regular and his many victories include Philippines, Singapore, Indian and Malaysian Opens.

ARMOUR, Tommy – *born Edinburgh, Scotland, 24 September 1896. Died 1968*
Had the unique honour of representing Britain and Ireland as an amateur in Walker Cup in 1922 and, after emigrating, the US as a professional against Britain in 1926. Later to become one of the game's great teachers, Armour won 1927 US Open, 1930 US PGA Championship and 1931 British Open and three Canadian Open titles between 1927 and 1934. He lost an eye in World War I.

ARMSTRONG, Wally – *born New London, Connecticut, USA, 19 June 1945*
This former Collegiate All-American amateur has chalked up a succession of top ten finishes since turning pro in 1973 and has steadily improved his top 60 money list placing.

AUCHTERLONIE, Willie – *born St Andrews, Scotland, 1872. Died 1963*
Used a set of seven home made clubs to celebrate his 21st birthday in 1893 by winning British Open at Prestwick, later founding world famous club-making business in his birthplace. Was professional to Royal & Ancient Golf Club from 1935 until he died.

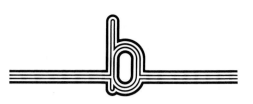

BACHLI, Douglas – *born Victoria, Australia, 2 April 1932*
British Amateur Champion 1954 and twice Australian Amateur Champion. Played regularly for his country from 1948 to 1962 and was a member of 1958 winning side in Eisenhower World Team Championships.

BAILEY, Diane – *born Wolverhampton, England, 1943*
The former Miss Robb and Mrs Frearson made a Curtis Cup comeback in 1972, ten years after her first appearance. Won English and British Girls' titles and was runner-up in British Championship in 1961 at the age of 18. Had three years as an England international and played in 1968 World Team Championship.

BAIOCCHI, Hugh – *born Johannesburg, South Africa, 17 August 1946*
This former South African amateur champion was second to Ballesteros in European order of merit in 1977. The slim six-footer won Sun Alliance PGA Match Play Championship and was runner-up in Portuguese, Scandinavian, Dutch and German Opens. He ended the year with official European prize-money of over £24,000. Baiocchi gave up an accountancy job to turn professional in 1971 at the age of 25. His first overseas victory came in 1973 Swiss Open and after several home circuit victories he took 1975 Dutch Open and 1976 Scandinavian Open. He has represented South Africa in World Cup and captained the Rest of the World in 1977 Double Diamond International in Scotland.

Left: US woman professional Debbie Austin shows her enormous power.

Below: Hugh Baiocchi is one of the most consistent of the younger South Africans.

AUSTIN, Debbie – *born Oneida, New York, USA, 1 February 1948*
She hinted at great things to come by finishing low amateur in five successive LPGA events before joining the professional ranks in 1968, having been the youngest finalist in New York State Amateur Championship at 15, and a sensational five victories in 1977 earned her $86,000 and pushed her career winnings to more than $230,000.

BAIRD, Butch – *born Chicago, Illinois, USA, 20 July 1936*
Only once since joining the tour in 1959 had Baird finished higher than 46th place in the 1976 money list, when he won San Antonio-Texas Open and tied fourth in US Open and seventh in Tournament Players' Championship. A shoulder injury handicapped him for several years.

BAKER, Vin – *born Durban, South Africa, 17 February 1946*
Winner of 1973 Benson and Hedges title and runner-up that year in South African Open, this all-round athlete was out of action for much of 1976 after a back operation, but he came back to finish joint third in 1977 Portuguese Open.

BALBUENA, Salvador – *born Torremolinos, Spain, 12 December 1949*
A club professional in Malaga, Spain, Balbuena was unknown internationally until he won 1976 Portuguese Open. He went on to finish second in French Open and ended the year in 20th place in the Order of Merit with £9000 prize-money, winning again in unofficial Moroccan Grand Prix. Top 12 finishes in 1977 Portuguese, Spanish, Italian and German Opens failed to prevent

Below: John Ball was the greatest amateur golfer of his time and was the first unpaid player to win the British Open Championship.

him slipping back to 51st in the point list. He played for Europe in 1976 Double Diamond and Hennessy Cup matches.

BALDING, Al – *born Toronto, Canada, April 1924*
Four times Canadian PGA and Match Play Champion. Highlighted US Tour career with three victories in 1957 and partnered George Knudson to victory in 1968 World Cup, finishing top individual.

BALL, John – *born Hoylake, Cheshire, England, 24 December 1861. Died 1940*
Sixth in British Open Championship while only 15. Took British Amateur title eight times between 1888 and 1912, despite spending three years fighting in the Boer War, and became first amateur and first Englishman to win Open Championship in 1890. Enjoyed a long spell as England captain.

BALLESTEROS, Manuel – *born Pedrena, Spain, 22 June 1949*
Elder brother of Severiano and a consistently successful European campaigner, finishing only once out of the top 50 since 1971 despite failing to secure a major victory. His best performances were second in 1971 Swiss Open and second in 1974 El Paraiso Open, when he lost a sudden death play-off to Peter Oosterhuis. Third in 1976 Spanish Open.

BALLESTEROS, Severiano – *born Pedrena, Spain, 9 April 1957*
'Seve' confirmed his superstar billing by finishing Europe's leading money winner for the second year running in 1977, earning around £70,000 prize-money world-wide. The handsome six-footer, a farmer's son from northern Spain, went to the top in 1976 after only two seasons on the Tour, winning Dutch Open and Lancôme Trophy event and finishing joint second with Jack Nicklaus to Johnny Miller in British Open. He finished out of the top 20 in PGA events only twice and won a record £39,500 in total. Later partnered Manuel Pinero to victory in World Cup in the US. Despite the demands of national service with the air force and a troublesome back, Ballesteros added brilliant victories in 1977 in French Open, Uniroyal International, Swiss Open and Braun International. Lost a play-off in the Lancôme event to Graham Marsh and shared second place in the Scandinavian Open and Belgium's Laurent Perrier event, and was third in Spanish Open and Colgate World Match Play Championship, beating Hale Irwin in a play-off to win £12,000. In April 1978 he became the youngest man to win an American tour title since Ray Floyd won the St Petersburg Open in 1963.

BANNERMAN, Harry – *born Aberdeen, Scotland, 5 March 1942*
Bannerman earned Scottish World Cup honours in 1967 and 1972 and a Ryder Cup place against the Americans in 1971, the year he achieved his highest placing in the Order of Merit – sixth. He won Northern Open title three times and was twice Scottish Professional Champion between 1967 and 1972.

BARBER, Jerry – *born Woodson, Illinois, USA, 25 April 1916*
Winner of seven Tour events in ten years from 1953, including 1960 Tournament of Champions and 1961 PGA Championship, Barber was America's Player of the Year in 1961, the year he captained his country's Ryder Cup team. He appeared among the top 60 money winners eight times and is a past PGA Tournament Committee chairman.

Left: Severiano Ballesteros, Europe's best professional, helped Spain to win the 1977 World Cup.

BARBER, Miller – *born Shreveport, Louisiana, USA, 31 March 1931*
Winner of over $1 million prize-money in 19 years on the pro circuit this bespectacled heavyweight with the unorthodox swing won a tournament a year from 1967 to 1974, including the eight round 1973 World Open, when a first prize of $100,000 helped him to best ever season's winnings of $184,000. His first four years on tour were so disappointing he took a club job but was persuaded to try again and won Ryder Cup recognition in 1969 and 1971. Outstanding score was a 23 under par 261 in 1971 Pheonix Open – the lowest winning aggregate on tour for 16 years.

BARBER, Sally – *born Chigwell, Essex, England, 9 April 1938*
Sister of Michael Bonallack, Mrs Barber was English Champion in 1968 and subsequently twice runner-up. After winning German Championship was ten times Essex Champion. Curtis Cup appearance in 1962. Played for England in home internationals and European team championships on nine occasions.

Below: Brian Barnes is one of Britain's leading professionals and Scotland's number 1.

BARNES, Brian – *born Addington, Surrey, England, 3 June 1945*
English-born son of Scots parents, the 6ft 2in, 210-pound Barnes took his career winnings in Europe past the £100,000 mark in 1977 when he finished sixth in the Order of Merit–his seventh successive top eight placing – to win an official £16,300. Barnes beat Jack Nicklaus twice on the last day of 1975 Ryder Cup match in America and defeated Johnny Miller 7 and 6 in Double Diamond event. Occasional verbal indiscretions have landed him several fines and reprimands. Barnes scored his first victory in 1967 Flame Lily Tournament in South Africa and his first British success in 1969 Agfacolor Tournament. He won 1970 Australian Wills Masters and his other victories include 1974 Dutch Open, 1975 French Open and 1976 Sun Alliance PGA Match Play Championship. Barnes has played in every Ryder Cup match since 1969 and represented Scotland in World Cup.

BARNES, James – *born Lelant, Cornwall, England, 1887*
Jim Barnes, a naturalized American, was three times a top six finisher before winning US Open in 1921, five years after taking US PGA title. He returned to win 1925 British Open.

BARNETT, Pam – *born Charlotte, North Carolina, USA, 2 March 1944*
A former North Carolina Champion, she joined the pro tour in 1966 and in ten years had won over $100,000 prize-money. After winning 1971 Southgate Open she tied second in US Open in 1972.

BARRIOS, Valentin – *born Madrid, Spain, 7 April 1942*
This handsome 6ft 4in Spaniard topped the Continental Order of Merit in 1967, 1969 and 1973, won 1972 Marlboro Nations Cup for Spain with Angel Gallardo and first played for Spain in World Cup in 1965. A prodigious hitter, he won Madrid and Bergamo Opens in 1971 and 1972 Algarve Open.

BARRON, Hermann – *born New York, USA, 1909*
Winner of 1942 Western Open, Barron was runner-up in 1945 Canadian Open and finished a stroke off a tie for US Open in 1946 after needing two pars to win. Gained Ryder Cup honours in 1946.

BARRY, Beth – *born Mobile, Alabama, USA, 1948*
She was beaten by one hole by Laura Baugh for US Womens title in 1971 and that year played in winning American Curtis Cup side.

BARTON, Miss Pamela – *born London, England, 4 March 1917. Died 1943*
At 19 won British and American Championships in 1936 after playing in her second Curtis

Cup match. Won French Championship in 1934 and British title again in 1939. She died aged 26 in a plane crash in Kent.

BAUGH, Laura – *born Gainesville, Florida, USA, 31 May 1955*
She joined LPGA circuit in the summer of 1973 after a distinguished amateur career in which she was National Pee-Wee five times, Junior World Champion in 1970 and US Amateur Champion in 1971 and a member of winning 1972 Curtis Cup side. She tied second in her first Tour event after heading the qualifiers at the LPGA school and a succession of high finishes had earned this stunningly attractive golfer nearly $150,000 winnings by the end of 1977.

BAYER, George – *born Bremerton, Washington, USA, 17 September 1925*
The winner of four US Tour titles, his best year was 1962 when he was placed 14th in the money list with $30,000. He finished in the top 60 for ten straight years from 1955.

BEAN, Andy – *born Lafayette, Georgia, USA, 13 March 1953*
This former All-America amateur, who joined the Tour in 1976, won his first title in Doral Eastern Open in 1977, going on to earn more than $120,000 compared with $10,000 in his rookie season. Bean turned professional after winning Eastern, Falstaff, Dixie and Western Amateur Championships and reaching semi-finals of 1975 US Amateur.

BEARD, Frank – *born Dallas, Texas, USA, 1 May 1939*
In 1969 this bespectacled six-footer won the first of two Ryder Cup caps and topped American money list with $175,000. Had won more than $100,000 the previous two years and did the same the following two years. Since then he has gradually slipped down the table. Between 1963 and 1971 won 11 tournaments, including two Tournament of Champions titles.

BECK, Dorothy – *born Cabinteely, Dublin, Eire, 1 July 1901*
Wife of former Walker cup captain John Beck, the former Dorothy Pim was Irish Champion in 1938 and four times Veterans' Champion. Completed a family double by captaining 1954 Curtis Cup team. Captained a team to South Africa in 1951.

BECK, John – *born Luton, England, 13 August 1899*
After playing in 1928 match, he was non-playing captain of the 1938 and 1947 British Walker Cup sides, steering Britain and Ireland to victory at St Andrews, Scotland, in 1938.

BEHARRELL, John – *born Solihull, England, 2 May 1938*
British Amateur Champion at the age of 18 – a record – in 1956, Beharrell won England and Britain and Ireland international honours before becoming an England selector.

BEHARRELL, Veronica – *born 1937*
As Miss Anstey she won Australian Championship, New Zealand Open Match Play Championship and Victoria State Open in 1955 at age of 18. Gained Curtis Cup honours a year later and played for and captained England in the home internationals.

Below: Child prodigy, Laura Baugh, is now a successful American woman professional.

BEMAN, Deane – *born Washington DC, USA, 22 April 1938*
Became US PGA Tour Commissioner in succession to Joe Dey in 1974 after distinguished playing career. British Amateur Champion 1959 and American Champion 1960 and 1963. Played in four successive Walker Cup sides from 1959 and four Eisenhower Trophy teams from 1960. Turned professional 1967. Won four US Tour events and was second in 1969 US Open.

BEMBRIDGE, Maurice – *born Worksop, Nottinghamshire, England, 21 February 1945*
After six seasons in which his worst placing was 19th (he was second in 1974 and third in 1971), the little Midlander crashed to 63rd in the 1976 European Order of Merit after a dramatic loss of form. But Bembridge, one of the world's most travelled campaigners, bounced back to take 30th spot in 1977. Winner of 11 major titles, including two Kenya Opens, German Open and British PGA Match and Stroke Play Championships, he equalled Augusta National course record with a 64 in 1974 US Masters and that year went on to win Britain's Piccadilly Medal, Viyella PGA Championship and Double Diamond Individual events and £12,000 prize-money, as well as winning all his matches in Japan v Britain international. A Ryder Cup and World Cup international, his best performance in 1977 was fifth place in the Swiss Open.

BENITO, Jaime – *born Madrid, Spain, 5 October 1933*
Winner of 1973 Portuguese Open and runner-up in 1965 Dutch Open, Benito was a fore-

Right: British professional, Maurice Bembridge, plays in tournaments worldwide, mostly in Australia and the Far East.

runner of Spaniards like Manuel Pinero and Severiano Ballesteros who dominated European circuit in 1976 and 1977.

BENKA, Pamela – *born Worthing, England, 17 June 1946*
As Miss Tredinnick was British and French girl champion in 1964 and played in 1966 and 1968 Curtis Cup matches.

BENKA, Peter – *born London, England, 18 September 1946*
British Youths' Champion, County Champions' Champion and leading amateur in British Open Championship in 1967, Benka added Walker Cup honours in 1969 to his England and British Boy and Youth caps.

BENTLEY, Arnold – *born Southport, England, 11 June 1911*
Winner of 1939 English Championship. Played alongside his more successful brother Harry for England in the '30s.

BENTLEY, Harry – *born Manchester, England, 13 October 1907*
Took English title three years before his brother, Arnold, in 1936 and won French, German and Italian Championships as well as making three Walker Cup appearances in the '30s. Played many times for England and was captain in 1954.

BERG, Patricia – *born Minneapolis, Minnesota, USA, 13 February 1918*
Winner of over 40 tournaments as an amateur, including US Championship. Twice a Curtis Cup cap. Turned professional in 1940 and

scored 41 Tour wins, including 1946 US Open. Twice won six events in a year and was three times leading money winner. First President of LPGA.

BERNARDINI, Roberto – *born Rome, Italy, 21 January 1944*
This husky Italian World Cup international won Swiss Open title in 1968 and 1969, Italian BP Open in 1968 and 1971, Walworth Aloyco event in 1969, Shell Trophy in 1972 and Garlenda Open in 1969 and has twice been Italian Professional Champion. Two brothers are also pros.

BERNING, Susie – *born Pasadena, California, USA, 22 July 1941*
She had won a dozen LPGA tournaments by the end of 1976, including three USGA Open Championships (1968, 1972 and 1973) and over $170,000 prize-money. First girl to attend Oklahoma State University on a golf scholarship, she turned professional in 1964 and although limiting her tour appearances for family reasons, has been consistently successful.

BERTOLACCINI, Silvia – *born Rafaela, Argentina, 30 January 1950*
Winner of 1972 Argentine National Amateur title and twice a member of her country's World Amateur Team, she turned professional in 1975 and underlined her class by finishing among top 20 money winners in 1976 with over $30,000. She was in top 12 in 1977 with $56,000 winnings.

BESSELINK, Al – *born Merchantville, New Jersey, USA, 1924*
Besselink, of Dutch ancestry, won six pro tournaments and typical of his extrovert personality was his much publicized $500 bet on himself to win 1953 Tournament of Champions, which he did.

BIES, Don – *born Cottonwood, Idaho, USA, 10 December 1937*
Success came late in life for the quiet, unassuming golfer with a love of fishing, who turned professional in 1957 but did not score his first victory until 1975 in the Sammy Davis Jr Greater Hartford Open.

BILLOWS, Ray – *born Wisconsin, USA, 1914*
Several times New York Champion, Billows was three times runner-up in US Amateur Championship and played in 1938 and 1949 Walker Cup matches.

BISGOOD, Jeanne – *born Richmond, Surrey, England, 11 August 1923*
Three times English Champion and three times a Curtis Cup international in the '50s. Non-playing Curtis Cup captain in 1970. Won Swedish, Norwegian, Italian, German and Portuguese titles and made eight appearances for England in the home internationals.

Left centre: Patty Berg was one of the early American women's tournament professionals.

BISHOP, Stanley – *born USA, 1923*
Followed a 37th hole victory over Smiley Quick in final of 1946 US Amateur Championship at Baltusrol by gaining Walker Cup honours in 1947 and 1949.

BLACKBURN, Woody – *born Pieville, Kentucky, USA, 26 July 1951*
He won 1976 Walt Disney World National Team Play Championship with fellow rookie Bill Kratzert six months after turning professional.

BLAIR, David – *born Nairn, Scotland, 25 August 1917*
Scottish Boys', Scottish and Scandinavian Champion – played in 1955 and 1961 Walker Cup matches – and regularly for his country between 1948 and 1957.

BLALOCK, Jane – *born Portsmouth, New Hampshire, USA, 19 September 1945*
This former New Hampshire and New England Champion topped $100,000 prize winnings in 1977 to take her total official earnings since turning professional in 1969 to $475,000. Her first eight years on tour brought her 16 victories. A former schoolteacher, she scored five wins in 1972 and four in 1974.

BLANCAS, Homero – *born Houston, Texas, USA, 7 March 1938*
On his first year on tour in 1965 Blancas won Mexican Open and was voted Rookie of the Year. His total prize-money was $26,000 – $5000 more than he earned in his worst year in 1976. In the early '70s he three times won around $100,000 and three victories came in that period. This former All-American amateur once scored a 55 and gained Ryder Cup honours in 1973.

BLAND, John – *born Johannesburg, South Africa, 22 September 1945*
This genial South African marked his return, after several years absence, to the European scene by finishing second in French Open in 1977, third in Madrid Open, ninth in German Open and tenth in Dutch Open, ending the summer with £5700 prize-money in 31st place in Order of Merit. Then he returned home to win first two events of new season, South African PGA Championship and Rhodesia's Victoria Falls Classic.

BOATWRIGHT, Purvis – *born Augusta, Georgia, USA, 1927*
A former Carolina Amateur and Open Champion, 'P J' became Executive Director of USGA in 1969 after ten years as Assistant on the departure of Joe Dey.

BOLT, Tommy – *born Haworth, Oklahoma, USA, 31 March 1918*
His 13 US Tour wins included US Open Championship in 1958, eight years after he joined the circuit. That was his best year. He finished seventh in the money list to earn nearly $27,000. Famed for his fiery temperament and big hitting – he was nicknamed 'Thunder' – Bolt won two Ryder Cup caps and 1969 World Seniors' title.

BOLTON, Zara – *born London, England, 16 March 1914*
After finishing runner-up in English Championship played in 1948 Curtis Cup match and was non-playing captain of 1956, 1966 and 1968 sides. Also captained England and a British Commonwealth team.

BONALLACK, Angela – *born Birchington, England, 7 April 1937*
Wife of Michael, Angela, 1955 British Girls' Champion, won two English Championships as well as Swedish, Scandinavian, German and Portuguese titles. Made six Curtis Cup appearances and played in 12 home internationals for England from 1956 before responsibilities of raising four children forced her to limit her golf.

BONALLACK, Michael, OBE – *born Chigwell, Essex, England, 31 December 1934*
Outstanding British amateur Bonallack highlighted a great career by leading Britain and Ireland to victory in Walker Cup at St Andrews

Below: Angela Bonallack, wife of the British amateur Michael Bonallack, is a champion golfer herself winning the English title twice.

in 1971 and subsequently was awarded OBE. Collected first of five British titles in 1961, the other four coming in a six-year period from 1965. Was five times English Champion in seven years from 1962 and four times English Open Stroke Play Champion. Member of seven Walker Cup sides and seven Eisenhower Trophy World Team Championship squads. Won more than 40 events in addition to major championships, was twice leading amateur in the Open, became chairman of R and A Selection Committee in 1975 and of PGA in 1976.

BOOMER, Aubrey – *born Jersey, Channel Islands, 1 November 1897*
Settled in Belgium after a spell in France but played for Britain in three Ryder Cup matches in the '20s. Won French Open five times, Dutch three times, Belgian twice and the Italian.

BOOTH, Jane – *born Whittier, California, USA, 1948*
The former Miss Bastanchory won Trans-Mississippi and National Collegiate titles before playing in US World Amateur Team of 1970 and 1970 and 1972 Curtis Cup sides.

BOROS, Julius – *born Fairfield, Connecticut, USA, 3 March 1920*
In 1950, at the age of 30, Boros gave up a career in accountancy to try his luck on the pro golf tour. Two years later he won US Open, and repeated the feat in 1963. In 1968, at the age of 48, he took US PGA title. Famed for his relaxed style of play, Boros was twice leading money winner in the '50s and has played in four Ryder Cup teams. Between 1952 and 1968 he scored 18 tour victories. Most recent win was US PGA Seniors' title, but was beaten by Ireland's Christy O'Connor for World Seniors' crown in 1977. Latterly troubled by back and hip injuries.

BOURASSA, Jocelyne – *born Quebec, Canada, 30 May 1947*
She won Canadian Open twice and was a member of Canada's World Cup winning team in 1970. New Zealand Amateur Champion in 1971, was named Pro Athlete of the Year in

Left: Michael Bonallack holds the British Amateur Championship Trophy. He won the championship five times.

18

1972, the year she turned professional. Her first five years on tour earned her $70,000 winnings.

BOUSFIELD, Ken – *born Marston Moor, Yorkshire, England, 2 October 1919*
One of Britain's most successful professionals in the '50s, Bousfield enjoyed his finest year in 1955, winning PGA Championship, German Open and PGA Match Play Championship. His other victories included 1958 Swiss and Belgian Opens and 1960 and 1961 Portuguese Opens. He was British Seniors' Champion in 1972. Bousfield was a member of six Ryder Cup teams including that which defeated the Americans at Lindrick, Yorkshire, in 1957 and played for England in Canada Cup.

BOYKIN, Gerda – *born Baden-Baden, Germany, 20 February 1938*
She was Germany's first woman pro and had to compete against the men. She joined US Tour in 1961 and has topped $100,000 in career winnings.

BOYLE, Hugh – *born Omeath, County Louth, Eire, 28 January 1936*
This England-based Irishman's tournament successes included victory in 1966 Yomiuri Open in Japan and 1966 Daks event in Britain. He won 1967 Irish Professional Championship and that year played for Britain and Ireland in Ryder Cup and Ireland in World Cup.

BRADLEY, Pat – *born Arlington, Massachusetts, USA, 24 March 1951*
Twice New Hampshire Champion in her teens, she was selected for first All-American Women's Collegiate Team in 1970. She became a professional in 1974 after winning two New England Championships and won 1975 Colgate Far East Tournament. Earnings of $84,000 in 1976 pushed her career winnings over the $100,000 mark and she collected another $78,000 in 1977.

BRADSHAW, Harry – *born Delgany, Wicklow, Eire, 9 October 1913*
Winner of Irish Professional Championship ten times, Irish Open and Dunlop Masters twice and PGA Close Championship as well as partnering Christy O'Connor to victory in 1958 World Cup in Mexico City. Bradshaw is best remembered for an incident in the 1949 British Open Championship when he played his ball out of a broken bottle where it had lodged, took 6 at a par 4, had to settle for a tie with Bobby Locke and lost the play-off.

BRADY, Michael – *born Massachusetts, USA, 1887*
One of the outstanding home-produced golfers in America in the early part of the 20th century, he was runner-up in the 1911 and 1919 US Opens, losing the latter in a play-off to Walter Hagen. He was also twice runner-up in Canadian Open and won 1917 North and South Championship.

BRAID, James – *born Elie, Fife, Scotland, 6 February 1870. Died 1950*
A member of the Great Triumvirate, with Harry Vardon and J H Taylor, which domi-

Right: Four famous veterans – left to right: Harry Vardon, Ted Ray, James Braid and J H Taylor.

nated golf for two decades before the outbreak of World War I. The first man to win Open Championship five times – a feat matched by Taylor and surpassed by Vardon. His five wins came in ten years from 1901. In nine years he won four British Match Play Championships.

BRASK, Bill – *born Annapolis, Maryland, USA, 18 December 1946*
Selected for the All-American golf team in 1967 and 1968, Brask turned professional in 1969 but after a year on the US Tour he elected to play world-wide and in 1975 won New Zealand Airlines Tournament.

BREER, Murle – *born St Petersburg, Florida, USA, 20 January 1939*
After joining US Tour in 1958 she scored her first victory in 1962 USGA Open Championship and by the end of 1976 this highly consistent professional had won more than $180,000.

BREWER, Gay – *born Middletown, Ohio, USA, 19 March 1932*
The highlight of Brewer's career was his victory in the 1967 US Masters but his biggest prize cheques have come on overseas soil – $65,000 for winning 1972 Taiheiyo Club Masters in Japan and $55,000 in both 1967 and 1968 for winning Alcan Championships in Britain. Has scored 11 US Tour victories, last of which was Canadian Open in 1972 after he had recovered from an operation.

BRITZ, Tienie – *born Johannesburg, South Africa, 14 May 1945*
This former South African PGA Champion, rated one of world's deadliest putters, bounced back to top form in 1977 by winning German Open. He led from start to finish and ended the year with £8600 prize-money in 19th place in Order of Merit. For Britz, who partnered Gary Player to third place in 1972 World Cup, it was his first success away from his home circuit.

BROOKS, Andrew – *born Lanark, Scotland, 22 December 1946*
A tall Scot, who turned professional after appearing in 1969 Walker Cup team, Brooks was a consistent performer in the early '70s, finishing in the top 50 in the Order of Merit for five straight seasons, his best being 26th in 1970 and 1974. As an amateur, represented Scotland at all levels and was undefeated in his Walker Cup match.

BROWN, Eric – *born Edinburgh, Scotland, 15 February 1925*
Once a railway stoker, Brown turned professional after winning 1946 Scottish Amateur Championship and went on to win 25 major events. They included Swiss, Italian, Irish and Portuguese Opens, Dunlop Masters and two PGA Match Play Championships. Played in

winning Britain and Ireland team in 1957 Ryder Cup and made three other appearances against the Americans, winning all his four singles encounters against Lloyd Mangrum, Jerry Barber, Tommy Bolt and Cary Middlecoff. Captained the 1969 side, which halved the match 13-all, and the 1971 squad, which put up the best ever performance in America. Was twice third in British Open Championship and shared record of 65, which was not broken until 1977 at Turnberry.

BROWN, Ken – *born Harpenden, Hertfordshire, England, 9 January 1957*
In only his second full season on Tour Brown, who stands 6ft tall but weighs under 126lb (9st) recorded five top ten finishes in Europe to win more than £8000 prize-money and earn a Ryder Cup debut against the US. Former England boy international highlighted 1977 with second place finishes in Zambian Open and Greater Manchester Open. Elected to represent his parents' country and was picked for Scotland in 1977 World Cup.

BROWN, Pete – *born Port Gibson, Missouri, USA, 2 February 1935*
Twice America's Negro National Champion, Brown's best year on US Tour was 1970 when he won Andy Williams San Diego Open and $56,000 prize-money to finish 35th in money list.

Above: Eric Brown was one of the most successful Scottish professionals. He was formerly the Scottish Amateur Champion.

Below: Pete Brown, one of the few top-class black golfers in the United States.

Top right: Jackie Burke won the US Masters in 1956 and the US PGA Championship the same year.

Right: James Bruen was a famous Irish amateur with a very unorthodox style.

BRUEN, James – *born Belfast, N Ireland, 1920. Died 1972*
Possessor of an eccentric looping swing, Bruen, one of the game's longest hitters, was 1936 British Boys' Champion. Took Irish Close and Irish Amateur titles in next two years and gained the first of his three Walker Cup caps in the victory of 1938 at the age of 18. British Amateur Champion in 1946. Wrist injury forced retirement at 31.

Top right: Jackie Burke won the US Masters in 1956 and the US PGA Championship the same year.

BRYANT, Bonnie – *born Tulare, California, USA, 5 October 1943*
Only left hander on the LPGA Tour, she did not take up golf until she was 20 but broke through to win 1974 Bill Branch Classic.

BULLA, Johnny – *born Newell, Virginia, USA, 2 June 1914*
Bulla was runner-up in 1939 and 1946 British Opens and 1949 US Masters and he had a third and fourth place finish in US Open.

BURFEINDT, Betty – *born New York City, USA, 20 July 1945*
One of the longest hitters in women's golf, she turned professional in 1969 and after surgery for thyroid trouble in 1970 has blossomed into one of the Tour's most successful campaigners, collecting over $175,000 prize-money between 1972 and 1977 and scoring a series of victories, including 1976 LPGA Championship.

BURKE, Billy – *born Connecticut, USA, 1902*
Of Lithuanian descent, his real name was Burkauskus. He had to work extra hard to win 1931 US Open at Inverness, Toledo, tying George von Elm and finally getting home by one stroke in a second 36-hole play-off after a tie in the first. North and South Champion in 1928, he played in 1931 and 1933 Ryder Cup matches.

BURKE, Jack Junior – *born Fort Worth, Texas, USA, January 1923*
US Masters and PGA Champion in 1956, when voted Player of the Year. Scored 15 US Tour victories, five in 1952. Played in four Ryder Cup sides from 1951, captaining 1957 team, and was non-playing captain 1973.

BURKEMO, Walter – *born Detroit, Michigan, USA, 1918*
Winner of 1953 US PGA Championship and twice runner-up, Burkemo was a consistent money winner on US Tour and played in 1953 Ryder Cup match.

BURNS, George – *born Brooklyn, New York, USA, 29 July 1949*
This hefty, blond six-footer turned professional after playing in 1975 Walker Cup and World Cup teams and immediately won Scandinavian Open and Ireland's Kerrygold event. He was runner-up to Jerry Pate at 1975 TPD School and on his first year on tour in 1976 finished an impressive 30th in the money list winning $85,000. He improved on that in 1977.

BURROWS, Gaylord – *born Saugor, India, 29 September 1943*
Educated and now living in America, Burrows, a professional since 1973, hinted at his potential by finishing second in 1974 Thailand Open and 1975 Hong Kong Open and fifth in Australia's Colgate Champion of Champions event in 1976. He won 1977 Indonesian Open and was runner-up in the Philippine Masters and earned over $20,000 prize-money in Asia that season. He opened 1977 British Open 69, 72, 68 to be up with the leaders but slipped to a closing 80.

BUSSELL, Alan – *born Glasgow, Scotland, 25 February 1937*
British Boys' and Youths' champion; gained Walker Cup honours in 1957 and figured in four home international series for Scotland.

BUTLER, Peter – *born Birmingham, England, 25 March 1932*
Despite restricting his tournament appearances because of a new club job and a back injury, Butler won almost £8000 in 1977, finishing joint runner-up in the Callers of Newcastle event after being involved in a play-off. Since his first win in 1959 Swallow Penfold event this former Captain of the PGA and four times Ryder Cup international has totalled 15 major victories, including 1963 Schweppes PGA Championship, 1968 French Open and 1975 Colombian Open. Butler has only twice finished out of the top 20 in the Order of Merit in the past 16 years, his highest placing being second in 1968. Career winnings top £90,000.

BYERS, Eben – *born Allegheny, Pennsylvania, USA, 1880*
After twice losing in the final Byers, a jockey-sized 5ft 4in, defeated Canadian Champion G S Lynn to win 1906 US Amateur title.

BYMAN, Bob – *born Poughkeepsie, New York, USA, 21 April 1955*
A product of Arnold Palmer's old school, Wake Forest, North Carolina, Byman failed to win his US players' card after turning professional in October, 1976, decided to tackle the European circuit instead and promptly won Scandinavian and Dutch Open titles. He was third in German Open and won almost £19,000 from only seven European outings. Byman, winner of 1972 US Junior Championship, won twice and was second three times in US mini-tour events before crossing to Europe.

CADDEN, Suzanne – *born Old Kirkpatrick, Dunbartonshire, Scotland, 8 October 1957*
Winner of 1973 World Junior Championship. Runner-up in the British and British Stroke Play Championships in 1975. Vagliano Trophy honours in 1975, Curtis Cup selection in 1976. A Scotland regular, was voted Daks Woman Golfer of the Year in 1975.

CADLE, George – *born Pineville, Kentucky, USA, 9 May 1948*
A fourth, a fifth and a ninth in US Tour events in 1976 left this former three times Kentucky amateur champion with $36,000 winnings, and he improved on that in 1977.

CALDWELL, Ian – *born London, England, 17 May 1930*
English Champion 1961, played in 1951 and 1955 Walker Cup matches, represented Britain against Europe and in the Commonwealth Tournament.

CAMPBELL, Dorothy – *born Edinburgh, Scotland, 1883. Died 1946*
The first British born golfer to win US Women's Amateur Championship and first to win the American and British Championships in the same year. That was in 1909 after she had won three Scottish Championships. Lived for 25 years on North American continent. Won British title again in 1911 and two more US Titles. Also two Canadian Opens.

CAMPBELL, Joe – *born Anderson, Indiana, USA, 1935*
After playing in 1957 Walker Cup match Campbell won three tournaments as a professional and a $50,000 hole-in-one prize before back trouble struck him in 1966.

CAMPBELL, William – *born West Virginia, USA, 5 May 1923*
Runner-up in British Championship 1954 and US Champion ten years later. North and South Champion four times and played in eight Walker Cup sides, captaining 1955 team. Won Bobby Jones Award in 1956 and captained 1968 Eisenhower Trophy side.

Above: Despite the restrictions in movement caused by the clothing of her time, Dorothy Campbell (Mrs Hurd) was a fine golfer.

Left: Bill Campbell, US amateur, appeared in eight Walker Cup matches, and in one of them as Captain.

CANIZARES, Josemaria – *born Madrid, Spain, 18 February 1947*
Winner of 1972 Lancia d'Oro event in Italy, this slim Spaniard from Madrid's Puerta de Hierro club twice finished in top 35 in the European Order of Merit between 1974 and 1977, each time winning over £6000. He represented the Continent against Britain and Ireland in 1974 and 1976 and played for Spain in 1974 World Cup.

CARNER, Jo Anne – *born Kirkland, Washington, USA, 4 April 1939*
The former Jo Anne Gunderson won US Amateur title five times between 1957 and 1968 and played in four Curtis Cup sides before turning

Above: Jo Anne Carner (formerly Gunderson) was a famous American amateur and is now a successful professional.

Far right: Joe Carr holds the British Championship Trophy he won three times.

ternational honours the year before. His best year since turning professional was 1974 when he finished 48th in Order of Merit.

CASPER, Billy – *born San Diego, California, USA, 24 June 1931*
One of America's all-time leading money winners with more than $1,600,000, who passes on a percentage of his prize-money to the Mormon Church. Has won 51 US Tour titles in 20 years, including two US Opens and a US Masters. He was leading money winner in 1966 and 1968, when he took home $205,000 after winning five tournaments. Only twice in ten years from 1966 did he fail to win more than $100,000. Casper earned the nickname 'Buffalo Bill' because of a diet which included buffalo steaks.

CAYGILL, Alex – *born Appleby, Westmorland, England, 22 August 1940*
He first came to notice by winning 1960 and 1962 British Youths' titles, and on turning professional won Assistants' Championship and Rediffusion Tournament in 1963. Caygill earned Ryder Cup recognition in 1969 after winning that year's Penfold event and tying for victory in Martini International. He won 1970 Dunlop Lusaka Open.

CERDA, Antonio – *born Argentina, 1921*
Runner-up to Britain's Max Faulkner in 1951 British Open and joint second behind Ben Hogan in 1953. Partnered Roberto de Vicenzo to victory in 1953 World Cup. Twice Argentine Open Champion and also took German, Spanish, Dutch, Italian and Jamaican Open titles.

CERDA, Antonio – *born Buenos Aires, Argentina, 24 April 1948*
Winner of 1968 Mexican Amateur Championship, 1971 Costa Rican National Amateur Championship and 1974 Mexican Tournament of Champions, Cerda joined US Tour in 1975.

professional in 1970. Has won well over $300,000 and many events, including two US Opens. Was leading money winner with six victories and $87,000 winnings and Player of the Year in 1974.

CARR, Joe – *born Dublin, Eire, 18 February 1922*
Winner of 1953, 1955 and 1960 British Amateur Championships. Was six times Irish Champion and four times Irish Open Amateur Champion. For 21 years a member of Irish international side and Walker Cup regular between 1947 and 1963. Won more than 30 titles in Ireland and was three times leading amateur in the Open. Reputation stretched across Atlantic. Won both Bobby Jones and Walter Hagen awards.

CARR, Roddy – *born Dublin, Eire, 27 October 1950*
Son of one of Ireland's most famous amateurs, Joe Carr, Roddy was a member of the side which beat the US in 1971 Walker Cup match at St Andrews, Scotland, having won Irish in-

CERRUDO, Ron – *born Palo Alto, California, USA, 4 February 1945*
A member of the 1966 US Eisenhower Trophy side and the 1967 Walker Cup side, Cerrudo joined US Tour in 1968 and won that year's Cajun Classic and 1970 San Antonio Open. His best year was 1970 when his winnings totalled $36,000.

CHAMBERS, Doris – *born Liverpool, England*
British Champion 1923, Veterans' Champion 1937, England international from 1906 to 1925. Captained British teams to South Africa and Canada in the '30s and was non-playing Curtis Cup captain in 1936 and 1948. Past President of LGU and ELGA.

CHAPMAN, Richard – *born Greenwich, Connecticut, USA, 23 March 1911*
Took US Amateur title in 1940 and after twice finishing runner-up, added the British in 1951. Also French, Italian and Canadian Champion. Played in four Walker Cup sides. Set a course record of 65 at Sunningdale, England, and carded 63 at Pinehurst, USA.

CHARLES, Bob – *born Cartenton, New Zealand, 14 March 1936*
Victory in the 1963 British Open and five US Tour wins established the former bank clerk as the world's leading left-hander. Only once between 1962, when he joined the tour, and 1972 did he finish outside the top 60 money winners,

Above: Dick Chapman won both the US and British Amateur Championships.

Left: Doris Chambers was one of the most famous British players of the first quarter of this century.

Above: Well known worldwide, left-handed New Zealand professional, Bob Charles.
Far right: Brian Barnes is one of the most popular and internationally successful professional golfers on the circuit today.

CHERRY, Don – *born Wichita Falls, Texas, USA, 1924*
Well known as a pop singer, Cherry turned professional in 1962 after winning Canadian Amateur title in 1953 and playing in two Walker Cup sides.

CHILLAS, David – *born Aberdeen, Scotland, 19 August 1953*
This husky Scot, who promised so much by winning over £7000 to take 20th place in the 1974 PGA Order of Merit while only 21 has since slipped down the table. Brother of a club professional, Chillas was also hit by injury after his fine 1974 season, when he was third in Dunlop Masters, fourth in Spanish Open and fifth in French Open.

CHRISTMAS, Martin – *born 1939*
Gained Walker Cup honours 1961 and 1963, Eisenhower Trophy place 1962. Played regularly for Britain and England until 1964.

CLARK, Clive – *born Winchester, Hampshire, England, 27 June 1945*
An outstanding amateur, Clark turned professional in 1965 following his heroic performance in the Walker Cup in America, where he holed a 30ft last green putt to halve his own and the overall match. He tied for third place in 1967 British Open and finished that year third in the Order of Merit. Played in the 1973 Ryder Cup match but cut down on his tournament appearances after becoming club professional at Sunningdale.

CLARK, Gordon – *born Northumberland, England, 15 April 1933*
Turned professional in 1974 at the age of 40 after a long and distinguished amateur career. The highlight was his victory in 1964 British Amateur Championship after being runner-up three years earlier. Made seven Home International appearances for England and played for Britain in Walker Cup and European Championships.

CLARK, Howard – *born Leeds, Yorkshire, England, 26 August 1954*
After playing in 1973 Walker Cup match Clark turned pro and broke through in 1976, winning TPD Under-25s title and finishing second in Dutch Open and Cacharel World Under-25s event to end in 22nd place in Order of Merit with more than £9000 prize-money. He made his Ryder Cup debut against the United States in 1977, in which year he won over £10,000 prize-money and finished in 16th place in the Order of Merit.

COCHRAN, Robert – *born St Louis, Missouri, USA, 1912*
Runner-up to Joe Carr at the age of 48 in 1960 British Amateur Championship. The following year made his Walker Cup debut.

his highest placing being 11th in 1967. His US winnings total $528,000. Winner of tournaments in New Zealand, Switzerland, Britain and South Africa, the lanky Charles is rated among the deadliest putters in the game.

CHEN, Chien-chung – *born Taipei, Taiwan, 1936*
Son of top teacher Chen King-shih, he has won a succession of Asian titles since turning professional in 1957, including Korean, Philippines and Indian Opens.

CHEN, Ching-po – *born Taipei, Taiwan, 1931*
For a decade he represented his country in the World Cup and his victories include Japanese and Kanto Opens and half a dozen other major Japanese events.

CHEN, King-shih – *born Taiwan, 1910*
Former caddie, widely known as 'Old Man Chen'; is one of his country's most celebrated golf coaches.

CHERIF el SAYED Cherif – *born Cairo, Egypt, 1923*
Played 13 times in World Cup and is a former Egyptian Open and Professional Champion.

Severiano Ballesteros is one of golf's superstars. Born in Spain in 1957, he has achieved success in most international tournaments. In 1977 he was Europe's leading money-winner for the second year in a row.

Above: Gaylord Burrows

Above: Manuel Ballesteros

Above: Hugh Baiocchi

Miller Barber won more than one million dollars in his 19 years of professional golf.

Above: Bobby Cole

COE, Charles – *born USA, 26 October 1923*
Twice US Amateur Champion and runner-up to Jack Nicklaus in 1959. Runner-up in the British Amateur Championship. Shared second place with Arnold Palmer a stroke behind Gary Player in 1961 US Masters. Played in five Walker Cup sides, captaining 1959 team, and in Eisenhower Trophy.

COLBERT, Jim – *born Elizabeth, New Jersey, USA, 9 March 1941*
Although he entered Kansas State University on a football scholarship, Colbert soon switched sports and since joining the Tour in 1966 he has won five US events and more than half a million dollars.

COLE, Bobby – *born Springs, South Africa, 11 May 1948*
Came to prominence by winning 1966 British Amateur Championship at the age of 18 and turned professional the following year. His many South African tournament wins include 1974 SA Open. He took World Cup individual title when South Africa won in 1974 – his best year financially on the US Tour when he totalled $59,600. Breakthrough came when he won 1977 Buick Open, his previous best being third in British Open in 1975 which was won by Tom Watson.

COLES, Neil – *born London, England, 26 September 1934*
Europe's leading prize-money winner with career earnings of more than £151,000, Coles has scored 26 major victories including three British PGA Match Play Championships. His first win was in 1961 Ballantine Tournament. Has made eight Ryder Cup appearances since 1961. An aversion to air travel has led him to concentrate his efforts in Europe. Best year financially was

1976 when he won over £20,500, £10,000 coming when he beat Gary Player and Eamonn Darcy in a play-off for Penfold PGA title.

COLLETT, Glenna – *born New Haven, Connecticut, USA, 1903*
Winner of six US Ladies' Amateur Championships between 1922 and 1935 and twice runner-up in that period, she also took two Canadian Championships as well as the French. Beaten in final of the British Championship by Joyce Wethered in 1929 and Diana Fishwick in 1930. Played in four Curtis Cup matches, three times as captain, and was non-playing captain of the side in 1950.

COLLINS, Bill – *born Meyersdale, Pennsylvania, USA, 23 September 1928*
Winner of four US Tour events between 1959 and 1962 and a Ryder Cup place in 1961, he finished eight times in the top 60 in the money list, best year being 1960 – 9th with $26,000.

COMBOY, Carol
Former Northern Champion. Curtis Cup captain 1978 after captaining England in 1975 and

1976, and Britain in 1977 in Vagliano Trophy. Served from 1976 as chairman of the English selectors.

COMPSTON, Archie – *born Penn, Wolverhampton, England, 14 January 1893. Died September 1962*
Before becoming a celebrated teacher, he enjoyed an outstanding playing career, finishing second in 1925 Open and third in 1928 to Walter Hagen, whom he had earlier crushed 18 and 17 in a challenge match. Twice British PGA Match Play Champion. Played in three Ryder Cup matches.

CONRAD, Joseph – *born San Antonio, Texas, USA, 1930*
While serving in Britain with the US Air Force in 1955 he played in his country's Walker Cup side, won the British Amateur Championship and finished top amateur in the Open. Turned professional in 1956.

COODY, Charles – *born Stamford, Texas, USA, 13 July 1937*
The tall Texan won 30 tournaments as an amateur before joining the Tour in 1963. Since

Right: Neil Coles is one of Britain's most consistently successful professionals.

then he has been a consistent top 60 money winner and victorious in three events, including 1971 US Masters. He won the World Series that year and a Ryder Cup place, and in 1973 won Britain's Wills Open and John Player Classic.

COOK, John – *born Wembley, Middlesex, England, 14 August 1949*
Winner of 1969 English Amateur Championship, Cook's victories since turning professional came in 1970 Nigerian Open and 1972 Southern Professional Championship.

COOPER, Harry – *born Leatherhead, Surrey, England, 1904*
After emigrating to America 'Lighthouse' Harry Cooper was pipped for the US Open titles of 1927 by Tommy Armour and 1936 by Tony Manero. He was among the country's top pros and wins included two in Canadian Open.

CORCORAN, Fred – *born Cambridge, Massachusetts, USA, 1905. Died 1977*
One of the professional game's best-known managers and promoters and an Executive Director of the US PGA, Corcoran, a former caddie, guided the business careers of Sam Snead, Tony Lema, Babe Zaharias and others. He helped build the men's and women's pro tours, managed four Ryder Cup teams and ran a succession of Canada (later World) Cups through the International Golf Association.

CORLETT, Elsie – *born Lytham, Lancashire, England, 2 September 1902*
Winner of English Championship and runner-up in the British in 1938. Twice played in Curtis Cup matches in the '30s and was non-playing captain in 1964. Played five times for Britain against France and 11 times for England.

CORNELIUS, Kathy – *born Boston, Massachusetts, USA, 27 October 1932*
Her US Tour victories include 1956 US Open in her first season but her career earnings of around $200,000 are sadly small, reflecting the fact that many of her most successful years came before the advent of big prize purses.

COSH, Gordon – *born Glasgow, Scotland, 26 March 1939*
Scottish Champion and runner-up in Scottish Open Amateur Stroke Play Championship 1968. Member of 1965 Walker Cup side, played for Britain in Eisenhower Trophy and Commonwealth Tournament and against Europe.

COTTON, Thomas Henry – *born Holmes Chapel, Cheshire, England, 26 January 1907*
Won 1934, 1937 and 1948 British Open Championships. Awarded MBE for services to sport in 1946. Won Belgian, French, German, Italian and Czechoslovakian Opens many times and was three times British PGA Match Play Champion. Made three Ryder Cup appearances and

twice captained Ryder sides. Turned Professional at 17 and was a full club professional at 19. More than 30 major victories including America's 1948 White Sulphur Springs event. Set many scoring records, including a 65 in 1934, which stood as an Open Championship record until 1977.

COURTNEY, Chuck – *born Minneapolis, Minnesota, USA, 11 October 1940*
Winner of 1964 St Paul Open, 1967 Puerto Rican Open and 1969 Tallahassee Open, Courtney's highest placing in the money list was 38th in 1964 and his best year financially was 1972 when he earned $52,000. His career earnings top $300,000.

COWAN, Gary – *born Kitchener, Ontario, Canada, 1938*
In 1971 Cowan became the first foreigner to win the US Amateur more than once (his first win was in 1966), and the first golfer to win the title in stroke play. He won America's North and South title in 1970 and New Zealand's Centennial Invitation event in 1971 and is a former Canadian Junior and Amateur Champion. Played in six World Cup teams.

Below: Henry Cotton, three-times winner of the British Open Championship, is considered to be one of the best British Golfers since the Triumvirate – Vardon, Taylor and Braid.

COWEN, Peter – *born Sheffield, Yorkshire, England, 7 January 1951*
Past winner of Yorkshire Professional Championship and Northern PGA Under-25s title, Cowan scored his first major win in 1976 Zambian Open.

COX, Bill OBE – *born Chalfont St Giles, Buckinghamshire, England, 18 March 1910*
Awarded OBE for services to sport in 1967. Played in 1935 and 1937 Ryder Cup sides. Established international reputation as teacher. Now retired.

COX, Wilfred – *born Brooklyn, New York, USA, 1897. Died 1969*
Cox won many tournaments in the '30s, five in 1931, including the North and South Open. He was fourth in that year's US Open, third in 1934 and fifth in 1932 and played in 1931 Ryder Cup match.

CRADDOCK, Tom – *born Malahide, Dublin, Eire, 16 December 1931*
After winning Irish Championship and Irish Open Amateur Championship in the late '50s, Craddock, capped 12 times for Ireland, earned a Walker Cup place in 1967.

CRAMPTON, Bruce – *born Sydney, Australia, 28 September 1935*
After Gary Player, Crampton has been most successful overseas competitor on US Tour, winning 15 times between 1961 and 1975, when he carried off the Vardon Trophy for the second time and became fifth of the Tour's million dollar earners. Crampton went eight straight years from 1968 with winnings in excess of $100,000, collecting $274,266 in 1973 when he won four tournaments and was second in five

others. Only Jack Nicklaus prevented him from topping earnings table. Crampton made his home in America.

CRAWFORD, Jean – *born Kansas, USA, 1939*
US Women's Amateur Champion in 1965 after beating Anne Quast in the final. Was runner-up to Jo Anne Gunderson in 1960 and to Mary Lou Dill in 1967. Played in three Curtis Cup matches and captained 1972 side.

CRAWFORD, Richard – *born El Dorado, Arkansas, USA, 28 June 1939*
Twice America's National Collegiate Champion, he joined the Tour in 1965 and his best year was 1970 when he was 51st in the money list with $46,000. His career winnings top $300,000.

CRAWLEY, Leonard – *born Nacton, Suffolk, England, 26 July 1903*
England international from 1931 until 1955 and member of four Walker Cup sides between 1932 and 1947. Won 1931 English Championship and 1934 Irish Open Amateur title.

CREAVY, Tom – *born Tuckahoe, New York, USA, 1911*
Matched Gene Sarazen's feat of winning US PGA title at the age of 20 in 1931. Confined himself to club affairs after an illness.

CREED, Clifford Ann – *born Alexandria, Louisiana, USA, 23 September 1938*
She gained Curtis Cup honours in 1962 after winning North-South and South Atlantic titles and finishing second in Southern Amateur and that year turned professional, since when she has won well over $200,000. Her 11 US Tour wins all came between 1964 and 1967.

CRENSHAW, Ben – *born Austin, Texas, USA, 11 January 1952*
His winnings in his first five years on the Tour topped half a million dollars. He went straight from winning the TPD card school by 12 strokes to win San Antonio Texas Open in 1973, then finished second in the eight-round World Open. A brilliant amateur career, in which he several times finished in the top ten in major pro events and won three NCAA Championships, earned him a World Team Trophy appearance in 1972. Finished runner-up to Jack Nicklaus in 1976 money list with $257,759 earnings after three victories and that year crossed the Atlantic to win Carrolls Irish Open.

CRITCHLEY, Diana – *born London, England, 12 April 1911*
British Champion in 1930 and twice English Champion, the former Diana Fishwick also took two British Girls' Championships and the French, German, Belgian and Dutch titles, made two Curtis Cup appearances in the '30s and was non-playing captain in 1950. Represented Britain against France four times and

Right: British amateur, Leonard Crawley, a famous all-round sportsman and later golf correspondent.

Canada twice and was an England international from 1930 to 1947.

CROSBY, Bing – *born Tacoma, Washington, USA, 1901. Died 1977*
Apart from being one of the world's greatest entertainers, singer Bing Crosby was an avid golfer. His sudden death after a game of golf at the Moraleja club, Madrid, Spain, in October, 1977, after completing a strenuous music-hall tour of Britain, was mourned by the world, but his wife Kathy said 'It would have been the way he would have wished to go.' Crosby took up golf at Lakeside in Los Angeles during 1930 when filming The King of Jazz, and a number of his successful films featured a golf scene, including *Going My Way*, for which he was awarded an Oscar. Holding at one time a handicap of 2, Crosby played in British Amateur Championship at St Andrews in 1950, and achieved a hole in one at the daunting 16th at Cypress Point. In 1936 he inaugurated Bing Crosby National Pro-Am tournament, with the proceeds going to charity, and this has become one of the most popular tournaments on the US Tour.

CRUICKSHANK, Robert – *born Grantown-on-Spey, Moray, Scotland, 1894*
After emigrating to America to turn professional he repeatedly went close to a major title. In 1923 US Open tied Bobby Jones but lost the play-off when he failed to get a par four at the last. Was second in the Championship to Sarazen in 1932 and twice 3rd later in the '30s.

CULLEN, Betsy – *born Tulsa, Oklahoma, USA, 14 August 1938*
This former Oklahoma State Champion topped $150,000 prize-money in her first 12 years on the US Tour, which she joined in 1962, three victories coming in five years from 1972.

CUMMING, George – *born Bridge of Weir, Renfrewshire, Scotland, 1879. Died 1949*
Went to Canada as a young man and was professional at Toronto GC for 50 years, teaching many top Canadian pros and amateurs, designing several courses and helping found the Canadian PGA; he was five times Captain.

CUPIT, Jack – *born Longview, Texas, USA, 1938*
First victory as a professional came in 1961 Canadian Open. He was Western Open Champion in 1962 and runner-up in US Open in 1963, tying with Julius Boros (eventual winner) and Arnold Palmer.

CURL, Rod – *born Redding, California, USA, 9 January 1943*
This threequarter Wintu Indian switched from baseball to golf at 19, turning professional in 1968. His best year was 1974 when he won Colonial National Invitation event and $120,000 in total to finish 17th in the money list.

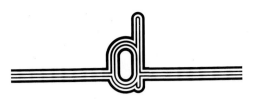

DABSON, Kim – *born Cardiff, Wales, 10 July 1952*
Runner-up in 1968 British Boys' Championship and, as a professional, in 1971 Classic International, Welshman Dabson was second once more in 1976 TPD Under-25s Championship.

DALY, Fred – *born Portrush, Northern Ireland, 11 October 1911*
Only Irishman to win British Open Championship – in 1947. Second in 1948 and twice third in subsequent years. Won Ulster Professional title 11 times, was PGA Match Play Champion three times in the space of six years in the late '40s and early '50s and made four successive Ryder Cup appearances from 1947, as well as twice playing in World Cup.

Below: Fred Daly won many championships in his extensive career. He is seen here in 1973.

Right: Irish World Cup player, Eamonn Darcy.

DAVIES, John – *born London, England, 14 February 1948*
Runner-up in both British and English Championships in 1976. Was a member of 1973, 1975 and 1977 Walker Cup sides and Eisenhower Trophy World Cup side in 1974 and 1976, when Britain and Ireland won.

DAWSON, Peter – *born Doncaster, Yorkshire, England, 9 May 1950*
In 1977 this strapping left-hander earned his first Ryder Cup cap, but he missed a chance to snatch his first major victory in the Tournament Players' Championship. Going into round four with a six stroke lead he took seven at the par four 18th to finish a stroke behind Neil Coles. A former England amateur Dawson, who won the 1975 36-holes Double Diamond individual event, finished third in Italian and Carrolls Irish Opens and was placed in the top ten in Uniroyal, Martini and Callers of Newcastle events to end 1977 season in seventh place with winnings of almost £16,000 – his best by some £10,000.

DARCY, Eamonn – *born Delgany, Dublin, Eire, 7 August 1952*
This 6ft Irishman based in Derbyshire, England, slipped down the Order of Merit in 1977, despite recording his first major victory – in the Greater Manchester Open. But illness and injuries did not stop him doing well enough to secure his second Ryder Cup appearance. Shot to prominence in 1975 when he was second to Arnold Palmer in British Penfold PGA Championship, second in French Open and third in Carrolls Irish Open, and had three other top ten finishes to end the year leading home campaigner in third place in Order of Merit with nearly £15,000 prize-money. Finished second to Severiano Ballesteros in 1976 money list with £25,000 winnings. An Irish World Cup international.

Right centre: Peter Dawson made history by being the first ever left-hander to play in Ryder Cup matches.

DARWIN, Bernard – *born Kent, England, 1876. Died 1961*
A grandson of Charles Darwin, he became the most celebrated writer about golf in the history of the game, after gaining eight England caps and playing in 1922 Walker Cup match. In 1937 was awarded the CBE for his services to sport and literature.

DASSU, Baldovino – *born Florence, Italy, 3 November 1952*
Winner of 1970 British Youths' Championship, the 6ft 2in Dassu finished third in 1971 Swiss Open, with the help of a record round of 60 at Crans-sur-Sierre, in his first professional season. In 1976 he won the last two 72-hole stroke play events of the season – Dunlop Masters and Italian Open – to push himself into ninth place in the Order of Merit and collect over £13,000 prize-money. Best performance in 1977 – third in Spanish Open.

DE BENDERN, Count John – *born 1907*
Former John de Forest. Was British Champion in 1932 and that year played for Britain and Ireland in the Walker Cup. Also won Austrian and Czechoslovakian Championships.

DeFOY, Craig – *born Pennsylvania, USA, 27 March 1947*
Born in America but taking the nationality of his Welsh father, DeFoy has several times represented Wales in the World Cup. Has recorded eight victories, five in Zambia, including two Zambian Opens, but has yet to improve on three under-25s title wins in Britain. He came closest in 1976 Sun Alliance PGA Match Play Championship, losing in the final to Brian Barnes. Finest performance was fourth place in 1971 British Open, three strokes behind winner Lee Trevino.

DEIGHTON, Dr Frank – *born Glasgow, Scotland, 21 May 1927*
Played in 1951 and 1957 Walker Cup matches, was a Scotland regular for ten years and represented Britain in the Commonwealth event and against South Africa, New Zealand and Scandinavia.

DEMARET, James – *born Texas, USA, 24 May 1910*
Won 28 US Tour events between 1935 and 1957, twice scoring five victories in one year. Took three US Masters titles between 1940 and 1950, covering the back nine in 30 strokes to win in 1940. Runner-up to Ben Hogan in 1948 US Open and won all his matches in Ryder Cups of 1947, 1949 and 1951.

DENT, Jim – *born Augusta, Georgia, USA, 11 May 1942*
One of the game's biggest hitters, Negro Dent's best year on US Tour was 1974 when he finished 59th in the money list with $48,000.

DEVLIN, Bruce – *born Armidale, Australia, 10 October 1937*
He won Australian Amateur and Open titles before turning professional and following Bruce Crampton to the US, where he settled. He has won over $700,000 and nine tournaments, including three in 1970. His best year was 1972 when he finished eighth in the money list with almost $120,000 winnings. In 1970 he partnered David Graham to victory in the World Cup. In recent years has spent more time on golf architecture.

Above: Jimmy Demaret, three times winner of the US Masters.

DEY, Joseph – *born Virginia, USA, 1907*
In 1968 he retired as Executive Director of the USGA to become Commissioner of the Tournament Players Division of the US PGA, a job he held until 1974. During 35 years with the USGA he gained a high reputation as an administrator and enhanced this with the PGA.

DICKINSON, Gardner – *born Dothan, Alabama, USA, 27 September 1927*
Won the first of eight US Tour events in 1956, four years after joining the circuit. Best year was 1968 when he was placed 16th in the money list with $73,000. He was a consistent top 60 cash winner between 1953 and 1971. Played in 1967 and 1971 Ryder Cup matches and was TPD Player Director in 1969. His career winnings top $533,000. He now concentrates on teaching.

DICKSON, Bob – *born McAlester, Oklahoma, USA, 25 January 1944*
After winning Oklahoma State amateur and open titles in 1966 the bespectacled Dickson took the British and US Amateur titles in 1967, a feat achieved previously by only three men – Harold Hilton, Bobby Jones and Lawson Little – and played in that year's Walker Cup match. He turned professional in 1968 and that year won Haig Open and $46,000 and landed Bob Jones Award. His best year was 1973 when he won Andy Williams San Diego Open and $89,000 to finish 28th in the money list.

Left centre: Bruce Devlin was originally an Australian professional but now bases himself in Florida, USA.

40

Right: Leo Diegel, the US professional with the eccentric but successful putting method.

DIEGEL, Leo – *born USA*
Twice US PGA Champion, Diegel, who adopted an unorthodox elbows out putting style, tied second in 1920 US Open and 1930 British Open and finished third in British in 1929.

DIEHL, Terry – *born Rochester, New York, USA, 9 November 1949*
After failing to qualify 17 times in his first year on the Tour in 1974 this former New York State Amateur Champion won the final event, the San Antonio Texas Open, to increase winnings of $1900 by $25,000. He tied Tom Kite in the IVB Philadelphia Classic in 1976 but lost the final play-off.

DILL, Terrance – *born Fort Worth, Texas, USA, 13 May 1939*
Among the top 60 money winners five times between 1964 and 1970, Dill's best year was 1970, when he finished 56th in the list with $41,000.

DOLEMAN, William – *born Musselburgh, Scotland, 1838. Died 1918*
One of four golfing brothers who exerted a powerful influence on the game in the second half of the 19th century, he was leading amateur in the Open Championship on nine occasions – five in succession.

DOUGLAS, Findlay – *born St Andrews, Scotland, 1874. Died 1959*
Emigrated to America in 1898 and that year won US Amateur title. Was runner-up the following two years and twice a semi-finalist. Took the US Seniors' title in 1932 after a spell as president of the USGA.

DOUGLASS, Dale – *born Wewoka, Oklahoma, USA, 5 March 1936*
Two victories in 1969 earned the 6ft 2in Douglass a place in the Ryder Cup side that fought a historic tie in Britain that year.

DRAPER, Marjorie – *born Edinburgh, Scotland, 18 June 1905*
Won the Scottish Championship, Curtis Cup place in 1954 and was Scottish international from 1929 to 1962.

DREW, Norman – *born Belfast, N. Ireland, 25 May 1932*
Played in 1953 Walker Cup match and six years later, as a professional, made his Ryder Cup appearance. In 1959 won Irish Championship, Irish Dunlop and *Yorkshire Evening News* events. Made two appearances for Ireland in Canada Cup.

DUDLEY, Edward – *born Brunswick, Georgia, USA, 1901. Died 1963*
Many times winner of Oklahoma, California, Pennsylvania and Philadelphia Opens, Dudley also took Los Angeles and Western Open titles. Played in three Ryder Cup matches. Was pro at Augusta National for 20 years and president of the USGA for six years in the '40s.

DUNCAN, Colonel Anthony, OBE – *born Cardiff, Wales, 10 December 1914*
Four times Welsh Champion and runner-up in 1939 British Championship. Made 17 appearances for Wales. Skippered 1953 Walker Cup side. Former chairman of Walker Cup Selection Committee.

DUNCAN, George – *born Oldmeldrum, Aberdeenshire, Scotland, 1893. Died 1964*
He called his Autobiography *Golf at the Gallop*, recalling his reputation for fast play. Won 1920 Open Championship with final rounds of 71, 72 after two opening 80s had left him 13 strokes off the lead, was runner-up to Walter Hagen in 1922 and won 1913 British Match Play title by beating James Braid on his own Walton Heath course in the final. Made three Ryder Cup appearances, captaining 1929 side.

DUNK, Billy – *born Gosford, New South Wales, Australia, 1938*
Winner of almost 100 tournaments, chiefly in Australia and New Zealand, Dunk has set or equalled over 50 course records at home and on trips to Malaysia, Japan and the US. He had a 60 in a 1970 Australian event. Many times a World Cup player, his titles include three Australian Professional Championships.

DUNLAP, George – *born USA*
Seven times winner of the North and South Championship following two National Collegiate title wins, he gained Walker Cup honours in 1932, 1934 and 1936. Won 1933 US

Amateur Championship, getting into the event only after a play-off.

DUNN, Willie – *born Musselburgh, Scotland, 1821. Died 1880*
Known as 'Old' Willie. Partnered twin brother Jamie in many challenge matches, the most notable being against the St Andrews pair of Old Tom Morris and Allan Robertson. Later became the first club professional at Royal Blackheath, near London.

DUNN, Willie – *born Musselburgh, Scotland, 1870, died 1952*
Son of 'Old' Willie, he won the first unofficial US Open in 1894 after crossing the Atlantic to lay out a course at Shinnecock Hills, New York, with the help of a Red Indian work force. Runner-up in the USGA Open in 1895. He pioneered steel shafts in clubs and introduced the first tee 'pegs', made of paper.

DUTRA, Olin – *born Monterey, California, USA, 1901*
Winner of 1934 US Open at Merion, he overtook Gene Sarazen with a closing 71, 72. Also won 1932 US PGA Championship, was third in 1935 US Masters and played in two Ryder Cup matches in the '30s, when he toured with Walter Hagen and had a spell as chairman of the US PGA tournament committee.

DYKES, John Morton – *born Bearsden, Scotland, 26 July 1905*
Winner of 1951 Scottish Championship. Was Walker Cup selector in the '40s and '50s after playing in the 1936 match. Made six appearances for Scotland.

EDWARDS, Danny – *born Ketchikan, Alaska, USA, 14 June 1951*
Edwards turned professional in 1973 after twice being named for the All-American team, winning 1972 North and South title and Walker Cup honours in 1973, when he finished low amateur in British Open. First victory came in 1977 Greensboro Open and he finished the year with around $100,000 prize-money.

EGAN, Chandler – *born Chicago, Illinois, USA, 1884. Died 1936*
Twice US Amateur Champion and three times Western Amateur Champion between 1902 and 1907, Egan 'dropped out' of top golf when he moved house in 1911 to Oregon. Came back in 1929 US Amateur and reached the semi-finals. Was selected for the 1934 Walker Cup side at 50. Died of pneumonia two years later.

EHRET, Gloria – *born Allentown, Pennsylvania, USA, 23 August 1941*
She won the US LPGA Championship in only her second season on tour in 1966 and finished in the top 12 in the prize-money list. Won again in 1973 and a series of second place finishes helped push her total winnings over the $150,000 mark.

EICHELBERGER, Dave – *born Waco, Texas, USA, 3 September 1943*
He turned professional after being a member of 1965 US Walker Cup and Americas Cup sides and won 1971 Milwaukee Open, finishing ninth in the money list with over $108,000. After several lean years he won 1977 Milwaukee Open.

ELDER, Lee – *born Dallas, Texas, USA, 14 July 1934*
He became the first black man ever to play in US Masters in 1975 after the first victory of his career in 1974 Monsanto Open, in which he beat Britain's Peter Oosterhuis in a play-off. He did not join the Tour until 1968 when in his thirties, and that year lost a play-off to Jack Nicklaus in the American Golf Classic. Has only once finished out of the top 60 money winners since 1971, accumulating over half a million dollars,

Below: The Late President Eisenhower was a keen golfer. Here he is seen at the Wentworth Club, Surrey, England in 1962.

Above: One of Britain's leading women amateurs, Mary Everard.

ESPINOSA, Al – *born Monterey, California, USA, 1892. Died 1957*
Suffered the shattering experience of tying Bobby Jones in 1929 US Open – then losing the 36 holes play-off by 23 strokes – 141 to 164. Was also runner-up in 1928 US PGA Championship, to Leo Diegel, but won many events, including Illinois, Ohio, Indianapolis and Mexican Opens, and played in two Ryder Cup matches.

EVANS, Albert – *born Brecon, South Wales, 28 August 1911*
A total of 25 Welsh caps, seven as captain, made Evans one of Wales's most honoured golfers between 1931 and 1965. Welsh Champion twice.

EVANS, Charles – *born Indianapolis, USA, 18 July 1890*
'Chick' pulled off the double of US Open and Amateur Championships in 1916, a feat matched only by Bobby Jones. Was US Amateur Champion again in 1920. Played in five Walker Cup matches and 50 consecutive US Amateurs. Gained Bobby Jones Award in 1960.

EVERARD, Mary – *born Sheffield, Yorkshire, England, 8 October 1942*
English Champion and British Ladies' Stroke Play Champion. Gained first of three Curtis Cup caps in 1970. Played for Britain in Vagliano Trophy, Commonwealth Tournament and World Team Championships.

$113,000 of which came in 1976. In 1971 he played in South Africa at Gary Player's invitation and later won Nigerian Open.

ELSON, Philip – *born Leamington Spa, Warwickshire, England, 14 April 1954*
Sixth place in Spanish Open set this former England Boys' and Youths' captain on his way to his best season as a professional in 1977. He finished 38th in the order of merit with close to £5000 prize-money. Only once since 1973 has he finished out of the top 60.

EMERY, Richard – *born Sheringham, Norfolk, England, 7 October 1942*
Winner of 1968 Piccadilly Fourball with Hugh Jackson, the 6ft 3in Emery combines a club job with tournament play and has represented Britain and Ireland against America's club professionals.

ENGLEHORN, Shirley – *born Caldwell, Idaho, USA, 12 December 1940*
Eleven US LPGA Tour victories included LPGA Championship in 1970 when she won three other tournaments and finished third in the prize-winners' list overall with $22,700. This bespectacled former Pacific Northwest, Oregon and Idaho Champion suffered serious injuries in a road accident in 1970 and had to undergo two major operations. Her comeback earned her the Ben Hogan award.

Far right: Charles Evans Junior, the first man to win the US Amateur and the US Open in the same year, 1916.

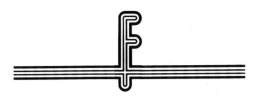

FALDO, Nick – *born Welwyn Garden City, Hertfordshire, England, 18 July 1957*

This former English Champion jumped 50 places in the Order of Merit in his second season as a professional in 1977, finishing eighth with official prize winnings of £14,750. He boosted this total to almost £30,000 by winning Belgium's Laurent Perrier event and appearing in the invitation Colgate World Match Play and Lancôme Trophy tournaments. He turned professional after winning the 1975 English Championship and British Youths' Championship. Faldo, 6ft 3in, tied with Spain's Severiano Ballesteros in Uniroyal International in 1977 but lost a sudden death play-off. He received his Ryder Cup baptism in 1977 and finished with three victories from three matches, partnering Peter Oosterhuis to foursomes and fourballs wins, then defeating Open Champion Tom Watson in the singles. In the same year represented England in the World Cup.

Left: Britain's brightest young professional star, Nick Faldo.

FALLON, John – *born Lanark, Scotland, 29 April 1913*
Played in 1955 Ryder Cup match after finishing runner-up in 1954 British PGA Match Play Championship. Was non-playing captain of 1963 Ryder side.

FARRELL, Johnny – *born New York, USA, 1901*
Farrell carved his name in golf history by defeating Bobby Jones in a 36-hole play-off to win 1928 US Open Championship, and was twice third in the event. Was a regular winner in the '20s and '30s and was second in British Open and US PGA Championships in 1929. Made three Ryder Cup appearances.

FAULK, Mary Lena – *born Thomasville, Georgia, USA, 1930*
Turned professional after winning 1953 US Amateur title and gaining a Curtis Cup cap in 1954 and was joint runner-up in 1955 US Women's Open.

FAULKNER, Max – *born Bexhill, Sussex, England, 29 July 1916*
Won 1951 British Open Championship. Three times Spanish Open Champion and other victories included Dunlop Masters and British PGA Match Play Championship. Made five Ryder Cup appearances.

FAZIO, George – *born USA*
Turned to golf course architecture after a successful career as a professional, highlighted by his tie with Ben Hogan and Lloyd Mangrum in 1950 US Open, when Hogan won the play-off.

FERGUSON, Bob – *born Musselburgh, Scotland, 1848. Died 19 May 1915*
Won the first of three successive British Open titles over his native links of Musselburgh in 1880 and tied with Willie Fernie in 1883, but a bout of typhoid cut short his career. He won the Leith Tournament against a strong field of top pros while only 18 and defeated Tom Morris six times in challenge matches.

FERNANDEZ, Vicente – *born Buenos Aires, Argentina, 5 April 1946*
The little Argentinian switched to the US circuit in 1977 after a series of good years in Europe. He won the 1970 Dutch Open and 1975 Benson and Hedges Festival in Britain and finished sixth in the 1974 Order of Merit, ninth in 1975 and 19th in 1976, totalling £27,000 prize-money in those three years. Has represented his country in the World Cup and the Rest of the World in Double Diamond Internationals.

FERNIE, Willie – *born St Andrews, Scotland, 1851. Died 1924*
Second in 1882 Open Championship; won 1883 British Open after a tie with Bob Ferguson. Became a club professional and a renowned teacher after finishing runner-up in the Open on four more occasions and taking part in many challenge matches against such players as Andrew Kirkaldy and Willie Park.

FERRARIS, Jan – *born San Francisco, California, USA, 2 June 1947*
A former North Carolina, Los Angeles, San Francisco, Western and National Junior Champion, she joined the LPGA Tour in 1966 and ten years later had won over $100,000 and three major events.

FERREE, Jim – *born Pine Bluff, North Carolina, USA, 10 June 1931*
Winner of 1958 Vancouver Open, 1961 Jamaica Open, 1962 Panama Open and 1963 Maracaibo Open, Ferree finished among America's top 60 money winners five times after joining the Tour in 1956, his best year being 1965 when he was placed 49th.

FERRIER, James – *born Sydney, Australia, 24 February 1915*
His 22 US Tour victories included 1947 PGA Championship and two Canadian Opens. Won four Australian Amateur titles and two Australian Opens in the '30s before joining the US circuit in 1941. Ferrier's best year in America was 1950 when he won $27,000 to finish runner up to Sam Snead in the money list. He finished among the top 60 12 times and totalled career earnings of $183,000.

FEZLER, Forrest – *born Hayward, California, USA, 23 September 1949*
In his second year on Tour in 1973 Fezler was runner-up to international stars Lee Trevino, Tom Weiskopf and Gary Player in big tournaments, but after another second to Hale Irwin in 1974 US Open he scored his first big win in that year's Southern Open. He won almost $200,000 in those two years.

FIDDIAN, Eric – *born Stourbridge, England, 28 March 1910*
English Champion and runner-up for British title in 1932. Won the first of two Walker Cup caps that year. Seven times capped by England.

FINSTERWALD, Dow – *born Athens, Ohio, USA, 6 September 1929*
Having played in four Ryder Cup matches himself Finsterwald, tournament winning star of the late '50s and early '60s, was named captain of America's successful 1977 Cup side. He won 12 US Tour events, gaining lifetime exemption from qualifying by taking 1958 PGA Championship. Was second twice and third three times in the money list in five years from 1956, winning Vardon Trophy in 1957 and being named Player of the Year in 1959.

FISCHER, John – *born Cincinnati, Ohio, USA, 10 March 1912*

US Amateur Champion in 1936. Played in three Walker Cup matches in the '30s and captained the side which drew with Britain and Ireland at Baltimore in 1965.

FITZSIMONS, Pat – *born Coos Bay, Oregon, USA, 15 December 1950*
His best year since joining the US Tour in 1972 was 1975 when he won the Glen Campbell Los Angeles Open and totalled $86,000 in earnings to finish 20th in the money list.

FLECK, Jack – *born Bettendorf, Iowa, USA, 8 November 1921*
In 1955, his first full year on the Tour, Fleck won the US Open. He also took the 1960 Phoenix Open and 1961 Bakersfield Open titles. His best year was 1960 when he was placed 18th in the money list.

FLECKMAN, Marty – *born Port Arthur, Texas, USA, 23 April 1944*
Turned professional in 1967 and in his first start on Tour won the Cajun Classic.

FLEISHER, Bruce – *born Union City, Tennessee, USA, 16 October 1948*
Turned professional in 1970 after winning 1968 US Amateur title and playing in 1969 Walker Cup and Eisenhower Trophy events.

FLOYD, Ray – *born Fort Bragg, North Carolina, USA, 4 September 1942*
This former Army officer's son, saddled for some years with a playboy image, wrote himself into the history books by equalling the record score of 271, 17 under par, in winning the US Masters in 1976. He won in the World Open and two more victories in 1977 took his total to ten in 15 years on Tour. Took three titles in 1969, including US PGA Championship, and that year made the first of three Ryder Cup appearances. His 1977 winnings took his career total over the million dollars mark.

FORD, Doug – *born West Haven, Connecticut, USA, 6 August 1922*
Former US Masters and PGA Champion won 19 Tour events between 1952 and 1963 and never finished worse than 21st in the money winners list. His best placings were second in 1953 and 1957, each time following three tournament wins, and he was third in 1955, when he was named Player of the Year after winning the All-American Championship, PGA Championship and Carling Open. Ford made four Ryder Cup appearances and served two terms on the PGA Tournament Committee.

FORSELL, Liv – *born Sweden, 1945*
Her country's outstanding woman golfer in the '60s and '70s, she was many times Scandinavian Open and Swedish Close Champion as well as winning Portuguese and Moroccan Opens. Named Woman Sports Personality of Sweden in 1966 and twice Swedish Golfer of the Year, she represented her country internationally for ten years.

FOSTER, Martin – *born Bradford, Yorkshire, England, 12 May 1952*
Injury and loss of form saw the 6ft 4in Yorkshireman slip from seventh in 1976 to 56th in the 1977 order of merit with a plunge in prize-

Below: Ray Floyd on the 18th tee as he wins the US Masters at Augusta in 1976.

money from £17,400 to £3300. This former British Boys' Champion and England international in only his third year as a professional in 1976 was second in the Uniroyal International and Carrolls Irish Open, third in the Piccadilly Medal and fourth in the Cacharel World Under-25s Championship. He played for England when they won the Double Diamond title, for Britain when they won the Hennessy Cup, and again played for England in the World Cup.

FOSTER, Rodney – *born Shipley, Yorkshire, England, 13 October 1941*
Member of winning Eisenhower Trophy team in 1964. Played in five Walker Cup sides and was England regular from 1963 to 1973. Won English Open Stroke Play title 1970.

FOULIS, James – *born Scotland, 1886*
Emigrated to America and won the 1896 US Open at Shinnecock Hills, tying for third place the following year.

FOURIE, John – *born Pretoria, South Africa, 23 August 1939*
Turned professional in his thirties after winning the South African Dunlop Masters by six strokes in 1970. Scored his first major victory beyond his native circuit in the 1977 Callers of Newcastle event after a sudden death play-off. His £5000 prize helped him to top £9000 in official winnings and take 18th place in the Order of Merit, his best since he joined the Tour in 1971. Fourie's South African victories include a further Dunlop Masters title in 1975 and the Transvaal (1973) and Western Province (1974) Opens.

Below: Scottish professional and British Ryder Cup man, Bernard Gallacher.

FOWNES, William – *born USA, 1878. Died 1950*
Won the US Amateur Championship in 1910, was a semi-finalist four times and played in two Walker Cup matches, captaining the first American side in 1922. A former USGA President, he was a prime mover in the development of the Oakmont course designed by his father.

FUNSETH, Rod – *born Spokane, Washington, USA, 3 April 1933*
Until a hand injury in 1974 Funseth's lowest finish in the US money list in ten years had been 66th. His two victories came in the 1965 Phoenix Open and 1973 Glen Campbell Los Angeles Open.

FURGOL, Ed – *born New York Mills, New York, USA, 22 March 1917*
Winner of the 1954 US Open, Furgol, who joined the Tour in 1945, also won the 1954 Phoenix Open, 1956 Miller High Life and Rubber City Opens and 1957 Caliente Open. His best year was 1956 when he finished seventh in the money list with $23,000. He was a top 60 money winner in all but one year from 1945 to 1957.

FURGOL, Marty – *born New York Mills, New York, USA, 1918*
No relation of Ed, although they shared the same birthplace, Furgol highlighted his pro career by finishing third leading money winner in 1954 and earned a Ryder Cup place in 1955. His title wins included the San Diego, Houston, El Paso and Western Opens.

GALLACHER, Bernard – *born Bathgate, Scotland, 9 February 1949*
The little Scot's Spanish Open triumph in 1977 was one of only four major victories by British based players that year in Europe. After only one finish outside the top 12 in the Order of Merit in seven seasons from 1968 Gallacher slipped to 30th in 1976 after cutting his schedule following his appointment as club professional at Wentworth, Surrey. He launched his winning career by taking two Zambian titles and Britain's Schweppes PGA Championship and Wills Open titles in 1969 when, at the age of 20, he topped the Order of Merit to win the Vardon Trophy with close to £7000 prize-money. His best year financially was 1974 when he won the Carrolls Celebration Open in Ireland and the first of two successive Dunlop Masters titles and more than £18,500 prize-money. He became the youngest British Ryder Cup international in 1969 and has played in every match since as well as appearing regularly for Scotland in the World Cup and Double Diamond International events.

GALLARDO, Angel – *born Barcelona, Spain, 29 July 1943*
Enjoyed his best season in 1977, winning the Italian Open after a sudden death play-off against Britain's Brian Barnes, and tying in the Callers of Newcastle event, only to lose a play-off to John Fourie of South Africa. Finished 10th in the Order of Merit with official winnings of almost £13,000. Gallardo, one of three golfing brothers, has captained the Continent in the Hennessy Cup and Double Diamond events as well as representing Spain in the World Cup. Victories include the 1967 Portuguese Open, 1970 Spanish Open and 1971 Mexican Open.

GANCEDO, Jose – *born Malaga, Spain, 1938*
Was Spanish Close and Open Amateur Champion in 1968 and 1969 and played in four Eisenhower Trophy World Team events as well as representing the Continent against Britain and Ireland three times.

GARDNER, Robert Abbe – *born Hinsdale, Illinois, USA, 1890. Died 1956*
Came to the fore by winning the US Amateur title in 1909 while still at Yale and took the title again in 1915. Was runner-up the following year and again in 1921, and lost at the 37th in the final of the 1920 British Amateur Championship to Cyril Tolley. Captained three Walker Cup sides after making his debut in 1922.

GARDNER, Robert W – *born USA, 1921*
Runner-up in the 1960 US Amateur Championship to Deane Beman, he was selected for that year's winning Eisenhower Trophy side. He was unbeaten on his Walker Cup appearances in 1961 and 1963 and was always a popular contestant.

GARNER, John – *born Preston, Lancashire, England, 9 January 1947*
Five highly successful European seasons from 1970 saw Garner total £20,000 prize-money. His best Order of Merit placing was sixth in 1972 when he won over £8000 and his worst 33rd. He won the 1971 Coca Cola Young Professionals Championship and the 1972 Benson and Hedges Match Play Championship and gained Ryder Cup honours in 1971 and 1973. He subsequently took up a club appointment.

GARRIDO, Antonio – *born Madrid, Spain, 2 February 1944*
Garrido was placed third in Europe in 1977 with official prize-money of £19,700. Little was heard of Garrido after he won the 1972 Spanish Open

Top left: Angel Gallardo is one of the senior Spanish professionals.

Far left: Bob A Gardner won the National Amateur in 1909 and 1915.

Left: Spanish international professional, Antonio Garrido.

and 1973 Madrid Open until 1976, when only three times in 12 stroke-play appearances in Europe did he finish out of the top ten, earning £13,000. He was in the forefront as Spain dominated the 1977 season, winning the Madrid Open and Benson and Hedges International. He has played for Europe in the Double Diamond and Hennessy Cup events.

GARRIDO, German – *born Madrid, Spain, 15 June 1948*
Younger brother of Antonio Garrido, he slipped from a career of best 45th in the 1976 order of merit to 91st in 1977 with only £918 official winnings. Has scored three victories – in the 1968 and 1973 Madrid Opens and the 1972 Portuguese Open.

Below: Philomena Garvey won the Irish Ladies' Championship 15 times between 1946 and 1970.

GARVEY, Philomena – *born Drogheda, Eire, 26 April 1927*
British Champion 1957 and four times runner-up. Took Irish title 15 times between 1946 and 1970. Had brief spell as professional in the '60s after making six Curtis Cup appearances.

GEIBERGER, Al – *born Red Bluff, California, USA, 1 September 1937*
For this 6ft 2in Californian five victories in the past three years have pushed his winnings past the million dollars mark. Geiberger had already won four times before he earned a lifetime exemption from qualifying by taking the US PGA title in 1966. It was eight years until his next victory in the Sahara, but he followed up in 1975 by winning two of the Tour's most important events, the Tournament of Champions and Tournament Players Championship. His best year was 1976 when he earned $194,000 from two wins and eight more top ten placings.

GERMAIN, Dorothy – *born USA*
Gained Curtis Cup honours in 1950 after winning the 1949 US Amateur Championship and was non-playing captain of the 1966 Curtis Cup side.

GHEZZI, Victor – *born Rumson, New Jersey, USA, 1911*
He and Byron Nelson finished a stroke behind Lloyd Mangrum in a 36 holes play-off for the 1946 US Open five years after he took the US PGA title by beating Mangrum in the semifinals and Nelson in the final. Ghezzi, whose victories included the Los Angeles, Maryland, New Jersey, North and South and Greensboro Opens, was picked for the 1939 and 1941 Ryder Cup matches, but they were never played owing to the War.

GIBBS, Carol – *born Jersey, Channel Islands, 18 October 1951*
As Carol le Feuvre made five appearances for England and was capped for Curtis Cup in 1974. Toured Canada and Australia with British sides. Won 1972 Dutch Championship.

GILBERT, Gibby – *born Chattanooga, Tennessee, USA, 14 January 1941*
Only once since he won the 1970 Houston Open had Gilbert finished worse than 48th in the US money list, so his performance in 1976 in winning the Danny Thomas-Memphis Classic and nearly $100,000 prize-money was no surprise.

GILDER, Bob – *born Corvallis, Oregon, USA, 31 December 1950*
Gilder followed up victory in the 1974 New Zealand Open by securing his player's card at the fourth attempt in 1975, then, in 1976, became only the fourth rookie pro in the history of the Tour to win more than $100,000, picking up the Phoenix Open title on the way.

Above: Antonio Garrido

*Above and left: Baldovino
Dassu*

52

Above: David Graham

Above: Bernard Gallacher

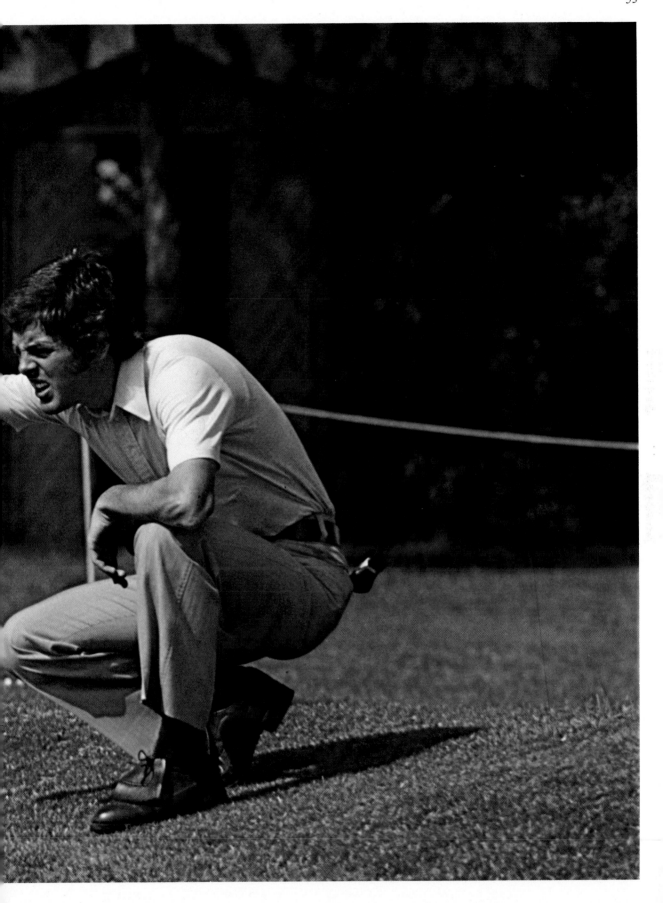

Above: Ray Floyd

Above: Martin Foster

GILES, Marvin – *born Charlottesville, Virginia, USA, 1943*
After being runner-up three years running, Giles took 1972 US Amateur title and added British title in 1975. Member of 1969, 1971, 1973 and 1975 Walker Cup sides and made three appearances in Eisenhower World Trophy teams, tying Britain's Mike Bonallack for individual top score in 1968, the year he finished low amateur in the US Masters. Low amateur in 1973 US Open.

GOALBY, Bob – *born Belleville, Illinois, USA, 14 March 1929*
Of his 11 victories in 20 years on the Tour, Goalby's success in the 1968 US Masters was the most memorable, with Argentinian Roberto de Vicenzo signing for a wrong score to miss a play-off. His career winnings top $600,000, his best year being 1967 when he finished tenth to earn $77,000.

GODFREY, Walter – *born Auckland, New Zealand, 1941*
Of Maori origin, Godfrey turned professional in 1963 after winning the 1958 New Zealand Open Amateur title and making two Eisenhower World Team Trophy appearances. Scorer of many victories in his home country, Australia and the Far East.

GOLDSCHMID, Isa – *born Italy*
Won ten Italian Women's Opens and 21 Italian Close Championships. Also past French and Spanish Champion. Played in five World Team and eight Vagliano Trophy matches.

GOODMAN, Johnny – *born Omaha, Nebraska, USA, 1908*
Goodman made three successive Walker Cup appearances after winning the 1933 US Open title. He added the US Amateur title in 1937 after a run of near-misses and scored other victories in the Mexican and trans-Mississippi Championships before turning professional.

GOURLAY, Mary, OBE – *born Basingstoke, Hampshire, England, 1898*
When Miss Gourlay retired aged 73 her handicap was four. Past chairman of LGU and past president ELGA. Twice English Champion in the '20s and took the French and Swedish titles. Made two Curtis Cup appearances in the '30s and was England international from 1923 to 1934.

GRAHAM, David – *born Windsor, Australia, 23 May 1946*
Victories in the Westchester Classic and American Golf Classic and seven other top ten finishes swept this American-based Australian into eighth place in the money list with $176,000 earnings in 1976, and victories overseas in Britain's Piccadilly World Match Play Cham-

Left: Vinny Giles won both the US Amateur (1972) and British Amateur (1975) Championships as well as many others.

Below: One of Australia's world class professionals, Dave Graham, is now based in the United States.

pionship and Japan's Chunichi Crowns invitational made him one of the world's top earners. It was a far cry from the days when, at 21, failure of his club pro business in Australia left him bankrupt. He joined the tour to pay off his debts and in the next two years was a winner in France, Thailand, Venezuela and Japan and he and Bruce Devlin carried off the World Cup. His first US win was in the 1972 Cleveland Open, when he 'baptised' a set of irons given him by Arnold Palmer.

Above: Lou Graham won the US Open Championship in 1975, 11 years after joining the tour.

GRAHAM, Lou – *born Nashville, Tennessee, USA, 7 January 1938*
Victory in the 1975 US Open helped this former army regular to his best season financially since joining the Tour in 1964. After beating John Mahaffey in an 18-hole play-off for the title, Graham went on to collect $96,425 prize-money for the year. He topped $100,000 in 1976 and improved considerably on that in 1977. His first win was in the 1967 Minnesota Classic. Only once since then – in 1969 when he underwent an operation for a hand injury – has he failed to make the top 50. He made his third successive Ryder Cup appearance in 1977.

GRAY, Downing – *born Pensacola, Florida, USA, 1938*
Runner-up in the 1962 US Amateur to Labron Harris, Gray played in the 1963 and 1964 Walker Cup matches.

GREEN, Charlie – *born Dumbarton, Scotland, 2 August 1932*
Scottish Champion 1970 and Scottish Open Amateur Stroke Play Champion 1975. Member of winning Walker Cup side in 1971 and of four other Walker sides in the '60s and '70s as well as two Eisenhower Trophy teams. Was Scotland regular from 1961 into the late '70s.

Centre right: Top US money winner Hubert Green. He is likely to finish up among the top dollar earners of all time.

GREEN, Hubert – *born Birmingham, Alabama, USA, 28 December 1946*
This lanky Alabaman is one of the most successful professionals of the '70s. His first major title

came in the 1977 US Open, but he had already established a reputation as a regular Tour winner, picking up two first prizes in 1973 to win over $100,000 for the first time, four in 1974, when his winnings topped $200,000, and three in three weeks in 1976 in the Doral-Eastern, Jacksonville and Sea Pines Heritage Classic. In that hot spell he won $118,000 towards his best grand total of $228,031. He was Rookie of the Year in 1971, won the 1975 Phoenix Dunlop event in Japan and the 1977 Carrolls Irish Open, gaining his first Ryder Cup cap a month later.

GREENE, Bert – *born Gray, Georgia, USA, 11 February 1944*
This former Tennessee State amateur champion won the 1973 L and M Open. His best year in a career blighted by injuries was 1969, when he had two seconds and a third and finished 23rd in the money list with $76,000.

GREENHALGH, Julia – *born Bolton, Lancashire, England, 6 January 1941*
English Champion 1966 and twice British Stroke Play Champion in the '70s. New Zealand title in 1963. First of five Curtis Cup appearances in 1964. Twice captained Britain and Ireland in the World Team Championship. England regular since 1960, Daks Woman Golfer of the Year 1974.

GREGSON, Malcolm – *born Leicester, England, 15 August 1943*
He was spectacularly successful in 1967 when, at the age of 23, he took the Vardon Trophy as leader of the Order of Merit after victories in the Schweppes PGA Championship and the Daks and Martini International events, earning close to £5000. He won the Daks title again in 1968 and partnered Brian Huggett to victory in the

1972 Sumrie Better Ball event. Gregson gained Ryder Cup honours in 1967. Until 1977, when he occupied 47th place, Gregson had never finished out of the top 40 in the Order of Merit since 1963. He won a Zambian event in 1974.

GROH, Gary – *born Chicago, Illinois, USA, 11 October 1944*
After winning four second tour events between 1973 and 1974, Groh took the 1975 Hawaiian Open title and that year finished 31st in the money list with $68,000.

GUILFORD, Jesse – *born Manchester, New Hampshire, USA, 1895. Died 1962*
Sprang to prominence by winning the New Hampshire Championship at 14 and went on to win the 1921 US Amateur title and play in the Walker Cup matches of 1922, 1924 and 1926.

GULDAHL, Ralph – *born Dallas, Texas, USA, 22 November 1912*
Won US Opens of 1937 and 1938, 1939 US Masters and three successive Western Opens over the same period and gained two Ryder Cup caps. Won ten US Tour events in five years from 1936. Was the first player not to go over par in any round when winning US Open in 1937.

GUNN, Watts – *born Macon, Georgia, USA, 1905*
Reached the final of the 1925 US Amateur Championship at Oakmont at the age of 20 – only to find himself up against his Atlanta Club colleague Bobby Jones, who beat him 8 and 7 over 36 holes. Winner of the Georgia and Southern Amateur titles and US National Collegiate Champion in 1927, he gained Walker Cup caps in 1926 and 1928 and was unbeaten.

HAAS, Freddie – *born Portland, Arkansas, USA, 3 January 1916*
Haas won the 1945 Memphis Invitational event as an amateur to end Byron Nelson's record run of 11 straight victories. He played in the 1953 Ryder Cup side and was World Seniors Champion in 1966.

HAGEN, Walter – *born Rochester, New York, USA, 21 December 1892. Died October 1969*
Hagen's millionaire lifestyle was exemplified by his hiring a Rolls Royce as a changing-room for Open Championships in the era when professionals were not permitted entry to most British clubhouses – and handing his caddie his first prize cheque. He won the first of his two US Opens at 21. After his second victory five years

later in 1919 he opted for the full time circuit. He finished 53rd in a field of 54 in his first British Open in 1920, but won the first of his four British titles in 1922 to become the first American to take both national titles. Hagen, who also won five US PGA Championships – four in a row – when match play decided the issue, five Western Opens, plus the French, Canadian and Belgian titles, was a revolutionary influence in raising the status of professional golf. He captained all the US Ryder Cup sides until 1937. He took golf to the world, playing in Australia, Japan, South America and Africa, often touring with trick shot specialist Joe Kirkwood.

HAGGE, Marlene – *born Eureka, USA, 16 February 1934*
She became a professional at 16 after winning the Western and National Junior Championships and a string of honours and was top prize-money winner in 1956 after scoring eight US Tour victories. She is one of America's all-time top money earners with more than $320,000 and by 1972 had scored 25 major victories, including the 1956 LPGA Championship, when she defeated Patty Berg in a play-off. She won five events in 1965.

HAHN, Paul – *born Charleston, South Carolina, USA, 12 June 1918. Died 1976*
Gave up a career as a tournament professional to tour the world giving exhibitions of trick shots.

HALIBURTON, Tom – *born Rhu, Dunbartonshire, Scotland, 1915. Died 1975*
Haliburton set a British record tournament score of 61 and a world two-round record of 126 at Worthing in 1952. Former Scottish amateur international, turned professional in 1933 and played in the 1961 and 1963 Ryder Cups as well as representing his country in the World Cup.

HAMILTON, Robert – *born Evansville, Indiana, USA, 1916*
Former Indiana Amateur and Open Champion, beat Byron Nelson in the final of the 1944 US PGA Championship, and after a run of victories, including the Charlotte, Nevada and New Orleans Opens, made his Ryder Cup debut in 1949.

HANSON, Beverly – *born USA, 1926*
Turned professional after winning the 1950 US Amateur title and gaining Curtis Cup honours that year, took the 1955 USLPGA title and was leading money winner in 1958.

HARBERT, Melvin – *born Dayton, Ohio, USA, 20 February 1915*
Winner of nine US Tour events between 1941 and 1958, including the 1954 PGA Championship. Followed appearance in 1949 Ryder Cup by captaining the 1955 side and was in America's winning World Cup team that year.

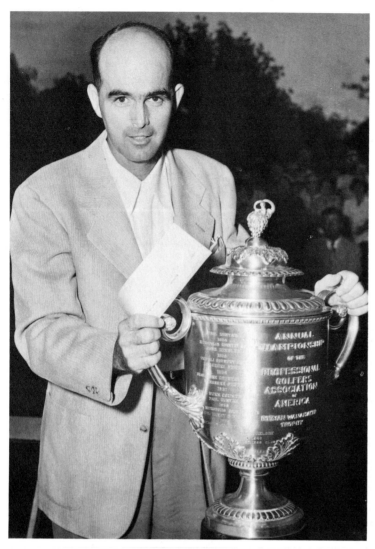

Above: Chandler Harper receives the US PGA Championship Trophy he won at Columbus in 1950.

HARRIS, Marley – *born 11 January 1928*
As Marley Spearman was British Champion in 1961 and 1962 and English Champion in 1964. Other titles included 1963 New Zealand Stroke Play Championship. Played in three Curtis Cup matches in the '60s as well as Vagliano and Commonwealth events. For ten years an England regular.

HARRISON, Ernest – *born Conway, Arkansas, USA, 29 March 1910*
'Dutch' won 19 major events on the US Tour between 1937 and 1958 including the All-American, Western and two Texas Opens. Was national Seniors' Champion five times in the '60s and Vardon Trophy winner in 1954.

HARROLD, Lynne – *born London, England, 9 November 1956*
After winning the 1976 English Championship and being first reserve for that year's Curtis Cup match, England international Miss Harrold turned professional.

HASSANEIN, Hassan – *born Cairo, Egypt, 1916. Died 1957*
Four times Egyptian Open Champion. Also won Italian and French Opens and played in the World Cup. Died in an explosion.

HAVERS, Arthur – *born Norwich, England, 10 June 1898*
Won British Open Championship 1923, two years after making the first of five Ryder Cup appearances. Qualified for Open at 16. Year after he won he crossed the Atlantic to challenge and defeat British-born Bobby Jones and American-born Gene Sarazen.

HAYES, Dale – *born Pretoria, South Africa, 7 January 1952*
Took the South African, Scottish, German and Brazilian titles as an amateur and as a teenage professional scored his first win in the 1971 Spanish Open. After finishing fourth in the 1973 European Order of Merit and second in 1974, Hayes finished top in 1975 with £20,000 prize-money to take the Vardon Trophy – the first overseas player to do so since countryman Bobby Locke in 1954. His 15 pro victories

HARMON, Claude – *born Savannah, Georgia, USA, 14 July 1916*
Harmon won 1948 US Masters and five major US Tour events and went close to winning his country's Open and PGA titles.

HARPER, Chandler – *born Portsmouth, Virginia, USA, 10 March 1914*
Won over 20 tournaments, including 1950 US-PGA Championship, 1954 Texas Open, when he returned a record score of 259, and 1968 World Seniors' Championship. Played in 1955 Ryder Cup. He once shot 58 on a 6100yd course.

HARRIS, Labron – *born Stillwater, Oklahoma, USA, 27 September 1941*
Winner of the 1962 US Amateur Championship and a member of the 1962 USA Eisenhower Trophy and 1963 Walker Cup sides, the 6ft 4in Harris turned professional in 1964 and won the 1971 Robinson Open. His best year was 1972, when he finished 36th in the money list to earn $65,000.

Right: Labron Harris won the US Amateur Championship in 1962. Here he is seen shaking hands with former president, Dwight D Eisenhower.

include the South African Open and PGA titles and the Swiss Open and British Young Professionals Championship. In 1974 he teamed with Bobby Cole to win the World Cup. Hayes, in his first year on the US Tour, finished 128th in the 1976 money list but improved to earn over $40,000 in 1977.

HAYES, Mark – *born Stillwater, Oklahoma, USA, 12 July 1949*
After an outstanding amateur career, Hayes turned professional in 1973. He was a quick success, winning the Byron Nelson and Pensacola events and over $150,000 in 1976 and taking the Tournament Players Championship in 1977.

HAYNIE, Sandra – *born Fort Worth, Texas, USA, 4 June 1943*
A former Texas State and Trans-Mississippi Champion, she scored a dazzling 39 major victories on the US LPGA Tour between 1962 and 1976 and is high in the all-time prize-money winners table behind Kathy Whitworth with almost half a million dollars. Her wins include two LPGA titles. She won four times in 1975 to collect over $61,000 – her best season – and 1976, when she suffered injury problems, was the first year since 1961 in which she had failed to score a victory.

HEAFNER, Clayton – *born USA, 1914. Died 1960*
Was unbeaten on his two Ryder Cup appearances in 1949 and 1951 – the two years in which he finished runner-up in the US Open to Cary Middlecoff and Ben Hogan.

Left: South African Dale Hayes was a successful amateur before turning professional.

HEARD, Jerry – *born Visalia, California, USA, 1 May 1947*
Son of a municipal golf course operator, Heard was playing par golf at the age of 12. In 1971, two years after joining the Tour, he won the American Golf Classic and $112,000 and in two of the following three years he collected three more Tour titles, as well as winning the Spanish Open. He subsequently slipped back, suffering the frightening experience of being struck by lightning, along with Lee Trevino and Bobby Nichols, in the 1975 Western Open, and having to leave the Tour for spells with severe back trouble.

HEATHCOAT-AMORY, Lady – *born Surrey, England, 17 November 1901*
One of the greatest women golfers of all time, the former Joyce Wethered was four times British Champion and English Champion five years in a row in the '20s. Played regularly for England in the '20s and appeared in the 1932 Curtis Cup match. Forfeited her amateur status in 1935 to tour the United States, playing matches against Bobby Jones, Babe Zaharias and Gene Sarazen among others.

HEBERT, Jay – *born St Montinville, Louisiana, USA, 14 February 1923*
Hebert was US PGA Champion in 1960, three years after his younger brother Lionel took the title. He scored seven Tour victories between 1957 and 1961, his best year when he finished fifth in the money list with $35,000 winnings. He was consistently a top 60 money winner between 1953 and 1966 and his career earnings total $289,000. Hebert played in the 1959 and 1961 Ryder Cup matches.

Below: One of the greatest women golfers of all time, Lady Heathcoat-Amory (née Joyce Wethered) is seen here putting .

HEBERT, Lionel – *born Lafayette, Louisiana, USA, 20 January 1928*
Hebert's first US Tour victory came in his debut year in the 1957 PGA Championship. He won four more titles up to 1966, the last year he finished among the top 60 money winners. He played in the 1957 Ryder Cup.

HEDGES, Peter – *born Kent, England, 30 March 1947*
English Open Stroke Play Champion 1976. Played in 1973 and 1975 Walker Cup matches and 1974 Eisenhower Trophy team.

HENNING, Harold – *born Johannesburg, South Africa, 3 October 1934*
Most successful of four golf professional brothers. South African Open Champion 1957 and 1962 and four times South African PGA Champion. Other victories include Italian, Swiss, German, Danish and Malaysian Opens, five events in Britain, two in the US and many on his home tour. Partnered Gary Player to victory in 1965 World Cup. In 1963 won £10,000 for a hole-in-one at Moor Park, England.

HENSON, Dinah – *born Dorking, Surrey, England, 17 October 1948*
Daks Woman Golfer of the Year in 1970, Mrs Henson, then Dinah Oxley, won that year's British Championship and the 1970 and 1971 English titles. Played in 1970 World Cup side and made her fourth Curtis Cup appearance in 1976 after a four year absence following marriage.

HERD, Alexander – *born St Andrews, Scotland, 1868. Died 1944*
Sandy's British Open Championship career began at 17, when he sported only four clubs, and ended at the age of 71. He won the title in 1902 and was runner-up four times between 1892 and 1920. Twice took the British Match Play title. Herd, who represented Scotland ten times, won the 1902 Open after adopting the new Haskell rubber-cored ball.

HERD, Fred – *born St Andrews, Scotland*
Brother of Sandy. Was winner of the 1898 US Open, the first to be played over 72 holes – 8 times round the nine-hole course of the Myopia Hunt Club in Hamilton, Massachusetts.

HERRON, Davidson – *born USA*
Davy Herron defeated the young Bobby Jones 5 and 4 to win the 1919 US Amateur Championship over his home course of Oakmont while himself only 20.

HEZLET, May – *born Ireland, 1882*
Won the Irish and British Championships in consecutive weeks at Royal County Down in 1899. Her 17th birthday fell between the two events and she remains the youngest double winner. Added two more British and three more Irish titles.

HIGGINS, Liam – *born Cork, Eire, 13 November 1944*
This husky former Irish amateur international has made a speciality of winning on the course to which he is attached, Waterville, County Kerry. He took the 1974 and 1977 Kerrygold titles there. Higgins made the top 60 in the Order of Merit for the third season running in 1977 after opening the year with victory in the Kenya Open, but official prize-money of £3000 was £2000 less than he earned in 1976.

Left: Alexander 'Sandy' Herd was an early Scottish professional.

Centre left: Dinah Henson was the British Ladies' Champion in 1970.

HIGGINS, Pam – *born Groveport, Ohio, USA, 5 December 1945*
Winner of more than $100,000 prize-money in nine seasons on the US Tour, this product of Jack Nicklaus's old college, Ohio State, scored her first victory in the 1971 Lincoln-Mercury event.

HIGUCHI, Chako – *born Tokyo, Japan, 13 October 1945*
Her first major victory outside her home country – she had scored three Japanese LPGA and Open wins – came in the 1976 Colgate-European Open in England. That year she finished 10th in the prize-money list with earnings of $57,000 to push her career winnings over the $100,000 mark in six years on the Tour. Wife of a golf pro, she is rated a superstar in Japan.

HILL, Dave – *born Jackson, Michigan, USA, 20 May 1937*
This million dollar US Tour earner was the man

Right: Consistent dollar earning American professional, Dave Hill.

Right: Chako Higuchi, Japanese woman professional, plays the United States circuit.

who clinched victory for the United States in the 1977 Ryder Cup match with his singles win over Tommy Horton. He has scored 13 victories since joining the Tour in 1959, four times winning the Memphis event. He was never out of the top 60 between 1960 and 1976, his best year being 1969, when he was second in the money list with $156,000 winnings, collected three titles, and took the Vardon Trophy with a stroke average of 70.344 for 90 rounds.

HILL, Mike – *born Jackson, Michigan, USA, 27 January 1939*
Younger brother of the more successful Dave, Mike Hill took his third Tour title, and his first for five years, in the 1977 Ohio Kings Island Open, a last round 64 giving him an impressive 269 total.

HILTON, Harold – *born West Kirby, Lancashire, England, 12 January 1869. Died 1942*
Won British Open Championships 1892 and 1897. He won four British Amateur Championships and took the American Amateur title in 1911 to become the first player and the only Briton to hold both national titles at the same time.

HINKLE, Lon – *born Flint, Michigan, USA, 17 July 1949*
This heavyweight six footer gained valuable experience playing in Australasia, Japan and Europe as a prelude to his best year on the US Tour in 1977 when he won more than $40,000.

HINSON, Larry – *born Gastonia, North Carolina, USA, 5 August 1944*
This 6ft 2in blond, who plays with a left arm withered after a bout of polio as a boy, won the Ben Hogan Award for triumphing over his handicap to earn over $120,000 and take eighth place in the 1970 money list. He won the 1969 New Orleans Open and finished in the top 60 money winners in six successive years.

HISKEY, Babe – *born Burley, Idaho, USA, 21 November 1938*
Winner of the 1965 Cajun Classic, 1970 Sahara Invitational and 1972 National Team event with Kermit Zarley, Hiskey's best year was 1972 when he finished 51st in the money list with $49,000.

HOBDAY, Simon – *born Mafeking, South Africa, 23 June 1940*
This former Zambian farmer became a victim of British Government sanctions against Rhodesia, his home being in Salisbury, and all his official prize-money was 'frozen' in a Channel Islands bank account. He unsuccessfully campaigned to be recognised as British, having been born of British parents. Hobday represented Zambia, then Northern Rhodesia, at rugby and won that country's amateur golf title. He was later expelled from Zambia for playing on the

South African circuit. After turning professional he won the 1971 South African Open, and his first European victory was in the 1976 German Open. His 1976 earnings after eight top ten placings topped £15,000 and left him 10th in the Order of Merit. Five top 12 placings in 1977 saw him finish 23rd in the table with £7600.

HOGAN, Ben – *born Dublin, Texas, USA, 13 August 1912*
A legend in his lifetime. Won 57 US Tour events between 1938 and 1959 – 12 in 1946 alone and four or more in six other years between 1940 and 1948. One of only four players to have taken all four of the world's major titles (Jack Nicklaus, Gary Player and Gene Sarazen are the others) and in 1953 took the British as well as his fourth US Open title. Was twice US Masters and twice US PGA Champion. Suffered multiple injuries in a car crash in 1949 and recovered to record victories in the 1950, 1951 and 1953 US Opens, the 1951 and 1953 US Masters and the 1953 British Open. Partnered Sam Snead to victory in Canada Cup at Wentworth in 1956, taking top individual prize. Hogan played in the 1947 and 1951 Ryder Cup sides, and was non-playing captain in 1949 and 1967. Was five times leading money winner, four times Player of the Year and voted Sportsman of the Decade in 1956. In 1965 he was voted the greatest professional of all time by US golf writers and he gained the Bobby Jones award in 1976.

Left: An action picture of the legendary Ben Hogan, one of the finest golfers ever to hit a ball.

HOMER, Trevor – *born Bloxwich, England, 8 September 1943*
Turned professional in 1974 after winning the 1972 and 1974 British Amateur Championships, representing England in the home internationals and European Championships and playing in the 1972 Eisenhower Trophy and 1973 Walker Cup sides.

HORTON, Tommy – *born St Helens, Lancashire, England, 16 June 1941*
Only twice in 14 years on the European circuit has the slim Channel Islands-based professional finished outside the top 20 in the Order of Merit and his career winnings top £86,000. His first victory came in Ireland's RTV Open and in only one year since has he failed to win a major title. Horton, who became the youngest ever Captain of the Professional Golfers Association in 1978, was runner-up in the 1967 Order of Merit and in the top ten in 1968, 1969, 1970, 1974, 1976 and 1977. He represented Britain and Ireland in the 1975 and 1977 Ryder Cup matches as well as the Hennessy Cup and has played for England in the World Cup and Double Diamond International. Horton's ten victories include 1970 South African Open and British PGA Match Play Championship, 1973 Nigerian Open and 1977 Zambian Open.

HOYT, Beatrix – *born USA, 1880*
At 16 won the first of three successive US Amateur titles. She won the medal for the best qualifying score each time and remains joint youngest winner of a major women's championship.

HSIEH, Min Nam – *born Tansui, Taiwan, 1940*
Holds the unique record of having taken top individual prize in the Eisenhower World Amateur and World Cup Professional team events in 1964 and 1972. He and Lu Lian Huan won the 1972 World Cup in Australia.

HSIEH Yung Yo – *born Taipei, Taiwan, 1934*
Four times top campaigner on the Asian circuit, his many victories include the Japan, Philippines, China, Thailand and Singapore Opens.

HUGGETT, Brian – *born Porthcawl, Wales, 18 November 1936*
The diminutive Welshman was honoured with the Ryder Cup captaincy against the United States at Royal Lytham in 1977 after six appearances in the side since 1963. His 16 major victories world-wide include the 1962 Dutch Open, 1963 German Open, 1967 PGA Close Championship, 1968 British PGA Match Play Championship, 1970 Dunlop Masters and 1974 Portuguese Open. After finishing third in the 1963 Order of Merit, he topped the table to take the Vardon Trophy in 1968 following three major victories and winning over £8000. He was placed third in the table in three of the next four years and his official career prize winnings are

close to £80,000. A Welsh World Cup regular, he has rationed his appearances in recent years, involving himself with golf course architecture.

HUISH, David – *born Edinburgh, Scotland, 23 May 1944*
Successfully combines a club job with tournament play. Won 1973 Northern Open and represented Scotland in the World Cup and Britain and Ireland in club professionals matches against the United States.

HUNT, Bernard – *born Atherstone, England, 2 February 1930*
Made eight Ryder Cup appearances between 1953 and 1969. Captain in 1973 and 1975. Won 26 major titles between 1953 and 1973 covering nine holes in 28 strokes en route to his first big win in the 1953 Spalding event. Other victories came in the Egyptian, German, Belgian, Brazilian, French and Algarve Opens and the Dunlop Masters. Won the Vardon Trophy in 1958, 1960 and 1965.

HUNT, Guy – *born Bishop's Stortford, England, 17 January 1947*
This 5ft 6in tall art master's son came back spectacularly to win 1977 Dunlop Masters, beating Brian Barnes in a play-off, and take 12th place in the Order of Merit with £12,700 total earnings. It was his first major victory. His best year was 1972 when he was runner-up to Tommy Horton in the Piccadilly medal and his consistency took him into second place behind Peter Oosterhuis in the Order of Merit with almost £10,000 winnings. He gained a Ryder Cup place in 1975 and also represented England in the World Cup.

HUTCHEON, Ian – *born Monifieth, Scotland, 22 February 1942*
Scottish and Scottish Open Amateur Stroke Play Champion. Two Walker Cup matches and two appearances in Eisenhower Trophy World Championship, including 1976 when Britain and Ireland won and Hutcheon finished joint best individual.

HUTCHINSON, Horace – *born London, England, 16 May 1859. Died 1932*
Was elected Captain of the Royal North Devon club at Westward Ho! at 16 – after winning the scratch medal. First Englishman to become Captain of the Royal and Ancient in 1908 after winning the British Amateur Championships of 1886 and 1887.

HUTCHISON, Jock – *born St Andrews, Scotland, 6 June 1884. Died December 1977.*
Settled in Pennsylvania, USA, in the early 1900s. Won 1920 US PGA Championship and 1921 British Open at his native St Andrews and finished second twice and third twice in the US Open. Other victories included two US Seniors' titles and two Western Opens.

Left: Jock Hutchison was the first American to win the British Open Championship when he returned to his native St Andrews in 1960.

HYNDMAN, William – *born USA, 25 December 1915*
One of America's foremost amateurs for 15 years. Earned five Walker Cup caps and two Eisenhower Trophy appearances, once as captain. Runner-up in British Amateur Championship three times and once in American Championship. He was US Seniors' Champion in 1973.

Left: American amateur Bill Hyndman misses a putt during the 1969 British Amateur Championship.

Far left: Brian Huggett, a top Welsh professional, has won many championships and has captained the Ryder Cup team.

INMAN, Joe – *born Indianapolis, Indiana, USA, 29 November 1947*
A product of Arnold Palmer's old school, Wake Forest, Inman's impressive amateur record included victory in the North-South Championship and a Walker Cup cap in 1969. He turned professional in 1973, his first victory coming in the 1976 Kemper Open.

IRVIN, Ann – *born Lytham, Lancashire, England, 11 April 1943*
Winner of the British Ladies' title in 1973, the British Ladies Stroke Play event in 1969 and twice English Champion. Daks Woman Golfer of the Year in 1968. Played in four Curtis Cup matches between 1962 and 1976.

IRWIN, Hale – *born Joplin, Missouri, USA, 3 June 1945*
Victories in the 1977 Atlanta Classic, Hall of Fame Classic and San Antonio-Texas Open ensured Irwin's season's winnings topped $200,000 for the third successive year. He won seven titles in that period, but his most outstanding victory came in 1974 US Open at Winged Foot. That year he also won Piccadilly World Match Play title at Wentworth, England and represented America in the World Cup. He made his second Ryder Cup appearance in 1977. Fourteen top ten finishes in 1975 and 12 in 1976 bear testimony to his outstanding ability.

IVERSON, Don – *born LaCrosse, Wisconsin, USA, 28 October 1945*
This former Wisconsin State amateur champion's best year on the US Tour was 1975 when he won the BC Open and $56,000 in total to finish 37th in the money list.

Below: Hale Irwin, winner of the US Open Championship and the Piccadilly World Match Play Championship, is one of the most successful of American professionals.

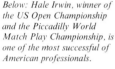

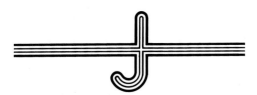

JACK, Robert Reid – *born Cumbernauld, Scotland, 17 January 1924*
British Amateur Champion in 1957 two years after taking the Scottish title. Played in the 1957 and 1959 Walker Cup sides and the 1958 Eisenhower Trophy team as well as representing Britain in European and Commonwealth events and Scotland throughout the '50s.

JACKLIN, Tony, OBE – *born Scunthorpe, England, 7 July 1944*
Second place a stroke behind Tom Watson in the Bing Crosby event in America early in 1977 suggested a return to the form that took him to a historic British and US Open double in the space of 11 months in 1969–70, but, apart from victory in the Rank Zerox English Championship, Jacklin was to endure another disappointing year. Jacklin's brilliant Open feats inspired a British golf 'boom', and earned him the Order of the British Empire, and world-wide fame and a fortune. He was the first home player to win the British Open since Max Faulkner in 1951. When at Hazeltine, Minnesota, he added the US title to the crown he won at Royal Lytham and St Annes, he became the first Briton to hold both major titles at the same time, and the first Briton since Ted Ray in 1920 to take the US title. He won six other titles before the Open, including the Dunlop Masters, New Zealand PGA, South Africa's Kimberley Tournament and America's Jacksonville Open. Following his US Open success he won a dozen more major events. He has divided his time between the US and European Tours, and has played in every Ryder Cup match from 1967 to 1977.

JACKSON, Bridget – *born Birmingham, England, 10 July 1936*
English Champion in 1956 and runner-up in British Championship in 1964. Won German and Canadian Open Championships. Made three Curtis Cup appearances and played in 1964 World Team event.

JACKSON, Hugh – *born Newtonards, N Ireland, 28 February 1940*
Consistently successful in the early '70s, finishing eighth in the 1970 Order of Merit with over £4000 prize-money and 16th, 26th and 19th in the next three years. Jackson, twice an Irish World Cup international, won the 1968 Piccadilly Fourball with Richard Emery and was Irish Professional Champion in 1970.

JACKSON, James – *born USA, 1924*
Played in 1935 and 1955 Walker Cup matches after being leading amateur in 1952 US Open.

JACOBS, John – *born Lindrick, Yorkshire, England, 14 March 1925*
Played in 1955 Ryder Cup match and for Britain three times against the Continent in the '50s. Victories include Dutch Open and South African Match Play Championship in 1957.

JACOBS, Tommy – *born Denver, Colorado, USA, 13 February 1935*
Winner of four Tour events and a member of the 1965 Ryder Cup side, this former Chairman of the PGA Tournament Committee had his best year in 1964, finishing 12th in the money list with $37,000 winnings.

JAECKEL, Barry – *born Los Angeles, California, USA, 14 February 1949*
This Hollywood actor's son came to prominence after winning the Southern California amateur championship by taking the 1972 French Open title. He joined the US Tour in 1975 and had three top ten finishes in 1976.

Below: Tony Jacklin, British Open Champion 1969 and US Open Champion 1970, held both titles at the same time.

JAGGER, David – *born Sheffield, Yorkshire, England, 9 June 1949*
Just squeezed into the top 60 in 1977 but, despite his second victory in the Nigerian Open, it was his most disappointing year in Europe since 1972. His highest Order of Merit placing was in 1973 when he finished 24th. He won the 1974 Kenya Open.

JAMES, Mark – *born Stamford, Lincolnshire, England, 28 October 1953*
James quickly made his mark after turning professional following a brilliant amateur career, which saw him take the 1974 English title and finish runner-up in the 1975 British Championship and gain Walker Cup honours against the Americans. His first victory came in 1977 Lusaka Open. Top ten finishes in three European events earned him a Ryder Cup debut.

JAMESON, Betty – *born Norman, Oklahoma, USA, 1919*
After winning the US Amateur Championships of 1939 and 1940 took 1947 US Open title, having been runner-up to Patty Berg in 1946. Won almost $100,000 in 17 years on proette tour.

JAMIESON, Jim – *born Kalamazoo, Michigan, USA, 21 April 1943*
Winner of 1972 Western Open, Jamieson also finished tied second in PGA Championship and fifth in the Masters and had five other top ten placings, ending up 15th in the money list with $109,000 and teaming up with Tom Weiskopf in the World Cup.

JANUARY, Don – *born Plainview, Texas, USA, 20 November 1929*
In 20 years after turning professional in 1955 January, who earned lifetime exemption from qualifying by taking 1967 US PGA title, scored

a dozen victories. He took 2½ years off from playing to build golf courses in 1972. He returned to win 1975 San Antonio-Texas Open and 1976 Tournament of Champions. He finished 9th in the 1976 money league after ten top ten placings with earnings of $163,000 – over $90,000 more than he had won in any previous season – and a stroke average for 96 rounds of 70.5. January's astonishing comeback earned him a return to Ryder Cup duty in 1977, after 12 years' absence, at the age of 47.

JENKINS, Tom – *born Houston, Texas, USA, 14 December 1947*
This former All-American golfer first appeared among the top 60 money winners in 1975 when he took the IVB Philadelphia Golf Classic title and won $45,000 for 52nd place.

JESSEN, Ruth – *born Seattle, Washington, USA, 12 November 1936*
She scored 11 US Tour victories between 1959 and 1971 and claims career earnings of around $150,000. A former Pacific Northwest and Washington State Champion, she earned the Ben Hogan award for her comeback in 1971 after repeated injury and illness. Her best year was 1964 when she won five times. She is co-holder of the LPGA 54-hole record of 200.

JOHNSON, Howie – *born St Paul, Minnesota, USA, 8 September 1925*
Victories in 1958 Azalea Open and 1959 Baton Rouge event helped Johnson to career earnings of over $280,000. He figured among the top 60 campaigners eight times, his best year being 1970 when he finished 26th with $66,000.

JOHNSTON, Harrison – *born Minnesota, USA, 1896*
Victorious in all his matches in the Walker Cups of 1924, 1928 and 1930, 'Jimmy' Johnston took 1929 US Amateur title. He was a major figure in American golf in the '20s despite suffering shell shock in World War I, which affected his nerves.

JONES, Grier – *born Wichita, Kansas, USA, 6 May 1946*
After winning 1968 National Collegiate Championship, Jones was the medallist at that year's pro qualifying school and after finishing 50th in the money list in his first year on Tour he was voted Rookie of the Year. His two victories came in Hawaiian Open and Robinson Fall Golf Classic in 1972, when he earned $140,000 and finished fourth in the money list.

JONES, Robert Trent – *born Ince, Lancashire, England 1906*
He moved to the United States with his parents while still a toddler and has emerged as one of the world's foremost golf course architects over the past 40 years. He has designed or remodelled over 300 courses around the world, many of them controversially long and difficult.

Right: Don January turned professional in 1955 and 20 years later he is still a top professional.

JONES, Robert Tyre – *born Atlanta, Georgia, USA, 17 March 1902. Died 1971*
Jack Nicklaus is the only man to challenge seriously the claim made of Bobby Jones – that he was the world's greatest golfer. His record up to his retirement in 1930 at the age of 28 was five US Amateur Championships, four US Opens, three British Opens and one British Amateur. He remained an amateur, yet, in eight years from 1923 took 13 major titles. His retirement came when he reached the pinnacle of achievement in 1930 by completing the original and unique Grand Slam of golf by winning the Amateur and Open Championships of the USA and Britain. Four times runner-up in the US Open. Jones played five successive Walker Cups from 1922, captaining the last two sides, romping to huge singles wins each time – by 13 and 12 over Tom Perkins, 12 and 11 over Cyril Tolley, 9 and 8 over Roger Wethered. He graduated in law, literature and engineering. Won his first title, the Georgia State Amateur,

Seen here in 1927, Bobby Jones is considered by many to be the greatest golfer ever born. The stone (above) marks an historic shot played by Jones in the 1926 British Open Championship at Royal Lytham, England.

Above: This portrait of Bobby Jones is located in the library of Golf House, the headquarters of the United States' Golf Association, New York. It was painted by T E Stephens and the framed letter beside it is from President Eisenhower.

at 14, was Southern Amateur Champion at 15 and runner-up in the US Amateur Championship at 17. His one mentor was Scots born Stewart Maiden, professional at the East Lake club. Jones preceded his first British Open win in 1926 with a qualifying 66 at Sunningdale. Jones created the Augusta National course following his retirement, with the help of Scottish architect Dr Alister Mackenzie, and Jones and the late Clifford Roberts developed the US Masters classic. Jones began suffering from a progressive spinal disease in the '50s and was reduced to a complete cripple. The Masters remains a living monument to a man honoured with the Freedom of St Andrews, where the 10th hole on the Old Course is named after him.

JONES, Stuart Gwynn – *born Hastings, New Zealand, 1925*
He took up golf after being badly scalded in an accident in 1947 and went on to win seven New Zealand Amateur Championships and many other events. He made seven appearances in the Eisenhower Trophy World Team Championship.

JURADO, Jose – *born Buenos Aires, Argentina, 1899. Died 1972*
Runner-up to Tommy Armour in 1931 British Open at Carnoustie, Jurado was the first Argentinian to make his mark in world golf. Six times his country's Open Champion, he captained an Argentinian side on a European Tour in 1939.

K

KAZMIERSKI, Joyce – *born Pontiac, Michigan, USA, 14 August 1945*
Steady success since she joined the LPGA Tour in 1968 has brought her well over $100,000 prize-money.

KEISER, Herman – *born Springfield, USA, 1914*
He was selected for 1947 US Ryder Cup side after pipping Ben Hogan for 1946 US Masters title. He won many major events in the '40s.

KIMBALL, Judy – *born Sioux City, Iowa, USA, 17 June 1938*
Her four major victories include 1962 LPGA Championship. That was in her second year on tour. In her first she won American Open. Her career prize winnings total around $150,000.

KING, Sam – *born Godden Green, Kent, England, 27 March 1911*
Two years after making the first of three Ryder Cup appearances, was third in 1939 Open. Victories include 1933 British Assistants' and 1961 and 1962 British Seniors' Championships.

KINSELLA, Jimmy – *born Skerries, Dublin, Eire, 25 May 1939*
A heart condition forced Kinsella, who won 1972 Madrid Open, two Irish Dunlop and two Irish Professional Championships, to cut down on tournaments after 20 years as a professional. Made four appearances for Ireland in World Cup and four in Double Diamond Internationals.

KIRBY, Dorothy – *born Atlanta, Georgia, USA, 1919*
She played in four successive Curtis Cup sides against Britain and Ireland from 1948 and won US Amateur Championship in 1951 after finishing runner-up in 1939 and 1947.

KIRKALDY, Andrew – *born Denhead, Scotland, 18 March 1860. Died 1934*
Tied with Willie Park for 1889 British Open but lost play-off. Spent most of his life in St Andrews, latterly being professional. Played many money matches, beating Open Champion J H Taylor by one hole in a £50-a-side affair in 1895.

KIRKWOOD, Joseph – *born Sydney, Australia, 1898*
He gained world-wide recognition as a trick shot artist on tours with Walter Hagen, specialising in hitting full-blooded drives off the face of a wrist watch. He was a fine golfer, too, and won both the Australian and New Zealand Open titles in 1920 when only 23. He was three

Above: Tony Jacklin

Above: Tommy Horton

Above: Hale Irwin

Above: Mark Hayes at the British Open in 1977 with a record round of 63.

Above: Hubert Green

Above: Graham Marsh

Above: Angel Gallardo

Above. Arthur D'Arcy 'Bobby' Locke

times fourth in the British Open and won California, Houston, Canadian and Illinois Opens.

KIROUAC, Martha – *born USA*
Victory in 1970 US Amateur Championship earned her the first of two Curtis Cup appearances and a place in America's victorious Espirito Santo World Amateur Team of 1970.

KITE, Tom – *born Austin, Texas, USA, 9 December 1949*
This bespectacled Texan entered pro golf with impressive credentials, having finished runner-up to Lanny Wadkins in 1970 US Amateur Championship, made that year's World Trophy side and 1971 Walker Cup team and tied Ben Crenshaw for 1972 National Collegiate title. He was 1973 Rookie of the Year, finishing 56th in the money list. He had eight top ten finishes in 1974 and nine in 1975, a prelude to his first victory in IVB-Bicentennial Golf Classic in 1976 when he finished with season's winnings of $116,000. He was into six figures again in 1977.

KNUDSON, George – *born Winnipeg, Canada, 28 June 1937*
Knudson, who always plays in dark glasses to counter an eye weakness, won 12 US Tour events between 1961 and 1972 and was never out of the top 60 in that period. His best year was 1972 when he won $74,000 to take 30th place in the table. He won the Canada Cup individual award in 1966 and partnered Al Balding to team victory in the 1968 event. Knudson's many Canadian wins include two PGA titles and his career earnings top half a million dollars.

KOCH, Gary – *born Baton Rouge, Louisiana, USA, 21 November 1952*
He turned professional after his second Walker Cup appearance in 1975, having also won World Amateur Team honours and a series of solo titles – including the 1970 US Junior Championship. Koch won the Tallahassee Open in 1976, in his fourth month on the Tour, and in 1977 he won the Citrus Open.

KOCSIS, Charles – *born Newcastle, Pennsylvania, USA, 1913*
'Chuck' Kocsis was US National Collegiate Champion in 1936 and two years later made the first of three Walker Cup appearances. He was runner-up to Harvie Ward in 1956 Amateur Championship and his victories included six in the Michigan Amateur Championship and three in the Michigan Open, one after a play-off against Tommy Armour. He was one of 12 children of Hungarian immigrants.

KONO, Takaaki – *born Hodogaya, Yokahama, Japan, 1940*
Son of an official of the Hodogaya Club, Kono played golf from childhood and took the 1968 Japanese Open title after elder brother Mit-

sukaka had twice won the Japanese Professional title. Four times a Japanese World Cup international he has also taken the Brazilian, Malaysian and Singapore Opens and twice been named outstanding Japanese athlete of the year.

KRATZERT, Bill – *born Quantico, Virginia, USA, 29 June 1952*
A former All-American amateur, he joined the US Tour in June 1976 and that year partnered Woody Blackburn to victory in the Walt Disney World National Team-Play event, having chalked up three other top ten finishes. In 1977 he won the Hartford Open with formidable rounds of 66, 66, 64, 69–265, finishing his second pro year with earnings of over $120,000.

KROLL, Ted – *born New Hartford, New York, USA, 1919*
Victory in 1953 George May World Championship earned him $50,000 and Kroll played in that year's Ryder Cup side, was runner-up in 1956 USPGA Championship, joint second in 1960 US Open to Arnold Palmer and winner of 1962 Canadian Open.

KYLE, Alex – *born Hawick, Scotland, 16 April 1907*
British amateur Champion 1939 and runner-up in 1946 Irish Open Amateur Championship and 1952 English Open Amateur Stroke Play Championship. Played in 1938, 1947 and 1951 Walker Cup sides. Played for Scotland 1938 to 1953.

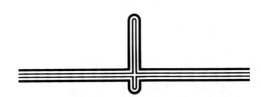

LACEY, Arthur – *born Burnham Beeches, Buckinghamshire, England, 20 May 1904*
Belgian and French Open Champion and a Ryder Cup player in 1933 and 1937 and captain in 1951. Played regularly for England and captained British side against Argentina in 1939. Now lives in United States.

LAFFOON, Ky – *born Zinc, Arkansas, USA, 1908*
Winner of a dozen pro events in the '30s and '40s – four in 1934 – Laffoon was twice runner-up in Canadian Open, a semi-finalist in 1937 USPGA Championship, fourth in 1946 US Masters and fifth in 1936 US Open.

LAMAZE, Henri de – *born Trelissac, Dordogne, France, 2 August 1918*
Outstanding French amateur. Won 25 French Open and French Native Championships between 1947 and 1971, as well as taking the Spanish, Portuguese, Belgian and Italian Amateur titles and Spanish Open.

Right: Charlotte Cecilia Leitch was a leading British player. Seen here is the young Miss Leitch of 1908.

LANGLEY, John – *born Northwood, Middlesex, England, 25 April 1918*
Won British Boys' title in 1935 and English Championship in 1950. Earned three Walker Cup caps, the first in 1936 while he was still a schoolboy.

LAUER, Bonnie – *born Detroit, Michigan, USA, 20 February 1951*
She turned professional in 1975 after winning the 1973 National Collegiate title and reaching the semi-finals of US Amateur Championship and making the 1974 Curtis Cup side. She was twice second and earned $15,000 in her first 12 months on the Tour to be named Rookie of the Year.

LEES, Arthur – *born Sheffield, England, 21 February 1908*
Winner of four Ryder Cup caps between 1947 and 1955. Won Dunlop Masters, Irish Open and British Seniors'.

LEE-SMITH, Jennifer – *born Newcastle on Tyne, England, 2 December 1948*
Voted joint Daks Woman Golfer of 1976 after winning the British Ladies Open Stroke Play title. Played in 1974 and 1976 Curtis Cup matches, European and 1975 Commonwealth Team events and 1976 World Team championships. Now a professional.

LEGRANGE, Cobie – *born Boksburg, South Africa, 22 October 1942*
Won four tournaments in Britain in the sixties – Dunlop Masters of 1964 and 1969 and Pringle and Senior Service events. Won eight events on home circuit, and scored victories in Australia, New Zealand and Switzerland.

Below: The late Tony Lema won the British Open in 1964 in his first attempt. Here he (left) receives the trophy from T F Blackwell, Captain of the Royal and Ancient Club.

LEITCH, Charlotte Cecilia – *born Silloth, Cumbria, England, 13 April 1891. Died 1977*
British Champion in 1914, 1920, 1921 and 1926. English Champion in 1914 and 1919. Was five times French Champion and also won Canadian Championship. Was England international from 1910 to 1928, winning 29 of her 33 matches.

LEMA, Tony – *born Oakland, California, USA, 1934. Died 1966*
The former caddie and US Marine was spectacularly successful before his tragic death in a private plane crash. After joining the US Tour in 1958 he was runner-up to Jack Nicklaus in US Masters and finished fourth in the prize-money list in 1963, and in 1964 he came fresh from winning three American events to take the British Open title by five strokes at St Andrews, despite the fact that he arrived on his first trip to Europe only 36 hours before round one over the testing Old Course. He played in the Ryder Cup matches of 1963 and 1965, won the World Series and Carling World tournaments, played for America in 1965 Canada Cup match and established a reputation of being a second Hagen because of his love of the high life.

LEONARD, Stan – *born Vancouver, Canada, 1914*
Nine times Canadian PGA Champion between 1940 and 1962, Leonard won three US events, including the 1958 Tournament of Champions. When in his forties, represented his country in seven Canada Cup team championships and was top individual in the 1954 event and joint best with Australian Peter Thomson in 1959.

LEWIS, Jack – *born Florence, South Carolina, USA*
A member of the 1967 Walker Cup side and 1968 Eisenhower World Trophy team, Lewis, winner of 1968 North-South Amateur title and a product of Arnold Palmer's old school, Wake Forest, turned professional in 1969.

LIETZKE, Bruce – *born Kansas City, Kansas, USA, 18 July 1951*
This husky former Texas Amateur Champion had two fourth places in 1975, his first year on the Tour. Two thirds, a fourth and three sixths in 1976 underlined his progress. But no one could have expected his explosive start to 1977, when he won two of the first five events, the Tucson Open and Hawaiian Open. A succession of high finishes improved earnings of $69,000 in 1976 to around $200,000 in 1977.

LISTER, John – *born Temuka, New Zealand, 9 March 1947*
Victories in New Zealand PGA Championship and two British events as well as World Cup appearances encouraged Lister to tackle the US circuit, but his first five years were frustrating. His highest placing in the money list was 94th and his best year financially yielded only $24,600. Lister broke into the top 60 in 1976 by winning the Ed McMahon-Quad Cities Open.

LITTLE, Sally – *born Cape Town, South Africa, 12 October 1951*
The former South African Match and Stroke Play Champion, who finished top individual in 1971 World Amateur Team Championships, enjoyed her best year in 1977 since turning professional six years earlier, collecting $67,000 prize-money to finish 10th in the LPGA list and push her career earnings to more than $150,000. The only South African on the Tour, she scored her first win in 1976 Ladies' Masters.

LITTLE, William Lawson – *born Newport, Rhode Island, USA, 23 June 1910. Died 1968*
Unique in golf history by winning British and US Amateur Championships of 1934 and 1935. En route to 1934 British title at Prestwick, Scotland, Little crushed local opponent J Wallace 14 and 13 after a morning 66. On Walker Cup debut that year in Britain defeated Cyril Tolley 6 and 5. Little turned professional in 1936 and immediately won Canadian Open. Four years later took US Open title after play-off against Gene Sarazen.

LITTLER, Gene – *born San Diego, California, USA, 21 July 1930*
After 24 Tour victories Littler's career looked to be over when he underwent surgery for cancer in 1972. But 'Gene the Machine', as the 1961 US Open Champion is known, came back the same year and in 1973 he won again in St Louis. In 1974 Littler, nine times among America's top ten money winners in 15 years from 1954, won more than $100,000, and in 1975 his comeback was complete when he won the Bing Crosby, Danny Thomas Memphis Classic and Westchester Classic events and $182,000. The 29th victory of a career that has yielded Littler

Below: Gene Littler, former US Open Champion, is one of the most stylish players of the game.

Centre right: Henry Longhurst, best known for his golf television commentaries both in the United States and Britain.

Below: South African Bobby Locke was four times winner of the British Open Championship.

around $1,400,000 winnings came in 1977's Houston Open and a series of high finishes, which ensured he again earned over $120,000. A year before turning professional Littler won 1953 US Amateur Championship. He has won in Japan and South Africa and made seven Ryder Cup appearances. His triumph over illness earned him the Bobby Jones and Ben Hogan awards in 1973.

LOCKE, Arthur D'Arcy – *born Germiston, South Africa, 20 November 1917*
First since the Great Triumvirate of Vardon, Braid and Taylor to record four British Open victories – in 1949, 1950, 1952 and 1957. Was South African Amateur and Open Champion while still a teenager in 1935 and 1937 and won his country's Open title six more times. Also took New Zealand, Canadian, French, German, Irish, Swiss and Egyptian Open titles and won five US Tour events in 1947, two in 1948, three in 1949 and another in 1950. British wins included two Dunlop Masters. Three times winner of the Vardon Trophy.

LONGHURST, Henry Carpenter – *born Bedford, 1909*
Longhurst was both the German Open Amateur champion and runner-up in the French Open Championship in 1936. He was golf correspondent for *The Sunday Times* for almost 30 years. He is well known on both sides of the Atlantic for his television commentaries. He has written several books on golf and golfing humour.

LOPEZ, Nancy – *born New Mexico, USA, 1957*
Nancy Lopez was runner-up in the 1975 US Women's Open Championship as an amateur. In 1977 she turned professional and again was runner-up in the same event. In 1976 as an amateur she played in the Curtis Cup match against Great Britain and Ireland at Royal Lytham. In 1977 as a professional, she won $23,138. In 1978 she won her first LPGA major title when she took the Bent Tree Classic.

LOTT, Lyn – *born Douglas, Georgia, USA, 9 April 1950*
This former Georgia State Open and Amateur Champion qualified at the first attempt at the 1973 School for the US Tour and his winnings have increased each year to over $75,000 in 1977.

LOTZ, Dick – *born Oakland, California, USA, 15 October 1942*
Winner of 1969 Alameda Open, 1970 Monsanto Open and 1970 Kemper Open, Lotz's most successful US Tour year was 1970 when he finished sixth in the Order of Merit with $125,000 winnings.

LU, Liang Huan – *born Taipei, Taiwan, 1936*
'Mr Lu' achieved fame outside his native land, where he has won a succession of tournaments, with his second place behind Lee Trevino in 1971 British Open. Member of 1972 winning World Cup team. Victories include the Philippines, Thailand, French and Hong Kong Opens as well as Japanese events.

LUCAS, Percy Belgrave, – *born Sandwich, Kent, England, 2 September 1915*
'Laddie' Lucas's Walker Cup career was interrupted by the War after he made his debut in 1936. Chosen again in 1947 and was non-playing captain in 1949. A former Member of Parliament.

LUNN, Bob – *born Sacramento, California, USA, 24 April 1945*
He enjoyed five oustanding years on the US Tour, winning the 1968 Memphis and Atlanta events, 1969 Hartford Open, 1970 Florida citrus, 1971 Los Angeles Open and 1972 Atlanta classic. His highest placing in the money list was 11th in 1968. Then and in 1970 his winnings topped $100,000.

LUNT, Michael – *born Birmingham, England, 20 May 1935*
Son of the 1934 English Champion, Stanley Lunt, Michael took the title in 1966, three years after winning the British Amateur Championship. Played in four successive Walker Cup matches from 1959 and was member of the winning Eisenhower Trophy World Team Championship side in 1964.

LYLE, Alexander – *born Shrewsbury, England, 9 February 1958*
Turned professional in 1977 after adding Walker Cup honours to three British appearances in the European and Commonwealth events. In 1975 represented England at boy, youth and full international level and took that year's English Open Amateur Stroke Play title.

LYON, George – *born Richmond, Ontario, Canada, 1858. Died 1938*
An all-round sportsman who did not take to golf until his late thirties, Lyon was eight times Canadian Amateur Champion between 1898 and 1914 and runner-up for the US Amateur and Canadian Open titles. A unique honour for Canada was the golf title he won in the 1904 Olympic Games in St Louis, USA, and he was many times Canadian and North American Seniors' Champion.

MCALLISTER, Susie – *born New Orleans, USA, 27 August 1947*
In 1977 she took her official winnings on the US Tour past the $100,000 mark despite two operations on her left arm in 1974.

McCANN, Catherine – *born Clonmel, Tipperary, Eire, 1922*
The former Catherine Smye added the British title to her two Irish Championship victories in 1951 and made her Curtis Cup bow in 1952. Irish international 1947 to 1962.

McCORD, Gary – *born San Gabriel, California, USA, 23 May 1948*
He was assured of his best year financially on the US Tour in 1977 when his winnings total passed his previous best of $43,000 in 1975.

McCORMACK, Mark – *born Chicago, Illinois, USA, 1931*
This qualified lawyer earned world-wide renown as manager of the 'Big Three' of Jack Nicklaus (who later left the organization), Arnold Palmer and Gary Player, and his world-wide company handles the business affairs of many golfers and other sportsmen.

McCREADY, Samuel – *born Belfast, N Ireland, 8 March 1918*
British Amateur Champion 1949. Made first of two Walker Cup appearances that year and represented Ireland 1947 to 1952.

Left: Nancy Lopez is a top dollar-earning American professional.

McCULLOUGH, Mike – *born Coshocton, Ohio, USA, 21 March 1945*
Joined US Tour in 1972 after winning Ohio State Amateur and West Palm Beach Open title in 1970, won 1974 Mini-Kemper Open on the second tour and moved into top 60 money winners with around $80,000 in 1977.

McDERMOTT, John – *born Philadelphia, Pennsylvania, USA, 1891. Died 1971*
He became the first home-bred American to win the US Open in 1911, having lost a play-off 12 months earlier, and successfully defended the title in 1912. He also won the Philadelphia, Western, Shawnee and North and South Opens, all his successes coming in the space of five years before illness cut short his career.

MACDONALD, Charles Blair – *born Niagara Falls, New York, USA, 1855. Died 1939*
He left America in 1872 to be educated at St Andrews University while living with his Scottish grandfather, took up golf and returned home to win the 1895 US Amateur title, found the Chicago Golf Club and build several courses, including the National Golf Links and Mid-Ocean.

Right: A pioneer and a rebel in the early days of American golf, Charles Blair Macdonald not only played the game well, he also designed courses.

McGEE, Jerry – *born New Lexington, Ohio, USA, 21 July 1943*
McGee's reward for consistent high finishing was a Ryder Cup debut in Britain in 1977. Earlier he had added the Philadelphia Classic title to the Pensacola Open title he won in 1975 to push his prize-money to more than $120,000,

for the second year running and to more than $500,000 in his career. McGee finished in the top ten 12 times.

McHALE, James – *born Stockton, California, USA, 1916*
He was a professional for a time after playing in 1949 and 1951 Walker Cup matches and reaching the semi-finals of the British and quarter-finals of the US Amateur Championships and in 1947 US Open set scoring records of 30 for nine holes and 65 for 18.

McINTIRE, Barbara – *born USA, 1935*
US Champion 1959 and 1964 and British Champion 1960. Lost play-off to Kathy Cornelius in 1956 US Womens' Open. Played in six Curtis Cup matches between 1958 and 1972.

McKENNA, Mary – *born Dublin, Eire, 29 April 1949*
Won Irish Championship 1969, 1972 and 1974. Played in four successive Curtis Cup sides from 1970 as well as in the Vagliano Trophy and World Championship teams.

MACKENZIE, Ada – *born Toronto, Canada, 1891. Died 1973*
Elected to Canada's Golf Hall of Fame, she was five times Canadian Open and Close Champion and a semi-finalist in the US Amateur Championship of 1927 and her country's outstanding woman golfer for many years.

MACKENZIE, Keith – *born Britain, 1921*
He became secretary of the Royal and Ancient Golf Club of St Andrews, ruling body of the game, in 1967 and has been instrumental in the dramatic growth of the British Open Championship.

MACKENZIE, Roland – *born Washington DC, USA, 1907*
He played in the 1926, 1928 and 1930 Walker Cup matches and won the District of Colombia, Middle Atlantic and Maine Amateur titles.

McCLELLAND, Doug – *born South Shields, Durham, England, 30 November 1949*
Never out of the top 60 in the European order of merit since 1971, McClelland enjoyed his best season for four years in 1977, finishing 26th in the table with over £7000 prize-money. His best year was 1973 when, after winning the Dutch Open, he ended in 14th place with over £7600 earnings.

McLENDON, Mac – *born Atlanta, Georgia, 10 August 1945*
In his first tournament after turning professional in 1968 this Louisiana State accountancy graduate won the Magnolia Classic – a second Tour event. He made the top 60 money winners in his first two seasons but only once in the next

five years did he repeat the feat. His two major victories came in the 1974 Walt Disney World National Team Championship with Hubert Green and the 1976 Southern Open.

McLEOD, Fred – *born North Berwick, Scotland, 25 April 1882*
Emigrated to United States in 1903 and became a prominent tournament professional, winning many events, including the 1908 US Open and two Western Opens. Was second and third in subsequent Opens and runner-up in the US-PGA Championship. Took USPGA Seniors' title in 1928.

Left: Freddie McLeod won the US Open Championship in 1908. He is seen here at the age of 81 acting as an honorary starter for the 1964 Masters at Augusta, Georgia.

McNAMARA, Thomas – *born USA, 1882. Died 1939*
One of the best of the early home-bred American golfers, he was runner-up in the 1909, 1912 and 1915 US Opens, his 69 in 1909 being the first in the event's history under 70.

McSPADEN, Harold – *born Rosedale, Kansas, USA, 1908*
He and Byron Nelson were tagged 'the Gold-dust Twins' during World War II because of their successes on the pro tour. 'Jug' McSpaden won more than 20 tournaments in the '30s and '40s, including 1939 Canadian Open, and he was runner-up in 1937 US PGA Championship.

MAHAFFEY, John – *born Kerrville, Texas, USA, 9 May 1948*
After winning the Sahara Invitational event and topping $112,000 winnings in 1973, Mahaffey earned over $120,000 in 1974. In 1975 he chalked up three second places, losing a play-off to Lou Graham in the US Open, and earned more than $140,000.

Centre left: Irish and British international, Mary McKenna, 1977.

88

MALTBIE, Roger – *born Modesto, California, USA, 30 June 1951*
This bespectacled former California State Open Champion's victory in the 1976 Memorial Tournament after a sudden death play-off against Hale Irwin, was his third in only two full years on the Tour, which yielded almost $200,000 prize-money. His first two wins came in successive weeks in 1975 in the Ed McMahon-Jaycees Quad Cities Open and Pleasant Valley Classic. He was the first rookie to win back-to-back since Bob Murphy in 1968.

MANERO, Tony – *born New York, USA, 1905*
US Open Champion in 1936 with a record 282 total, he was a contemporary of Gene Sarazen and the Turnesa Brothers in the Westchester area. He reached the semi-finals of 1937 US-PGA Championship, played in that year's

Ryder Cup match and won over a dozen tournaments.

MANGRUM, Lloyd – *born Trenton, Texas, USA, 1914. Died 1973*
Picked for the 1939 Ryder Cup match (not played because of the War), Mangrum made four successive appearances in the contests from 1947, captaining the 1953 side. He was runner-up after a record 64 in 1940 US Masters before war service and won US Army Championship in Paris and British GI Championship at St Andrews, Scotland in 1945 before returning to take the 1946 US Open title after a play-off with Byron Nelson and Vic Ghezzi. He was defeated by Ben Hogan in a play-off for the 1950 title. His victories include the Pennsylvania, Argentine and All-American Opens as well as the 1948 World Championship.

Right: American Ryder Cup Captain, Lloyd Mangrum, with the trophy at Wentworth Club, Surrey in 1953.

MANN, Carol – *born Buffalo, New York, USA, 3 February 1941*
Has scored 40 US Tour victories and won almost half a million dollars prize-money since turning professional in 1961. Won ten tournaments in 1968 and eight in 1969, earning close to $100,000 in that spell. US Open Champion in 1965.

MARR, Dave – *born Houston, Texas, USA, 27 December 1933*
Most outstanding of his four US Tour wins was the PGA Championship in 1965. For nine years from joining the Tour in 1960 he was never out of the top 60 money winners, his best placing being seventh in 1965, when he gained Ryder Cup recognition. Marr is now a well known TV golf broadcaster.

MARSH, David – *born Southport, Lancashire, England, 29 April 1934*
English Champion, 1964 and 1970. Selected for 1959 and 1971 Walker Cup sides and was non-playing captain in 1973 and 1975. Captained Britain against Europe and England in four home internationals as well as playing in the sides from the '50s.

MARSH, Graham – *born Kalgoorlie, Western Australia, 14 January 1944*
One of the world's most successful golfers. He won seven tournaments on three continents in 1976, then qualified for his US players' card, and in 1977 he finished fifth three times, sixth and 12th in his first five American events, going on to score his first US victory by a stroke from Tom Watson in the Heritage Classic, finishing his debut year with $107,000 prize-money. Since 1970 Marsh has won in Australia, New Zealand, Switzerland, India, Germany, Thailand, Scotland, Malaysia, England and France. He has twice topped the Asian Order of Merit. He won four Japanese tournaments in both 1974 and 1976 and by the end of 1977 had chalked up 27 victories world-wide, collecting close to $200,000 prize-money in the space of just over 12 months. His most profitable win came in the 1977 Colgate World Match Play Championship in Britain where he collected £30,000. A week later he won the Lancôme Tournament in Paris and another £10,000.

MARSTON, Maxwell – *born USA, 1892*
A member of the 1922, 1924 and 1934 Walker Cup sides, he was US Amateur Champion in 1923, beating Bobby Jones in an early round and Jess Sweetser in the final. He was runner-up in the 1933 Championship and won many invitation events.

MARTI, Fred – *born Houston, Texas, USA, 15 November 1940*
This former National Collegiate Champion and All-American had his best year in 1971 when he finished 39th in the money list with $58,000.

MARTIN, Steve – *born Dundee, Scotland, 21 December 1955*
Won Scottish Open Amateur Stroke Play title and East of Scotland Open Stroke Play Championship in 1976. Played in that year's winning Eisenhower Trophy side. Now a professional.

MASON, Carl – *born Goring, Berkshire, England, 26 June 1953*
British Youths' Champion in 1973, Mason was voted Professional Rookie of the Year in 1974. He won the Lusaka Open in 1975 and finished 38th in the Order of Merit.

MASSENGALE, Don – *born Jacksboro, Texas, USA, 23 April 1937*
Elder brother of Rik, he took the Bing Crosby and Canadian Open titles in 1966, his best year on the Tour when he won $38,000 for 26th place in the money list.

Below: Australian Graham Marsh is a world-ranked international professional.

MASSENGALE, Rik – *born Jacksboro, Texas, USA, 6 February 1947*
Rik kept up his record of winning a tournament a year with success in 1977 Hope Desert Classic, having taken 1975 Tallahassee Open and 1976 Sammy Davis Jr Greater Hartford Open titles. He entered the top 60 money winners list in 1975, won over $124,000 in 1976 and improved on that in 1977. He joined the Tour in 1970.

MASSY, Arnaud – *born Biarritz, France, 1877. Died 1958*
First overseas golfer to win British Open – in 1907. Tied for the title with Vardon in 1911 but lost play-off. Won four French Open titles, three Spanish and the Belgian.

MASSY, Debbie – *born USA, November 1950*
Three times Canadian Champion and a Curtis Cup international, she marked a highly impressive rookie year on the US Tour in 1977 by collecting $47,000 prize-money and winning a Japanese tournament.

MASTERS, Margie – *born Victoria, Australia, 24 October 1934*
She became a professional in 1965 after a distinguished amateur career highlighted by victories in the Australian, New Zealand, Canadian and South African Championships and many international appearances. She took her prize winnings past the $100,000 mark in 1974, having scored two major victories.

MAXWELL, William – *born Abilene, Texas, USA, 1929*
US Amateur Champion in 1951, he became one of America's most successful tour professionals, finishing fifth in the 1962 US Masters and 1963 US Open and US PGA Championships. He won seven major events and played in the 1963 Ryder Cup match.

MAYER, Dick – *born Stamford, Connecticut, USA, 29 August 1924*
In 1957 won US Open, was Player of the Year, leading money winner and gained a Ryder Cup place. Won four other major events and collected a $50,000 prize for a hole-in-one in a 1962 tournament.

Right: Cary Middlecoff won two US Open Championships in his lengthy professional career. Before turning professional he was a successful dentist.

MELHORN, William – *born USA, 1898*
Twice third in US Open and runner-up in 1925 US PGA Championship, 'Wild Bill' Melhorn's

American Tour victories included the Western, Hawaiian and Texas Opens and he played in the 1927 Ryder Cup match. He won 18 major events.

MELNYK, Steve – *born Brunswick, Georgia, USA, 26 February 1947*
Winner of the 1969 US Amateur title and the 1971 British Amateur title, Melnyk played in the 1969 and 1971 Walker Cup matches before turning professional, since when his best year was 1974, when he won over $53,000 and made the top 60 for the first time.

MENNE, Bob – *born Gardner, Massachusetts, USA, 19 February 1942*
Four years after joining the US Tour he broke through to win 1974 Kemper Open after a play-off and finished 40th in the money list with $61,000.

METZ, Dick – *born Arkansas City, Kansas, USA, 1909*
A highly successful US Tour campaigner in the '30s, he won more than 15 major events – six in 1939, when he was a semi-finalist in US PGA Championship and gained Ryder Cup honours. He was runner-up to Ralph Guldahl in 1938 US Open after losing a four stroke lead and was 1960 US PGA Seniors' Champion.

MICKLEM, Gerald, CBE – *born Burgh Heath, Surrey, England, 14 August 1911*
Winner of English Championship 1947 and 1953. Played in four Walker Cup sides from 1947 and was non-playing captain in 1957 and 1959. Twice captained Britain against Europe and led 1958 Eisenhower Trophy side. Served R and A Club as Chairman of Rules of Golf Committee and Championship Committee and as Captain. Won Bobby Jones Award 1969.

MIDDLECOFF, Cary – *born Halls, Tennessee, USA, 6 January 1921*
Named for first postwar Walker Cup side but declined in order to turn professional. In 1949 won first of his two US Opens. Won US Masters in 1955 and was runner-up in the Open, Masters and US PGA Championships. Won 34 US Tour events between 1947 and 1961, including six in 1955 when he gained the Byron Nelson Award. Made three Ryder Cup appearances in the '50s.

MIGUEL, Angel – *born Madrid, Spain, 1929*
Elder of two golfing brothers. Twice Spanish Open Champion. Won three British tour events in as many years in the '60s. Took the Argentine, Dutch and three Portuguese Open titles and top individual honours in the 1958 World Cup.

MIGUEL, Sebastian – *born Madrid, Spain, 7 February 1931*
Represented his country 11 times in World Cup. Took the Portuguese and Peru Open titles as well as three Spanish Open and four Spanish Professional crowns.

MILLER, Allen – *born San Diego, California, USA, 10 August 1948*
He played in the 1969 and 1971 Walker Cup matches and won the Canadian Amateur Championship before turning professional in 1971, and scored his first victory in 1974 Tallahassee Open.

MILLER, Johnny – *born San Francisco, California, USA, 29 April 1947*
1974 was Johnny Miller's year. His first 23 rounds were of par or better and he won the Bing Crosby, Phoenix and Tucson events in the opening three weeks, adding the Heritage Classic and Tournament of Champions top checks before the end of April and taking his year's

Below: Johnny Miller is a high-ranking modern American professional.

total to eight with wins in the Westchester Classic, World Open and Kaiser International. Official earnings of $353,000 beat Jack Nicklaus' record by more than $30,000 and after topping the table he finished second in 1975 with $226,000 earnings, winning three of his first four tournaments – Phoenix Open, Dean Martin-Tucson Open and Bob Hope Desert Classic – by margins of 14, nine and three strokes and with totals of 24, 25 and 21 under par. Rounds of 61 helped him to his first two 1975 wins, and later in the year he again won the Kaiser event. The 1973 US Open Champion pushed his total winnings in an amazing eight year career over the million dollar mark in 1976, winning the British Open and two more US titles to take his American total to 17. Other achievements of the 6ft 2in blond were victories in the 1964 USGA Junior Championship and 1968 Californian Amateur Championship, the World Cup individual and team titles (with Nicklaus) in 1973, and a 1975 Ryder Cup appearance.

MILLER, Sharon – *born Marshall, Michigan, USA, 13 January 1941*
She was twice Michigan State Champion and won the Trans-Mississippi title before joining the LPGA Tour in 1966 and, helped by two victories in 1973 and 1974, she had well over $100,000 to show for her first ten years on Tour.

MILLS, Mary – *born Laurel, Mississippi, USA, 19 January 1940*
Winner of the Mississippi State title eight consecutive years before turning professional in 1962, she had recorded eight victories by the end of 1973, including the 1963 US Open and 1964 and 1973 LPGA Championships. She was

among the top 20 money winners in 12 of her first 13 seasons and is among the all-time leading money winners with over a quarter of a million dollars.

MILNE, Willie – *born Perth, Scotland, 13 July 1951*
Followed Scottish International honours with Walker Cup recognition in 1973 and since turning professional has won the 1973 Lusaka Open and the 1973 and 1974 Northern Opens.

MILTON, Moira – *born Scotland, 18 December 1923*
The former Moira Paterson enjoyed her best year in 1952, winning the British Championship and a Curtis Cup place. Played for Britain and Scotland between 1949 and 1952 and was non-playing captain of Scotland's European Championship team 1973.

MITCHELL, Abe – *born East Grinstead, England, 1887. Died 1947*
Winner of three British Match Play Championships. Described by J H Taylor as 'the finest player who never won an Open Championship.' Was in the top six five times. Runner-up in 1912 British Amateur Championship losing at the 38th to John Ball. Made three Ryder Cup appearances.

MITCHELL, Bobby – *born Chatham, Virginia, USA, 23 February 1943*
A former Virginia Open Champion, Mitchell won 1971 Cleveland Open and 1972 Tournament of Champions. He finished in the top 60 in 1969, 1971 and 1972 – his best year with $113,000 winnings for 11th place.

Below: Abe Mitchell was an outstanding British Professional after World War I but he never succeeded in winning the British Open Championship. He is seen here driving off in his 1929 attempt at the Open.

MIYAMOTO, Tomekichi – *born Rokko, Japan, 1902*
A former caddie, he was one of his country's outstanding performers in the early days of tournament golf, winning the Japanese Open six times and the Professional Championship four times, and playing a series of challenge matches in America in the '30s.

MOE, Donald – *born USA, 1909*
He played in the Walker Cup matches of 1930 and 1932 and won the Western Amateur Championship twice, Pacific North West title three times and Oregon Amateur Championship twice.

MOHAMMED, Said Moussa – *born Egypt, 1933*
Egyptian Open Champion a dozen times and a regular representative in the Canada (World) Cup contest since the '50s, he has been a regular campaigner on the European tournament circuit.

MOLINA, Florentino – *born Cordoba, Argentina, 30 December 1938*
Winner of 1970 Argentina PGA Championship and 1971 and 1973 Argentina Opens, Molina took 1975 Pine Tree Open, a second tour event, in his first year on the US circuit.

MOODY, Orville – *born Chickasha, Oklahoma, USA, 9 December 1933*
Moody left the US Army to turn professional in 1967 at the age of 34 and two years later took his solitary Tour title – the US Open. He won the World Series that year and the World Cup with Lee Trevino and was named Player of the Year. Moody never had a golf lesson. His two best years were 1969 and 1973 when he topped $70,000 winnings.

MOONEY, Maisie – *born Dublin, Eire, 11 June 1952*
Winner of the Irish, Dutch and Australian Championships in 1973. Played in that year's Vagliano Trophy and European Team Championships, toured Canada and Australia with LGU sides and was voted Daks Woman Golfer of the Year.

MORELAND, Gus – *born USA, 1911*
He came to notice when he tied second place in the Texas Open in 1932 and that year won the Texas, Trans-Mississippi and Western titles as well as the first of two Walker Cup caps, winning all four of his matches. He turned professional in his fifties after winning several more amateur titles.

MOREY, Dale – *born USA, 1919*
He was picked for the 1965 Walker Cup side ten years after his first appearance in the match after winning 1964 North and South Amateur Championship. Morey, a professional for a spell, came to the fore by winning the 1950 Southern title. He was Western Amateur Champion in 1953 and runner-up in that year's US Amateur Championship to Gene Littler.

MORGAN, Gil – *born Wewoka, Oklahoma, USA, 25 September 1946*
This former Collegiate All-American enjoyed his best year since joining the US Tour in 1973 when he scored his first victory in the BC Open and finished 1977 with more than $100,000 earnings. Morgan, a Doctor of Optometry, scored six top ten finishes in 1976.

MORGAN, John Llewellyn – *born Llandrindod Wells, Wales, 23 June 1918*
Winner of the 1950 and 1951 Welsh Amateur Championships, Morgan made three successive Walker Cup appearances from 1951 and played for Wales from 1948 to 1967.

MORGAN, Wanda – *born Lymm, Cheshire, England, 22 March 1910*
British Champion 1935 and three times English Champion. Made three successive Curtis Cup appearances in the '30s as well as playing for Britain against France and Canada. An England regular for many years.

Left: Fashion of yesteryear modelled by Wanda Morgan – cardigan and ankle-length skirt.

MORLEY, Mike – *born Morris, Minnesota, USA, 17 June 1946*
This former winner of North Dakota Amateur Championship and three events on America's second tour made the top 60 money winners' list in 1976 after two seconds, a third and a fourth – six years after joining the circuit. In 1977 he recorded his first big win in the Quad Cities Open and for the second year running earned more than $80,000 prize-money.

Right: Tom Morris Senior and Tom Morris Junior, two of the best known professionals of the early days of golf.

MORRIS, (Old) Tom – *born St Andrews, Scotland, 1821. Died 1908*
One of the father figures of golf, Old Tom began life as an apprentice ball and club maker to the great Allan Robertson. They played as partners in challenge matches. Old Tom won the British Open Championship four times between 1861 and 1867, his son Young Tom then taking over the title. After a spell at Prestwick he returned to work out his life as greenkeeper to the Royal and Ancient Golf Club.

MORRIS, (Young) Tom – *born St Andrews, Scotland, 1851. Died 1875*
Continued the great tradition of championship golf begun by his father. Set a record still standing by following his father to victory in the British Open while only 17 in 1868. Old Tom was runner-up. Young Tom won again in 1869, 1870 and 1872. Three wins in a row earned him the Championship Belt, which still hangs in the R and A Clubhouse. Won scores of challenge matches and after one against Willie and Mungo Park in 1875 in partnership with his father, Young Tom was told his wife and newborn baby had died. He never recovered from the shock, dying on Christmas Day that year at the age of only 24.

MOUSSA, Mohammed – *born Alexandria, Egypt*
Won 17 successive Egyptian Championships and made as many World Cup appearances.

MURPHY, Bob – *born Brooklyn, New York, USA, 14 February 1943*
This heavyweight New Yorker turned professional in 1967 after winning 1965 US Amateur Championship and a 1967 Walker Cup place and in his first year on the Tour he won the 1968 Philadelphia and Thunderbird events in successive weeks and over $100,000 to finish tenth in the money list. In his first eight years on tour he finished outside the top 35 in the money list only once, his best being ninth for $120,000 in 1970. A thumb injury saw him slip to 44th overall in 1974 but he was back to his best in 1975, winning the Jackie Gleason Inverary Classic, a career best $127,000 and a Ryder Cup place. Further injuries hindered him in 1976 and 1977.

MURRAY, Ewen – *born Edinburgh, Scotland, 7 October 1954*
Murray turned professional in 1971 after winning the World Junior Championship and the Scottish Boys' Stroke and Match Play titles.

MURRAY, Gordon – *born Paisley, Scotland, 19 December 1936*
Twice Scottish Champion. Added a Walker Cup place in 1977 to a string of Scotland appearances from 1973.

MURRAY, Stuart – *born Paisley, Scotland, 10 November 1933*
Scottish Champion. Gained Walker Cup honours in 1963 and played for Britain in Commonwealth and European Team Championships as well as for Scotland from 1959 to 1963, when he turned professional.

NAGLE, Kelvin – *born Sydney, Australia, 21 December 1920*
Won 1960 centenary British Open at St Andrews in his 40th year. In 1965 tied Gary Player for US Open but lost play-off. Second in 1962 British Open. British and Irish Tour victories included Irish Hospitals event in 1961 with a record score of 64, 65, 66, 65 – 260. Nagle, three times British Seniors' Champion and World Seniors' titleholder in 1971, won 1959 Australian Open and was New Zealand Open winner six times, as well as taking the Canadian and French titles and helping Australia to victory in 1954 and 1959 World Cups.

NEEDHAM, Sandra – *born Bishopton, Renfrewshire, Scotland, 8 March 1946*
1976 Scottish Champion. Twice played in Vagliano trophy and established herself as Scotland international in '70s, touring South Africa with LGU team in 1974.

NELSON, Byron – *born Fort Worth, Texas, USA, 4 February 1912*
Won 11 consecutive US Tour events between March and August 1945 and a total of 18 tournaments that year. Won the first of two US Masters titles in 1937, four years after turning professional. Two years later won US Open title. First of two US PGA Championship wins came in 1940. Beat Ben Hogan in a play-off for 1942 Masters title. He preceded his remarkable feats of 1945 by winning 13 of the 23 events he entered in 1944. He averaged 68.33 in his formidable 1945 campaign and won a record $60,000. Made two Ryder Cup appearances.

NELSON, Larry – *born Fort Payne, Alabama, USA, 10 September 1947*
Nelson took up golf after a chance visit to a driving range in 1969 – at the age of 22 – and four years later he qualified for his players' card. His first three years on Tour earned him $24,000, $39,000 and $66,000 and in 1977 he topped $100,000 despite failing to record his first victory.

NEWTON, Jack – *born Sydney, Australia, 30 January 1950*
Newton came within a hairsbreadth of winning the 1975 British Open at Carnoustie, Scotland. American Tom Watson holed a long last green birdie putt to force a play-off, which he won 71 to 72. Newton was outstandingly successful in Europe, finishing fifth in the 1972 Order of Merit, and 10th, 14th and eighth in the following three years, winning more than £45,000 prize-money. His first European victory came in 1972 Dutch Open. His other wins include 1974 Nigerian Open and Benson and Hedges PGA Match Play Championship, and 1972 Benson and Hedges Festival and City of Auckland Classic. Newton transferred to the US circuit but a crop of injuries restricted his progress after he won twice in Zambia early in 1976.

Far left: Veteran Australian professional Kel Nagle created a surprise when he won the Centenary British Open Championship at St Andrews.

Above: World War II deprived the great American, Byron Nelson, of further golfing honours as so many of the tournaments were cancelled.

Left: The young Australian, Jack Newton, was runner-up to Tom Watson in the 1975 British Open Championship.

NICHOLS, Bobby – *born Louisville, Kentucky, USA, 14 April 1936*
Nichols joined the US Tour in 1960 and in his first 16 years was never out of the top 60 money earners. His best was 1964 when he took fifth place in the table after winning the PGA Championship and the World Open. His best year financially was 1974 when he won twice in a season for the third time and collected over $124,000. He had to have hospital treatment in 1975 after being struck by lightning in the incident in the Western Open which also involved Lee Trevino and Jerry Heard. Nichols, a 1967 Ryder Cup player, has won 12 times and accumulated total prize-money of close to a million dollars.

NICKLAUS, Jack – *born Columbus, Ohio, USA, 21 January 1940*
Undisputedly the world's number one golfer, Nicklaus took his official winnings in 16 years on the Tour to more than three million dollars and his total of victories to 63 in 1977 when he won the Inverrary Classic, an event he won again in 1978, Tournament of Champions and Memorial event to beat Arnold Palmer's total by two. Nicklaus has been leading money winner eight times and never finished worse than fourth despite rationing his tournament appearances. He has won a record 16 major titles. Winner of the 1959 and 1961 US Amateur crowns, Nicklaus has won the US Masters five times, the US PGA Championship four times, the US Open and the British Open three times each. His 1973 US PGA win broke Bobby Jones's 43 year old record of 13 majors. Only once since 1963 has Nicklaus finished worse than sixth in the British Open. His first US Open win in 1962 came only months after he joined the Tour after two Walker Cup appearances. He has played in the last five Ryder Cup matches. He is the only player to win the four major championships, termed 'The Grand Slam', twice. He has played in six winning US World Cup teams. His overseas victories include five Australian Opens. Nicklaus toiled in the shadow of the folk hero figure of Palmer in his early years, but he has improved his public image by slimming and changing his hair and clothes styles. In recent years, as well as spending more time with his wife and five children and in pursuing his hobbies of hunting, fishing and tennis, Nicklaus's 'Golden Bear' business interests have mushroomed and he has become heavily involved in golf course architecture, his prize creation being Muirfield Village near his Ohio home. He won the British Open in 1978.

Below: Jack Nicklaus, winner of the US Open Championship, the British Open Championship and the US Masters. Many consider him to be the best living golfer.

NIDA, Norman von – *born Sydney, Australia, 14 February 1914*
Pioneer of Australian golf after the war. Made an immediate impact in Britain in 1946, winning two tournaments, then took four of the six first prizes of 1947 to earn record prize-money and take the Vardon Trophy. Won three Australian Opens and was third in 1948 British Open.

NIEPORTE, Tom – *born Cincinnati, Ohio, USA, 21 October 1928*
He won the 1959 Rubber City Open, 1960 Azalea Open and 1967 Bob Hope Classic and figured in the top 60 between 1957 and 1960, his best year being 1959, when he finished 18th in the table.

NORMAN, Greg – *born Queensland, Australia, 1955*
As a relative unknown of 21 Norman won 1976 West Lakes Classic on his native circuit after finishing joint third on his pro debut in the Queensland Open a month earlier. After winning Japan's Kusuha Classic and representing Australia in the World Cup, he moved to Britain and almost immediately won the Martini International. Norman ended a spectacular debut year in Europe in 20th place in the Order of Merit with over £8200 prize-money, having helped Australasia into second place in the Double Diamond Internationals behind the USA.

Above: Jack Nicklaus

*Above: Christy O'Connor
Junior*

Right: Nancy Lopez

Above: Arnold Palmer

Above: Peter Oosterhuis

Above: Johnny Miller

Above: Kel Nagle

NORTH, Andy – *born Thorp, Wisconsin, USA, 9 March 1950*
As a schoolboy of 13 he was ordered to use crutches for 18 months when it was found a bone in a knee was disintegrating. He gave up football, baseball and basketball but was permitted to play golf so long as he rode in a cart. Fortunately the knee trouble cleared up. After winning the Wisconsin and Western Amateur titles he joined the US Tour in 1973, moved into the top 60 money winners list in 1974 and scored his first big victory in 1977 Westchester Classic, first prize of $60,000 helping him to top $100,000 for the first time.

O'CONNOR, Arnold – *born Sligo, Eire, 15 February 1946*
This former Irish amateur international based in Cheshire, England, enjoyed his best year on the European circuit in 1976 when he finished 37th in the Order of Merit with close to £6000 prize-money after four top 15 finishes.

O'CONNOR, Christy – *born Galway, Eire, 21 December 1924*
At the age of 53 this evergreen Irishman retained his British and World Seniors' titles (beating American Julius Boros) in 1977 to take his total of major victories to 27 since 1955. Only Neil Coles and Tony Jacklin in Europe can beat his postwar money winnings total of £121,485. His £31,532 total winnings in 1970, when he took top prize of £25,000 in the John Player Classic, has been bettered only twice – by Peter Oosterhuis (£32,127) in 1974 and Severiano Ballesteros (£39,504) in 1976. O'Connor won the Vardon Trophy as Order of Merit leader in 1961 and 1962, finished in the top ten for 16 straight years and from 1955 (he was only twice out of the top three in ten seasons from 1961) and has never finished out of the top 40. O'Connor's victories include two Dunlop Masters, the British PGA Match Play Championship, three Gallaher Ulster titles and four Carrolls Internationals in Ireland. He has had ten Ryder Cup outings and he partnered Harry Bradshaw to victory in the World (then Canada) Cup in 1958, tying for the individual title. In 1977 he finished the European season in 37th place with £4700 winnings.

O'CONNOR, Christy Jr – *born Galway, Eire, 19 August 1948*
Young Christy followed his famous uncle into the Ryder Cup team in 1975 after winning the Carrolls Irish Open and Irish Match Play Championship and tying Australian Ian Stanley for victory in the Martini International. He won 1974 Zambian Open and partnered Eamonn Darcy to victory in the 1976 Sumrie Bournemouth Better-ball event. He has only once finished outside the top 50 in the Order of Merit since 1971, his best placing being seventh in 1975 with almost £12,000 winnings. He has represented Britain and Ireland against the Continent of Europe and South Africa, and Ireland in the World Cup.

O'LEARY, John – *born Dublin, Eire, 19 August 1949*
The big Irishman turned professional a year after representing his country in 1969 European Team Championships. He entered the top 50 in the Order of Merit in 1972 and has stayed there, his best placing being 16th in 1976, when he won the Greater Manchester Open and over £12,000 prize-money. O'Leary's first victory came in the 1975 Holiday Inns event in South Africa, and later that year he partnered Australian Jack Newton to victory in the Sumrie Better-ball event. O'Leary has represented Ireland in the Double Diamond Internationals and played for Britain and Ireland in the Ryder Cup in 1975.

OLIVER, Ed – *born Delaware, USA, 1916. Died 1961*
So far as golf major events are concerned it was a case of 'always the bridesmaid' for 'Porky' Oliver – runner-up in 1946 US PGA Championship, 1952 US Open, and 1953 US Masters. Ben Hogan pipped him in the PGA and Masters Championships and Julius Boros in the Open. He was second in many more events, including the Canadian Open, and in 1940 US Open Oliver tied Gene Sarazen and Lawson Little but was disqualified with two other players for starting round four before the official hour to beat a storm. However Oliver won ten US Tour events, including the Bing Crosby, Phoenix, Texas and Western Opens, and played in three Ryder Cup matches.

Below: Irishman Christy O'Connor, winner of the 1977 World Senior Championship in the United States.

ONO, Koichi – *born Dairen, Manchuria, 1919*
Japanese Open and Professional Champion in 1955, the former caddie was in the winning Canada Cup side of 1957 – a success which sparked the country's golf explosion.

ONSHAM, Sukree – *born Prachuap, Khiri Khan, Thailand, 1944*
One of the smallest professionals in the world at 5ft 3in, ex-caddie Onsham has been a steady money winner on the Asian circuit since turning professional in 1967. He was joint third in the 1969 World Cup event and has scored top three finishes in many tournaments in Asia, Japan and Australia.

OOSTERHUIS, Peter – *born London, England, 3 May 1948*
Britain's most successful golfer since Tony Jacklin, Oosterhuis dominated the European circuit before transferring to the US Tour in 1975. He topped the European Order of Merit four years in a row from 1971, his prize-money totalling a record £32,000 in 1974 after victories in the French, Italian and El Paraiso Opens. He took his prize-money in Europe since turning professional in 1968 to around £100,000 in 1977. As an amateur he played for his country at

boys', youths' and men's level, winning the British Youths' title and playing in the Walker Cup in 1967 and the Eisenhower trophy in 1968. The 6ft 5in, 210 pound giant chalked up 19 major victories around the world before heading for the US Tour. They included five in South Africa. In his last full season in Europe, as well as his three victories, he was second in the Open Championship behind Gary Player. His French Open win was his second in successive years. In 1975, his first full season in America, Oosterhuis was second in the NBC New Orleans Open and seventh in the US Open and finished 34th in the money list with almost $60,000. Despite three more top ten finishes he slipped to 66th with only $41,000 winnings in 1976. But two second place finishes in 1977 swept him back into the top 60. Now based in United States.

OOSTHUIZEN, Andries – *born Pretoria, South Africa, 11 August 1953*
Winner of 1973 South African Amateur Championship, Oosthuizen was quick to make an impact in Britain, finishing 14th in the 1975 Order of Merit with over £8000 prize-money. He slipped to 42nd in 1976 but topped £6000 earnings to finish in 27th spot in 1977, recording seven top 15 finishes.

OPPENHEIMER, Raymond – *born London, England, 1905*
A golfer of international class himself, he went on to captain the 1951 Walker Cup side and make a major contribution to British amateur golf as an administrator and chairman of the British and English selectors. He is a former President of the English Golf Union.

ORCUTT, Maureen – *born USA*
Four times selected for Curtis Cup internationals, she was runner-up in 1927 and 1936 US Amateur Championships and won Canadian title twice and US Senior title as well as a host of regional events like the North and South, Eastern and Women's Metropolitan Championships.

OUIMET, Francis – *born Brookline, Massachusetts, USA, 1893. Died 1967*
Winning career began in 1913 US Open in his home town of Brookline when, aged 20, he defeated top Britons Harry Vardon by five strokes and Ted Ray by six in a play-off for the title. A year later he added the US Amateur title, and he won again in 1931. Member of every Walker Cup team from 1922 to 1934 and non-playing captain from then until 1949. In 1951 he became the first non-Briton to be appointed Captain of the Royal and Ancient Golf Club.

OWEN, Simon – *born Wanganui, New Zealand, 10 December 1950*
The slim six-footer was Europe's most successful newcomer when he followed an appearance in the World Cup by finishing the 1974 season in

Below: British Peter Oosterhuis is now a regular contestant on the American tournament circuit. Here he plays a bunker shot.

11th place in the Order of Merit with over £10,000 prize-money, £4000 of which came in two weeks, when he beat Peter Oosterhuis in a play-off for the German Open title, then finished joint second in the Dutch Open. He slipped back in 1975 but in 1976 won the 36-hole Double Diamond event and scored three other top ten finishes in Europe. The former New Zealand PGA Champion returned home to win his country's Open Championship.

OZAKI, Masashi – *born Tokushima, Japan, 1947*
One of Japan's most successful professional sportsmen, 'Jumbo' Ozaki was a baseball star before turning to golf in 1969 and in 1971 he won 17 million yen prize-money – a foretaste of this big hitter's many victories to come.

PAGE, Estelle – *born USA*
She defeated Patty Berg 7 and 6 to win 1937 US Amateur Championship but was runner-up the following year to Miss Berg. She was a semi-finalist in three other US Championships and played in 1938 and 1948 Curtis cups.

PALMER, Arnold – *born Latrobe, Pennsylvania, USA, 10 September 1929*
The most exciting golfer the sport has known won 61 US Tour events between 1955 and 1973. His total winnings top $1,750,000 but he is a multi-millionaire as a result of building a business empire embracing commodities ranging from dry cleaning to driving ranges. Palmer possesses a capacity for turning tragedy into triumph, with a muscular frame, massive hands and a gambler's fearlessness. He turned professional after winning the 1954 US Amateur title and was the Tour's top money winner four times in the space of six years from 1958. He

won the US Masters four times, the British Open twice and the US Open in a seven year period from 1958. Palmer's decision to cross the Atlantic to play in the British Open, which he won in 1961 and 1962, launched the 'invasion' of American stars, who have dominated the game's oldest championship with 11 victories in the last 17 years. Palmer proved he can still win by taking the 1975 Spanish Open and British PGA titles. He made five Ryder Cup appearances and was twice captain. He played seven times in the Canada and World Cup. His best financial year on Tour was 1971 when he won four times and earned $209,000.

PALMER, Johnny – *born Eldorado, North Carolina, 1918*
He was runner-up to Sam Snead in 1949 US PGA Championship and that year gained Ryder Cup recognition. His victories include the Canadian, Western and Mexican Opens and he was among America's top half dozen earners in the late '40s.

Top centre: Harry Vardon (left), Francis Ouimet (centre) and Ted Ray after their play-off in the US Open Championship of 1913 which Ouimet, a young amateur, won.

Below: The great American golfing favourite, Arnold Palmer.

PALMER, Sandra – *born Fort Worth, Texas, USA, 10 March 1941*
She recorded her tenth successive top ten finish in the LPGA Tour prize-money list in 1977 with winnings of $82,000 and stretched her record of being a winner every year since 1971. High on the all-time money winners' list with career earnings of around $500,000, her victories include 1970 Japan Open and US Open in 1975, when she topped the money list. She won five times in 1973. Although only 5ft 1in tall she hits the ball prodigious distances.

Centre right: One of Scotland's best professionals of this century, John Panton. Below: The small but powerful US woman professional Sandra Palmer is an accomplished money-winner. She is seen here in 1975.

PANTON, Catherine – *born Bridge of Allan, Stirlingshire, Scotland, 14 June 1955*
Won 1976 British Championship. Member of the 1973 LGU Under-25 tourists to Canada. 1969 Scottish Girls' Champion, and a Scotland international since 1972. Daughter of John Panton.

PANTON, John – *born Pitlochry, Scotland, 9 October 1916*
Won nine major events, including 1956 PGA Match Play Championship. Eight times Scottish Professional Champion and seven times Northern Open Champion. Winner of 1951 Vardon Trophy. Made three Ryder Cup appearances and represented Scotland 13 times in the Canada (now World) Cup. Panton was British Seniors' Champion in 1967 and 1969 and World Seniors' Champion in 1967, beating Sam Snead.

PARKS, Sam – *born USA*
Taught golf by Gene Sarazen in the Pittsburgh area, Parks was the surprise winner of 1935 US Open Championship.

PASCASSIO, Bernard – *born Ciboure, France, 23 May 1947*
French PGA Champion 1972 and 1973 and World Cup international. Partnered Jean Garaialde to victory in the 1975 Philip Morris International team event.

PATE, Jerry – *born Macon, Georgia, USA, 16 September 1953*
Things began happening in a big way for the slim six footer in 1974 when he won the US Amateur Championship and played in the winning Eisenhower World Amateur Team for his country. In 1975 he helped America retain the Walker Cup before turning professional. Pate made an explosive start to his pro career winning 1976 US Open and Canadian Open and finishing tenth in the money list with $153,000.

He scored nine top ten US finishes, and won Japan's Pacific Masters. Pate proved it was no flash in the pan by winning the first event of 1977, the Phoenix Open, adding the Southern Open title and again totalling

PATTON, William Joseph – *born North Carolina, USA, 1922*
For this Wake Forest University graduate 1954 was an outstanding year. He won the first of three North and South Championships, was third behind Sam Snead and Ben Hogan in the US Masters and low amateur (as he was again in 1957) in the US Open. He played in five Walker Cup matches in the '50s and '60s and captained the 1969 side.

PEARCE, Eddie – *born Fort Myers, Florida, USA, 16 March 1952*
As an amateur Pearce was 1968 USGA Junior Champion, 1971 North-South Champion and runner-up in 1971 US Amateur. In 1974, his first full season as a pro, he finished 47th in the money list with more than $50,000 winnings and improved to 39th in 1975.

PERKINS, Tegwen – *born Cardiff, Wales, 2 October 1955*
Runner-up in 1974 British Ladies' Stroke Play Championship at 19. Took 1976 Welsh title. Played in 1974 and 1976 Curtis Cup matches as well as the 1974 World Team Championships' Vagliano Trophy and Commonwealth Team events. First Welsh player to win Curtis Cup place in 1974.

PERKINS, Thomas – *born Birmingham, England, 1904*
Won 1927 English Championship. Added British title the following year, as well as finishing runner-up in the US Amateur following the 1928 Walker Cup match. Bobby Jones crushed him 10 and 9 for US title after inflicting a 13 and 12 defeat on him in the Walker Cup. Turned professional in America in 1932 and was joint runner-up to Gene Sarazen in that year's US Open.

PHILLIPS, Frank – *born Australia, 1932*
Twice Australian Open Champion and winner of the New Zealand Professional and Singapore and Hong Kong Open titles, the bespectacled Phillips represented Australia in the World Cup and played all over the world.

PICARD, Henry – *born Plymouth, Massachusetts, USA, 1907*
In a 20-year career he won more than 20 tournaments, including 1938 US Masters and 1939 US PGA Championship and played in the Ryder Cup matches of 1935, 1937 and 1939. He was a top six finisher in the British and US Opens in the mid-'30s. He was America's leading prize-money winner after six major wins in 1939.

PICKWORTH, Ossie – *born Australia, 1920. Died 1969*
Winner of four Australian Open and three Australian Professional titles, Pickworth took the Irish Open title in 1950 on one of his frequent visits to Europe and played in the first Canada Cup in 1953.

PINERO, Manuel – *born Puebla de la Calzada, Spain, 1 September 1952*
In the forefront of the Spanish 'revolution' in professional golf, the diminutive ex-caddie took

Below: Manuel Pinero is another member of Spain's team of young professionals. He is seen here in July 1976.

fourth place with close to £20,000 prize-money in both the 1976 and 1977 European Orders of Merit. Twice Spain's Professional Champion in the early '70s, Pinero took the Madrid Open title in 1974 and the Swiss Open title in 1976, going on that year to partner Severiano Ballesteros to victory in the World Cup in the United States, and finishing joint second in the individual event. He captained the Continental team against Britain and Ireland in the Hennessy Cup in 1976. Pinero's brilliant £10,000 victory by three strokes in the Penfold PGA Event was one of eight triumphs for Spain in 1977.

PLATTS, Lionel – *born Sheffield, Yorkshire, England, 10 October 1934*
Only once out of the top 60 in the order of merit between 1959 and 1976, Platts was among the most consistent British campaigners, although he won only twice – the 1964 Braemar event and 1971 Portuguese Open. His highest placings were seventh in 1964 and 1965, when he gained Ryder Cup recognition.

PLAYER, Gary – *born Johannesburg, South Africa, 1 November 1936*
One of the game's smaller exponents at 5ft 8in, Player came back after major surgery in 1973 to win that year's Southern Open in America, and

score his fifth victory in the gruelling 36-holes a day Piccadilly World Match Play event in Britain. The following year he took his total of American Tour victories to 18 by winning the Masters for the second time and the Danny Thomas-Memphis Classic, taking his third British Open title and also winning the Brazilian (with the help of a 59) and Australian Opens. He has scored well over 100 major victories around the world's circuits, including nine South African and seven Australian Opens. Player's great achievement has been to keep up his spectacular victory spiral while still maintaining his base with his wife and six children in South Africa. He is one of only four men to have won all four of the world's major championships. Indeed he needs only one more US Open win to complete a second 'Grand Slam'. Player's winnings topped $100,000 for the sixth time in nine years in 1977 and his career winnings in America top $1,300,000. He headed the money list in 1961 and has four times finished fifth. He, Palmer and Nicklaus became known as golf's 'Big Three' in the '60s.

POLLAND, Eddie – *born Newcastle, Co Down, N Ireland, 10 June 1947*
Twice Irish Stroke and Match Play Champion, this cheerful Ulster protégé of former Open

Below: South Africa's greatest player Gary Player includes among his successes the US Open Championship, the British Open Championship, the US Masters and the US PGA Championship. He is seen here during the Piccadilly Match Play contest of 1974.

Champion Fred Daly earned a Ryder Cup cap in 1973, when he achieved his highest placing in the Order of Merit – sixth. After taking the 1971 Parmeco Classic title, his first major victory came in the 1973 Penfold Bournemouth event. Despite a wrist injury in 1975 he won the Sun Alliance PGA Match Play title and a fortnight after returning to action following an operation on his wrist won the 1976 Spanish Open, going on that year to collect £16,700 prize-money. He has represented Britain and Ireland in the Hennessy Cup against the Continent and Ireland in the World Cup and Double Diamond Internationals.

PORTER, Joe – *born Pasadena, California, USA, 5 June 1945*
After winning 1973 United Airlines Open on America's second tour Porter scored five top ten finishes in major Tour events in 1976.

PORTER, Ruth – *born Chesterfield, England, 6 May 1939*
1956 British Girls' Champion. Won 1959, 1961 and 1965 English Championships and was runner-up in 1963 Australian Championship. Played in 1960, 1962 and 1964 Curtis Cup matches and 1964 and 1966 World Team Championships. Represented Britain in the Vagliano Trophy and Commonwealth team events. Played for England from 1959 to 1975.

POST, Sandra – *born Oakville, Ontario, Canada, 4 June 1948*
Three times winner of the Canadian and Ontario Junior Championships, she joined the US LPGA Tour in 1968 with spectacular success, winning that year's LPGA Championship after an 18-hole play-off against Kathy Whitworth, which earned her Rookie of the Year honours. She won the Colgate Far East event in 1974 and $77,000 prize-money in 1977 took her career winnings to more than $250,000.

POTT, Johnny – *born Cape Girardeau, Montana, USA, 6 November 1935*
Winner of 1963 American Golf Classic and 1968 Bing Crosby National, Pott, who made three Ryder Cup appearances in the '60s, enjoyed his best year in 1965, finishing 14th in the order of merit to earn $50,000. He finished in the top 60 for 12 straight years.

POVALL, John – *born Cardiff, Wales, 18 December 1938*
Welsh Amateur, Close and Stroke Play Champion, runner-up in 1962 British Championship, voted Welsh Sportsman of the Year in 1962. Represented Britain against Europe and was a regular for Wales from 1960, captaining the side in 1975 and 1976.

POWELL, Renee – *born Canton, Ohio, USA, 4 May 1946*
Winner of dozens of junior titles, this Negro professional's daughter became the only regular black player on the LPGA Tour, scoring several top ten finishes before moving her home to England.

PRADO, Catherine de – *born Paris, France, 27 June 1945*
As Catherine Lacoste, highlighted a remarkable career by beating the world's best amateurs and professionals to take the 1967 US Women's Open title. Won the French, Spanish, British and American amateur crowns in 1969. Came to prominence in 1964 at 19 when she helped France win the Espirito Santo world team event. Retired in 1970 following her marriage.

PRENTICE, Jo Ann – *born Birmingham, Alabama, USA, 9 February 1933*
In 21 years on the LPGA Tour she has accumulated winnings of over $300,000. Her best year was 1974 when she finished fourth in the prize-money list with $67,000 earnings.

Below: Eddie Polland from Northern Ireland is one of golf's modern personalities.

112

PREUSS, Phyllis – *born Detroit, Michigan, USA, 1939*
She played in five successive Curtis Cup matches from 1962 after finishing runner-up in 1961 US Amateur Championship. She was a semi-finalist in 1962 US and 1964 British Championships, twice low amateur in US Women's Open and Southern Champion in 1968.

Above: Elizabeth Price-Fisher holds the trophy she won as British Ladies' Golf Champion, May 1959.

PRICE-FISHER, Elizabeth – *born London, England, 17 January 1923*
British Champion 1959 and twice runner-up. Played in every Curtis Cup match from 1950 to 1960 and regularly appeared for Britain and England in internationals. Turned professional in 1968, reinstated as amateur in 1971.

PUNG, Jacqueline – *born Honolulu, Hawaii, USA, 13 December 1921*
She won five US Tour events in the '50s, turning professional after winning 1952 US Amateur Championship and four Hawaiian Amateur titles. In 1957 she missed victory in US Open Championship by signing for a wrong score.

PURTZER, Tom – *born Des Moines, Iowa, USA, 5 December 1951*
Turned professional after winning the 1972 Arizona State amateur championship and South West Open. He was runner-up in 1975 Thailand Open and scored a second and a third in 1976, his first full season on the US Tour. Purtzer's breakthrough came early in 1977 when he won the Los Angeles Open and he finished the season with over $80,000 earnings.

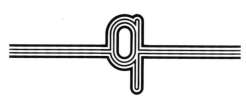

QUICK, Smiley – *born Centralia, Illinois, USA, 1907*
Only a missed short putt at the 37th in the final against Ted Bishop prevented Quick from adding the US Amateur title to the US Public Links crown he won in 1946. He gained Walker Cup honours the following year, then turned professional.

RAGAN, Dave – *born Daytona Beach, Florida, USA, 1935*
He gained Ryder Cup honours after being runner-up to Jack Nicklaus for the US PGA title in 1963. He won several events after joining the US Tour in 1956.

RANKIN, Judy – *born St Louis, Missouri, USA, 18 February 1945*
She threatens to overtake Kathy Whitworth as the US Tour all-time top money winner after topping the prize league for the second year running in 1977 with almost $123,000. She was a six-time winner in 1976 and earned over $150,000 – an LPGA record. Her career winnings total over $600,000. She has been winning titles since she was eight and was the youngest Missouri State Champion at 14. She turned professional in 1962, scored her first victory in 1968 and has been a winner every year since 1970 and in six years a multiple winner. In 1976 she became the first woman ever to win $100,000 in a season. One of the smallest players on tour at 5ft 3½in, her 25 victories include two in the Colgate European Open in England.

RANSOM, Henry – *born Houston, Texas, USA, 1911*
He was a late arrival on the US Tour in his thirties but won a dozen major events and gained Ryder Cup honours in 1951.

RAWLINS, Harold
This young English professional emigrated to the USA and won the US Open at the age of 19 in 1895, the first year that the US Open was a stroke-play event.

RAWLS, Elizabeth – *born Spartanburg, South Carolina, USA, May 1928*
Scored 55 US Tour victories, including four US Open and two LPGA Championships. Earned more than $300,000 prize-money. Turned pro-

fessional in 1951 and had her most outstanding year when winning ten out of 26 events in 1959 to earn almost $27,000 prize-money – a record. First Open win came in her rookie year, 1951.

RAY, Ted – *born Jersey, Channel Islands, 1877. Died 1943*
Old photographs of Ray wearing collar and tie, suit, trilby hat, smoking a pipe – and swinging a golf club – look incongruous, but he won the 1912 British and 1920 US Open titles. Captained the 1927 Ryder Cup side. Until Tony Jacklin's 1970 win Ray remained the last Briton to take the US Open crown. Only one other Briton, Harry Vardon (also from Jersey) has won both national titles.

REDDAN, Clarrie – *born Drogheda, Eire, 3 July 1916*
Irish Champion in 1936 and runner-up for British title in 1949, Clarrie Reddan, formerly Tiernan, won 1937 New Jersey State title, was runner-up for 1938 Canadian title and played in 1938 and 1948 Curtis Cup matches. Played regularly for Ireland in '30s and '40s.

REES, David James, CBE – *born Barry, South Wales, 31 March 1913*
Won first of four British PGA Match Play titles in 1936. Made first of nine Ryder Cup appearances in 1937. Captained the side at Lindrick, Yorkshire, England in 1957 when Americans were beaten for the last time. Also captain in 1955, 1959 and 1961 and non-playing captain in 1967. More than 40 victories included two in Dunlop Masters as well as Irish, Egyptian, Swiss, New South Wales and Belgian Opens, PGA Close Championship and Seniors' Championship. Played nine times for Wales in Canada (later World) Cup and skippered Britain against the Commonwealth and Europe.

REGALADO, Victor – *born Tijuana, Mexico, 15 April 1948*
In second full year on US Tour Regalado, former Mexican Amateur, PGA and Masters Champion, World Amateur and World Cup international, tasted more success by winning 1974 Pleasant Valley Classic. A series of high finishes swept him to his best US season in 1977, when he won more than $75,000.

REVOLTA, Johnny – *born St Louis, Missouri, USA, 1911*
Joined the Tour after beating the best ball of touring stars Gene Sarazen and Tommy Armour in the '30s and was leading money winner in 1935 after taking US PGA and Western Open titles and winning a Ryder Cup place that year. Won a succession of Tour titles.

Below: A photograph probably taken at a US Open Championship. In front is Harold Rawlins who won the very first championship in 1895.

RIEGEL, Robert – *born New Bloomfield, Pennsylvania, USA, 1914*
Gained first of two Walker Cup caps in 1947 after winning that year's US Amateur Championship and was successful in all his four international matches. Turned professional and finished a stroke behind winner Ben Hogan in 1951 US Masters.

RILEY, Polly – *born Fort Worth, Texas, USA*
Runner-up in 1953 US Amateur Championship, she made six successive Curtis Cup appearances from 1948 and was non-playing captain in 1962.

ROBBINS, Hillman – *born Memphis, Tennessee, USA, 1932*
Turned professional in 1958 after winning US Amateur title and Walker Cup recognition in 1957 to climax a career which saw him win the National Collegiate and North and South Championships.

ROBERTS, Sue – *born Oak Park, Illinois, USA, 22 June 1948*
This former telephone operator ended 1976 – her eighth year on tour – with more than $90,000 career earnings after four major victories. Her breakthrough came with wins in 1974 in Niagara Classic and Southgate Open.

ROBERTSON, Allan – *born St Andrews, Scotland, 1815. Died 1858*
Outstanding golfer of his time as well as leading ball and clubmaker in St Andrews. Often partnered Old Tom Morris, his former apprentice, in challenge matches but they parted after a dispute over the rival merits of the old feather and new gutta balls.

ROBERTSON, Isabella, MBE – *born Southend, Argyll, Scotland, 11 April 1936*
The former Isabella McCorkindale won the Scottish Championship four times. She was twice British Stroke Play Champion and won 1971 New Zealand Match Play title. After playing in 1960, 1966, 1968, 1970 and 1972 Curtis Cup matches was non-playing captain in 1974 and 1976. Also captained British sides in World Team and Commonwealth Championships, and Scotland in European Championships. Daks Woman Golfer of the Year in 1971.

RODGERS, Phil – *born San Diego, California, USA, 3 April 1938*
Five victories in as many years on US Tour from 1962. Lost 36 holes play-off for British Open title in 1963 to New Zealand's Bob Charles. Best year, financially, was 1971 when he won over $71,000.

RODRIGUEZ, Juan – *born Puerto Rico, 23 October 1935*
'Chi Chi' bounced back to form in 1977 with earnings of over $55,000. First of seven victories on US Tour came in 1963 Denver Open. Highest placing in money list was ninth in 1964 when he won twice, but his best years financially were 1972 $113,000 and 1973 $91,000. Played in 1973 Ryder Cup.

Right: Isabella Robertson, a Scottish and British international, was four times Scottish champion.

ROGERS, Bill – *born Waco, Texas, USA, 10 September 1951*
Member of 1973 US Walker Cup side and 1972 Southern Amateur Champion. Won 1976 Sun City Open on second tour in America and a series of high placings earned him over $85,000 prize-money in 1977.

ROMACK, Barbara – *born Sacramento, California, USA, 16 November 1932*
Made three successive Curtis Cup appearances from 1954, the year she won US Amateur Championship. Was runner-up for 1958 title, four times California State and three times South Atlantic Champion. She was soon a successful proette, following two seconds and a third with her first victory in 1963 Rock City Open. Her career earnings top $60,000.

ROSBURG, Bob – *born San Francisco, California, USA, 21 October 1926*
Seven victories, including 1959 PGA Championship, helped him to career earnings of over $400,000 in 21 years on Tour. Best year financially was 1972 $78,000 winnings. Won Vardon Trophy in 1958. Highest money list placing was 7th in 1959. Member of 1959 Ryder Cup side.

ROSS, Donald – *born Dornoch, Sutherland, Scotland, 1873. Died 1948*
Emigrated to the United States and became one of that country's great golf architects, designing more than 500 courses, among them Pinehurst, Brae Burn, Seminole, Scioto and Inverness. He originally trained under Old Tom Morris at St Andrews.

ROSS, Mackenzie – *born Edinburgh, Scotland, 1890. Died 1974*
Became one of the world's leading golf architects, designing or re-designing courses all over Britain – the rebuilding of Turnberry, Scotland after the war was perhaps the outstanding achievement – Belgium, France, Portugal and Spain.

ROTAN, George, – *Born Waco, Texas, USA, 1886*
Three times Texas Amateur Champion. He gained Walker Cup honours in 1923 and was a USGA Executive member in 1927 and 1928.

RUDOLPH, Mason – *born Clarksville, Tennessee, USA, 23 May 1934*
In his first 17 years on US Tour won six tournaments, first being the 1959 Golden Gate event. Best years were 1963 and 1964, when he finished 7th and 8th in the money list. Winner of 1950 US Junior Championship, he gained Walker Cup honours in 1957 and in 1971 added a Ryder Cup cap.

RUNFELT, Erik – *born Sweden, 1893*
Ten times Swedish Amateur Champion between 1911 and 1938 and four times Scandinavian Champion, Runfelt, a former secretary of the Swedish Golf Union and editor for 20 years of its magazine, played a dozen times for his country and captained two Eisenhower Trophy teams. An expert on the rules, he won 11 consecutive Swedish Seniors' titles.

RUNYAN, Paul – *born Hot Springs, Arkansas, USA, 1908*
Winner of US PGA Championship in 1934 and 1938 and of Ryder Cup caps in 1933 and 1935, Runyan beat Craig Wood and Sam Snead in his two PGA finals and won many major tournaments, including seven in 1934 when he was America's leading prize-money winner. The former US and World Seniors' Champion subsequently became one of his country's top teachers.

SADDLER, Sandy – *born Forfar, Angus, Scotland, 11 August 1935*
Captained 1977 Walker Cup team beaten 16–8 by USA at Shinnecock Hills. Played in 1963, 1965 and 1967 Walker Cups and 1962 Eisenhower Trophy. Represented Britain in Commonwealth team in several matches. Scottish international regular between 1959 and 1965; non-playing captain in 1974 and 1975.

SANDERS, Doug – *born Cedartown, Georgia, USA, 24 June 1933*
Won 1956 Canadian Open as an amateur and then turned professional -- joining the tour in 1957. Soon established himself a consistent winner and blossomed into one of golf's most colourful characters. Has won a total of 19 tour

Left: Famous American professional Doug Sanders. In the British Open Championship at St Andrews in 1970 he missed a short putt which cost him the championship.

events but a 'Major' title has eluded him although he was twice runner-up in the British Open – in 1966 and 1970. His best year financially was 1967 when he won $109,455 and his career earnings stand some $200,000 short of the one million mark.

SANUDO, Cesar – *born Navojoa, Mexico, 26 October 1943*
Turned professional 1966, joined tour in 1969 and won 1970 Azalea tournament.

SARAZEN, Gene – *born Harrison, New York, USA, 27 February 1902*
Grand Slam golfer – he won US Open (1922 and 1932), US Masters (1935), US PGA (1922, 1923 and 1933) and British Open Championship (1932). One of only a few who have captured Open titles of Britain and America in same year

(1932). Also won Australian Open in 1936, 15 US Tour events and US PGA Seniors in 1954 and 1958. Six successive Ryder Cup appearances between 1927 and 1937.

SAUNDERS, Vivien Inez – *born Sutton, England, 24 November 1946*
Turned professional 1 January 1969. Runner-up in 1966 British Ladies'. In 1973 won two professional events in Australia – Schweppes-Tarax Open and Chrysler Open – and in 1977 lifted British Women's Open.

SCHLEE, John – *born Kremmling, Colorado, USA, 2 June 1939*
Joined tour in 1965 one year after turning professional. Won 1973 Hawaiian Open. Named Rookie of the Year in 1966 and has career earnings of half a million dollars.

One of the greatest of all professionals, Gene Sarazen, won the British and American Open titles in the same year 1932. In the photograph below he is seen clutching the US National Pro Championship Trophy after his victory in 1933. On the left, he is seen still swinging 40 years later.

SEGARD, Mme Patrick (formerly Vicomtesse De St Sauveur née Lally Vagliano)
Outstanding French amateur who represented her country every year between 1947 and 1965. Her first appearance for France was in 1937; her last in 1970. Won French Ladies' Open (1948, 1950, 1951, 1952), French Ladies' Close (1936, 1946, 1949, 1950, 1951, 1954), British Ladies' (1950), Swiss Ladies' (1949, 1965), Luxemburg Ladies' (1949), Italian Ladies' (1949, 1951) and Spanish Ladies' (1951). Captained Vagliano Trophy teams of 1959 and 1961, also played in teams of 1963 and 1965 and non-playing captain in 1975.

SEMPLE, Carol
Member of 1974 Curtis Cup and winning 1975 World Team Championship team. US Ladies' Amateur Champion in 1973 and British Ladies' champion 1974.

SEWELL, Douglas – *born Woking, England, 19 November 1929*
Won English Amateur Championship 1958 and 1960 and English Open Amateur Stroke Play title in 1957 and 1959. Walker Cup player in 1957 and 1959 and earned a series of other international honours before turning professional in 1960. Tied for Martini International 1970.

SHADE, Ronnie David Bell Mitchell, MBE – *born Edinburgh, Scotland, 15 October 1938*
Outstanding amateur with three English open Amateur Stroke Play titles (1961, 1963, 1967), five Scottish Amateur titles (1963, 1964, 1965, 1966, 1967) and a runners-up spot in British Amateur Championship (1966) among his individual achievements. Earned Walker Cup recognition in 1961, 1963, 1965 and 1967 and also played in four Eisenhower Trophy teams (1962, 1964, 1966, 1968). Leading amateur in 1966 Open Championship and turned professional in 1968. Won Carrolls (Ireland) in 1969 and Mufulira Open (Zambia) in 1975.

Represented Scotland in 1970, 1971 and 1972 World Cups and 1971, 1972, 1973, 1974 and 1975 Double Diamond World Golf Classic matches.

SHAW, Bob – *born Sydney, Australia, 24 December 1944*
A professional since 1965, he joined US Tour in 1969 and won 1972 Tallahassee Open. Also won 1968 New Zealand PGA title.

SHAW, Tom – *born Wichita, Kansas, USA, 13 December 1942*
Turned professional and joined tour in 1963 and has won four times – Doral Open and Avco Classic in 1969 and Bing Crosby and Hawaiian Open in 1971.

SHEAHAN, Dr David – *born Southsea, Hampshire, England, 25 February 1940*
Won Irish Amateur Championship 1961, 1966 and 1970 and won international honours for Ireland and Great Britain. Member of 1963 Walker Cup.

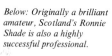
Centre left: British woman professional Vivien Saunders has competed (often successfully) in most of the US Women's championships.

Below: Originally a brilliant amateur, Scotland's Ronnie Shade is also a highly successful professional.

118

SHEARER, Bob – *born Melbourne, Australia, 25 May 1948*
A desperate illness which momentarily not only threatened his career but also his life ruined his hopes of making a bold showing in the US Tour in 1977 after a satisfactory rookie year in 1976. Now appears ready to prove his potential in the States and win again following his early career victories in the Chrysler Classic (Australia) in 1974, Madrid Open, Piccadilly Medal (England) and Westlakes Golf Classic (Australia) in 1975 and New Zealand Airlines Classic and Chrysler Classic in 1976. Finished second in European Order of Merit in 1975 when he won £16,040 and runner-up that same year in the World Cup Individual.

Right: Australian professional Bob Shearer is a consistent money winner in many countries.

SHROEDER, John – *born Great Barrington, Massachusetts, USA, 12 November 1945*
Turned professional in 1969, joined tour the same year and in 1973 won US Professional Match Play title.

SIDEROWF, Dick
Canadian Amateur champion in 1971 and British Amateur Champion in 1973 and 1976. Played in the 1969, 1973 and 1975 Walker Cups.

SIFFORD, Charles – *born Charlotte, North Carolina, USA, 3 June 1923*
Turned professional in 1948 but did not join US Tour until 11 years later. Won 1967 Hartford Open and 1969 Los Angeles Open.

SIKES, Dan – *born Jacksonville, Florida, USA, 7 December 1930*
In sight of reaching one million dollars in career earnings but without a US Tour win since 1968 when he won Florida Citrus and Minnesota. Before that lifted Doral (1963), Cleveland (1965) and in 1967 Jacksonville and Philadelphia. Best seasons – 1967 $111,508 and 1968 $108,330. Won All-Army Championship and US Public Links title before turning professional in 1960. Ryder Cup team member in 1969.

Far right: Great Britain's best post World War II player, Frances Smith.

SIKES, R H – *born Paris, Arkansas, USA, 6 March 1940*
Turned professional and joined tour in 1964 and gained victories in 1964 Sahara Invitational and 1966 Cleveland Open.

SIMONS, Jim – *born Pittsburgh, Pennsylvania, USA, 15 May 1950*
First came to prominence in 1971 when he gained Walker Cup recognition, reached final of British Amateur Championship and led US Open at Merion after three rounds before eventually finishing top amateur in fifth place. Turned professional the following year but waited until April 1977 for first victory when he won first NBC New Orleans Open.

SIMPSON, Jack – *born Earlsferry, Fife, Scotland*
Won British Open Championship at Prestwick in 1884.

SKALA, Carole Jo – *born Eugene, Oregon, USA, 13 June 1938*
Turned professional in 1970 following successful amateur career. She has won four times on the US circuit and banked almost $150,000.

SKERRITT, Patrick Joseph – *born Lahinch, County Clare, Eire, 30 May 1930*
Won Alcan International in 1970 following successes in Southern Ireland Professional Championship (1966, 1967) and Carrolls Irish Match Play (1970). Represented Ireland in 1971 Double Diamond World Golf Classic.

SMITH, Mrs Frances – *born Lancashire, England, 1924*
Won British Ladies' (1949 and 1954) and English Ladies' (1948, 1954, 1955) during outstanding career in which she also took the French Ladies' title in 1949 and played in six Curtis Cup

matches (1950, 1952, 1954, 1956, 1958, 1960). Non-playing captain of 1962 and 1972 Curtis Cup teams and also of England in 1973 European Team Championship. Regular England international.

SMITH, Horton – *born USA, 1908. Died, aged 55, October 1963*
Collapsed and died in a Detroit Hospital in 1963 one day after attending Ryder Cup match at Atlanta. Ironically it was at Atlanta that he enjoyed his most memorable successes – winning the first US Masters in 1934 and repeating that triumph two years later. In all he won more than 30 major events, including capturing the French Open on his 21st birthday, and made three Ryder Cup appearances – in 1929, 1933 and 1935. President of American PGA (1952, 1954).

SMITH, Macdonald – *born Carnoustie, Scotland, 1890. Died Los Angeles, USA, 1949*
Crossed the Atlantic before his 20th birthday and enjoyed tremendous success. Won several tournaments including Canadian Open in 1926. Twice Open Championship runner-up (1930, 1932) and thrice third, his best chance to win came in 1925 when he led by five shots entering the last round. A huge partisan Prestwick crowd, however, produced unruly scenes which disturbed his concentration and led to the introduction of entrance money the following year.

SMITH, Marilynn – *born Topeka, Kansas, USA, 13 April 1929*
Won 22 tour victories between 1954 and 1972 and accumulated almost $300,000 in prize winnings. President of LPGA 1958–60.

Left: Horton Smith was the winner of the first US Masters in 1934. He repeated this feat again in 1936. In his career, he won more than 30 major tournaments.

SMITH, William Dickson – *born Glasgow, Scotland, 2 February 1918*
Won Indian Amateur (1945), Scottish Amateur (1958) and Portuguese Amateur (1967 and 1970) and earned Walker Cup place in 1959. Scottish international who finished fifth – leading amateur – in 1957 Open Championship.

SNEAD, J C – *born Hot Springs, Virginia, USA, 14 October 1941*
The nephew of Sam, Jesse Carlyle Snead turned professional in 1964 but failed to get on the circuit until 1968. Three years later he finally won – taking the Tucson and Doral-Eastern events in a dizzy three week spell. Earned Ryder Cup recognition that same year (1971) and also in 1973 and 1975. In 1972 won Philadelphia, the next year lifted Australian Open Championship and in 1975 landed Andy Williams San Diego Open. Best year was 1976, when he won Andy Williams again and Kaiser International, accumulated $192,645 and took his career earnings past the three quarter of a million dollars mark.

SNEAD, Sam – *born Hot Springs, Virginia, USA, 27 May 1912*
One of the true Greats of international golf.

Below: Sam Snead, winner of almost every major national championship except the US Open. He is one of the world's all-time Greats and is famous for his long drives.

Credited with 135 tournament triumphs by independent record markers – 84 of his wins on the US Tour. First victory in 1936 in Virginia Closed Professional title – last US success in 1965 when he won Greensboro Open for the eighth time in his career. That stands as record for most victories in a single event by any player on the US Tour. Snead also runner-up in that unique department with six wins in Miami Open. In first full season (1937) on US Tour he won St Paul Open, Nassau Open, Miami Open and Oakland Open and banked $10,243. Leading money winner in 1938 and again in 1949 and 1950 – his best year. In 1950 Snead won ten tournaments, a calendar record beaten only by Byron Nelson, and recorded the best ever Vardon Trophy scoring average (69.23 with 6646 strokes in 96 rounds). Winner of seven 'Majors' – US Masters (1949, 1952 and 1954); US PGA Championship (1942, 1949 and 1951) and British Open (1946). Grand Slam foiled by no US Open win. Eight times a Ryder Cup team member (1937, 1939, 1941, 1947, 1949, 1951, 1953 and 1955) and won 10 and halved one of 13 matches. Captained Ryder Cup team in 1959 and 1969. Member of winning Canada Cup (now World Cup) team in 1956, 1960 and 1961 and individual champion in 1961. Has won six PGA Senior and World Seniors' titles – the last in 1973. Other unique achievements include round of 60 at Glen Lakes Country Club, Dallas, Texas, in second round of 1957 Dallas Open and 36-holes scores of 126 in 1950 Texas Open (63, 63) at Brackenridge Park, San Antonio, Texas, and in 1957 Dallas Open (60, 66). Career earnings of just over $600,000.

SNEED, Ed – *born Roanoke, Virginia, USA, 6 August 1944*
Turned professional in 1967 but waited until 1973 before winning in unique fashion. Won New South Wales Open Championship in Australia and then flew straight to San Francisco – gaining a day through international dateline – and qualified for Kaiser International Open. Following Sunday beat John Schlee in play-off for that title. Won Milwaukee title in 1974 and gained third US Tour win in Tallahassee Open in April, 1977. Made debut in US Ryder Cup team at Royal Lytham and St Anne's, England, in September 1977.

SNELL, David – *born Whitwell, nr Worksop, England, 10 October 1933*
Represented England in 1965 World Cup. As individual won British PGA Match Play (1959).

SOMERVILLE, Charles Ross – *born London, Ontario, Canada, 4 May 1903*
US Amateur Champion in 1932 and Canadian Amateur Champion in 1926, 1928, 1930, 1931, 1935 and 1937. Won several other Canadian titles including Seniors' in 1960, 1961 (tied), 1965 and 1966 (tied). President of Royal Canadian Golf Association in 1957.

Above: Tom Watson

Above and inset: Tom Weiskopf

124

Above: Judy Rankin

Above: Lee Trevino

Above and inset: Gary Player

Above: Vincent Tshabalala

Above: Bob Shearer

SOTA, Ramon – *born Pedrena, Spain, 23 April 1938*
Winner of several Open titles – Spanish (1963), Portuguese (1963, 1969, 1970), French (1965), Brazilian (1965), Dutch (1966, 1971) and Italian (1971).

SOUCHAK, Mike – *born Berwick, Pennsylvania, 10 May 1927*
Turned professional in 1952 and won a total of 16 US Tour events – the last in 1964. Gained a Ryder Cup place in 1959 and 1961 and was runner-up in the 1960 US Open.

SPRAY, Steve – *born Des Moines, Iowa, USA, 16 December 1940*
Turned professional in 1964, joined tour one year later and won San Francisco Open in 1969.

SPUZICH, Sandra – *born Indianapolis, Indiana, USA, 3 April 1937*
Turned professional in 1962 and four years later lifted US Open Championship – one of four tour victories during a career in which she has earned almost $200,000.

STACEY, Hollis – *born Savannah, Georgia, USA, 16 March 1954*
Turned professional in 1974 and achieved enormous breakthrough in 1977 when she won US Women's Open.

STADLER, Craig – *born San Diego, California, USA, 2 June 1953*
Turned professional in late 1975 following outstanding amateur career during which he won World Junior Championship (1971) and US Amateur (1973) and represented US in Walker Cup in 1975.

STANLEY, Ian – *born Melbourne, Australia, 14 November 1948*
Australian World Cup player who enjoyed a brief period of success in 1975 when he won Queensland Open in his native country and tied for Martini International in England.

STEPHENSON, Jan – *born Sydney, Australia, 22 December 1951*
Followed outstanding career as an amateur by turning professional in 1973 and since joining the US Women's Tour she has won two tournaments and more than $100,000.

STILL, Ken – *born Tacoma, Washington, USA, 12 February 1935*
Joined professional ranks in 1953 but waited until 1969 before winning. In that year he took two events – Florida Citrus and Milwaukee – and gained Ryder Cup call-up. Totals three US tour wins with almost half a million dollars in career earnings.

STOCKTON, Dave – *born San Bernardino, California, USA, 2 November 1941*
Turned professional in 1964, joined the tour the following year and a regular top 60 money winner since first victory in 1967. Totals 11 US Tour wins with highlights – two US PGA triumphs in 1970 and 1976. That last win at the Congressional Country Club lifted his career winnings close to the one million dollar mark. He made his Ryder Cup debut in 1971 and gained a second appearance in 1977. He was a member of America's World Cup team in 1970.

Far left: Ramon Sota's success spurred on many young Spanish golfers to get to the top.

Left: Professional Dave Stockton has been a consistent US money winner for the last ten years.

STOREY, Eustace Francis – *born Leicester, England, 30 August 1901*
Walker Cup player in 1924, 1926, 1928 and runner-up in 1924 British Amateur Championship.

STOWE, Charles – *born Sandyfields, Sedley, England, 11 January 1909*
Won English Amateur Stroke Play in 1948 and 1953 and played in 1938 and 1947 Walker Cup teams. England international.

Right centre: Louise Suggs as she appeared in her early amateur days. She became a leading US money winner after turning professional in 1948.

Below: Jesse Sweetser was the winner of the US Amateur Championship in 1922 and the British Amateur Championship in 1926.

STRANAHAN, Frank – *born Toledo, Ohio, USA, 5 August 1922*
Turned professional in 1954 following a fine amateur career during which he appeared in Walker Cup teams of 1947, 1949 and 1951 and won British Amateur Championship (1948 and 1950) and Canadian Amateur (1947 and 1948). Won no less than 21 other amateur titles and as an amateur was twice second in Open Championship (1947 and 1953). He won two events on US Professional tour.

STREIT, Marlene Stewart – *born Cereal, Alberta, Canada, 9 March 1934*
Won Canadian Ladies' open 11 times and Canadian Ladies' Close on nine occasions. Also won British Ladies' (1953), US Ladies' (1956) and Australian Ladies' (1963). Voted Canadian Athlete of the Year 1951, 1953, 1956.

STUART, Hugh Bannerman – *born Forres, Scotland, 27 July 1942*
Outstanding performance in 1971 Walker Cup when he won all his matches for Great Britain. Also member of 1973 and 1975 teams. Scottish Amateur champion 1972.

SUGGS, Louise – *born Atlanta, Georgia, USA, 7 September 1923.*
Won US Ladies Amateur (1947) and British Ladies' (1948) and represented country in Curtis Cup before turning professional in 1948. Won US Womens' Open 1949 and 1952 and leading money winner of US circuit in 1953 and 1960. Won 50 events on US tour. Also winner of 1957 LPGA Championship.

SWEENEY, Robert – *born Pasadena, California, USA, 25 July 1911*
Won British Amateur Championship in 1937. Runner-up US Amateur 1954.

SWEETSER, Jess – *born St Louis, Missouri, USA, 18 April 1902.*
US Amateur Champion in 1922 and British Amateur Champion in 1926, he played in Walker Cups of 1922, 1923, 1924, 1926, 1928 and 1932 and captained the side in 1967 and 1973.

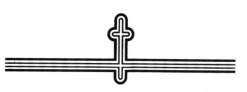

TAIT, Frederick Guthrie – *born Edinburgh, Scotland, 11 January 1870. Died Koodoosberg Drift, South Africa, 7 February 1900*
He was killed in the South African war but had already left his mark by twice setting the course record for an amateur at St Andrews – 77 in 1890 and 72 in 1894. Won British Amateur Championship in 1896 and 1898.

TAYLOR, John Henry – *born Northam, North Devon, England, 19 March 1871. Died Devon, February 1963, aged 92.*
Won British Championship five times in 1894,

1895, 1900, 1909, 1913, tied but lost play-off with Harry Vardon in 1896 and was also runner-up in 1904, 1905, 1906, 1914. Also included victories in the French and German Opens among his many triumphs and he finished runner-up in the 1900 US Open. One of the front-runners in the organization of the Professional Golfers' Association in Great Britain, he was awarded honorary membership of the Royal and Ancient Golf Club in 1949 – an honour that emphasised his position as one of the greatest golfers in the history of the game.

THIRLWELL, Alan – *born 8 August 1928*
English Amateur champion in 1954 and 1955. Member of ten England Home International teams and also played in 1957 Walker Cup.

THOMAS, David – *born Newcastle upon Tyne, England, 16 August 1934*
Lost to Peter Thomson in play-off for 1958 British Open Championship and second again in 1966. Won the Open championships of Belgium (1955), Holland (1958) and France (1959). Won 13 other major titles including British PGA Match Play (1963), Caltex (New Zealand, 1958 and 1959) and Olgiata Trophy (Rome, 1963). Ryder Cup player in 1959, 1963, 1965 and 1967 and represented Wales in 11 World Cups between 1957 and 1970. Won qualifying competition for 1964 US Open.

THOMPSON, Leonard – *born Laurinburg, North Carolina, USA, 1 January 1947*
Wake Forest University graduate who turned professional in 1970, joined tour in 1971 and won Jackie Gleason-Inverary in 1974 – his best year with winnings of $122,349.

THOMSON, Hector – *born Machrihanish, Argyll, Scotland, 21 November 1913*
Won British Amateur Championship in 1936, Scottish Amateur in 1935 and Irish Open Amateur in 1934 and 1935. Scottish international between 1934 and 1938 and member of 1936 and 1938 Walker Cup sides. Turned professional in 1940 and won Scottish Professional Championship in 1953.

THOMSON, Peter, MBE – *born Melbourne, Australia, 23 August 1929*
Completed a hat-trick of British Open victories in 1954, 1955, 1956 and followed with further successes in 1958 and 1965 to establish a record

Left: British professional Dave Thomas now devotes most of his efforts to golf course architecture.

Above: J H Taylor was one of the great early professionals at the turn of the century. He is seen here in 1945.

Left: Five-times winner of the British Open Championship, Australian Peter Thomson is a brilliant golfer with many international successes to his credit.

Above: Scottish professional, Sam Torrance's best performance to date occurred in 1976 when he finished the season in third place.

Below: Lee Trevino is one of today's best known golfers. Among the most successful of professionals, Trevino's earnings are near the two-million-dollar mark.

unequalled since the event became international. He was also runner-up in 1952 and 1957. Has also won the Opens of Australia (1951, 1967, 1972), New Zealand (1950, 1951, 1953, 1955, 1959, 1960, 1961, 1965, 1971), Italy (1959), Spain (1959), Hong Kong (1960, 1965, 1967), Germany (1960), India (1963) and the Philippines (1964). His amazing record also includes no less than 25 other major victories including two US Tour events, the PGA Match Play (England) (1954, 1961, 1966, 1967) and the Dunlop Masters (1961, 1968). Member of Australia's winning World Cup teams of 1954 and 1959.

THORNHILL, Jill – *born 18 August 1942*
Won Belgian Ladies' title in 1967. England international.

TOLLEY, Major Cyril James Hastings, MC – *born London, England, 1895 Died May 1978*
Gifted golfer who rose to become a member of the Royal and Ancient Rules of Golf Committee and Championship Committee. He was Chairman of the Walker Cup Selectors 1938–47 and Captain of the Royal and Ancient in 1948–49. Won the British Amateur Championship in 1920 and 1929 and the Welsh Open

Amateur in 1921 and 1923. Also won the French Open in 1924 and 1928. Member of the 1921, 1922, 1923, 1924, 1926, 1930 and 1934 Walker Cup teams and a regular England international throughout the '20s and '30s.

TORRANCE, Sam – *born Largs, Scotland, 23 August 1953*
Joined European tour in 1972 after two years as assistant professional and won Lord Derby's Under-25 Match Play Championship and Radici Open in Italy. Blossomed in 1976 when he landed Piccadilly Medal and Martini International and finished season in third place in European Order of Merit with £20,917.

TORRANCE, Thomas Arthur – *born Edinburgh, Scotland, 13 March 1891*
Irish Open Amateur Champion in 1925 and German Amateur Champion in 1927 and 1929, he was a Walker Cup player in 1924, 1928, 1930, 1932 (Captain) and 1934. A regular Scottish international in the '20s and early '30s.

TOUSSAINT, Philippe – *born Brussels, Belgium, 30 June 1949*
Outstanding amateur who turned professional in 1970 and won 1974 Benson and Hedges Festival event on the European tour.

TOWNSEND, Peter – *born Cambridge, England, 16 September 1946*
British Boys' champion in 1962 and 1964, British Youths' champion in 1965 and English Amateur Stroke Play champion in 1966, he enjoyed an outstanding career as an amateur winning a number of major events and representing Great Britain in 1965 Walker Cup. Also played in 1966 Eisenhower Trophy. Turned professional in December 1966 and christened his new career with victory in 1967 Dutch Open. In 1968 won Coca Cola Young Professionals' Championship and Piccadilly PGA Close Championship in England and also Western Australian Open. Landed Caracas open in 1969 and in 1971 won Walworth Aloyco (Italy) and Swiss Open.

TREVINO, Lee – *born Dallas, Texas, USA, 1 December 1939*
Modern day golf's most magnetic character who plays as fast as he talks. Rapid rise to fame charted by incredible US Open progress. Tied 54th in 1966 – his first and only appearance that year on circuit – then finished fifth a year later and in 1968 took the title at Oak Hill Country Club in Rochester, New York. That was his first of five 'major' successes and 20 US Tour wins. He added another US Open victory in 1971, won British Open that year and again in 1972 and took US PGA Championship in 1974. Followed his US and British Open 'double' in 1971 by winning Canadian Open to complete a memorable five week spell which earned him US Player of the Year title. Won Canadian Open

again in August 1977, to complete a marvellous recovery after a nightmare brush with lightning during 1975 Western Open and surgery in November 1976, to correct a herniated disc. Widely referred to as Super-Mex, he is now fast approaching two million dollar mark in official US Tour earnings. Gained Ryder Cup recognition in 1969, 1971, 1973 and 1975. Was a member of the US World Cup team in 1968, 1969, 1970, 1971 and 1974. Other achievements include winning World Series of Golf in 1974 and Mexican Open in 1975.

TSHABALALA, Vincent – *born Soweto, South Africa*
Surprise winner of 1976 French Open, he earned £5704 and a 27th place finish on his first European venture but dropped to 79th in the 1977 Order of Merit.

TUCKER, William Iestyn – *born Nantyglo, Monmouth, Wales, 9 December 1926*
Welsh Amateur Champion of 1963 and 1966, he holds the remarkable record of 24 successive appearances for Wales in the Home Internationals between 1949 and 1972. At Cardiff Golf Club (SSS 68) he shot a 59 in a medal round on 25 October 1972.

TURNESA, William – *born New York, USA, in 1914*
Won US Amateur title in 1938 and 1948 and British Amateur Championship in 1947. Member of 1947, 1949 and 1951 (captain) Walker Cup sides.

TWEDDELL, William MC – *born Wickham, County Durham, England, 21 March 1897*
British Amateur champion in 1927. Walker Cup player-captain in 1928 and non-playing captain 1936.

TWITTY, Howard – *born Phoenix, Arizona, USA, 15 January 1949*
One of the tallest professionals on the US Tour – he stands at 6ft 5in – he turned professional in 1973, joined the circuit in 1975 and won $54,268 to finish 51st in 1976 Order of Merit. Winner of Thailand Open in 1975 but still seeking first US Tour victory.

VALENTINE, Jessie, MBE (née Anderson) – *born Perth, Scotland, 18 March 1915*
Turned professional in 1959 following outstanding amateur career. Won British Ladies' 1937, 1955, 1958, New Zealand Ladies' in 1935 and French Ladies' in 1936. Appeared in seven Curtis Cup teams and was a regular for Great Britain and Scotland in international events during the '30s, '40s and '50s. Won several events as a professional including 1969 Babe Zaharias Trophy.

VAN DONCK, Flory – *born Tervueren, Brussels, Belgium, 23 June 1912*
Much respected player who won his own Belgian Open five times and Belgian Professional title 16 times and also 21 Open titles – the Dutch (1936, 1937, 1946, 1951, 1953), Italian (1938, 1947, 1953, 1955), Spanish (1951), Swiss (1953, 1955), French (1954, 1957, 1958), German (1953, 1956), Uruguay (1954), Portuguese (1955), Danish (1959) and Venezuelan (1957). Won a number of other events including World Cup individual title in 1960.

Below: Belgian Flory van Donck has been a leading European professional for many years.

*Above: The Vardon Trophy.
Below: l–r: Gene Sarazen,
Joyce Wethered (Lady
Heathcoat-Amory), Glenna
Collett Vare and Johnny
Dawson, May 1935.*

VARANGOT, Brigitte – *born Biarritz, France, 1 May 1940*
Outstanding amateur career in which she won French Ladies' Open (1961, 1962, 1964, 1965, 1966, 1973), French Ladies' Close (1959, 1961, 1963, 1970), British Ladies' (1963, 1965, 1968) and Italian Ladies' (1970) and a number of other titles. Represented France between 1956 and 1973, made six Vagliano Trophy appearances and six World Team Championship appearances. Member of 1964 winning World Team Championship side.

VARDON, Harry – *born Grouville, Jersey, 9 May 1890. Died 20 March 1937*
Ill-health and World War I did not stop Vardon creating golf history by winning British Open Championship six times – in 1896, 1898, 1899, 1903, 1911 and 1914. He also won the US Open in 1900 but it is generally considered that his victory roll call would have been much longer but for a serious illness in 1901. Nevertheless, he set standards that modern day golfers are still seeking to equal and gave the sport the upright swing and the Vardon grip.

VARE, Glenna (née Collett) – *born New Haven, Connecticut, USA, 20 June 1903*
Won six US Ladies' Amateur (1922, 1925, 1928, 1929, 1930 and 1935), two British Ladies' (1929, 1930) and two Canadian Ladies' (1923, 1924) titles. Made four Curtis Cup appearances in 1932, 1936, 1938 and 1948 (captain) and non-playing captain in 1950.

VAUGHAN, David – *born St Helens, Lancashire, England, 26 June 1948*
Welsh World Cup player and Double Diamond World Golf Classic representative who won 1971 Lord Derby's Under-23 Championship.

VENTURI, Ken – *born San Francisco, California, USA, 15 May 1931*
Won 14 tournaments between 1957, when he joined the tour, and 1966 but there can be no doubt that 1964 was his most memorable year.

He landed US Open title and won a total of $62,465 – his best ever one year earnings. He was also named Player of the year in 1964 and the following year played in the Ryder Cup.

VICENZO, Roberto de – *born Buenos Aires, Argentina, 14 April 1923*
One of the best loved golfers in the world with an incredible record of having won no less than 165 tournaments including 39 National Championships. His record could have been even better because although he won the 1967 British Open Championship becoming, at the age of 44 years and 93 days, the oldest winner of the 'Cup', he was also second in 1950 and third on no less than six occasions. Also missed chance of play-off for 1968 US Masters when he signed for a four at the last hole instead of three. Won Argentine Open nine times and Argentine Professional seven times and other victories include Chile Open (1946), Colombia Open (1947), Uruguay Open (1949), Belgian Open (1950), Dutch Open (1950), French Open (1950, 1960, 1964), Mexican Open (1951, 1953), Panama Open (1952, 1973, 1974), Jamaica Open (1956, 1957), Brazilian Open (1957, 1960, 1963, 1964, 1973), Caracas Open (1973), German Open (1964), Spanish Open (1966) and Bogota Open (1969). Won six US Tour events and in 1974 captured US PGA Seniors' and World Senior Professional titles. Member of winning 1953 Argentine World Cup team and individual winner in 1962 and 1970.

Left: The great Argentinian Roberto de Vicenzo is the oldest man to win the British Open Championship. At 55 he is still playing in tournaments with some success.

took the Portuguese Ladies' (1972), US Trans-Mississippi (1972) and Spanish Ladies' (1973) titles. Member of 1972 Curtis Cup team when she was undefeated. Turned professional August 1973 and won United States Ladies' PGA card in 1974.

WADKINS, Lanny – *born Richmond, Virginia, USA, 5 December 1949*
Brilliant amateur who attended Wake Forest University. Won 1970 US Amateur Championship and in the same year also won Western Amateur and was a member of US World Amateur team. A Walker Cup representative in 1969 and 1971, he turned professional and joined the tour in 1971. Won 1972 Sahara Invitational and a year later lifted Byron Nelson Golf Classic and USI Classic. Earned $200,455 to finish fifth in US Order of Merit in 1973 but career ground almost to a halt until 1977 when within a month he won the US PGA Championship and the World Series to accelerate his career earnings past the half a million dollar mark. Also earned his debut as a Ryder Cup player in 1977.

WALKER, Carol Michelle (Mickey) – *born Alwoodley, Leeds, Yorkshire, England, 17 December 1952*
As an Amateur won British Ladies' in 1971 and 1972 and English Ladies' in 1973 and overseas

Left: Lanny Wadkins, one of the younger stars on the US circuit, won the US Amateur Championship before turning professional.

WALKER, J B, MBE – *born Ireland, 21 June 1896*
Won Irish Ladies' 1930, Australian Ladies' in 1935 and appeared in three Curtis Cup teams (1934, 1936, 1938).

WALL, Art (Jr) – *born Honesdale; Pennsylvania, USA, 25 November 1923*
Ten years after turning professional in 1949 he experienced an incredible year by winning US Masters, Crosby National, Azalea and Buick tournaments, amassing $53,167 to lead the money winners. Also earned the Vardon Trophy for the best stroke average and was named PGA Player of the Year. Sixteen years later he was in the news again when, at the age of 51, he gained his first victory for nine years by triumphing in the Greater Milwaukee Open. That was his 14th US tour win. He has won more than half a million dollars and gained Ryder Cup recognition in 1957, 1959 and 1961 – winning four of his six matches.

Below: Tom Watson won the British Open Championship in 1975 and again in 1977.

WARD, Charles Harold – *born Birmingham, England, 16 September 1911*
Three times Ryder Cup player (1947, 1949,

1951), he finished third in 1948 and 1951 British Open Championships. Won ten major events including Dunlop Masters in 1949 and British PGA Close in 1956.

WARD, Harvie – *born USA, 1926*
Winner of British Amateur Championship (1952), US Amateur (1955, 1956), and Canadian Amateur (1954), he played in the Walker Cups of 1953, 1955 and 1959 before turning professional in 1973.

WATROUS, Al – *born Yonkers, New York, USA, 1 February 1899*
Won 1922 Canadian Open and finished runner-up in 1926 British Open Championship. Ryder Cup player in 1926, 1927 and 1929. Later won the US PGA Seniors' title three times – 1950, 1951, 1957.

WATSON, Tom – *born Kansas City, Missouri, USA, 4 September 1949*
By the end of the 1977 season he had established himself as one of the finest golfers of the current decade. But the manner in which he held off the challenges of Jack Nicklaus in the US Masters and the British Open at Turnberry suggested that he had the potential to become one of the world's top all-time performers. Introduced to the game at the age of six by his father, a scratch golfer, he won the Missouri Amateur Championship four times and for three years played for Stanford University where he studied for a degree in psychology – graduating in 1971. He turned professional the same year but waited until 1974 before winning his first tournament – taking the Western Open only one week after a last round 79 cost him victory in the US Open which he led after three rounds. But Watson's name was soon on a 'Major' trophy because 12 months later he won the British Open at Carnoustie – beating Australian Jack Newton in a play-off. That year he earned $153,795 on the US circuit, won the Byron Nelson Golf Classic and also lifted the $50,000 top prize in the World Series of Golf. Success eluded him in 1976 although he had 11 top ten finishes on the US tour but in 1977 he began brilliantly by winning the Bing Crosby National and the Andy Williams Open and later added the Western Open en route to winning more than $300,000 and leading the money winners. It took his career earnings in six years to within sight of one million dollars but it was those victories in the US Masters and British Open which confirmed his arrival as one of the world's golf superstars. In 1977 he also made his debut as a Ryder Cup player.

WEAVER, DeWitt – *born Danville, Kentucky, USA, 14 September 1939*
Turned professional in 1963 and joined tour the following year. Won 1971 US Professional Match Play Championship and 1972 Southern Open.

WEISKOPF, Tom – *born Massillon, Ohio, USA, 9 November 1942*
In 1977 he won the Kemper Open to record his 12th tour victory but it is generally considered that Weiskopf possesses the talent to have won much more. Certainly during an eight week spell in 1973, he emphasised his prodigious ability by winning five tournaments which included the British and Canadian Opens. That year was certainly his best on the US Tour for he won the Colonial, Kemper and IVB-Philadelphia tournaments and accumulated $245,463 to finish third in the Order of Merit. He turned professional in 1964 – one year after winning the Western Amateur Championship – but waited until 1968 to win. Then the 6ft 3in graduate of Ohio State University won the Williams-San Diego and Buick events and totalled $152,946 to come third in that year's money list. But although he won the Kemper and IVB-Philadelphia in 1971 and the Jackie Gleason in 1972 it was not until 1973 that he exceeded that sum. In 1975 he earned $219,140 and won the Greater Greensboro Open and the Canadian Open and his career earnings have now passed the one and a half million dollar mark. His other victories include success in the 1972 Piccadilly World Match Play Championship at Wentworth, England, and in the 1973 South African PGA Championship. He represented his country in the 1973 and 1975 Ryder Cups and in the 1972 World Cup. His fine record also includes being runner-up no less than four times in the US Masters – in 1969, 1972, 1974 and 1975.

WESTLAND, Jack
Became the oldest player to win the US Amateur when at the age of 47 he captured the 1952 title and earned himself a return to international golf by playing in the 1953 Walker Cup following earlier appearances in 1932 and 1934. Won French Amateur in 1929.

WETHERED, Roger Henry – *born Maldon, Surrey, England, 3 January 1899*
British Amateur champion in 1923, runner-up in 1928 and 1930 and tied first for Open Championship in 1921 but lost play-off. Member of 1921, 1922, 1923, 1926, 1930 and 1934 Walker Cup teams. Captain of Royal and Ancient in 1946.

WHITCOMBE, Charles Albert – *born Burnham, Somerset, England, 21 September 1895*
First holder of the Vardon Trophy (1937), he made six successive appearances in the Ryder Cup between 1927 and 1937. Won Irish Open (1930), third in British Open Championship (1935) and winner of eight major tournaments including PGA Match Play (1928 and 1930).

WHITE, Ronald James – *born Wallasey, England, 9 April 1921*
English Amateur champion in 1949 and English Open Amateur Stroke Play champion in 1950 and 1951. Walker Cup player in 1947, 1951, 1953 and 1955.

WHITWORTH, Kathy – *born Monahans, Texas, USA, 27 September 1939*
By the end of the 1977 season she was approaching the three quarter of a million dollars mark in career earnings on the US Women's pro circuit –

Above: Tom Weiskopf, winner of the British Open Championship in 1973, is a brilliant and stylish player with a long record of successes to his credit.

Centre left: Roger Wethered, brother of Joyce Wethered (Lady Heathcoat-Amory) as he appeared in the British Open Golf Championship of 1928.

Above: Enid Wilson, one of Britain's finest women golfers, was a magnificent iron club player.

a figure unequalled. She turned professional in 1959 and has now won no less than 80 tour events including the 1967, 1971 and 1975 LPGA Championships.

WILL, George – *born Ladybank, Fife, Scotland, 16 April 1937*
Appeared in three successive Ryder Cup matches (1963, 1965, 1967) and represented Scotland in 1963, 1969 and 1970 World Cups.

WILSON, Enid – *born Stonebroom, near Alfreton, Derbyshire, England, 15 March 1910*
British Ladies' champion 1931, 1932, 1933; English Ladies' 1928, 1930 and Curtis Cup player in 1932.

WOLSTENHOLME, Guy – *born Leicester, England, 8 March 1931*
A British Boy international in 1946, 1947, 1948, he won the English Amateur Championship in 1956 and 1959, the English Open Amateur Stroke Play Championship in 1960 and the German Amateur Championship in 1956. Also represented Great Britain in the 1957 and 1959 Walker Cup matches and appeared in the Eisenhower Trophy team of 1958 and 1960 and the Great Britain Commonwealth team of 1959. Finished sixth in the Open Championship in 1960 as an amateur but turned professional later that year. Represented England in 1965 World Cup but emigrated to Australia in mid-1960s.

WOOD, Craig Ralph – *born Lake Placid, New York, USA, 18 November 1901. Died in 1968*
Came close to being a Grand Slam golfer. He won US Open in 1941 and US Masters in 1941 but had to settle for runners-up berths in British Open Championship (losing 1933 play-off) and US PGA (1934). Won Canadian Open in 1942 and played in Ryder Cup teams of 1931, 1933 and 1935.

WOOD, Norman – *born Prestonpans, Scotland, 8 January 1947*
Turned professional in 1965 but waited until 1972 to win on European tour when he lifted Italian Open title. Won £6945 and finished 18th in the Order of Merit in 1975 when he registered Ryder Cup debut and beat Lee Trevino at Laurel Valley. Also won Jamaican Open in 1973.

WORSHAM, Lewis – *born Alta Vista, Virginia, USA, 5 October 1917*
US Open champion in 1947, he earned Ryder Cup recognition that same year and won a total of six US tour events. Leading US money winner in 1953.

WRIGHT, Innes – *born Glasgow, Scotland, 7 January 1935*
Scottish Ladies' champion in 1959, 1960, 1961 and 1973. Appeared in 15 Scottish Homes International teams from 1952 to 1973 and was

a Curtis Cup player in 1954, 1956, 1958 and 1960.

WRIGHT, Mickey – *born San Diego, California, USA, 14 February 1935*
Holds records for most wins (82) during career and most wins (13) during one season on US Women's PGA Tour. Won four US Opens (1958, 1959, 1961, 1964) and four LPGA Championships (1958, 1960, 1961, 1963). Career earnings of £350,000.

WYLIE, Phyllis (née Wade) – *born Essex, England, in 1911*
Won English Ladies' title in 1934 and appeared in 1938 Curtis Cup team.

WYNN, Bob – *born Lancaster, Kentucky, USA, 27 January 1940*
A professional since 1959, he only joined the tour in 1971 and achieved a breakthrough in 1976 when he won BC Open. Earlier he had won 1975 Magnolia Classic, a second Tour event, and a hat-trick of Ohio Opens in 1970, 1971 and 1972.

YANCEY, Bert – *born Chipley, Florida, USA, 6 August 1938*
Turned professional in 1961 and won seven events after joining US Tour in 1964. Landed Azalea, Memphis and Portland Open in 1966, Dallas in 1967, Atlanta in 1969, Crosby National in 1970 and American Golf Classic in 1972. Career earnings of more than $650,000.

Centre right: Bert Yancey won several events in the sixties and early seventies.

YATES, Charles Richardson – *born Atlanta, Georgia, USA, 9 September 1913*
Won British Amateur Championship in 1938 and played in Walker Cup sides of 1936 and 1938. Non-playing Walker Cup captain in 1953.

YOUNG, Donna Caponi – *born Detroit, Michigan, USA, 29 January 1945*
Has won more than $350,000 on the US Ladies' PGA Tour since turning professional in 1965 – her career profiting from back to back US Open wins in 1969 and 1970.

ZAHARIAS, Mildred (née 'Babe' Didrikson) – *born Port Arthur, Texas, USA, June 1915. Died Galveston, Texas. USA, September 1956*
Competed in 1932 Olympic Games, establishing women's world records in 80m hurdles, javelin and high jump, before devoting her attention to golf and setting record after record. She won US National Women's Amateur in 1946, became first American to win British Ladies' Championship when she took that title in 1947, and then turned professional in August that year and won the US National Women's Open in 1948 and 1950. Top money winner on the US circuit from 1948–1951, she was voted in 1949 the Greatest Female Athlete of the Half-Century and later became the first woman to hold the position of head professional at a golf club.

ZARLEY, Kermit – *born Seattle, Washington, USA, 29 September 1941*
Since turning professional in 1963 and joining the tour one year later he has numbered three tour victories – the Kaiser in 1968, Canadian Open in 1970 and National Team Championship in 1972 with Babe Hiskey. His career earnings total more than half a million dollars.

ZIEGLER, Larry – *born St Louis, Missouri, USA, 12 August 1939*
One of 13 children, it was ten years after turning professional in 1959 that he scored a first tour victory – winning the Michigan Classic. It was not until 1975 that he won again – taking the Greater Jacksonville Open – but in 1976 he had a couple of 'highs' – finishing third in the US Masters and three weeks later winning the First NBC New Orleans Open en route to personal record winnings that season of $84,165. He has now won half a million dollars and other honours include victory in the 1974 Morocco International Grand Prix.

ZIOBRO, Billy – *born Elizabeth, New Jersey, USA, 11 September 1948*
Turned professional in 1971, joined tour following year and won 1973 Carlton Oaks Open and 1974 Mini Nelson.

ZOELLER, Fuzzy – *born New Albany, Indiana, USA, 11 November 1951*
Turned professional in 1973 but still seeking first tour victory despite a sensational display in 1976 Ed McMahon-Quad Cities Open when he carded a record equally eight birdies in succession for a first round 63. He finished second in the tournament.

Centre left: Donna Young is a powerful and successful American professional.

Left: Babe Didrikson Zaharias on her way to becoming the first American woman to capture the British Women's Championship in 1947.

courses

Aberdeen, Royal, *Balgownie, Aberdeen, Scotland*
6451yd, 5899m
Ranked as the sixth oldest club in the world, Aberdeen GC came into existence in 1815 although golf had been played on the links in the late 16th century and a club was founded in 1780 by the Society of Golfers of Aberdeen. It was accorded Royal recognition by King Edward VII in 1903. It has a longer outward nine holes, especially testing in the wind, with a fine par 5 second hole of over 500yd. The course has staged the Scottish Amateur Championship, the Northern Open, the Scottish Professional and the British Boys' Championships.

Aberdovey, *North Wales*
6406yd, 5858m
This club dates back to 1886, when the uncle of famed golf writer Bernard Darwin borrowed flower pots to cut into the first green. It was officially formed in 1892 and the first scratch medal was won by young Darwin with a return of 100. Looking out over Cardigan Bay and exposed to the winds, it lies between the railway and sandhills, and boasts a famous short third hole, 'Cader', with a completely blind shot of 165yd over a massive sandhill, with a tough sleepered bunker ready to catch anyone short who fails to reach the small green. A fine course, it has been the venue of the Welsh Amateur and Welsh Ladies' Championships.

Acapulco, *Mexico*
Pierre Marques: 6723yd, 6148m
Princess: 6355yd, 5811m
Mexico's famous city can boast of two outstanding courses, fronting a beautiful palm-tree-lined beach. A short drive from the airport, they are away from the hustle of the city. The Princess features numerous dog-legs and water on twelve holes, while the Pierre Marques, longer and more demanding, has five lakes and wide bunkers.

Addington, *Surrey, England*
6216yd, 5684m
Only ten miles from the centre of London, this course of heather, pine and silver birch was laid out by J F Abercromby, one of Britain's great golf course architects, in 1914, and is notable for having six short holes, starting off with a 166yd uphill 1st hole. A second course, the New, which Abercromby laid out, was taken over for housing by the local council after World War II, but the Old remains a fine test of golf.

Adelaide, Royal, *Seaton, South Australia,* par 72
7010yd, 6410m
One of two South Australian clubs given cham-

pionship status, Adelaide GC was founded in 1870, went out of existence for a few years, and has changed its course on a few occasions. It was established at Seaton in 1904, and given Royal recognition by King George V in 1923. Subject to wind as it is not too far from the coast and well bunkered, it is a testing course, and has been the venue of the Australian Open Championship on many occasions – the first was in 1910.

Aldeburgh, *Suffolk, England*
6502yd, 5945m, par 68
A heathland course, although close to the sea, it dates from 1884, and at times gives an impression of links characteristics. One of East Anglia's best-known courses, it has been the venue of the English Ladies' Championship. Conspicuous are the plentiful masses of yellow gorse. It features several outstanding holes, especially on the second half.

Alnmouth Village, *Northumberland, England*
6020yd, 5505m
This is one of the oldest golf clubs in England formed in 1867; the game has been played here possibly longer than anywhere else in England, except Westward Ho! in Devon. A nine-hole course of links character by the sea, it may owe its early beginnings to players from Scotland as it is located close to the border between the two countries. The fact that it is a short course does not detract from its attractiveness.

Aloha, *Marbella, Spain*
7029yd, 6427m
One of the newest courses along the Costa del Sol, this course is of championship standard; the complete automatic watering system leaves its

Preceding page: The new and unranked Woburn golf course built on the estate of the Duke of Bedford.
Left: Aloha is one of the new, well planned Spanish courses.

fairways and greens in fine condition. Carefully designed as a test for the best golfers, it has an undulating surface and offers some quite excellent and challenging holes.

Alwoodley, *Leeds, Yorkshire, England*
6755yd, 6177m
Founded in 1907, the club was entirely private for many years. However from 1965 it has staged many events including the county championship of Yorkshire, the English Ladies' Championship and the 1971 British Ladies' Championship, won by Michelle Walker. A moorland course, its layout owes much to two famous architects, H S Colt, who had a share in the first designs, and Alister Mackenzie, the club's first secretary, who later was responsible for two of the world's finest courses, Pebble Beach and Augusta National. The course calls for accuracy at several fine holes, notably the 5th, with a fairway sloping steeply away to the right, and the 15th, a testing dog-leg.

Antwerp, Royal, *Belgium*
6675yd, 6104m
Founded in 1888, the club moved to Kapellenbos in 1910 when an English architect, Tom Simpson, laid out the course; later a nine-hole course was added. It has been the venue of the Belgian Open Amateur and Women's Open Championships.

Ashburnham, *Pembrey, Dyfed, South Wales*
6814yd, 6231m
One of the oldest clubs in Wales, Ashburnham was founded in 1894; its opening holes are inland, the others are of seaside links character. The inward nine has some notable holes, particularly the par 5 14th. It has been the venue for the Welsh Amateur Championship, the PGA Close Championship and the Martini International Tournament.

Ashdown Forest, Royal, *near East Grinstead, Sussex*
6525yd, 5966m
Founded in 1888, the course is unusual in that it has no artificial bunkers, but abounds in hazards such as streams, heather, bracken, hollows and severe slopes. It was granted its Royal title after the Duke of Cambridge, having commanded troops at a review by Queen Victoria in the forest, drove a ball wearing full uniform. The 140yd 6th, the Island Hole, its green guarded by a stream, was endowed in the sum of £5 by a visitor intrigued by its charm, with the accumulated interest to go to anyone holing in one at any of three specified meetings. When it was first won in 1947, about £30 was paid out, but when the feat was repeated a few months later, there was only a few pence available. The Artisans Club has produced fine players, including Abe Mitchell and Open champion Alfred Padgham. Recently Royal Ashdown New (6025yd, 5509m) has been added.

Ashridge, *Berkhamsted, Hertfordshire, England*
6453yd, 5901m
A parkland course of great splendour, with fairways cut between stately trees in a forest maintained by the National Trust, the course spreads out from the clubhouse in a star shape. Tom Scott says it has 'the most perfect setting and is unquestionably the best-kept'. It has achieved great popularity among golf societies for its splendid facilities and testing golf. One of its most notable holes is named 'Cotton's', after Henry Cotton, professional from 1937 to 1943, who found the line from the tee at the 361yd 9th for the ball to run up to the slope and on to the green.

Atalaya Park, *Estepona, Spain*
6935yd, 6340m
One of the famed Costa del Sol's most popular courses, it is one of great character with an open parkland layout and a wide variety of trees and shrubs backed by the Sierra Bermeja mountains. The length of the holes on what is a tough championship course can be altered to make it an easier test; the front tees can be changed to shorten the total distance by 900m. Streams cross three of the fairways. The few existing bunkers are cunningly placed. Gently undulating fairways lead to fine greens, and the course is complemented by luxurious clubhouses.

Atlantic City, *New Jersey, USA*
This flat course is subject to high winds as it is part of a low-lying sandy island. The word 'birdie', to describe a hole played one stroke under par, is reputed to have originated here. After one player had hit a bird in flight with his ball from the tee, he put his second shot inches from the hole; one of his companions exclaiming that it was 'a bird of a shot'.

Auckland, *North Island, New Zealand*
6565yd, 6002m
Although the club dates from 1894, the present course was opened in 1910, and alterations were made between the two wars. A parkland type of course, it has been the venue for the New Zealand Open Championship, the first in 1909. The country's most famous player, Bob Charles, won one of his titles there in 1970. The club staged the Commonwealth Tournament in 1971, the centenary year of New Zealand golf.

Augusta National, *Georgia, USA*
7030yd, 6428m
The home of the famous Masters Tournament, the club was established in 1931, the year after the great Robert T (Bobby) Jones achieved his Grand Slam of the Open and Amateur titles of Britain and the USA. Having retired from competitive golf, Jones set out to achieve his aim of building a dream course and was invited to view a stretch of land west of Augusta which had been a horticultural nursery. At once he knew the site was ideal with its trees and shrubs

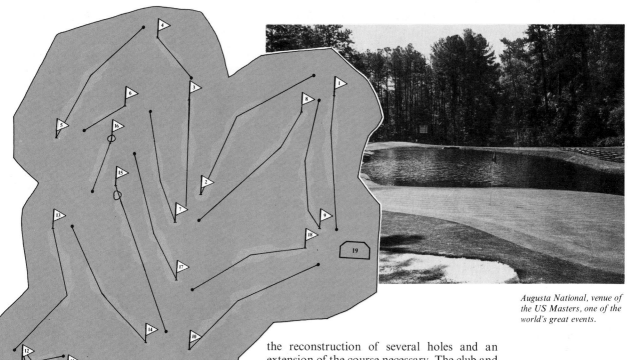

Augusta National, venue of the US Masters, one of the world's great events.

and streams. Jones engaged Yorkshire-born Alister Mackenzie, who had designed Cypress Point, and together they constructed a course of great beauty, but one which was a stern but fair test of the tournament golfer without being penal for the average player. The Augusta National Invitation Tournament, which became known as the Masters, was inaugurated in 1934 with a friendly gathering of professionals and amateurs. Horton Smith was the winner, and Jones, persuaded to play competitively again, shared thirteenth place. Jones and his friend Clifford Roberts, one of the founders of Augusta, decided to continue the tournament the following year, when Gene Sarazen, the winner, holed his second shot on the par 5 15th for an albatross and made the tournament front-page news. Its prestige grew and after some years it became acknowledged as one of the world's four major championships. Jones died in 1971 and Roberts in 1977. A riot of colour in spring when the tournament is held, its holes are appropriately named after flowers, shrubs and trees. Its most famous member was former President of the US, General Dwight D Eisenhower.

Australian, The, *Sydney, New South Wales, Australia*
7148yd, 6536m
First established in 1882 and one of the oldest clubs in Australia, the course has few trees, is subject to winds from the sea and is sandy in nature. In 1968 the building of a new road made

the reconstruction of several holes and an extension of the course necessary. The club and Royal Sydney formed the New South Wales Golf Association, and it has been the venue of the Australian Open Championship attracting famous American players including Jack Nicklaus, winner in 1975 and 1976. In 1975 Nicklaus had made alterations to the course. It was the venue of the 1977 Australian Open Championship won by Dave Graham. Nicklaus shot a last round of 80 on the course he had redesigned.

Bahamas Princess, *Grand Bahama Island, Bahamas*
7000yd, 6400m
Golf originated in the Bahamas at Nassau in the late 1920s, and it was not until 1960 that courses were developed on Grand Bahama Island. However the development of a number of superb courses has been so rapid that they have attracted visitors from all over the world. The Princess complex provides two courses – Emerald (6650yd, 6081m) and Ruby (6700yd, 6126m) – featuring pine trees and large lakes. Both provide excellent tests of golf. Also in Grand Bahama Island are the Lucaya and Shannon courses. Lucaya (6805yd, 6222m) was designed by American Dick Wilson, who also built other Bahamas courses. Opened in 1964, Lucaya was the venue for the 1971 Bahamas

Island Open won by Bob Goalby. Nearby Shannon (6700yd, 6126m) designed by Joe Lee is an even more delightful course. Not far from Nassau on New Providence is South Ocean Beach (6707yd, 6133m) which opened in 1973 and is one of the best in the Caribbean, with its undulating fairways densely wooded on either side, water hazards and large bunkers. It was designed by American Joe Lee.

Ballybunion, *County Kerry, Ireland*
6417yd, 5868m
A links course of the highest standard, its records go back to 1896. In more modern times Christy O'Connor has said of it 'Anyone who breaks 70 here is playing better than he is really able to'. In recent years, a fine new clubhouse has been built, resulting in a re-numbering of the holes, and in most people's opinions, providing a more attractive layout. Fairways thread between giant sandhills near the sea and when the westerly winds blow, it is a daunting prospect even for the most experienced players. In recent years the course has been threatened with course erosion but thanks to financial help from all over the world, especially the US, the course has been saved.

Baltimore, *Five Farms, Maryland, USA*
6659yd, 6089m
Founded before the turn of the century, Baltimore Country Club has had three courses. The present one at Five Farms is some miles from the centre of Baltimore. Designed by A W Tillinghast, architect of Winged Foot and other famous courses, it is not as long as many American courses, but offers interesting and challenging holes, notably the long 6th, the Barn Hole, a right-to-left dog-leg where the bold player will try to hit over the maintenance buildings, to be rewarded by an easy approach to the green. However disaster awaits those who fail! Baltimore has been host to great championships, dating from the US Open of 1899 won by Willie Smith by a record margin of 11 strokes. The 1899 contest was on the original course. Later events have included the 1928 US PGA Championship won by Leo Diegel, the 1932 US Amateur Championship won by Canadian Ross Sommerville, and in 1965, a Walker Cup match in which Great Britain and Ireland tied with the US.

Baltusrol, *Springfield, New Jersey, USA*
With two championship courses, the Upper and the Lower, Baltusrol has been host to many national championships, including the US Open on several occasions. The first occurred in 1903 when Willie Anderson won the second of his four titles, and the most recent occurred in 1967 when Jack Nicklaus set the lowest 72-hole aggregate for the championship with 275 on the Lower Course. The Upper Course staged the 1936 Open won by Tony Manero. The Lower

Below: The picturesque American club, Baltusrol (Springfield, New Jersey), which was founded in 1895.

Course is more suited to present-day championship demands although both were laid out by A W Tillinghast who was responsible for Winged Foot among others. It has a variety of testing holes, finishing with two par 5 holes which are lengthened for championships; the 17th alone stretches over 600yd. The short 4th over water is one of its most notable holes. A famous professional, since 1934, Johnny Farrell, US Open Champion of 1928 and a member of the first Ryder Cup team in 1927, often gave lessons to the late Duke of Windsor on this course. Farrell made a nostalgic return to Britain in 1977 when he was a guest at the Golden Jubilee Ryder Cup contest at Royal Lytham and St Annes.

Banff Springs, *Alberta, Canada*
6731yd, 6155m
Located in the spectacular Canadian Rockies complete with glorious mountain scenery and the wild life of a huge National Park, this is a course of championship standard, though it mainly plays host to summer visitors from all over the world. Built as a nine-hole course in 1911 by the Canadian Pacific Railway, it was extended to 18 holes by the end of World War I and re-designed in 1927. Skirted by the Bow River, there are many quite awe-inspiring as well as challenging holes; possibly the most famous is the 8th or Devil's Cauldron, a par 3 which calls for a carry of 175yd from an elevated tee over a lake to a well-bunkered green, with varying winds setting problems for the player. One of the great holes of golf, it is a tribute to Stanley Thompson, the Canadian architect, who re-designed the course. For those touring the Rockies, a 160 mile journey to Jasper Lodge provides another glorious setting for golf which is truly out of this world.

Basel, *Near Hagenthal, France*
6700yd, 6126m
One of Switzerland's newer courses, it is actually located over the French frontier in Alsace. A gently sloping, modern championship course, open from April to October it is noted for out of bounds hazards on the opening holes, and with its wealth of trees and bunkers, offers a real test.

Bastad, *Sweden*
6300yd, 5760m
Laid out by J H Taylor, the holes on this course up in the hills are quite intriguing and provide a good test, especially when subject to wind and rain. It was founded in 1928 with Ludvig Nobel, (nephew of Alfred Nobel of Nobel Prize fame) taking a leading part, and helped to create interest in the game in Sweden. It has staged several Swedish championships.

Bay Hill, *Orlando, Florida, USA*
This is one of several courses built in Florida by one of America's outstanding architects, Dick Wilson, after he had made his home in Delray

Beach. In 1969 the course was bought by Arnold Palmer and associates and comprised 27 holes set out in three loops, two of which made up the championship course. Dick Tiddy, who first met Palmer at Wake Forest College in the early '50s, moved from Charlotte, North Carolina, where he had been a professional for 20 years, to become head professional at Bay Hill. It is now the centre for the Arnold Palmer Golf Academy, a venture started by Palmer in Vermont to provide courses of instruction for boys 11 to 17. The boys who attend receive attention from Palmer himself.

Bel-Air, *Los Angeles, California, USA*
Founded in the 1920s, the course is located in the attractive community of Los Angeles which bears its name, and has many people in the film industry as members. It staged its most famous tournament, the American Amateur Championship, in 1976; the winner was Bill Sander. With the clubhouse on top of a hill, players walk from the 9th green through a tunnel to an elevator that takes them to the clubhouse, and from there to the 10th tee.

Belfry, The, *Sutton Coldfield, England*
Brabazon: 7182yd, 6567m
Derby: 6082yd, 5561m
This is a £3-million golfing development which opened in 1977 comprised of two outstanding courses and a hotel. The headquarters of the British Professional Golfers' Association is established here. The courses were designed by former Ryder Cup players, Peter Alliss and Dave Thomas, and are named after Presidents of the PGA. The Brabazon is modelled on Augusta and features natural water hazards and specially designed American-style greens to encourage attacking golf. The shorter Derby course also features water hazards and challenging bunkers. The standard of the courses so impressed the PGA, that the Belfry has already been named as the venue of the 1981 Ryder Cup matches between the USA and Great Britain and Ireland.

Belgique, Royal, *Tervuren, Belgium*
6627yd, 6060m
While England has many former stately homes converted into clubhouses, this course, built by Royal command, has a clubhouse listed as a national monument, a château built by the Infanta Isabella of Spain in the 17th century. King Leopold II ordered the course to be laid out in 1904 so that visitors, mainly British businessmen, would be able to play golf. Royal interest in the club has helped to popularise the game in Belgium.

Belvedere, *Prince Edward Island, Canada*
6372yd, 5827m
In beautiful surroundings, the course was established in 1906 as a nine-hole course, but was extended 20 years later. It has staged some

important tournaments including the 1964 Canadian Junior Championship. The fairways are lined by tall spruce trees and lead to greens rather on the small side, calling for careful approach play.

Berkshire, *Ascot, England*
Red: 6356yd, 5811m
Blue: 6258yd, 5722m
Set deep in the Berkshire countryside, these two courses must be among the most delightful in England with fairways running between pine trees, and heather and ferns lining the springy turf. There is little to choose in the excellence of both courses, though perhaps the Red would be the first choice, offering some superb short holes, none an easy par 3. There are three in each half, and these are balanced by the same number of par 5s. Herbert Fowler laid out the courses after World War I in a perfect setting, remote and peaceful. Two outstanding tournaments are held annually, the Berkshire Trophy, and for ladies, the Avia International Tournament. The English Amateur Championship was held at Berkshire in 1965 over a selection of

Above: The 1971 British Open was played at Royal Birkdale. Trevino is driving watched by the British amateur, Michael Bonallack.
Right: Royal Birkdale.

holes from both courses, and was won by Michael Bonallack, who in the same year won one of his six Berkshire Trophy titles.

Birkdale, Royal, *Lancashire, England*
6727yd, 6151m
Founded in 1899 and one of the oldest clubs in the North of England, this famous course among the sandhills on the Lancashire coast is rated by many as the most popular venue for the Open Championship. Certainly, Americans, including Jack Nicklaus, look on it as an outstanding test among Britain's championship links courses. It was granted its Royal title in 1951, and three years later took its place on the rota of Open Championship courses, with the event being staged there again in 1961, 1965, 1971 and 1976. It has also been the venue for the Ryder Cup matches of 1965 and 1969 (the only tie of the series occurred in 1969), the Walker Cup, the Curtis Cup, the Amateur and English Amateur Championships, as well as many other outstanding tournaments. The championship length of the course is extended to over 7000yd, par 74, and in recent years, one or two holes have been altered, not all to the liking of the world's most famous golfers. Royal Birkdale was the scene of Australian Peter Thomson's first Open Championship victory in 1954 and in 1965 he won his fifth title there – the only player to achieve five victories since the championship became an international event. A plaque on the course marks the spot where Arnold Palmer played a superb six-iron shot out of deep rough to the 15th green (now the 16th) which proved a decisive stroke in his 1961 Open victory. Although a great seaside links course, the fairways offer fair lies, and off them, willow scrub has ruined many a golfer's hopes.

Blackheath, Royal, *London, England*
6024yd, 5508m
Golf was played on Blackheath in the early 17th century when the thrones of Scotland and

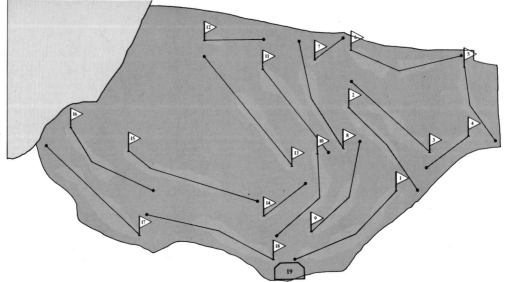

England were united under James I, but the actual establishment of the club is not known, although a society was known to exist in 1766 when a silver club was presented to the captain. The club can claim to be the oldest in England, but as James played the game in Scotland before moving south – where golf had been played for some time – it seems likely Scottish clubs then existed. Golf was played at Blackheath over five holes at first and later over seven and play survived until World War I. The club later merged with Eltham, and James Braid laid out a new course at Eltham Park, a fine test set in wooded parkland. The superb clubhouse, the 17th century Eltham Lodge, houses a fine collection of trophies including the Knuckle Club (the old Winter Club) dating back to 1790, paintings and china. Its most famous member was George Glennie from St Andrews who held the amateur record there for 24 years. He was captain of Royal Blackheath and later secretary until his death in 1886.

Blairgowrie, *Perthshire, Scotland*
6309yd, 5769m
(Second course under construction)
Founded in 1899, with a nine-hole course on land leased from the Marquess of Landsdowne, the course was extended to 18 holes in 1927, and a few years later, partly re-designed by James Braid. In its glorious setting of birch and pine trees, it is considered the best inland course in Scotland. About half the holes are dog-legs, and

and superb greens from mid-March through to the end of October.

Bloemfontein, *Orange Free State, South Africa*
7014yd, 6496m
Founded in 1895, the club enjoyed several courses before finally being established on its present site in the early 1950s. With a wealth of trees, it has matured considerably, and is a pleasant course, with large greens and wide fairways. It has been the venue for all major South African amateur, ladies' and professional tournaments, including the South African Open, won in 1964 by Alan Henning.

Bombay Presidency, *India*
6230yd, 5697m
Only one Bombay course remained by the 1920s, surviving all others including the Royal Bombay GC. Initially called the New Golf Club, its name later was changed to its present title, and the course moved to the suburb of Chembur. The influence of the great Australian player Peter Thomson has been of value in bringing the course to fine condition with some challenging holes and fast greens. It has been the venue of the All-India Amateur Championship.

Brae Burn, *Massachusetts, USA*
No 1: 6516yd, 5958m
No 2: 5120yd, 4682m
Scots-born Donald Ross, designer of many famous American courses, designed the course,

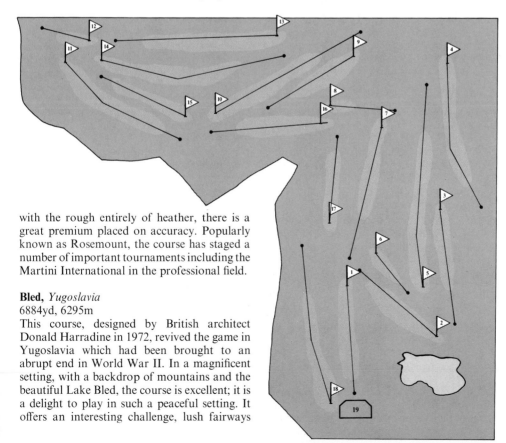

with the rough entirely of heather, there is a great premium placed on accuracy. Popularly known as Rosemount, the course has staged a number of important tournaments including the Martini International in the professional field.

Bled, *Yugoslavia*
6884yd, 6295m
This course, designed by British architect Donald Harradine in 1972, revived the game in Yugoslavia which had been brought to an abrupt end in World War II. In a magnificent setting, with a backdrop of mountains and the beautiful Lake Bled, the course is excellent; it is a delight to play in such a peaceful setting. It offers an interesting challenge, lush fairways

Left: Brae Burn, Massachusetts.

amending it over the years; trees are important features of play. It has a number of notable holes, one being the 255yd (233m) 17th, downhill from tee to fast green. It has staged a number of major events, including the US Open (won by Walter Hagen in 1919), the American Amateur (won by Bobby Jones in 1928), the Women's Amateur of 1906 and the Ladies' Championship of 1975. It was also host to the Curtis Cup in 1958 and 1970.

Brantford, *Ontario, Canada*
6601yd, 6036m
Founded in 1879, the club settled on its present site in 1906, overlooking the Grand River, and it was extended from the original nine holes to 18 holes in 1920. The course has outstanding natural features, as it is situated on a headland. A hoist has been provided for those golfers who wish to avoid a climb from the 18th green back to the 1st tee and clubhouse. Among other events, it staged the Canadian PGA Championship, won by Al Balding in 1970.

Bruntsfield Links, *Edinburgh, Scotland*
6369yd, 5823m
The Bruntsfield Links Golfing Society dates back to 1761; its links are in Edinburgh. It was originally the Bruntsfield Association and had connections with that body of golfers who became the Royal Burgess Golfing Society which claims an even earlier date for its foundation. After more than 100 years at Bruntsfield Links, the society was forced by housing encroachment to move to Musselburgh in the 1870s, and later to a stretch of beautiful parkland at Davidsons Mains where the course was laid out by Willie Park in 1898. Since then it has been altered several times.

Bulawayo, *Rhodesia*
Golf in Rhodesia began at Bulawayo in 1895, and the Rhodes Cup, still contested today, was originally presented by Cecil Rhodes. The course became 18 holes in 1910. The first Rhodesian Amateur Championship was played there in 1912 and the winner's trophy, the Gladstone Cup, was presented by the High Commissioner, Lord Gladstone. The course is frequently the venue for professional tournaments during the South African tournament season. On the club's 75th anniversary a new clubhouse was opened in 1970.

Burnham and Berrow, *Somerset, England*
6612yd, 6046m
(Second course under construction)
One of England's oldest courses, Burnham and Berrow was founded in 1890. The great J H Taylor was appointed its first professional and, although a number of blind holes of those days have been reconstructed, his comments still apply. The course gave him the opportunity to develop his mashie play and he commented, 'It is one of the most sporting courses conceivable, with its large sandhills and small greens, necessitating very accurate approach play'. Within sight of the Bristol Channel with Wales in the distance, it is a testing seaside course; the wind is a big factor. It has been the venue of the English Amateur Championship and the Ladies' Championship, and annually stages the West of England Open Amateur Championship. In recent years, a nine-hole course has been added.

Caernarvonshire, *Conway, North Wales*
6656yd, 6086m
One of the oldest and best courses in Wales, the course has existed since 1890, and is delightfully situated on the estuary of the River Conway close to the ancient Conway Castle and famous suspension bridge. Alterations to holes from the 6th to 9th by Frank Pennink have improved and lengthened the links course to championship standards, and it was the venue of the Martini International tournament in 1970, as well as national championships. Towards the finish, there is the added hazard of banks of gorse to punish the wayward shot. The famous George Duncan had his first professional post here, but it ended when he chose to play soccer on Saturday afternoons.

Calcutta, Royal, *India*
6968yd, 6372m
The club was founded in 1829 and its Royal title was conferred by King George V during the Delhi Durbar. India was the first country outside Britain where golf was played and Calcutta the country's first club. In 1885 the R and A played its first Calcutta Cup event; the trophy was presented by the Calcutta club. In 1892 the first Amateur Championship of India was played at Calcutta, and has been staged there ever since. The Indian Open, first played at New Delhi, now alternates with Royal Calcutta and has become part of the Asian golf circuit. Notable features of the course are large tanks (or ponds, two across the 10th fairway) and small but tricky greens.

Calgary, *Canada*
6260yd, 5724m
Founded a year or two before 1900, the club moved to its present site near the Elbow River in 1911. The course was laid out by Willie Park on different levels for each half; an escalator now links the 10th green and 11th tee, eliminating quite an uphill climb. Great efforts over the years have transformed the poor terrain into lush fairways with many trees and shrubs, and fine if small greens. It has been the venue of the Canadian Amateur, Ladies' Open and PGA Championships.

Canberra, Royal, *Australia*

7116yd, 6507m

Founded in 1926, the present course was designed by the late John Harris at Yarralumia after the government ordered the members to quit their course by the Molonglo River because a lake scheme had been planned. The club was offered a 50-year lease on the new course in 1960, and Harris completed an impressive job developing the course in between protected trees. It has staged a number of important events, notably the Australian Professional Championship in 1969. It gained its Royal title in 1955.

Canterbury, *Ohio, USA*

In his home state of Ohio, Jack Nicklaus established a new golfing record at Canterbury when in 1973 he won his third PGA title here to bring his total of major championship victories to 14, passing Bobby Jones's record. Over this course, with its formidable finish, Nicklaus won by four strokes with a seven under par total of 277; three of his rounds broke 70. The US Open has been played twice at Canterbury in 1940 and 1946; both required play-offs. The course has also twice staged the US Amateur.

Carnoustie, *Scotland*

6809yd, 6225m

One of the world's greatest golfing tests and a links course of infinite variety, Carnoustie presents all sorts of challenges, especially when the wind blows. No two holes are similar, the rough can be penal, and the Barry Burn winding across the course affects particularly the 1st, 10th, 17th and 18th holes. Golf was played here long before the Carnoustie Club was formed in 1842, and although famous players like old Tom Morris, Young Tom Morris and Willie Park played here, it was not until after James Braid

had altered the course and lengthened it in 1926, that it was considered for the Open Championship. In 1931 Tommy Armour won the first Open there, and since then only the greatest golfers have triumphed – Henry Cotton (1937), Ben Hogan (1953), Gary Player (1968) and Tom Watson (1975). The last three holes present an awesome finish, with the Barry Burn having to be crossed twice at the 17th and 18th, often proving the downfall of even the greatest golfers. Perhaps the victory of Ben Hogan made the most impact at Carnoustie. Arriving early and determined to win, he was inexhaustible in his preparation, and after an opening 73, produced a lower score each round, finishing with a record

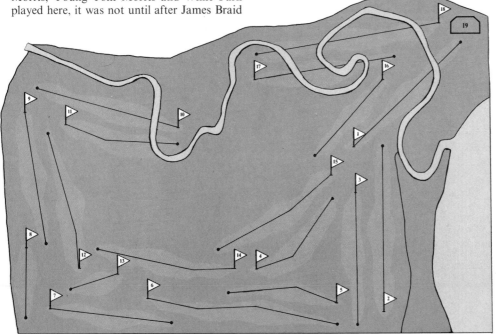

Above: The last green at the Calgary Golf and Country Club, Alberta, Canada.
Left: Carnoustie, Scotland.

68, to record an emotional win and complete a Grand Slam of major victories. Cotton claims his second Open win here as his greatest partially because it was achieved in torrential rain. Player will be remembered for a brilliant 3-wood to the 14th green, leaving him a 2ft putt for an eagle, and in 1975, Watson's long putt on the 18th to force a play-off with Jack Newton and go on to victory. Carnoustie has produced more than 300 professionals who took the game to all parts of the world. Perhaps the best known was Macdonald Smith.

As well as the championship course, which can be stretched to over 7000yd, there is the Burnside (5935yd, 5427m), which although not as tough, has many fine holes.

Castletown, *Isle of Man, Great Britain*
6804yd, 6221m
Founded in 1892, it is the island's second oldest course (Ramsey was the first in 1890), and is probably the best known. It is popular with players from the mainland. It is a true seaside links course of championship standard, with dunes, beach and rocks inviting trouble; its setting, with spectacular views, is highlighted by the closing holes which sweep to the cliff edge.

Cerdana, *Gerona, Spain*
6466yd, 5913m
Founded in 1945 and designed by a former Spanish golf champion, Don Javier Arana, it was initially a nine-hole course and was extended to 18 holes in 1964. Against a background of the Pyrenees, it is one of the best mountain courses in Europe and is nearly 4000ft above sea level. With snow covering its fairways for many months of the year, it is nevertheless in good condition throughout the summer. While not the most testing of courses, it offers wide fairways, bunkers and water hazards.

Below: Cerromar Beach, Puerto Rico.

Cerromar Beach, *Puerto Rico*
6298yd, 5725m
Cerromar Beach is another of Robert Trent Jones's fine courses. Similar to his course at Dorado Beach, he created lots of water hazards on this course also but it is not so terrifying

because it is not so long. Cerromar Beach is another of the Trent Jones courses in which the greens are a predominant feature.

Champions, *Houston, Texas, USA*
6986yd, 6388m
Two famous American players, Jimmy Demaret and Jackie Burke, realised their dream in 1960 when this Cypress Creek course was opened. It was planned as a championship course of exceptional quality and nine years later it became the venue of the US Open Championship. Thousands of trees were planted to create interesting layouts and dog-leg holes. Two longish par 3s, the 4th and the 12th, have proved the undoing of many famous players, including Ben Hogan. It was also the venue of a Ryder Cup match in 1967.

Chantilly, *France*
6835yd, 6250m
Though the name may be more famous in connection with horse racing, the club, founded in 1906, has established a reputation as one of the country's best-known courses, and has been the venue for all the national championships including the French Open and French Amateur Championships. Located in an area of woodland inhabited by wild game, the course itself is like a park and when stretched to championship length is a severe test with a number of outstanding holes. Two great French professionals of the past, Arnaud Massy and Jean Gassiat, played an exhibition match to mark the opening of the course.

Cherry Hills, *Denver, Colorado, USA*
7000yd, 6401m
Venue for the 1938 and 1960 US Open Championships, this course, nearly 2000ft above sea level, has some outstanding holes, one being the long par 4 14th, a dog-leg, which has tested the greatest players, and the 18th, another long par 4, with a lake on the left of the fairway. In the 1960 Open Arnold Palmer started his last round seven strokes off the lead, but after six birdies in the first seven, returned 65 to win by two strokes.

Chicago, *Illinois, USA*
One of the five clubs that formed the US Golf Association in 1894, this course was founded in 1892 at Belmont before moving to its present site at Wheaton. It was laid out by a famous

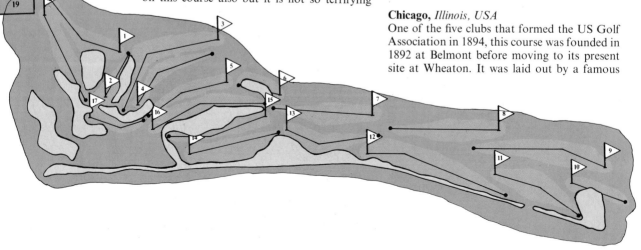

figure in early American golf, Charles Blair Macdonald, who was responsible for the 'National' at Long Island. It has staged three US Open and four US Amateur Championships, and also a Walker Cup match in 1928. Harry Vardon won the US Open here in 1900.

Christchurch, *New Zealand*
7005yd, 6405m
This, the second oldest club in New Zealand, celebrated its centenary in 1973, and moved to its present location at Shirley in 1900, with sand dunes and a creek among its features. After the New Zealand Open had been played there in 1910, the course was altered and lengthened. It has been the venue of the New Zealand Open on several occasions since then, and has also staged the Professional, Amateur and Ladies' Open Championships. It was the home course of the world's most famous left-handed golfer, Bob Charles.

Colombo, Royal, *Sri Lanka*
6286yd, 5748m
Founded in 1882 for the European community in Ceylon (now Sri Lanka), this course features water, trees, a railway line and variable winds, but has attracted players because of its great character. Famous statesmen and politicians and military leaders have played here. It has been the venue of the country's Amateur Championship, alternating with Nuwara Eliya annually since 1891. Native players have gained notable victories; the best known was W P Fernando, winner on ten occasions.

Colonial, *Fort Worth, Texas, USA*
7000yd, 6400m
Established in 1936, this club has been the home of the great Ben Hogan, and his knowledge of the course, which calls for great accuracy, resulted in his winning the Colonial National Invitation on five occasions. Narrow fairways thread through woods and a river flows through the course; both hazards occur before the player reaches the greens on the small side. The course was host to the US Open Championship in 1941, won by Craig Wood, and after flooding some years ago, has been restored to its former supreme standard.

Columbia, *Chevy Chase, Maryland, USA*
6400yd, 5852m
Within easy reach of the White House, this club, as might be expected, has many politicians among its players, and has a distinguished record over many years. The fact that the course is not too long is counteracted by hills which present problems for many players. It was the venue for the 1921 US Open Championship, won by Jim Barnes, and the 1955 Canada (now World) Cup, won by America, with Ed Furgol taking the individual title after a play-off with Peter Thomson and Flory van Donck, who set a course record of 66.

Congressional, *Bethesda, Maryland, USA*
7000yd, 6400m
The Congressional was the idea of two Congressmen who wanted a club where Congress members could play. The course was opened in 1924 in the valley of the Potomac River within easy distance of the Capital, Washington. Set in pleasant woodland, it was altered by Robert Trent Jones, and now includes a number of doglegs and a daunting par 5 of up to 600yd, with the green fronted by a ravine. The US Open Championship was played here in 1964, and a fine par 4 at the 9th gave Ken Venturi a lead which he held although troubled by illness and affected by the intense heat. The PGA Championship was played here for the first time in 1976 and Dave Stockton marched in triumph up to the imposing clubhouse to celebrate a second victory. Members of the club have included Presidents and multi-millionaire financiers.

Copenhagen, *Denmark*
6426yd, 5876m
Denmark's oldest club was founded in 1898; it was established in its present setting in Klampenborg deer park a few years later. Lying eight miles north of Copenhagen, it has staged a number of Danish championships, and is a popular venue. Roaming deer add to its natural attractions, and a pleasant clubhouse has replaced one destroyed in the German occupation of the last war.

Corfu, *Greece*
6767yd, 6189m
Opened in 1972, and built to championship standards, the course, laid out by architect Donald Haradine, is located in a superb setting near the sea, bordered on one side by mountains and on the other side a steep cliff with the remains of a monastery. On this romantic island off the Greek mainland, where the shipwrecked Ulysses first saw his Naussica, there is a magical

Below: The Corfu Golf Club in Greece is one of the best maintained courses in Europe.

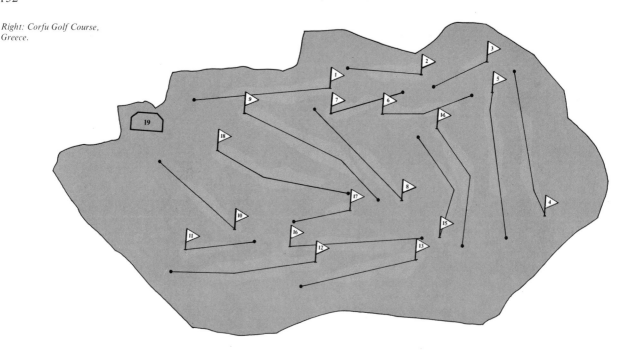

quality, and it offers a superb setting for golf.
Fully automatic watering keeps the course,
especially the greens, in excellent condition, and
a gentle breeze from the Ionian Sea makes
playing conditions perfect, even during the
hottest summer. The course has several lakes
and a winding stream which is a feature of many
holes; the short holes are played over water (the
16th, in particular, 225yd long, provides a fine
test). Adding to its attractions is the magni-
ficently equipped clubhouse.

Country Club, *Brookline, Massachusetts, USA*
This club, begun in 1882, has the distinction of
being the first country club to be formed in
America but golf was not played until ten years
later. In 1894 it joined with four other clubs to
form the US Golf Association. Seven miles from
Boston, the course is set in quiet grounds, has
many trees, and has small sloping greens. Today
there are 27 holes, and when it staged its second
US Open Championship in 1963, the 18 holes
were selected from the three separate 'nines'.
The first Open, won by Francis Ouimet, is
claimed as the most famous of all, for the 20-
year-old local amateur tied two of the greatest
British professionals of the day, Harry Vardon
and Ted Ray, on a day of soaking rain and went
on to win the play-off with a round of 72 against
Vardon's 77 and Ray's 78. The Country Club's
second Open was staged to celebrate the jubilee
of Ouimet's victory and was won by Julius
Boros, again in a play-off, after he had tied with
Jacky Cupitt and Arnold Palmer. This club was
the first club to have staged the Walker Cup on
two occasions: the first in 1932, the second in
1973.

County Down, Royal, *Northern Ireland*
6651yd, 6082m
Backed by the Mountains of Mourne and
looking out over Dundrum Bay, the course is
rated as one of the severest tests of golf in the
world, but because of its inaccessibility has sadly
never staged a British Open Championship
although it has been a most worthy venue for
other championships. Founded in 1889 it was
laid out by Tom Morris with instructions 'not to
exceed £4'. Harry Vardon improved the course
in 1908, and in the same year it received its
Royal title from Edward VII. Laid out in
differing circuits of nine holes, the course presents large carries from the tees, with heather
and gorse ready to punish the wayward shot in
one half, and sandhills and dunes in the other.
As well as the venue for the Irish Amateur,
Professional and Ladies' Championships, it was
chosen for the British Amateur Championship
in 1970, when Michael Bonallack won his fifth
title. In the 1933 Irish Open Amateur Championship final, English Amateur champion Eric
Fiddian achieved a hole in one in each of the two
rounds – yet lost to Scotsman Jack McLean. The
course has also staged the British Ladies'
Championship and the Curtis Cup was played
here in 1968.

A No 2 course (4100yd, 3750m) is a pleasant
and less strenuous test.

County Louth, *Baltray, Irish Republic*
6712yd, 6137m
This links course features a number of challenging holes, (particularly the finishing two) which
become even more challenging when the wind
blows from the sea. Established in 1892, it has

been the venue for a number of Irish championships including the Irish Open, won in 1947 by one of the best-known of the country's professionals, Harry Bradshaw. When the Irish Amateur Close Championship was played here in 1962, the finalists, Michael Edwards and Jack Harrington, were level after 36 holes and the match was finally decided in Edwards's favour on the 42nd hole, which established a record.

County Sligo, *Rosses Point, Republic of Ireland*
6436yd, 5885m

This natural links course with an abundance of space has no exceptionally long holes, though the wind can be a factor in play. With some of the holes on higher ground, there are some fine views of the Ox Mountains, the sea and rolling countryside. One of its greatest holes is the 440yd 14th, double dog-leg with a river running across the fairway. Founded in 1894, it was the home club of two famous Irish players, Cecil Ewing, a Walker Cup player, and James Mahon, also an international. It has been the venue for the Irish Amateur Close Championship and other major national events.

Crail Golfing Society, *Fife, Scotland*
5739yd, 5248m

One of Britain's oldest clubs, dating from 1786, it survived several crises in the early part of the following century when for brief periods membership lapsed. Tom Morris laid out the present course at Balcomie, which, though not long, has plenty of interest, and is only a few miles south of the home of golf, St Andrews.

Crans, *Valais, Switzerland*
6813yd, 6230m

Surrounded by snow-capped mountains on a plateau 5000ft above the Rhône Valley, this course provides excellent golf in one of the most spectacular settings in the world, with the towering Alps in the distance. It is now the permanent venue of the Swiss Open Championship, attracting the world's best golfers each year to the Crans-Montana resort, famous for winter sports and summer golf. In the rarefied atmosphere, the ball flies long and true, and its longest hole, the 634yd 9th, has been reached in two in the championship. Before the advent of the big ball, the 1971 winner Peter Townsend

Below: Crans Sur Sierre set high in the Swiss Alps is the venue for the Swiss Open Championship.

154

returned a round of 61 – only to have Baldovino Dassu follow with 60. The club was founded in 1905.

Cypress Point, *Pebble Beach, California, USA*
6464yd, 5911m

Scots architect Alister Mackenzie was responsible in the 1920s for this magnificent course with its great variety of holes which includes some of links character. It is one of America's most exclusive clubs with a beautifully kept course in a fine setting where the waves of the Pacific Ocean beat on the rocks. It offers some spectacular holes, in particular the 230yd 16th, with a carry of over 200yd across the Pacific, an expanse of shore, rocks and sea to the green located on a piece of land which is virtually an island, a formidable hole that has become famed world-wide. Some of its holes have links characteristics, and others are set among pine trees. The 15th, leading to the formidable 16th, is a delightful short hole, with a generous green, well bunkered, on the very edge of the sea.

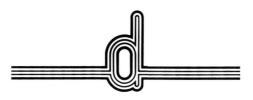

Dalmahoy, *Midlothian, Scotland*
East: 6639yd, 6071m
West: 5212yd, 4766m

The two courses were laid out by James Braid in 1927 on part of the estate of the Earls of Morton, but the club dates back to 1908. The longer East course, heavily wooded and in a parkland setting, has staged a number of championships and is a stern test. It features only three par 3 holes and many of its par 4 holes are

Below: Dalmahoy Country Club near Edinburgh Scotland has many hazards such as this lake.

over 400yd. The 423yd 7th is an outstanding hole, with a ridge, a lake, and ravine among its hazards. Among the professional tournaments staged here was the Wills Open, won by Tony Jacklin in 1970, and the World Senior Professional Championship, and among amateur events, the British Boys' and Youths' Championships. The shorter West course has many interesting features and offers a good test. The mansion house was converted for golfers and is reputed to be the only Adam clubhouse in the country. The present Earl of Morton has now taken over after the club's 50 year lease expired and the course is now being run on country club lines.

Dar es Salaam, Royal, *Rabat, Morocco*
Red: 7307yd, 6825m
Blue: 6780yd, 6205m

This course is set in the forest of Zaers a few miles out of the capital city of Rabat. American architect, Robert Trent Jones, created the courses in a wonderful setting among cork and eucalyptus trees, and some of its holes, with lakes, water fowl and colourful foliage, are quite picturesque. King Hassan II was the prime mover behind the creation of this country club complex, and as a keen player is often seen on the course with his entourage. Trent Jones has provided a challenging layout for the courses, with wide lush fairways lined by trees, dramatically designed bunkers and sloping greens often offering only the narrowest of openings. Automatic watering throughout the course keeps the grass lush, with little run for the ball but always perfect lies. The Moroccan Grand Prix for the King Hassan Trophy has been played here since it was inaugurated by the King in 1971. The Americans have won all but one of the tournaments, with Billy Casper a winner on two occasions.

Deal, Royal, *Cinque Ports, Kent, England*
6680yd, 6108m

Founded in 1892, this famous links course is renowned for its humps and hollows, its awkward stances, requiring equal parts luck and skill of a high order for success, especially over the back nine holes into a south-west wind. Even so, it is a course which provides excellent golf for every type of player, and famous players have written in its praise. Bernard Darwin said of it 'Deal is a truly great course'. It has a magnificent long par 4 at the 16th of 470yd, and the approach to a plateau green against the wind is a test of any golfer. The club was accorded its Royal title in 1908 when the Prince of Wales became president. In the Open Championship of 1920, George Duncan made up 13 strokes on Abe Mitchell to take the title, and on that occasion Walter Hagen played in his first Open in this country. In its first Open in 1909, J H Taylor was the winner for the fourth time. It has also been the venue of the Amateur Championship.

Delhi, *India*
6972yd, 6375m
Founded in 1928, the course was extensively improved, extended and relaid in 1950. It is located on the site of the burial ground for Mogul emperors and followers and interesting relics still remain round the course. The course provides an excellent test of golf. The famous Australian player, Peter Thomson, inaugurated the Indian Open Championship here and the match became part of the Asian Circuit, alternating with Royal Calcutta. It was fitting that Thomson should win the first Open, played at Delhi; he again triumphed here in 1966.

Detroit, *Michigan, USA*
6875yd, 6286m
The Country Club at Grosse Point Farms was founded in 1911, and the course was re-designed by Robert Trent Jones in the 1950s into an attractive layout on fairly flat parkland, well bunkered and with a longer second half. Here, in 1954, a young Arnold Palmer saw the start of a spectacular career when he won the American Amateur Championship by one hole from former British Amateur Champion, Robert Sweeny.

Divonne, *Divonne-les-Bains, France*
6573yd, 6010m
Situated near the border with Switzerland, the course has breathtaking views of snow-capped mountains and looks across to Lake Geneva. Indeed, it is only a short drive from the centre of the Swiss capital, but is completely remote, and is a course which delights all who visit it. Fast flowing streams create many problems for players, especially at the long 8th, where an elevated green needs a careful approach shot to avoid the rushing water. It was the venue in 1976 for the Philip Morris International team tournament when the US beat Scotland in the final.

Dorado Beach, *Puerto Rico, West Indies*
7005yd, 6405m
This is one of the masterpieces of architect Robert Trent Jones. The East course runs along the edge of the Atlantic and is one of four he designed in the area. It was created out of mangrove swamps. In a superb engineering feat, countless tons of earth were excavated to provide lagoons throughout the course and landscape the remainder; the fairways are lined by trees. The sun sparkling on the blue sea creates a perfect setting and varying breezes stiffen the

Below: Royal Dar es Salaam in Morocco is a unique course in many respects.

156

challenge one can always expect from a Jones course. It was the venue for the Canada Cup (now World Cup) in 1961, won by the US team of Sam Snead and Jimmy Demaret (with Snead the individual winner) over a composite course, as only nine holes of the East course had been completed at that time.

Doral, *Miami, Florida, USA*
7008yd, 6426m

The Blue course which is the principal of the five Doral courses, is the scene of one of the early-season tournaments on the US Tour, the Doral Eastern, with Billy Casper, Doug Sanders and Jack Nicklaus each claiming two victories. A flat course, it is notable for eight lakes which call for accurate play both on fairways and to the greens; the 8th, a par 5, and the 9th, a par 3, present long carries over water to peninsula greens. Course improvements have recently been introduced. With the other four courses, Doral is possibly the biggest golf complex in the US.

Dornoch, Royal, *Sutherland, Scotland*
6533yd, 5974m

Golf was played here as long ago as the early 1600s, but the club was not founded until 1877, and it was not long after that it became one of the outstanding links courses. Though a superb course, its remoteness has probably prevented it being chosen for Open Championships, which its standard certainly warrants. Though far north, it is favoured by an equable climate, making play possible all the year round. Located between the Dornoch Firth and the

mountains, it has attracted many famous players, from Vardon to the Wethereds, Roger and Joyce. Four of the last five holes are demanding par 4s and the 14th a great natural hole of 450yd – a test for the best. It has been the venue of the Scottish Professional and Ladies' Championships.

Downfield, *Dundee, Scotland*
6883yd, 6294m

Founded in 1932, this fine inland course provides a great test of golf with trees and a burn always coming into the reckoning. Five holes in the first nine are all par 4s of over 400yd, and in the second half, there are several severe doglegs. It has been the venue for many championship events including the British Youths' and Boys' Championships and for professional tournaments, such as the World Senior Professional Championship and the PGA Match Play Championship.

Drottningholm, *Stockholm, Sweden*
6469yd, 5915m

Set in a beautiful parkland estate near a royal palace, the course is one of 11 in the Stockholm area, but has become best known for the quality of play it demands in championship events. It has been the venue of the Scandinavian Enterprises Open on three occasions since its inauguration in 1973.

Dublin, Royal, *Republic of Ireland*
6657yd, 6087m

Founded in 1885, the oldest club in Eire and the second oldest in Ireland, it moved to Dol-

Right: Drottningholm Club in Sweden is one of the best known in a country where golf is increasing in popularity.

lymount in 1889 and acquired its Royal title in 1891. Lying on an island connected to the mainland by a bridge, it is a first-class links course, often with the wind in opposition to the inward half. The par 5 finishing hole offers a carry over out of bounds for those prepared to risk it: the reward is a short approach to the green. The venue for most of the country's major amateur and professional championships, it had the great Christy O'Connor as its professional for many years.

Dunbar, *East Lothian, Scotland*
6407yd, 5858m
Cromwell's army camped on the land where this historic course was constructed before the Battle of Dunbar in 1650. It is known that golf was played here possibly as early as 1700. The present club was founded in 1856. The course was laid out by Tom Morris and is of true championship standard with a variety of holes both inland and seaside, made all the more formidable when the wind blows. It has been the venue for the Scottish Amateur Stroke Play and Scottish Amateur Championships, the Scottish Ladies', Scottish Professional and Scottish Boys', as well as the British Boys' in 1968 and the Schweppes Championship the same year.

Durban, *Natal, South Africa*
6574yd, 6011m
Gary Player created history at this country club, when in 1976 he won the South African Open Championship for the tenth time, beating Bobby Locke's record and achieving the feat on the course where he won his first title in 1956. Laid out on sandhills running by the seashore, it was founded in 1920, and has been the venue of every national championship.

East London, *Cape Province, South Africa*
After winning the South African Amateur Championship here in 1937, Bobby Locke turned professional and became one of the world's greatest golfers, returning to the course to win the South African Open for the first time as a professional, having won it previously as an amateur. Plenty of hard toil by members went into creating the course out of bush among sandhills overlooking the Indian Ocean, and since those early days, many improvements have been made, resulting in its championship standard.

Eindhoven, *Valkenswaard, Holland*
6487yd, 5932m
Founded in 1930, this is one of the best courses in the Netherlands, designed by H S Colt with fairways laid through pine woods. Its high standard is reflected in the championships held here, including the Dutch Amateur and Dutch Open events. The Natal-born 'Papwa' Sewgolum was the first non-white to win an European major championship in Holland, capturing the Dutch Open title three times with two of the victories at Eindhoven in 1960 and 1964.

Eldorado, *Palm Desert, California, USA*
6840yd, 6254m
Opened in 1957 in a desert region renowned for its attractive climate, the course became the venue in the remarkably short time of two years

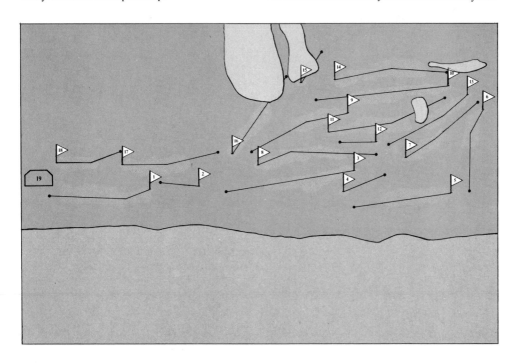

Left: Durban, Natal, South Africa.

158

for a Ryder Cup match, the Americans regaining the trophy lost at Lindrick by 8½–3½. It is one of a number of courses on which a round of the Bob Hope Desert Classic is played and it has links with former President Dwight Eisenhower who had a home by the course. It is located in a canyon with lakes and mountains in the background; its fairways are lined by palms and orange groves. It is a delightful course to play.

Elephant Hills, *Victoria Falls, Rhodesia*
7868yd, 7194m
This is the longest course in Africa and is a formidable test, set among thick bush with impenetrable rough, and wild game often presenting an unexpected and unnerving hazard. The thundering Victoria Falls is not far away with the wide Zambezi river forming a line of demarcation from neighbouring Zambia. With temperatures often over 30°C, it is a gruelling course, but one which attracts many fine players including Gary Player, Bob Charles and Tony Jacklin, who competed in the Victoria Falls Classic.

Elie, Golf House Club, *Fife, Scotland*
6253yd, 5718m
Founded in 1875, the course was developed to 18 holes by Tom Morris and altered in 1921 by James Braid, a native of Elie (who is commemorated by a plaque in the town). Mounds on the links course are the relics of open-cast coal mining, and like many a seaside course, it has humps and hollows and awkward stances as well as blind holes to test the player. It has been the venue for the Scottish Professional and Ladies' Championships.

El Paraiso, *Estepona, Spain*
6444yd, 5892m
One of the newer courses on the Costa del Sol, it was designed by South African Gary Player and his company (Davies-Kirby and Player) and opened in 1974. In a broad, sweeping valley, designed so that most tees and greens are visible from the clubhouse, it is kept in magnificent condition with superb greens and rolling fairways. It promises to be one of the most outstanding in what has become a golfer's paradise of courses along this attractive stretch of coast. The 1st and 10th holes sweep down from a hill, to which the 9th and 18th return, the last hole being a tough par 5 uphill to a two-tiered green.

El Prat – Real Club de Golf, *Barcelona, Spain*
6529yd, 5970m
Designed by leading Spanish architect, Javier Arana, and opened in 1954, the course is of championship standard, and in two years became the venue for the Spanish Open. It has also been host for the country's Amateur and Ladies' Championships. A flat course by the sea many of its narrow fairways have been skilfully carved out between the umbrella pines. It is located near Barcelona Airport.

El Saler, *Cullera, Spain*
7108yd, 6500m
One of Spain's two state-managed courses, it was built in 1967. It has no club as such and is open to all as a public course. The work of Javier Arana, and located a few miles from Valencia, it is one of Spain's longest courses, fairly flat, with pine trees and sandhills among its features, and is rated as a course of high standard. Run by the Ministry of Tourism, it includes motel-type accommodation in a state-owned guest house.

Engadine, *Samedan, Switzerland*
6529yd, 5970m
Founded in 1898, this is the oldest course in Switzerland, and the highest in Europe at 5700ft above sea level. Like most Swiss courses, play is possible for only a few months of the year and snow falls earlier here than elsewhere. Subject to strong wind, the course is flat and includes pine trees. It is located near St Moritz. Both the Swiss Amateur and Ladies' Championships have been played here.

Estoril, *Portugal*
5698yd, 5172m
Heavily wooded with fragrant pine trees, this short but challenging course was laid out by Mackenzie Ross in 1938, although it dates from 1928. It became the centre of golf in Portugal until more recent courses were built, and all the country's major championships have been held here continuously until the last few years. Nestling at the base of the Sintra mountains with a profusion of mimosa and looking out to the Atlantic, its setting is superb. Its short 9th hole has a plateau tee from which one looks down to the green 200ft below. There is also a nine-hole course.

Evian, *France*
6398yd, 5850m
Situated close to the border with Switzerland, the course wanders around gently rising ground 1500ft above Lake Geneva and looks across to Montreux and Lausanne. Apart from a few holes on steepish ground, it is not too strenuous and is kept in superb condition, offering enjoyable and testing golf in a parkland setting. It was the venue in 1976 for the Cacharel World Under-25 Championship won by Irishman Eamonn Darcy.

Falsterbo, *Sweden*
6400yd, 5852m
Situated on a peninsula 20 miles south of Malmö, the club was founded in 1909 and is the country's only real links course which offers a

similar test to the championship links of Britain. It has been the venue of both the Scandinavian Men's and Ladies' Open Amateur Championships, and the 1963 European Amateur Team Championship, which England won with Michael Bonallack as captain.

Firestone, *Akron, Ohio, USA*
South: 7180yd, 6565m
North: 7100yd, 6492m

Harvey Firestone, founder of the well-known company, built a course in the 1920s for his employees. With the boom in professional golf, the main South course was re-designed 30 years later by Robert Trent Jones, who lengthened the course, incorporated water and sand hazards and enlarged the greens. The majority of the holes run side by side but are separated by trees; the result is a test of championship standard, impeccably maintained. The US PGA was staged here first in 1960 and again in 1966 and 1975. The course has also staged the American Golf Classic and the World Series of Golf. The Classic event has also been played on the North course which opened in 1968 and has water from a reservoir coming into the layout on more than half the course.

Formby, *Lancashire, England*
6700yd, 6126m

A fine links course, with lush turf, great sand-hills and tall pine trees, it offers a variety of superb golf in a peaceful setting, although fairly close to the centre of the city of Liverpool. Founded in 1884, its clubhouse was opened in 1901 by the late Lord Derby; the present Lord Derby continues as president of the club. The flat opening by the railway gives way to testing golf among the sandhills, and the finishing hole, one of over 400yd and well bunkered, has a massive green. Coast erosion has resulted in a new layout for a few holes, with no reduction in the standard of play. Formby staged its first British Amateur Championship in 1957 when the venue was changed from Sandwich because of the Suez crisis and it was again staged there ten years later. It has also been the venue for the English Amateur Championship, the Boys' and Youths' Championships and the Home Internationals. Formby has also its own Ladies Club, formed in 1896 and completely separate, with a course of 6021yd, 5506m.

Foxhills, *Ottershaw, Surrey*
Chertsey: 6890yd, 6304m
Longcross: 6731yd, 6158m

These are two of Surrey's newest courses, designed by British architect Fred Hawtree and reflect American influence in their design. Both are parkland courses; the longer Chertsey course was the venue for the first European Tournament Players Championship in 1977 won by Neil Coles and is the more open but heavily bunkered. The Longcross course is the tighter and calls for accuracy from the tee. One of its most testing holes is a par 3 calling for a carry over a lake to a green 200yd away and well guarded by bunkers. Both courses are testing

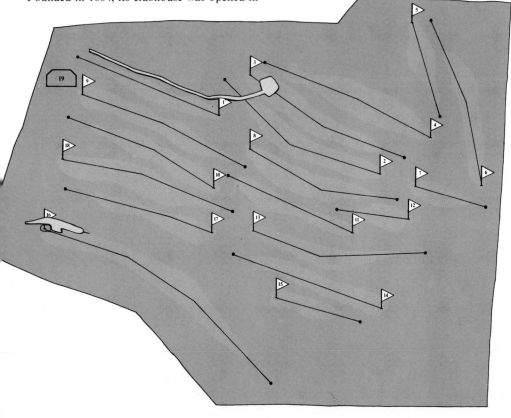

Left: Firestone, Akron, Ohio.

and have been designed to finish on a massive double green. The par 4 18th on the Chertsey course, a slight dog-leg left from a high tee, cost British World Cup player Peter Dawson the Tournament Players' title because, although he had two strokes to spare over Neil Coles on the 17th, he drove into the trees on the left and took 7 strokes.

Frankfurt, *Germany*
6445yd, 5893m

Opened in 1928, this is one of Germany's best courses and the venue for all the country's championships including the German Open. It is only a few kilometres from both the city centre and the airport. A course located in an attractive forest, it is not too long but its skilfully designed holes call for accuracy.

Ganton, *Yorkshire, England*
6677yd, 6105m

Although nine miles from the sea, Ganton has many of the characteristics of a links course, and has proved a worthy championship venue. Founded in 1891, its professional from 1896 was Harry Vardon who was later succeeded by Ted Ray. Vardon won three of his British Open titles and the US Open in 1900 while at Ganton, and Ray later also won both titles. With many daunting holes, it is perhaps its great finish which has established its reputation. In winning the Dunlop Masters here in 1975 for the second year in succession, Bernard Gallacher put in a storming finish to take the title from South African Dale Hayes by two strokes, after having been two strokes behind with five holes to play. It has been the venue for countless important events, including the British and English Amateur Championships, the British Ladies' Championship, the English Ladies' Championship, and the Ryder Cup in 1949.

Gavea, *Rio de Janeiro, Brazil*
6032yd, 5516m

Founded in 1923, the club is the second oldest in Brazil, and has been the venue of the Brazilian Open and Amateur Championships. In the 1974 Open, Gary Player returned a second round of 59 on his way to winning the title for the second time. The course was laid out by a young Scotsman Arthur Davidson, who became the club professional, and has a number of hilly holes in its attractive valley setting. On his home course, Brazilian player Mario Gonzales captured the Open title on seven occasions.

Geneva, *Switzerland*
6835yd, 6250m

Established in 1923 and designed by American Robert Trent Jones, the course commands a view of Lake Geneva and the city. Its layout features examples of his typical design, with water, sand hazards and trees cunningly placed to dictate the play. The 9th green, which comes back to the clubhouse, is shared with the 18th as one big surface.

Glen Abbey, *Oakville, Ontario, Canada*

This Jack Nicklaus-designed course, similar in many respects to his own Muirfield Village course in Ohio, was opened in 1976 and cost eight million dollars; it is now the permanent venue for the Canadian Open Championship and the home of the Royal Canadian Golf Association. It staged its first Canadian Open in 1977 which was won by Lee Trevino giving him his second Canadian Open victory. Favourable reactions to the course augur well for its future. When the RGCA decided on Glen Abbey as their Open venue, Nicklaus was the man chosen to re-design a course owned by the Abbey Glen Property Company, and built in the late 50s. As with his Memorial course, Nicklaus built Glen Abbey with the spectator in mind. Three large lakes were excavated and the earth from them used to create mounds around the greens, providing fine vantage points. Play at six holes is visible from the mound behind the ninth green. Five valley holes, the most spectacular on the course, wind through a ravine; most of them require the player to negotiate a creek. A

Far right, top: The clubhouse at Sunningdale (Berkshire, England), from behind the 18th green.
Far right, bottom: The clubhouse at St Andrews in Scotland.
Right: The Ganton Golf Club in Yorkshire, England has an attractive clubhouse and an excellent golf course.

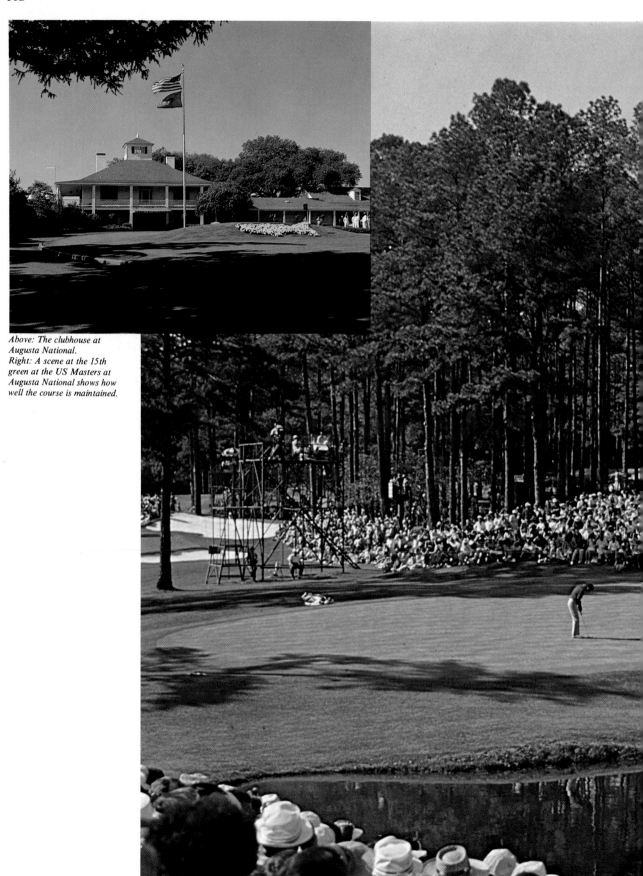

Above: The clubhouse at Augusta National.
Right: A scene at the 15th green at the US Masters at Augusta National shows how well the course is maintained.

massive horseshoe-shaped green, well bun-kered, is the feature of the 17th, and the par 5 18th hole has a lake guarding the front and right of the green and bunkers on the left. Perfectly conditioned and impressively designed, Glen Abbey may even one day surpass the course which Nicklaus holds most dear, his own Muir-field Village. The site at one time of a religious order, the Glen Abbey's reconstructed club-house was once a monastery.

Gleneagles Hotel, *Perthshire, Scotland*
King's: 6705yd, 6131m
Queen's: 6335yd, 5793m
Prince's: 4678yd, 4277m
To play golf in the autumn at Gleneagles, with the purple of the heather blending with the varied hues of landscape and woodland, is to enjoy an experience never to be forgotten. No wonder it attracts golfers from all over the world, many of whom stay in the five-star hotel run by British Transport Hotels. The longest King's course offers the sternest test but the Queen's is not far behind; in both, there is plenty of variety in the excellent holes. Both courses

(the Queen's initially being nine holes), were laid out by James Braid and opened in 1919. In recent years the Prince's course was built and a fourth 18-hole course is available. Although it has staged only one major tournament, the British Ladies' Championship of 1957, many important events have been played over the King's course, such as the Curtis Cup matches of 1936. The Double Diamond World Golf Classic was staged here on three occasions before the event was discontinued after the 1977 matches, won by America.

Glyfada, *Athens, Greece*
6715yd, 6140m
Glyfada opened as a nine-hole course in 1962. A further nine holes were added four years later and it became the first 18-hole course in the country and established the game in Greece. Carved out of a forest, the fairways wind between the pine trees and evergreens, and as well as offering a keen test, present picturesque views of the sea and mountains. It is located only a short distance from the airport and a few miles from Athens.

Preceding page, top: The favourite holiday course, Vilamoura, on the Algarve in Portugal.
Preceding page, bottom: Golf in the Emerald Isle – Killarney, County Kerry, Eire.
Below: The world famous Gleneagles Hotel in Scotland which attracts golfers from all over the world.

Gothenburg, *Sweden*
5935yd, 5427m
Sweden's oldest course, dating from 1902, was established on its present site two years later, and it was the country's only championship venue for many years. Then events moved to newer, longer and more modern courses, although championships still took place at Gothenburg until 1938. Scandinavian tournaments are staged there to the present day. It is a course with plenty of character and lies a few miles south of Gothenburg.

Guadalajara, *Mexico*
6912yd, 6320m
This magnificent country club offers one of the finest courses in Mexico. Built in 1942, it is peaceful and serene, with lush vegetation. Profusely planted with trees, it is incredibly colourful with two million rose bushes intermingling with the trees to line the fairways. An outstanding course, it is the venue for an important national amateur tournament.

Guadalmina, *Marbella, Spain*
6808yd, 6225m
This was the first golfing development on the Costa del Sol, where today golf courses abound. In recent years, great improvements have been made and new greens laid. A generally high standard has been achieved with an extra 11 holes towards a further 18 being added. Now well matured, it is an excellent test of golf, situated on undulating ground bordered by a river and the sea. Broad fairways contrast with others which are well sheltered and require accurate shot-making.

Gullane, *East Lothian, Scotland*
No 1: 6444yd, 5892m
No 2: 6090yd, 5568m
No 3: 5004yd, 4576m
Located in one of Scotland's great golfing centres, the Gullane No 1 course ranks almost as high as nearby Muirfield, the British Open Championship venue. Indeed, the No 1 course stages qualifying rounds for the Open when it moves to Muirfield, and has also staged the home internationals, the British Ladies', British Boys' and Scottish Ladies' Championships. Apart from the pleasure of playing up Gullane Hill, there is a fine panoramic view stretching from Edinburgh, the Firth of Forth and its famous bridges along the coast past Muirfield and North Berwick. The course offers many really fine holes, for example, the 390yd 17th has its tee on top of a hill and the green below, protected by huge bunkers. While the No 2 course is easier, it has some very testing holes, two of which run through a nature reserve. The No 3 course is ideal for more relaxed golf, although Gullane Hill still plays its part. Golf has been played at Gullane for well over a century, though the present club was founded in 1882. A notable event in its history was the

victory of Babe Zaharias in the British Ladies' Championship of 1947, the first American to win the title.

Haagsche, *The Hague, Holland*
6076yd, 5556m
It was not until after World War II that the present course was built with undulating fairways among sand dunes. The club is the oldest in the Netherlands, originating in 1889, and the original course which was extended to 18 holes in 1920, came under the German occupation. As a links course calling for accurate play, it has been the scene of a number of Dutch Open Championships; the first after the war was won by Jimmy Adams in 1949. It has also staged the Dutch International Amateur Championship.

Hamilton, *Auckland, New Zealand*
6619yd, 6052m
When New Zealand celebrated a centenary of golf in 1971, the Hamilton club played host to the Women's Commonwealth Tournament. This club, which dates back to 1896, has been the scene of all New Zealand's major tournaments including the New Zealand Open and Professional Championships, as well as the amateur and ladies events. One of its famous characters was H T Gillies, who was responsible for the site and its layout beside the Waikato River. His testing course has, over the years, lost much of its penal rough but had added more bunkered greens.

Harbor Town, *Hilton Head Island, South Carolina, USA*
6655yd, 6085m
Jack Nicklaus helped to design this course, laid out by American architect Pete Dye. Narrow fairways and smallish greens make it a great challenge, even though considerably shorter than most American championship courses. Its finishing hole calls for great accuracy, for both drive and approach to the green have to be played across the water of the Calibogue Sound. Gene Littler says of the course 'Precision means something here – you have to play every club here'. While not staging a major championship, it is the venue of the Sea Pines Heritage Classic, and it provided a notable first victory for Australian Graham Marsh in his first full year on the American Tour in 1977.

Hazeltine National, *Chaska, Minnesota*
Britain's most famous player of the modern era, Tony Jacklin, became the first of his countrymen to triumph in 50 years in the US Open when it was staged here in 1970. Jacklin, then holder

of the British Open title which he had won the previous year at Royal Lytham, returned four sub-par rounds for an aggregate of 281 and a winning margin of 7 strokes over Dave Hill. This 7 stroke margin had only been exceeded by Jim Barnes in 1921. Thus Jacklin became the first British player since Harry Vardon to hold the US and British Open titles at the same time. His victory was achieved in difficult weather conditions over a course which did not find favour with many of the players. Hill, in particular, strongly criticised it as a 'cow pasture', a description which brought censure from the authorities and which was far from fair. Certainly, Jacklin showed the course could be played, and he holed a string of fine putts on the greens for birdies. Hazeltine had previously been the venue for the American Women's Championship of 1966.

Hillside, *Southport, Lancashire, England*
6850yd, 6264m

A next-door neighbour to Royal Birkdale, Hillside has seen many changes since it was founded in 1912, and now ranks as one of the best of the chain of courses which stretch along the Lancashire coastline. Fred Hawtree was responsible for major alterations in 1967, and now the course stages many important events; the qualifying rounds for the British Open Championship were held here in 1971 and 1976; Michael Bonallack won the Brabazon Trophy in 1971 and in 1970, the Boys' Championship was staged here. The second half of the course is particularly testing, notably the 548yd 17th which features a raised green at the end of towering sandhills and a variety of bunkers, including a large cross bunker on the way to the green. Jack Nicklaus made his first appearance in Britain in the first Piccadilly Tournament staged here in 1962.

Hilversum, *Holland*
6805yd, 6222m

Founded in 1910 and established on its present site seven years later, this inland course, although flat, has plenty of trees, and since the last reconstruction in 1952, is of quite high standard. Before and since the alterations, it has been the venue of the Dutch Open Championship on a number of occasions, as well as the International Amateur Championship.

Hirono, *Kobe, Japan*
6950yd, 6314m

English architect C H Alison was responsible for the layout of the course in 1932; since then it has been the venue for both the Japanese Open and Amateur Championships. Although many new courses have appeared with the boom of golf in Japan, Hirono can still claim to be one of the finest. Although flat, it features streams and ponds with fairways lined by pine groves and the deepest of bunkers. It has always been one of the most popular of Japanese courses.

Hobart, Royal, *Tasmania, Australia*
6636yd, 6068m

Since being founded early in 1900, the club – which gained its Royal title in 1925 – moved to its present location at Seven Mile Beach, and was officially opened in 1963. Its high standard soon attracted championship events, and it was the venue of the Australian Amateur in 1968 and 1974, the Ladies' Open in 1969, and the Australian Open in 1971, won by Jack Nicklaus with an aggregate of 269.

Hong Kong, Royal, *Hong Kong*

Members once arrived at the clubhouse in rickshaws to start their game of golf. Now cars are the more common form of travel, but the game is still the same, though the club has been greatly developed since the formation meeting of 1899. Today the club has three courses in fine condition, a tribute to the work that followed the Japanese occupation during the war. The club gained its Royal title, conferred by Queen Victoria, in 1897. As progress continued, it established three course sites: Fanling, Happy Valley and Deep Water Bay. At the start of the war, there were 45 holes at Fanling, but the war brought everything to a halt. Now, Fanling is the regular venue for the Hong Kong Open Championship.

Honourable Company of Edinburgh Golfers, *Muirfield, East Lothian, Scotland*
See **Muirfield.**

Houghton, *Johannesburg, South Africa*

Every South African amateur and professional championship has been played over this fine parkland course, and great feats have been achieved by famous names like Brews, Locke and Player. British-born Sid Brews was professional here for over 30 years and dominated the country's golf until he had to give way to Bobby Locke. Brews, who died in 1972, won the South African Open eight times, and claimed the last of his Open titles in 1952 at the age of 53; he won, in all, more than 40 tournaments during his career. Brews was responsible for bringing the course up to its present high standard.

Hoylake – see **Liverpool, Royal**

Humewood, *Port Elizabeth, South Africa*
6777yd, 6197m

The unusual feature of Humewood is that it was constructed as a links course. Its skilful design and unusually strong winds provide the sort of challenge more customary along Britain's coasts. Since being built in 1930, it has staged every South African major amateur and professional championship; the late Sid Brews won one of his eight Open titles here in 1952.

Hunstanton, *Norfolk, England*
6670yd, 6099m

Not only is this one of the finest courses in East

Anglia, it is a links course which compares favourably with some of the country's best. Founded in 1891 as a nine-hole course, it was extended to 18 by James Braid, improved by James Sherlock and later the 17th and 18th were replaced by new holes. It features a great sandhill ridge stretching to the 9th green, dividing the inland first half from the second nine among the dunes. Sherlock, who died aged 91, was club professional who served the club for many years. Hunstanton has staged many championships. Joyce Wethered won the third of five successive English Ladies' Championship victories here in 1922. It has also been the venue of the British Ladies' and the English Amateur Championships. In 1960 Doug Sewell was taken to the 41st hole before overcoming Martin Christmas in the English Amateur.

Interlachen, *Minneapolis, Minnesota*
Although Interlachen has been the venue for only one major championship, it shared a record that will remain one of the oustanding events in the history of golf. Robert Tyre Jones Jr came here three weeks after winning the British Open at Hoylake and before that the British Amateur Championship. It was 1930, and Interlachen gave him his fourth US Open title and he went on to win the US Amateur at Merion and achieve the grand slam of the Open and Amateur titles of the two countries. After that, Bobby Jones retired from championship golf. Founded in 1917, the course was rebuilt by Donald Ross eight years later to become an attractive and exacting test.

Invercargill, *Otatara, New Zealand*
6511yd, 5954m
Established on its present site in 1911, the completion of 18 holes came in 1924, and just before World War II the course was lengthened to its present measurement. In a fine setting, its high standard was recognized when the New Zealand Ladies' Open became its first major championshp in 1949, and since then other championships have followed. In 1960, when the club celebrated 60 years' existence, the New Zealand Amateur, Professional and Open Championships were held here.

Inverness, *Toledo, Ohio, USA*
This club, founded in 1903, takes its name from the Scottish town. Ten years later a Scot, Donald Ross, re-designed the course and in 1914 it staged the US Open Championship, when Ted Ray became the second Briton to win the title. (Harry Vardon had been successful in 1900.) The US Opens of 1931 and 1957 were also staged here; before the event the course was

altered and improved. It was also the venue for the American Amateur Championship in 1973.

Inwood, *Long Island, New York, USA*
This course, founded in 1901, provides varied but exacting golf over inland and seaside holes and has the proud claim of being the venue for Bobby Jones's first US Open Championship victory in 1923 when he won the tie-breaking play-off. His victory came two years after Walter Hagen had won the first of his five US PGA titles here, and though it has disappeared from championship rotas, it remains not only an attractive course, but one of the highest standard.

Is Molas, *Cagliari, Sardinia*
6992yd, 6393m
The club celebrated its opening in 1976 with an outstanding Pro-Am tournament which attracted great players like Gary Player and Tony Jacklin, and later in the year staged the Italian Open Championship won by Italy's popular Baldovino Dassu. Set on undulating land away from the sea with a backcloth of mountain scenery, it provides a challenging test, with several water hazards and plateau greens. One of its most challenging holes is the par 4 9th, uphill with a tight fairway and an approach over water to the well-bunkered green. Another 18-hole course has been laid out as part of an impressive golf complex which includes a residential development, hotel and shopping precinct.

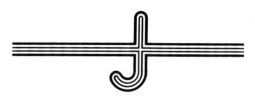

Jersey, Royal, *Channel Islands, Great Britain*
6128yd, 5603m
This course was founded in 1878 on sandy, low-lying links at Grouville Bay in this attractive island. The first nine holes of the course start along the shore and then move inland where more rough is encountered. Two of Britain's most famous golfers, Harry Vardon and Ted Ray, were born here, and the island produced other great players – Aubrey and Percy Boomer, the Gaudins, Renoufs and Chevaliers. The tradition has been carried on by Ryder Cup player Tommy Horton, now professional to the club. It was accorded its Royal title by Queen Victoria a year after its foundation.

Jockey Club, *San Isidro, Argentina*
6699yd, 6125m
The great Argentinian golfer Roberto de Vicenzo achieved a memorable victory on this course, one of the country's most famous and exclusive, when he won the individual title in the

1970 World Cup. De Vicenzo and his partner, Vicente Fernandez, finished runner-up in the team event to Australia's David Graham and Bruce Devlin. The great British architect Alister Mackenzie, famed for his work at Augusta National and Cypress Point, laid out two courses which were opened a year after his death in 1934. They are a fine testament to his genius, for he transformed the flat land of the site to provide an intricate test. The Red championship course calls for great skill. In the 1970 World Cup, Vicenzo played superbly for an aggregate of 269 and 19 under par. Eight years before Vicenzo's victory at the Jockey Club, he had also taken the individual title, again in his own country, at Buenos Aires, with Sam Snead and Arnold Palmer taking the team title.

Johannesburg, Royal *South Africa*
East: 7323yd, 6696m
West: 6850yd, 6264m
Founded in 1890, the club settled in its present location in 1906, and the first course was laid out. In 1933 the championship East course was built, and has since been the venue for all the country's major championships. The fairways are very long, but the ball flies farther because of the high altitude so that the course can be mastered, as Bobby Cole proved in the South African Open in 1972. Although returning two rounds in the 70s, he shot a brilliant last-round 64 against the par of 74 to win the title by four strokes. Bobby Locke and Gary Player both won two of their Open titles here.

Karen, *Nairobi, Kenya*
6839yd, 6254m
Founded in 1938, this course, although nine holes initially, was built with greens laid with grass (as distinct from the 'browns' generally found) and was extended later to 18 holes. Located not far from the centre of Nairobi, its popularity has grown and it has now become a country club complex. It is one of the country's best courses, up to championship standard, and has been the venue for the Kenya Amateur Championship.

Karlova Vary, *Carlsbad, Czechoslovakia*
6695yd, 6122m
Henry Cotton considers this one of the most beautiful courses on the Continent. It is located in a spa town founded by a King of Bohemia in the 14th century and dates from 1904 although not until 1935 was it extended to 18 holes, set among forests and mountains. The course was reclaimed after World War II and the club was re-formed in 1948. It is a testing course for the golfer, and is physically demanding as it is quite hilly.

Kasugai, *Nagoya, Japan*
6900yd, 6309m
Venue for the 1975 Japan Open Championship, the course favours the long hitters with its undulating grounds and quite steep hills. Trees and small ponds laid out among hills provide the hazards, and the greens require skilful reading. All adds up to a par 72 course with a variety of challenging holes. A second course, the West, is of similar character: 6825yd, 6241m.

Kasumigaseki, *Japan*
East: 6933yd, 6340m
West: 6660yd, 6090m
Founded in 1929, this is one of Japan's best-known courses, located in wooded country about 30 miles from Tokyo. The East championship course was followed two years later by a slightly shorter West course. While both courses are flat with generous fairways, they are well bunkered. As early in its history as 1933, the Japanese Open Championship was played here, and the winner was K Nakamura. The Open returned here in 1956 and the Japan Amateur Championship has also been played here. The Canada Cup (now World Cup) was staged in 1957, the home team of Torakichi Nakamura and Koichi Ono taking the title from the Americans, Sam Snead and Jimmy Demaret. Jack Nicklaus, Arnold Palmer and Gary Player are among a number of famous players who have made celebrity appearances.

Kawana, *Japan*
Fuji: 6691yd, 6118m
Oshima: 5711yd, 5222m
While the Oshima course was built first, in 1928, the championship Fuji course – named after Japan's famous mountains, Fujiyama, soaring in the distance – was laid out in 1936 by English architect C H Alison. The original course takes its name after Oshima Island, lying off the coast, and was built by a local man, a former student in London. It has many daunting features, particularly the short 6th over a ravine, which has to be crossed by suspension bridge. The Fuji course is truly championship standard, and has been host to the Amateur, Open and Professional Championships of Japan, and also to the Eisenhower Trophy matches.

Kennemer, *Zandvoort, Holland*
6296yd, 5757m
One of the oldest clubs in the Netherlands, the work of English architect H S Colt, it was established in 1928, although golf had been played only a few miles away before then. With its testing qualities, it was chosen for the Dutch Open Championship only five years after its opening. During the German occupation the

course was used for fortifications which put an end to golf during the war, and it was some years before it was restored to championship standard. Brigadier General A C Critchley won the last Dutch Amateur title in 1939 at Zandvoort before the war intervened and it was 1954 before the Championship returned here. Bobby Locke won the Dutch Open in 1939, and when the Open returned to Zandvoort in 1951, the winner was Flory von Donck. Since then, it has been a popular venue for both Championships.

Killarney, *County Kerry, Republic of Ireland*
Mahony's Point: 6734yd, 6158m
Killeen: 6893yd, 6303m

When the sun shines over Killarney's famous lakes and the rhododendrons are a blaze of colour in the spring, there is no lovelier place on earth than this course. If the views are breathtaking, both these courses demand plenty of concentration and skill, but provide testing yet enjoyable golf. The 17th and 18th on Mahony's Point offer an exciting challenge with the finishing hole calling for a 202yd shot over water from tee to green banked by rhododendrons and pines. Founded in 1891, it was not until just before World War II that the original course was laid out by Sir Guy Campbell for Lord Castlerosse, later Lord Kenmare, who had inherited the estate facing Lough Leane. In 1949 it staged the Irish Open Amateur Championship won by Dr W M O'Sullivan (a popular local victory) and later the Irish Ladies' Championship and home internationals. Demand to play the course resulted in the Killeen course being constructed in 1970, and from the two, a composite course was laid out for the European Amateur Team Championship in 1975, won by Scotland.

Kingston Heath, *Victoria, Australia*
6797yd, 6215m
Opened in 1925 when it moved from its original site at Elsternwick, the course has been the

Right: The golf course at Killarney is one of the most beautiful in the world and also provides a good test of a player's golfing abilities.

venue for many national championships, and provides a fine test, with many tree-lined fairways. Its deep bunkers were the result of advice given by Alister Mackenzie, creator of Augusta National and Cypress Point. The Australian Open has been staged here, and also the Australian Amateur, Professional and Ladies' Championships. The course lies 15 miles south of Melbourne.

Kittansett, *Marion, Massachusetts, USA*
This course, with its sand dunes and varying winds, has many characteristics of a links course, and provides many features of British seaside golf. A pleasant and popular course, its one real claim to fame was to be selected for the Walker Cup matches of 1953, won by the USA by nine matches to three. Among those who played were Gene Littler, US Amateur Champion of that year, and Ken Venturi, both of whom went on to turn professional and win the US Open title. Among the British players were

some well-known names including J B Carr and G H Micklem.

Krefelder, *Krefeld, West Germany*
6704yd, 6130m
The present course, lying seven kilometres from the industrial town of Krefeld, has been in existence for nearly 40 years, though its original course was established over nine holes in 1930. Most holes have wide fairways and flat terrain; its most severe hazard is the occasional thick rough. It has been the venue of all the country's national championships including the Amateur and Open Championships.

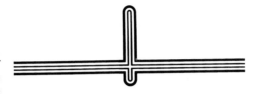

La Baule, *Côte d'Amour, Brittany, France*
7409yd, 6775m
This new club, situated about two miles from the town of La Baule at the entrance to the Loire Valley, is in an attractive setting of rich verdant countryside, designed by Peter Alliss and Dave Thomas, Britain's former Ryder Cup players. Planned around a lake, the course rates as one of the most challenging in Europe, with well-varied and testing holes. It was the venue of the 1978 French Open Championship.

Lagunita, *Caracas, Venezuela*
6895yd, 6305m
The newest of the three courses in the capital city of Caracas, this is an excellent test, and certainly one which offered a challenge to the players in the World Cup when it was held here in 1974. Only three players, Bobby Cole of South Africa who won the individual title with a score of 271, Hale Irwin of America and Masashi Ozaki of Japan, beat the four-round par of 280. It has also been the venue of the country's National Amateur Championship and also the Simon Bolivar International Trophy, and is recognized as a course offering a fair but tough challenge. Opened in 1962, it was designed by Dick Wilson with five demanding short holes, three of them over 200yd and the shortest 170yd. One of the toughest is the 445yd 12th, a dog-leg right with out-of-bounds all the way, and an approach shot over a lake.

Lahinch, *County Clare, Irish Republic*
6300yd, 5761m
Old Tom Morris laid out the course in 1893, and when the great course architect Alister Mackenzie – creator of Augusta National among others – re-designed it in 1927, he said 'Lahinch will make the finest and most popular course that I, or I believe, anyone else, ever constructed.' The course is among the best in Ireland, featuring

natural hills, hollows and sandpits. Its two most famous holes are the par 5 5th, named Klondyke, and the short 3rd, The Dell. The 1st requires a second shot over a great sandhill and another hole has a completely blind tee shot over high sandhills. The home of Ireland's oldest championship, the South of Ireland Open, since 1895, it has also been the venue for other championships, including the Irish Amateur, Professional and Ladies' events. Because of its popularity, a nine-hole course was added, and this has now been extended to 18 holes of 5340yd, 4882m.

Lakes, *Sydney, New South Wales, Australia*
6833yd, 6248m
Founded in 1930, the course was re-designed after a motorway sliced across it in 1968. As its name suggests, natural lakes are the main feature laid out by American architect Robert Von Hagge. Completed in 1970, a new clubhouse was opened a year later. It has been the venue for several championships and important tournaments, and staged the Australian Open in 1964.

La Manga Campo de Golf, *Cartagena (Murcia), Spain*
South: 6855yd, 6268m
North: 6455yd, 5902m
South African Gary Player, who became Director of Golf at La Manga on its opening in 1972, describes these courses as 'the best manicured, most superbly maintained I have ever played'. Unique among the golf resorts of the world, La Manga was designed so that each of the four nines ends at the clubhouse. Selected as the site of the Spanish Open Championship for five consecutive years from 1972, the par 72 South course and the par 71 North course are dotted with 14 lakes and 3000 palm trees. A 50yd ravine traversed by 25 natural stone bridges winds through both courses, confronting the player with demanding shots requiring anything from long woods to short irons.

La Moye, *Jersey, Channel Islands*
6055yd, 5536m
One of two excellent courses on the island of Jersey, it is a links type, set among sandhills with outstanding views over St Ouen's Bay. Founded

Below: A composite view of the latter holes of the South course of La Manga Campo de Golf in Spain, taken from behind the clubhouse. The palm trees were imported from Africa and transplanted.

in 1902, the course was laid out by the headmaster of La Moye School, George Boomer, and he and later his son both became professionals. Son Aubrey moved to the St Cloud club in Paris, became a leading tournament professional, and was runner-up in the British Open in 1927. Henry Cotton re-designed the course some years ago and the 14th and 15th holes, which cross and recross a ravine, are both outstanding tests.

Las Palmas, *Canary Isles*
6130yd, 5605m
A group of Englishmen founded the course in 1891 and until 1957 it was a sand course with 'browns' instead of greens. In 1957 it moved to a location 1300ft above sea level on a plateau overlooking an extinct volcano. Fairly flat, with fairways lined by heavy rough, it has some notable short holes, and three greens bring the player back under the shadow of the clubhouse which stands high above the course.

Laurel Valley, *Pennsylvania, USA*
7100yd, 6492m
Built early in the 60s by Dick Wilson, it has an exclusive membership of executives and millionaires including the great Arnold Palmer. It was the venue for the 1975 Ryder Cup matches and with the lush and green undulating fairways set among rolling wooded hills, its length was too much for the British players, who went down 21–11, although Britain's Brian Barnes

gained two outstanding singles victories in one day over Jack Nicklaus. Arnold Palmer with his home town of Latrobe nearby, was a proud recipient of the trophy as the US non-playing captain. The course has also staged the US PGA Championship in 1965 and the PGA Team Championship.

Le Touquet, *Côte d'Opale, France*
Sea: 6717yd, 6142m
Forest: 6461yd, 5908m
Founded in 1908, the course was devastated during World War II by the Germans and it was not until 1958 that Le Touquet saw the complete re-opening of the Forest and Sea courses and the return to championship standard. One of the nearest Continental courses to Britain, it offers golf of a links variety among sand dunes swept by the wind, or among the pines. It first staged the French Open Championship in 1914, and it returned to the course three times up to 1939. In 1976 the French Open returned to Le Touquet for the first time since the war and history was made when the first black South African, Vincent Tshabalala, captured the title.

Lindrick, *Worksop, Nottinghamshire, England*
6613yd, 6047m
An exceptionally fine inland course, it was the scene of a memorable Ryder Cup Victory when the British under Dai Rees triumphed over the Americans in 1957. On that occasion, the American captain Jackie Burke described the course

Below: The 18th green at Laurel Valley, Ligonier, Pennsylvania. The course was built in 1960 but has already hosted several important events.

as 'a golfing paradise', with perfect turf and flawless greens. Founded in 1891 as the Sheffield and District Golf Club, its 4th hole, on the borders of Nottinghamshire, Yorkshire and Derbyshire, was once a cock-fighting arena. The course has been the venue for many leading tournaments, including the Dunlop Masters, and the Youths' Championship, as well as staging the Curtis Cup in 1960. Its unusual feature is that a main road cuts through the course. Three of the five holes played away from the main part of the course (which includes the clubhouse), are lengthy. The road is then re-crossed to return to a fine short 18th of 206yd.

Little Aston, *Sutton Coldfield, Staffordshire, England*
6717yd, 6142m

The course was founded in 1908 and designed by the great Harry Vardon; it has seen alterations since. Its professional for many years, M J Lewis, has been responsible for some of the changes. In a fine parkland setting, it is one of the best courses in the Midlands, having some testing par 4s in its first half. There is only one long hole in each half. The 17th of 379yd, has excellent features. Looking from the tee, there are trees on the right and out-of-bounds on the left leading to a well-bunkered green with a lake on the left. The course has been the venue for many important tournaments, including the English Amateur Championship and Stroke Play Championship, and the Dunlop Masters.

Liverpool, Royal, *Hoylake, Merseyside, England*
6737yd, 6160m

One of the toughest and most demanding of all links courses, Hoylake has no great beauty to commend it, but its character is such to impress all who play here. It celebrated its centenary in 1969. In its early history great amateurs such as John Ball, Harold Hilton and Jack Graham rose

to prominence on these links. Its many dog-legs, its flat terrain and sandhills and its winds blowing from the Wirral peninsula make it a challenging course. The course has been subject to many changes of layout during its history, but can boast a challenging finish over its last five holes. Here the British Amateur Championship was inaugurated in 1885 and the first international match between England and Scotland was played in 1902. Hoylake staged its first British Open Championship in 1897 when local player Harold Hilton was a popular winner. Alex Herd, J H Taylor and Walter Hagen followed and in 1930 the great Bobby Jones gained his third Open victory in the year of his grand slam. It was a regular venue for the Open Championship until 1967 when the great Argentine player Roberto de Vicenzo was given a tremendous ovation on capturing the title at the age of 44. Bernard Darwin wrote of the course 'it belongs to the whole world of golf, for it has played a great part in the history of the game.' It was awarded its Royal prefix in 1872, the year it was extended to 18 holes.

Lytham & St Annes, Royal, *Lancashire, England*
6673yd, 6102m

One of Britain's great seaside championship links which dates back to 1886, it differs from other famous links courses as it is enclosed by a housing development and out of sight of the sea. But its fast-running fairways and its many sand-traps and sandhills make this one of the finest courses, and it is one of the regular venues for the British Open Championship. Its first hole is a testing par 3, and four of the next eight holes have menacing out-of-bounds with a railway line running on the right. One of its most testing holes is the par 5 11th, with a blind tee shot over a ridge of bunkers. The long par 4 17th is possibly the most famous, for it was here that the great Bobby Jones hit a great iron shot from

Below: One of the hazards of the famous English course, Royal Lytham – a railway runs alongside the opening holes.

a sand bunker to win the 1926 British Open; a bronze plaque at the spot commemorates the achievement. New Zealander Bob Charles became the first left-handed player to win the Open here in 1963, and other great overseas players, Bobby Locke, Peter Thomson and Gary Player, have also won Open titles over these great links. But possibly its most glorious moment, at least for British supporters, was when Tony Jacklin strode majestically to his Open victory of 1969, the first home player to capture the title since Max Faulkner in 1951.

Machrihanish, *Argyll, Scotland*
6228yd, 5695m
Founded in 1873, this splendid course by the Atlantic is natural links running by a sandy beach, with the sea intervening between tee and green to provide a dramatic opening hole. Old Tom Morris completed an 18-hole layout six years after its formation, and the result is a superb course with fine lies on the splendid turf of the fairways. It has all the hazards of links courses, made all the more testing when the wind blows, and undulating greens, many of generous dimensions. It has been the venue of the Scottish Professional and Scottish Ladies' Championships.

Mauna Kea, *Hawaii, USA*
6900yd, 6310m
American architect Robert Trent Jones's courses are notable for their extra-long tees, and this aspect is typical of this island masterpiece, with the course length able to be varied from a maximum of over 7000yd, down to less demanding proportions for the average player, with some formidable holes to negotiate. One of the toughest is the 215yd 3rd, with a daunting carry over the Pacific to a green perched on volcanic rock – a green with deceptive slopes to make putting a hazardous operation. Developed in the mid-1950s on rolling land beneath the snow-capped Kea volcano, it has all the lush vegetation typical of these islands.

Mayfair, *Edmonton, Alberta, Canada*
6632yd, 6064m
Heavily wooded having been carved out of a forest, the course was opened in 1922 by the Governor General of Canada, Lord Byng, and is located in an attractive setting on the banks of the North Saskatchewan River. Alterations were made some years after its opening, and the result is an excellent course winding through the trees. It was the venue for the Canadian Open Championship of 1958, won by Wes Ellis, and also for the Canadian Amateur and PGA Championships.

Left: Britain's most modern golf clubhouse, the Meon Valley Golf and Country Club in Hampshire, England. One of its amenities is an indoor swimming pool.

Medinah, *Chicago, Illinois, USA*
7032yd, 6430m
Founded in the 1920s this course is one of the toughest of those chosen as the venue for the US Open Championship and also one of the most controversial. It staged its first Open in 1949, when Dr Cary Middlecoff was the winner; it was not until 1975 that the Open returned, the winner being Lou Graham with an aggregate of 287, three over par. Built by the Shriners, an Arabic order, it has been completely altered over the years – the last alteration was made by George Fazio, course adviser to the USGA before the 1975 Open. It has severe dog-legs and nearly all the fairways are hemmed in by dense trees, with the 2nd and 17th holes being played across a lake. The 17th, the most spectacular and toughest on the course although only 220yd, calls for a carry across the lake and a ribbon bunker fronting the bunker-enclosed green. Here, Sam Snead in 1949 was tied for the lead, and having missed the bunker from the tee, elected to run the ball through grass rather than chip up, left the ball short, missed the putt – and was left still seeking the Open victory he was never to achieve. From start to finish, this is a course which never offers anything but the severest of tests and probably more than any other calls for complete accuracy and concentration throughout.

Melbourne, Royal, *Victoria, Australia*
6946yd, 6351m
Founded in 1891 and the oldest club in Australia, the present site was laid out in 1901 and in 1926 British architect Dr Alister Mackenzie aided by Alex Russell, a former Australian Open Champion, carried out extensive alterations to the course, named the West course. Russell later designed and built the East course, and a composite of the two (avoiding roads which cut into both courses), makes up the championship course, the length of which is given above. Located near the sea, the Melbourne courses are built on sand, giving ample scope for large fairway and greenside bunkers; the latter guarding greens are renowned for their pace. In its early days and since the course alterations, it has been the venue for many championship events, including the Australian Open and Amateur events and the Australian Professional Championship. The World (Canada) Cup was played here in 1959 and 1972; on the first occasion Australians, Peter Thomson

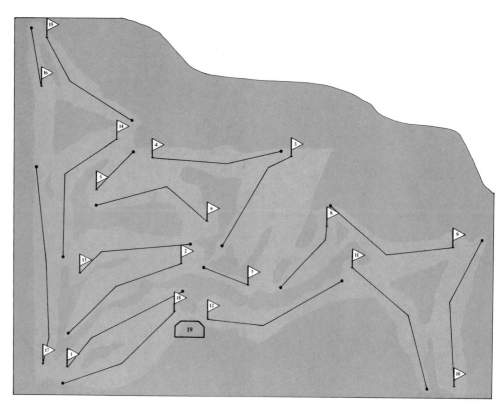

Above: The layout of the Royal Melbourne course in Australia.

and Kel Nagle pushed the USA team of Sam Snead and Cary Middlecoff into second place. On that occasion, Sam Snead returned a record round of 65. The World Amateur Team Championship of 1968 resulted in a victory for USA over Great Britain. Gary Player, winner of seven Australian Opens, triumphed at Royal Melbourne in 1963.

Meon Valley, *Hampshire, England*
6830yd, 6247m

This magnificent course designed by one of Europe's best known golf course architects, Hamilton Stutt, is the newest belonging to the Ashton Court Leisure Group, leaders in Britain's Golf and Country Club field. (The most famous of their clubs is St Pierre, venue of several leading tournaments.) Meon Valley, however, looks as if it will be the Group's *best* course. The clubhouse with swimming pool, squash courts and so on is built on American lines providing something for all the family.

Merion, *Ardmore, Pennsylvania, USA*
6544yd, 5984m

When members of Merion Cricket Club, founded in 1965, turned to golf, they chose an immigrant Scot, Hugh Wilson, to lay out their new course in 1910; this famous East course has seen few changes over the years. While it lacks the length of many championship courses, it has offered a severe challenge to the world's great golfers, and when Lee Trevino won the US Open here after a play-off in 1971, only he and Jack Nicklaus had matched the par of 280. In

the US Amateur Championship of 1916, the 14-year-old R T (Bobby) Jones took part, and he returned in 1924 and 1930 to win the title, the second occasion being the last event in the year of his Grand Slam. In 1950 Ben Hogan made his comeback here after his near-fatal car crash the previous year, playing in considerable pain and in the last round nearly giving up. He finished in a three-way tie and won the play-off to demonstrate remarkable courage in securing the second of his four Open titles. Merion's compact course is bounded by an avenue on one side and woods on the other, with tight greens and natural features of streams and a quarry. It has no fewer than 120 bunkers, all adding up to a challenging course. The 11th, calling for a downhill tee shot and an approach over a creek to the green, was the scene of Jones's 8 and 7 win over Gene Homans in the 1930 Amateur final, and a plaque there records the event. Gene Sarazen took seven here to lose the 1934 Open to Olin Dutra.

Mexico (Club de Golf), *Mexico City, Mexico*
7250yd, 6629m

Designed by Percy J Clifford and American architect Laurence Hughes, the course is located at an altitude of over 7000ft (2100m). The length is not quite as severe as it sounds because balls will travel further at high altitudes. Clifford, former Mexican Amateur champion, found the site south of Mexico City in the late 1940s, and it was carved out of a grove of cypress, cedar, eucalyptus and pine trees with a creek running through it. With its fairways lined by dense trees, the course calls for accurate driving, and its greens are well guarded by bunkers. It has been the venue for two World Cup tournaments; Christy O'Connor and Harry Bradshaw gave Ireland its only win in 1958. In 1967 the US team of Jack Nicklaus and Arnold Palmer held on to the trophy they won the previous year in Tokyo. Palmer took the individual title with an aggregate of 276, 12 under par, and the pair finished 13 strokes ahead of runners-up, New Zealand. The World Amateur Team Championship was played here in 1966, the US being runners-up to Australia.

Mid Ocean, *Bermuda*
6547yd, 5987m
The best-known of this beautiful Caribbean island's courses, Mid Ocean was laid out in 1924 by Charles Blair Macdonald, and altered in 1953 by Robert Trent Jones, with the skills of both men blending to provide some intriguing and testing holes with water playing a crucial part in some. The 5th, in particular, of 433yd, calls for as long a carry over water as the player dares – the longer the carry, the closer to the green. With the Atlantic shimmering in the sun, this is a perfect setting for the game and the standard of the course measures up to the wonderful surroundings.

Mid-Surrey, Royal, *Richmond, Surrey, England*
6385yd, 5838m
Founded in 1892, the club acquired its Royal title when the Prince of Wales (who abdicated as King in 1936, taking the title of the Duke of Windsor) became captain in 1926. The great British player J H Taylor, five times British Open champion and runner-up in the US Open, was professional here for 47 years, and brought about some alterations to the parkland course, which is notable for its fine trees. It was the venue for the English Amateur Championship in 1946 and the PGA Close Championship in 1968.

Minikahda, *Minneapolis, Minnesota*
The great Bobby Jones came here three years before his appearance at the other Minneapolis course, Interlachen, when he won the US Open in the year of his Grand Slam. At Minikahda in 1927, he won the third of his five American Amateur Championships. Over this picturesque course, founded in 1898, the famous amateur Chick Evans won the US Open Championship in 1916 – winning the Amateur title also in the same year. Evans's US Open aggregate of 286 after leading from the start set a record for the lowest total, equalled in 1932 by Gene Sarazen at Fresh Meadow and beaten by Tony Manero at Springfield in 1936. The course also staged the Walker Cup in 1967, when the United States beat Great Britain 8–3. In the American team were two players who later became US Open champions, Gene Littler and Ken Venturi.

Mission Hills, *Palm Springs, California*
7000yd, 6401m
This rolling course, designed by Desmond Muirhead, is owned by the Colgate-Palmolive company, who in recent years has expanded its interest in golfing activities, particularly in tournament sponsorship. Mission Hills is the

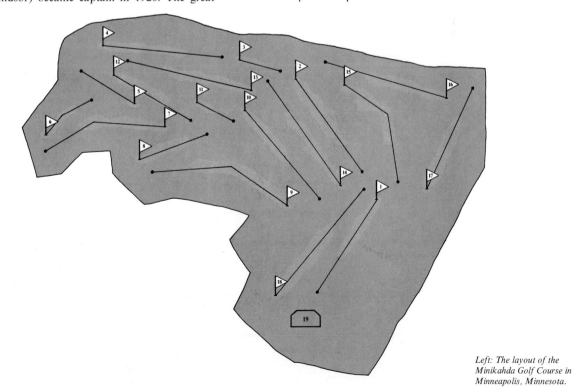

Left: The layout of the Minikahda Golf Course in Minneapolis, Minnesota.

site for the company's premier LPGA promotion, the Colgate-Dinah Shore Winner's Circle held each spring. In 1976 it was the venue for the World Cup, when the young Spanish pair of Severiano Ballesteros and Manuel Pinero gave Spain its first win in this event, the superb desert course, in perfect condition, providing a fine test for the players of the world's golfing countries.

Mississauga, *Toronto, Ontario, Canada*
6820yd, 6236m

Founded in 1905, the course is on the site of a former Indian village, and being located in a valley features many testing holes which are played across a river. Its challenging nature resulted in it being chosen for the first Canadian PGA Championship in 1912, and it has also been the venue for six Canadian Opens, the first in 1931 being won by Walter Hagen after a play-off, and other winners being Sam Snead, Gene Littler and latterly, Bobby Nichols in 1974.

Monte Carlo, *Monaco*
5950yd, 5440m

Founded in 1910, this is an ideal holiday course, laid out on a plateau over 2600ft (800m) above sea level, surrounded by snowy Alpine slopes and overlooking the sea and the beautiful resort of Monte Carlo. Each half of the course starts at the clubhouse, and although relatively short, the course provides an excellent and enjoyable test of golf in an ideal climate all the year round.

Montreal, Royal, *Quebec, Canada*
Blue: 6487yd, 5932m

Founded in 1873 by a group of Scots immigrants, this oldest of clubs on the North American Continent was established some years before the first to appear in the United States. It moved from its original site in 1896 out of Montreal to Dixie, ten miles away, and then again because of urban expansion, it settled at Ile Bizard early in the 1950s. The two courses were laid out by architect Dick Wilson, and together with a nine-hole course were completed in 1959. Against a view of the Lake of Two Mountains, both courses feature skilful use of trees, water and sand, with massive greens. The Dixie course was the venue for the Canadian Open Championship, and the 'Blue Monster' course now stages the Open again. In 1975 the championship finished in a tie between Tom Weiskopf and Jack Nicklaus, with the former taking the title in a sudden-death play-off. The Red course, slightly shorter, is equally testing, but lacks the Blue's challenging finishing holes.

Moor Park, *Rickmansworth, Hertfordshire, England*
High: 6663yd, 6093m
West: 5815yd, 5317m

Hertfordshire's only championship course, this must rank as one of the most attractive parkland courses in Britain, with its pleasant rolling landscape, wooded copses and magnificent trees. The High course has been the scene of

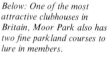

Below: One of the most attractive clubhouses in Britain, Moor Park also has two fine parkland courses to lure in members.

many famous tournaments dating back to the formation of a members' club in 1936, although golf had been played since 1923, four years after Lord Leverhulme bought the estate. Laid out by H S Colt, it has proved a severe test even to the top professionals. In 1976, the first Uniroyal International tournament was staged here, with Arnold Palmer among the competitors and Tommy Horton the winner in one of the most successful events in its history. It has a fascinating history, for throughout the centuries Moor Park and its impressive mansion, which now serves as a clubhouse, has seen the famous among its owners and visitors – Cardinal Wolsey, Henry VIII, Catherine of Aragon, the Duke of Monmouth to name but a few. A second course, the West, though less demanding, is equally attractive, and like the High is notable for its finishing holes.

Moortown, *Leeds, Yorkshire, England*
6604yd, 6039m

Venue for many championship dramas, one of the most outstanding events staged here was the 1929 Ryder Cup match between the American team captained by Walter Hagen and the British team with George Duncan as captain, leading his side to one of the rare victories by six matches to four, with two halved. The English Amateur and Ladies' Championships have been played here, and in 1976, the club professionals of Britain and America met in the 'mini' Ryder Cup match in appalling weather conditions, with victory going to the USA. Founded in 1909, and laid out on peaty moorland by the renowned Alister Mackenzie, the club's one-time secretary, it has gorse, heather, silver birches and narrow streams.

Muirfield, *East Lothian, Scotland*
6892yd, 6302m

The home of the Honourable Company of Edinburgh Golfers, this is one of the world's great tests of golf. The Honourable Company, probably the oldest golf club in the world, dating from before 1774, was concerned in 1754 with forming the first set of Royal and Ancient rules, and founding golf's ruling body. They moved from their golf house in Leith to Musselburgh in 1836, where the Open Championship of 1874 was staged there for the first time. When the course, which they shared with the Edinburgh Burgess and Bruntsfield Links societies, became too crowded, they moved to Muirfield in 1891, and since then it has been the venue for British Open and Amateur Championships and Ryder Cup, Walker Cup and Curtis Cup matches. Lying on the shores of the Firth of Forth, it is not a true links course in the accepted sense, although it has many of its typical characteristics. It has short holes full of character, testing long holes, and rough which can ruin a round, as it did to Arnold Palmer in 1966. The first Open Championship there in 1892 was won by the great amateur Harold Hilton and four years

later Harry Vardon gained one of his six titles to establish a record never equalled. After Walter Hagen had won the Open of 1929, during which he birdied the long par 4 8th hole twice on the last day, trees were planted to prevent a repeat of his short cut to the green. King George VI wished Henry Cotton good luck on the 1st tee in 1948 – and Cotton went on to win his third Open. Gary Player and Jack Nicklaus were subsequent winners.

Muirfield Village, *Dublin, Ohio, USA*
7072yd, 6467m

This course was designed and built by Jack Nicklaus. It is his own course and one in which he takes great pride. In creating the course, Nicklaus had spectators as well as the players in mind, and the course features fine vantage points. Each nine starts and finishes at a central point, and in each half, lakes and creeks are vital features in its layout. Water awaits the weak approach at the 3rd, and at the 430yd 6th a giant poplar, on an island in a lake fronting the green, blocks the approach, and a cluster of bunkers cut into the hillside is equally threatening to the left. The 10th of 441yd is one of the toughest par 4s on the second nine, especially when playing into the wind, with sand guarding both sides of the driving zone and a large bunker fronting the green. The short 12th of 158yd calls for a tee shot over the largest lake, with the smallest putting surface, a two-tiered kidney shaped green. Of two tough finishing holes, the 17th is outstanding, with a massive bunker set about 150yd from the tee stretching along the fairway for more than 100yd on the left. In 1976 the first Memorial Tournament – an event to honour an outstanding player, living or dead – was played here, with the name of Robert Tyre Jones Jr being honoured. The winner on that occasion was Roger Maltbie, but in 1977 came one of the most memorable occasions in Nicklaus's illustrious career when he triumphed in his own tournament on his own course.

Musselburgh, Royal, *East Lothian, Scotland*
6207yd, 5675m

One of Scotland's oldest clubs, it dates back to 1774 and possibly earlier. The Honourable Company of Edinburgh Golfers played over the original course from the 1830s until 1891, when they moved to their present course at Muirfield. In 1874, the course was shared with the Bruntsfield Links Society and the Royal Burgess club. The course took its place on the rota of the British Open Championship in 1874 but came off the list following the move of the Honourable Company to Muirfield. The site was acquired for a new course at Prestongrange in 1924, and James Braid laid out a splendid course in a parkland setting. Records show that an annual New Year's Day women's competition among the fishwives of Musselburgh was played about the time of the club's formation. It was granted its Royal title in 1876.

Muthaiga, *Nairobi, Kenya*
6710yd, 6136m
Opened as a nine-hole course in 1913, it was extended to 18 holes in 1927, and later became a frequent venue for the Kenya Amateur Championship. It staged the first Kenya Open in 1967, which was won by former British Walker Cup player Guy Wolstenholme, now living in Australia, and most of the later Opens have been held there. Grass greens have been laid on the course, which is over 5000ft above sea level, and with its own water supply, greens, tees and fairways are kept in fine condition.

Nairn, *Scotland*
6544yd, 5984m
Occupying a superb position on the Moray Firth, with a panorama of sea and mountains, this is a course of championship standard, with its fairways winding east and west through colourful broom in the spring and heather which turns the course purple in the autumn. Founded in 1887, the course was laid out by Archie Simpson and later altered by old Tom Morris and James Braid, with deep bunkers and large undulating greens. One of its finest holes is the 381yd 5th, requiring a drive partly over the sea when a north wind blows. Henry Cotton helped establish the Nairn Golf Week in May, a popular event in which Dai Rees and other professionals are tutors to an enthusiastic gathering of amateur players. The course has been the venue for the Scottish Ladies' Championship and Jessie Valentine has won the title here on two occasions. It has also staged the Scottish Amateur and Professional Championships. Located 15 miles east of Inverness, the area is noted for its low rainfall.

Nairobi, Royal, *Kenya*
6900yd, 6309m
Formed in 1906 with nine holes, the course was extended to 18 holes two years later, and after World War I gained greatly in popularity. It was granted its Royal title in 1935, and two of its members who became captain, J D Leonard and A C Tannahill, were largely responsible for the formation of the present Kenya Golf Union. The course was chosen for the first Kenya Amateur Championship, and has been its venue on many subsequent occasions. With its tree-lined fairways, the course provides an excellent test.

Nassau, *New Province Island, Bahamas*
6812yd, 6229m
This was the first course to be opened in the Bahamas, and in recent years the islands have become universally popular for the number of fine courses which have followed its lead. Originally nine holes, which opened in the late 1920s, the course later moved to its present site, and in recent years has been greatly improved, with a complete course watering system installed. Bordering a delightful beach, the course features a number of lakes and many bunkers. Courses which have been developed, notably in Grand Bahama Island, have attracted golfers from all over the world.

National Golf Links of America, *Long Island, USA*
6745yd, 6167m
This is one of the great courses of America, which the designer, Charles Blair Macdonald, intended should be a replica of the finest holes on British courses, and indeed there are holes reminiscent of those at Prestwick, North Berwick, Royal St George's and St Andrews, among others. Macdonald, an American who attended St Andrews University in Scotland, took up the game there to become possibly America's best player in the early 1900s before its popularity began to grow in the US. For a number of years, he regularly returned to Britain, visiting the most famous links courses, and picking out the most challenging holes, like the Redan at North Berwick. Then, aiming to create the perfect golf course, he found a site at Long Island and in 1909 his course was complete, although it did not then measure the length it ultimately reached. The result was described by writer Charles Darwin as 'a truly great course', and it is one which calls for the highest skill, as it constitutes a really severe test, especially in the wind. Although it lacks the formidable sand dunes of British courses, it has many links characteristics, and several holes are across water, with the most testing being the 14th, where a daunting carry has to be made. The National was the venue for the first Walker Cup match in 1922 between the USA and Great Britain, won by the Americans by eight matches to four, but despite its testing qualities, it has not staged any other major event.

Navatanee, *Bangkok, Thailand*
6985yd, 6388m
Golf in Thailand achieved world recognition in 1975 when the Navatanee course was chosen for the World Cup, with victory going to the US team of Johnny Miller and Lou Graham. This is an outstanding course, designed by Robert Trent Jones, and is a demanding championship test. It was built from rice fields and transformed into a lush course, with plenty of water hazards. These call for expert play at many holes, particularly the final hole, a par 5 of almost 600yd, which features a double water carry. The Thailand Open, now included in the Asian Circuit, won here by Philippines player Ben Arda in 1974, has helped to foster golf in Thailand, which was first played when the Royal Bangkok club was founded in 1890.

Above: The Mount Irvine Bay Hotel overlooks the tropical golf course of Tobago.

Above: The popular golf course of Gleneagles in Scotland.

Left: The 1971 British Open Championship at Royal Birkdale.

184

Above: The par 4 17th hole at Winged Foot, Mamaroneck, New York.

Above: The 9th hole at Muirfield Village, Dublin, Ohio.

Newport, *Rhode Island, USA*
The first US Amateur and Open Championships were played at the same time over the Newport course, in 1895, giving the club a unique place in the history of golf. It was the Amateur Championship and the first official Open Championship, played over 36 holes, with British player Horace Rawlins returning 173 – at 19, the youngest player to win the Open title. The previous year, in an unofficial Open with four competitors, young Scottish immigrant Willie Dunn, who built Shinnecock Hills, defeated Willie Campbell by two holes at New York. The original nine holes at Newport have disappeared, leaving a pleasant 18 holes of quite testing, if not too demanding golf, laid out near the beaches popular with the wealthy who patronize the resort.

North Berwick (West), *East Lothian, Scotland*
6317yd, 5776m
A links course founded in 1852, it lies by the Firth of Forth, with views of the Bass Rock and rocky islets. The present course, completed in 1895, has been little altered over the years, and is notable for one hole in particular, the Redan, the 15th of 192yd, which has been copied at several courses in the USA including the National. The 14th of 382yd, called Perfection, is another hole which has its counterparts overseas, calling for an accurate drive to a fairway sloping to the right and a blind pitch towards the sea. In 1972 the course was chosen for qualifying rounds of the British Open Championship.

North Devon, Royal, *Westward Ho!, Devon, England*
6639yd, 6070m
The oldest links course in England, it celebrated its centenary in 1964, having a vicar as its founder, the Reverend I H Gossett, of Northam, birthplace of one of Britain's greatest golfers, J H Taylor, one of the great three of Vardon, Braid and Taylor. Born at Northam, Taylor, who learned his golf on the course, won the British Open five times and was runner-up in the US Open in 1930. On his retirement, he was honoured with the presidency of the club in 1957, and lived in his native village until his death in 1966 at the age of 92. Originally designed by Old Tom Morris, the course was redesigned in 1908 by Herbert Fowler and has changed little since then. Mainly flat and sheltered from the sea by the great Pebble Ridge, it has fast greens. Its main features are sharp, tough sea rushes, burns and hidden bunkers. It has a massive bunker to be cleared from the tee at the 4th, although the 11th is probably the toughest hole – a drive over sea rushes, with more rushes lining the undulating fairway, and a sloping, well-bunkered green. It was the venue for the British Amateur Championships of 1912, 1925 and 1931; on the first occasion, John Ball, one of Britain's most famous amateurs, beat Abe Mitchell at the 38th hole. It has also staged the British Ladies' and English Ladies' Championships, and in professional events, the *Daily Mail* tournament of 1920 and the Martini International of 1975.

Below: The 18th hole and clubhouse of the Navatanee Golf Club in Bangkok, Thailand.

Northumberland, *Newcastle upon Tyne, England*
6644yd, 6075m
A parkland course, founded in 1898, it is the work of H S Colt, with later alterations by James Braid and again by Colt providing a number of dog-leg holes, including the 1st, which is followed by three long holes. One of the most testing holes is the 363yd 12th, a fairway lined by heather leading to a banked green with daunting bunkers. It has been the venue of the English Amateur Championship and professional tournaments include the Dunlop Masters.

Notts, *Hollinwell, England*
6965yd, 6369m
A heathland course of championship quality, it was founded in 1887, and was designed on its present site by Willie Park Jr and opened about 1900. Sand, gorse and heather feature on this undulating course, a fine test of golf winding through silver birch and oak trees. Of its many fine holes, the 8th of 393yd, demands a long carry over a lake. The English Amateur Championship has been played here, and professional events such as the Dunlop Masters and the first John Player Classic, with Irishman Christy O'Connor winning the then record first prize of £25,000.

Nueva Andalucia, *Marbella, Spain*
6813yd, 6230m
Designed by Robert Trent Jones in 1968, this is a severe championship test and was recognized as such when it was the venue for the World Cup in 1973, won by the United States' team of Jack Nicklaus and Johnny Miller. On that occasion Miller established a professional record, returning 65 against the par of 72. Fairways are long, as in most Jones courses, and similarly water features a great deal in play. Automatic watering keeps fairways and greens in perfect condition, the latter being very fast, but all holding approach shots. Cunning bunkers demand accurate shots at most holes, particularly the 580yd 5th. Backed by the Sierra Blanca mountains, its attractions are enhanced by colourful shrubs and trees. The Spanish Open Championship marked its official opening in 1970, when the popular Spanish player Angel Gallardo was the winner.

Oak Hill, *Rochester, New York, USA*
6900yd, 6309m
As its name suggests, the course features innumerable sturdy oaks, as well as other trees, to line the fairways, and is overlooked from the hill on which the clubhouse stands. Laid out by

Donald Ross, the course was lengthened and re-designed by Robert Trent Jones, and is notable for its final three punishing holes, all long and difficult par 4s. Ben Hogan went through the green at the 16th in the 1956 US Open and took three more strokes to lose any chance of forcing a tie with Cary Middlecoff. The US Open returned in 1968 to give Lee Trevino his first title with an aggregate of 275 which equalled the lowest Open total, a record set the previous year by Jack Nicklaus at Baltusrol.

Oakland Hills, *Birmingham, Michigan, USA*
7054yd, 6450m
When the great Ben Hogan won the US Open Championship at Oakland Hills in 1951 with a brilliant last-round 67, he said he was glad to have brought 'this monster course' to its knees. For the original course designed by Donald Ross had been toughened by Robert Trent Jones for the championship into a menacing test with masses of bunkers cutting into both sides of fairways and surrounding the greens. Hogan was caught by these hazards as he bogeyed the first five holes in the opening round of 76 and going into the last round trailed Bobby Locke and Jimmy Demaret by two strokes. Then Hogan produced one of his most brilliant displays of nerveless, attacking golf for his third US Open victory in four years. Before the course assumed its 'monster' title, it had been the venue of the 1924 and 1937 US Opens, and after Hogan's victory, the US Open returned ten years later when the course was slightly less severe and Gene Littler triumphed with a total of 281, six strokes better than Hogan. South African Gary Player equalled Littler's aggregate to win the US PGA Championship in 1972, ensuring victory at the 408yd 16th when hitting a blind shot to the green with a 9-iron high over trees and lake, perfectly executed to 4ft for a birdie 3. Without doubt Oakland Hills is now a superb course, having matured since Hogan's victory over the 'monster' to become a challenging but fair test.

Oakmont, *Pittsburgh, Pennsylvania, USA*
6800yd, 6218m
Although not a long course by championship standards, Oakmont is a severe test. Its severely-bunkered greens rate as among the world's fastest. Founded in 1903 and laid out by H C Fownes, the course owes much to his son William, a noted player, winning the US Amateur Championship in 1910, and in later years becoming president of the USGA. He brought it up to its high standard, and its razor-fast greens are a byword among the world's golfers. When the US Open Championship was held here in 1973, it equalled the record of Baltusrol as the only club to stage five US Opens. It has been the venue also for the US Amateur Championship and the US PGA Championship. Johnny Miller's 63 in his last round in 1973 was the lowest round returned in a US Open, but

possibly the most eventful moment in its history came in the 1962 Open when Jack Nicklaus tied Arnold Palmer's aggregate of 283 and then beat him in the play-off, scoring 71 to Palmer's 74. Nine years earlier, Ben Hogan returned the same aggregate to take the title, with Sam Snead runner-up. Tommy Armour won his US Open title after a play-off with Harry Cooper when the event was first played here in 1927, and Sam Parks Jr was the other winner in 1935. Johnny Miller's 279 at Oakmont was the lowest championship return, and without detracting from his superb last round performance, he had the advantage of greens made slower by a violent storm which preceded play. Sam Snead's 1953 failure to win the Open followed his victory here two years earlier in the PGA event, though the tournament was then match-play, with Snead winning 7 and 6 against Walter Burkemo.

Olgiata, *Rome, Italy*
6860yd, 6273m
Designed by British architect C K Cotton, the course was completed in 1961 and is an outstanding championship test, with its varied, spacious layout, with some holes heavily wooded but others offering open fairways on different levels. It has three testing opening holes, and many holes feature strategic fairway bunkers, notably at the 8th, 9th and 10th. The 16th, a par 3 of 192yd, is the most picturesque, but requires a well-placed tee shot to a well-bunkered green. It was the venue for the World Amateur Team Championship in 1964 won by Britain, with one of the American team being Deane R Beman, now Commissioner of the US PGA Tour. In 1958, Canadians Al Balding and George Knudson won the World Cup here, starting the last day two strokes behind Lee Trevino and Julius Boros of the USA, and finishing two ahead. It has also been the venue

for the Italian Amateur and Open Championships, the latter in 1973 being shared with the Roma Club, the winner being Britain's Tony Jacklin.

Olympic, *San Francisco, California, USA*
6748yd, 6170m
The Lakeside course of the Olympic Country Club is one that plays very long, although not up to major championship length. When it was bought by Olympic in 1922, it was planted profusely with pines, cypress and eucalyptus trees to create thickly wooded areas on the fairways which slope towards Lake Mercred. Towering trees create the hazards on holes which twist and turn, and punishing finishing holes saw two of the world's most famous players, Ben Hogan and Arnold Palmer, forfeit strokes which eventually cost them victory in the US Open Championships of 1955 and 1965. The unknown Jack Fleck tied with Hogan on the first occasion, and in the play-off was never in awe of his opponent, holding a one-stroke lead with one hole to go and taking the title when Hogan hooked into rough from the last tee. Palmer incredibly lost a seven-stroke lead which he held after nine holes of the last round in 1965 and was still five strokes ahead with four holes to go. He took 4 to Casper's 2 at the short 15th, 6 to Casper's 4 at the long 16th and when he drove into the rough at the 18th, Casper drew level. In the play-off Palmer led by two strokes at the turn, but eventually finished with 73 to Casper's 69. As Palmer found, it is a course which severely punishes the player bold enough to take a risk which fails to come off.

Otago, *Dunedin, New Zealand*
6383yd, 5837m
This, the oldest club in New Zealand, was founded in 1871 as the Dunedin club. It went

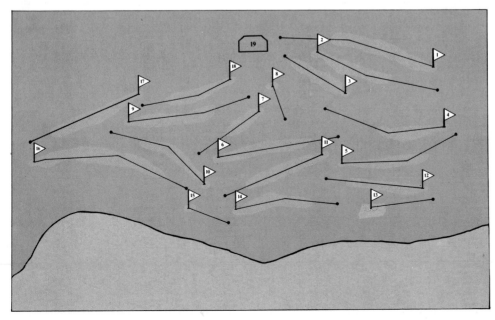

Left: The layout of the Olympic Golf Course, San Francisco.

out of existence, and re-emerged as the Otago club in 1892. It moved to its present site at Balmacewen in 1895, and the undulating course has many great holes. One of its most beautiful, though not the most demanding, is the 11th, with the drive from a high tee between gorse bushes, down into 'the Glen' with gorse and trees completely enclosing the fairway and green. It has a great finishing hole, with an elevated undulating green making the approach and final putts a great test. The course has been the venue of many championships; Australian Peter Thomson won the third of his nine New Zealand Opens here, as well as a New Zealand Professional title.

Ottawa, Royal, *Quebec, Canada*
6285yd, 5747m
Though established in 1891, it was some years later before the course was established on its present site, only a short distance from the city. Fairways on differing levels present a constant test, as does a gully running through the course. It has been the venue on a number of occasions for the Canadian Amateur Championship, and the Canadian Open. This last was won on the first two occasions in 1906 and 1911 by Charles R Murray. Its last Open was in 1932. The club received its Royal title in 1912.

Pebble Beach, *California, USA*
6815yd, 6232m
Founded in the early 1920s on the Monterey Peninsula, Pebble Beach has achieved world fame not merely on account of its demanding course, a superb test of golf, but through the Bing Crosby National Pro-Am Championship, which, through television, has gained golf's biggest audience. Bing Crosby, whom the world mourned when he died suddenly after playing golf in Spain in 1977, started his tournament in 1936, and after World War II it achieved such popularity that its opening rounds had to be spread round the adjoining courses, first of Cypress Point and later of Spyglass Hill, with the final rounds centred on Pebble Beach. It was the venue for the US Amateur Championships of 1929, 1947 and 1961, but not until 1972 did it stage the US Open Championship, won by Jack Nicklaus, who had already won the Crosby tournament on three occasions. Spectacular by any standards, Pebble Beach's fame is centred mainly on its stretch of tough seaside holes, starting at the 4th, all outstandingly beautiful, and all presenting the severest of challenges, and in gusty winds in that US Open Nicklaus completed a fine last-round 74 to take the title. He

had previously won the US Amateur title there in 1961. Pebble Beach was again the venue for a major tournament in 1977, when the US PGA Championship there resulted in a tie, with Lanny Wadkins winning a sudden-death play-off against veteran Gene Littler. The succession of holes along the shore, finishing on the 18th green, with the Monterey bay as the backdrop, spell disaster in windy conditions, with the sea, beach and rocks creating a constant threat. At the 218yd 17th, Arnold Palmer once took nine, and in another Crosby tournament, Jack Nicklaus crashed to a last-round 82. In the 1929 US Amateur, Bobby Jones failed to reach the last round. Pebble Beach remains an outstanding tribute to its creator, Jack Neville, aided by consultant Douglas Grant.

Penina, *Algarve, Portugal*
7450yd, 6812m
When Henry Cotton, three times British Open Champion, designed this course in 1964, he included tees 100yd long so that from its championship length, given above, it could be reduced as desired, the medal tees giving a test of 6889yd (6300m). Cotton resided here for many years before moving for a short spell to Sotogrande in Spain, but returned to his famous course in 1977. In its construction, he included 360,000 trees and flowering shrubs and created a course full of character on a completely flat area of ground. It was the venue for the Algarve Open in 1969 and 1972, the Portuguese Open in 1973, 1974, 1975 and 1977, and the European Team Championship in 1973. Hal Underwood became the first American winner of the Portuguese Open there in 1975.

Pevero, *Costa Smeralda, Sardinia*
6800yd, 6218m
In a beautiful setting between two bays, offering panoramic views, against the background of the blue Mediterranean, American architect Robert Trent Jones has created one of his most outstanding courses. The fairways run from a valley into the hills, between rocks, shrubs and wild flowers, with water often a hazard, and end with testing shots to varied greens typical of Jones's layouts. Opened in 1972, this is not only one of the most spectacular courses, but one calling for fine shot-making, with large bunkers and penal rough, although generally the fairways are open and inviting. It was the venue of the 1978 Italian Open Championship.

Pinehurst, *North Carolina, USA*
7028yd, 6426m
Pinehurst's first course was built just before 1900 after Boston chemist J W Tufts had visualized it as a winter resort, but its famous No 2 course was not completed until seven years later, after a young Scot, Donald Ross, arrived to become resident professional and laid out the new course. Ross achieved fame as one of golf's finest course architects and certainly No 2 has

gained renown as a great test of golf, calling for skill and precision along its pine-tree-lined fairways to small raised greens ringed by large bunkers. As an inland parkland course, it is unusual in that the terrain is entirely sandhills, giving it a linksland character. Pinehurst today is less demanding than the course Ross created, with new grass on fairways and greens of different texture, and in tournaments in recent years, low scores of 62 have been recorded. It was the venue for the US PGA Championship in 1936, followed by the Ryder Cup match between America and Britain in 1951, when a home win of nine matches to two, with one halved, was achieved. Ben Hogan, who was a member of the US team, had two great victories, in one of which he had a remarkable birdie at the longest hole, the 596yd, 10th. After driving in the trees, he hit a brilliant third shot to reach the elevated green, strategically guarded by bunkers, and then holed a 20yd putt. In 1962 the No 2 course staged the US Amateur Championship, in 1973 the first World Open, and in 1977, the first Colgate Hall of Fame Classic. In the World Open, Gibby Gilbert set a new course record of 62, nine under par, and Tom Watson later equalled that score. Then in winning the Colgate event, Hale Irwin also returned a round of 62 and finished with a superb 20 under par aggregate for 72 holes, surpassing the previous lowest total of ten under par. Pinehurst is the centre for the World Golf Hall of Fame, commemorating the names of famous men and women golfers from all over the world. It was opened by US President Gerald Ford in 1974.

Pine Tree, *Delray Beach, Florida, USA*
7000yd, 6400m
After architect Dick Wilson settled at Delray Beach in the 1950s, he built a number of courses in Florida, of which Pine Tree ranks as the most outstanding, and is always maintained in superb condition. The course calls for finely executed approach shots to greens severely bunkered to the front, sides and rear, and whether stretched to its limit to test the ability of the professional, or made less demanding in its length for the amateur, great skill is needed to pinpoint shots to the greens.

Below: Pinehurst is one of the greatest golf centres in the United States. This photo shows the clubhouse and the bowling green.

Pine Valley, *New Jersey, USA*
6765yd, 6186m

Regarded as the most challenging inland course in the world, it has unfortunately never been tested in a major championship because of lack of space for spectators. Its only major event was the 1936 Walker Cup match when the USA gained an overwhelming victory over Great Britain by nine matches to nil, with three halved. Its originator was Philadelphia hotelier George Crump, who had completed 14 of the 18 holes he had designed when he died in 1918 and British architect H S Colt and Hugh Wilson, of Merion fame, both had a hand in the final tough course, with its sandy stretches, tricky slopes and pines, oaks, firs and beaches. Some of its holes are quite terrifying to many players, notably the 7th of 585yd, which calls for complete precision play to reach the green in three strokes, with an aptly named Hell's Half-Acre of sand and scrub to be negotiated with the second shot and then a deeply bunkered green. Another stringent test is the 446yd, 13th, which like most of the other holes offers only a short patch of fairway to aim at from the tee, the rest being a wasteland of sand. Despite its fearsome challenge, this is a superb course, in a beautiful setting – and one player who conquered it in his early days was the great Arnold Palmer, who beat its par of 70 by two strokes.

Porthcawl, Royal, *Glamorgan, Wales*
6605yd, 6040m

Founded in 1891 with nine holes, the present course was laid out seven years later on a rough triangle of land looking out to the Bristol Channel, with the sea visible on every hole and subject to westerly winds. Although a seaside course, it has inland characteristics on a number of holes, with bracken, gorse and heather. The first three holes run along the shore, then the course turns inland and at the 5th slopes uphill to a plateau, before returning at the 8th to the sea. The second half has several challenging par 4s, and a tough finish of three long par 4s and a par 5. The premier course in Wales, it gained its Royal status in 1909, and has been the venue for many Welsh championships. It also staged the British Amateur Championship in 1951, when former US Amateur Champion Richard Chapman achieved victory after twice being runner-up. The Amateur championship returned to Porthcawl in 1965 and 1973, giving British player Michael Bonallack the second of his five titles on the first occasion, and resulting in a win in 1973 for American Dick Siderowf, who followed by winning his second title at St Andrews in 1976.

Portland, *Oregon, USA*

This course gained recognition as a venue for important events when it was chosen in 1947 to stage the first Ryder Cup match between the USA and Great Britain and Ireland to follow World War II. In the American team, which gained an overwhelming victory by 11 matches to one, were Ben Hogan, Byron Nelson, Sam Snead, Jimmy Demaret and Lloyd Mangrum, with the captains Ben Hogan and on the British side Henry Cotton. It was also the venue for one of the tournaments in the short-lived Alcan Golfer of the Year event, when Billy Casper gained a dramatic victory in 1969. He went into the last round six strokes behind Lee Trevino, who was still three strokes ahead with three holes to play. But Casper picked up three birdies as Trevino first dropped a shot and then slumped to a triple bogey to lose by only one stroke.

Portmarnock, *County Dublin, Ireland*
7097yd, 6489m

One of the finest of links courses, Portmarnock lies on a narrow spit of low-lying land some ten miles north of Dublin, surrounded on three sides by sea, and open to all the winds that blow. It owes its origin to two men named Pickeman and Ross, who took a boat from Sutton and rowed across the narrow entrance of the inlet and in a beautiful wilderness of bracken, rolling dunes and natural bunkers established the club in 1893.

On Bernard Darwin's first visit, when no access was possible by road and he had to sail across a stretch of water, he said he knew of no greater finish in the world, beginning with the 14th, a superb two-shotter called Ireland's Eye – 'five holes all different and all diabolically difficult'.

When the Irish Open Amateur Championship was held there in 1899, and won by the great amateur John Ball, the links immediately became famous, and in the years that followed the Irish Open and Irish Close Amateur Championships were staged there, the first Irish Open Championship in 1927 and the British Amateur Championship in 1949. In the 1960 World (then Canada) Cup, Arnold Palmer made his first appearance in Europe and Gary Player set a course record of 65. A round that will rank as one of the greatest was by George Duncan in winning the first Irish Open in 1927, for in a great gale with driving rain, he returned 74 and was the only player to break 80. After a lapse of some years, the cigarette firm of P J Carroll revived the Irish Open in 1975, and when the American Open Champion Hubert Green won the Championship in 1977, he returned a new winning aggregate for Portmarnock of 283.

Port Royal, *Southampton, Bermuda*
6541yd, 5981m

American architect Robert Trent Jones built this course in 1970 and it is now one of the finest of the island's excellent courses. It is set in rolling country by the sea, with many challenging holes, particularly the par 3 15th skirting a steep cliff. Its large greens, in fine condition, are outstanding. With play taking place throughout the year, golf in the Bahamas is a constant attraction to visitors, many of whom come from the United States.

Portrush, Royal, *County Antrim, Northern Ireland*
6809yd, 6226m

This is one of the finest courses to be found in Great Britain and Ireland, offering a superb challenge by the sea, and also spectacular scenery. Founded in 1888, and given its Royal title in 1893 by King Edward VII, the same year the first Irish Open Championship was played here, the course has been altered over the years, finally being re-designed by architect H S Colt to provide fairways threading between the sand dunes, calling for the most accurate driving. Its greens are surrounded by mounds and hollows, natural hazards which outnumber the bunkers. The British Ladies' Championship was staged here for the first time in 1895, returning on several occasions afterwards, and it was the venue in 1951 for the first and only British Open Championship to be held in Ireland, an event notable for the victory of Max Faulkner, the last Englishman to win the title until Tony Jacklin's triumph in 1969. In the British Amateur Championship played here in 1960, Irishman Joe Carr was in commanding form to gain a runaway victory by 8 and 7 over American Robert Cochran. Of the many great holes to test the best of players at Portrush, one of the most notable is the 206yd 14th hole. It is appropriately named 'Calamity Corner' for, depending on the wind, the shot from the tee can be made either with a driver or a middle iron, and unless it is straight to the green, disaster awaits the player in the form of violent slopes and bumpy hillocks on either side.

Preston Trail, *Dallas, Texas, USA*
7031yd, 6429m

Byron Nelson, one of America's greatest players, helped in the creation of this excellent course, which was designed by Ralph Plummer. The club stages an annual Byron Nelson Classic as a tribute to Nelson's help and advice. Built in 1962, the course provides a severe test, starting with three demanding long holes, and including two par 3s of over 200yd, before the first nine have been completed. Though the second-half is slightly easier, the course can rightly be described as difficult.

Prestwick, *Ayrshire, Scotland*
6544yd, 5984m

The first British Open Championship was held here in 1860, nine years after the course of 12 holes had been opened. First holder of the trophy, then the Championship Belt, was Willie Park, but young Tom Morris of St Andrews won the Belt outright in 1870 after three successive victories, and when the present championship cup was offered for competition two years later, he was again the winner. St Andrews and Musselburgh then alternated with Prestwick in staging the Open, and Prestwick saw its last Open in 1925 when American Jim Barnes was the winner. Problems over crowd control

Below: The clubhouse of the Prestwick Club where the first British Open was played.

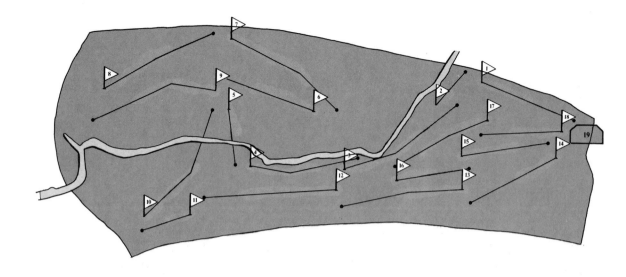

Above: The layout of the challenging Prestwick Golf Course in Scotland.

resulted in Prestwick being removed from the rota, for in that 1925 championship, Macdonald Smith, who as a teenager had left Scotland to live in America, went into the last round with a lead of five strokes, but was almost trampled to defeat as an enthusiastic crowd of 20,000 engulfed him in their efforts to see him win. But Prestwick's reputation as an outstanding course was never in doubt, for it is a superb example of a links course, with its sandhills, humps and hillocks, and its winding Pow Burn. Among its many testing holes, the third of 482yd, the 'Cardinal', is outstanding. A massive sleepered bunker across the fairway calls for a positive second shot to clear it; on the right is the added hazard of the Pow Burn and ahead lies a tiny green. In 1914 Prestwick saw history made when the great Harry Vardon achieved his sixth and last British Open victory – a record that has never been equalled. Prestwick has also staged the British Amateur Championship on many occasions, the last being in 1952 when the winner was former US Amateur Champion Harvie Ward, who was runner-up the following year.

Prince's, *Sandwich, Kent, England*
7130yd, 6520m
American Gene Sarazen won his British Open title here in 1932, with what was then a record score of 283, but the present links bears no resemblance to the course then. A battle training area in World War II devastated the links course, and it was completely re-designed, starting a new life over 40 years after its original foundation, with a layout of 27 holes to provide the championship course and also an 18-hole combination of shorter distance. Although many of the old features no longer exist, and the terrain is flat, the course is true linksland, with shallow valleys, plateau greens and a wealth of bunkers, with the few remaining areas of the old course, which survived, being included. Joyce

Wethered won one of her British Ladies' titles at the old course in 1922 and the British ladies defeated their American counterparts in the Curtis Cup at the new course in 1956.

Puerta de Hierro (Real Club de la), *Madrid, Spain*
7042yd, 6439m
Founded in 1904, this is the oldest course in Spain, though golf was first played in Spanish territory in the Canary Isles at Las Palmas in 1891. Formerly the Madrid Polo Club, it was laid out on land given by the King of Spain, but suffered in the Spanish Civil War and was brought back to championship condition afterwards. Early in its history, it was the venue for the first Spanish Open Championship in 1912, over the old course, the winner being Arnaud Massy, an outstanding French player who had won the British Open title. The Spanish Open continued uninterrupted over the course until 1941 – except for the civil war period – and since then has alternated with other courses. The World Amateur Team Championship was played here in 1970, with the American team, which included Tom Kite and Lanny Wadkins, being the winners. It is also one of the venues for the Madrid Open. One of the features of the course, which is fairly hilly, is the variety of attractive trestle bridges spanning small valleys, starting with one at the short 1st, separating tee from green.

Quaker Ridge, *New York, USA*
Though not as famous as its close neighbour Winged Foot, this course, set in rolling wooded

land north of New York City and designed by A W Tillinghast in 1916, is one of outstanding character. While not staging the major championships or tournaments which have been played at Winged Foot, including the US Amateur and Open, the course at Quaker Ridge has had its moments of glory, notably when Byron Nelson, then an assistant professional, won the Metropolitan Open here in 1936, only two years before he triumphed in the US Masters, and was chosen for his first Ryder Cup appearance. One of the course's most testing holes is the 431yd 7th, a 90-degree dog-leg left, with the green 200yd away guarded by bunkers on three sides.

Quebec, Royal, *Quebec, Canada*
6550yd, 5989m
Founded in 1875, this is the second oldest golf club in Canada and came into being two years after the Royal Montreal. After several moves over the years, the course came to Boischatel, overlooking the St Lawrence River, in 1925, and was laid out in thickly wooded land. Scots architect Willie Park Jr, a former British Open champion, who had designed the Montreal courses of that time, was engaged, but died at the age of 61 before the Quebec course was completed. The club was granted its Royal title in 1933, and in recent years a second course (6448yd, 5896m) has been added. Both are fine tests, with undulating fairways bordered by thick trees. The major course was the venue for the Canadian PGA Championship of 1968, won by George Knudson, who that year won the Phoenix and Tucson Opens and with Al Balding, the World Cup in Rome.

Quinta do Lago, *Algarve, Portugal*
6940yd, 6346m
American course architect Bill Mitchell laid out this fine course on undulating ground, cutting through wooded areas of umbrella pine trees, to create three separate nine holes, which are interchangeable, and will eventually be expanded to two courses of 18 holes. Developed in the early 1970s, the course quickly became established and was chosen for the 1976 Portuguese Open Championship. Many of the fairways provide plenty of space from the tee, and a number feature dog-legs, with the Bermuda grass offering perfect lies on springy turf. Perfect texture greens require a deft touch on the variable slopes.

Riviera, *Pacific Palisades, California, USA*
7084yd, 6440m
In 1974 Riviera was revived following massive reconstruction work during which 17 acres of land were reclaimed. This was necessary be-

cause, since the course was designed by George Thomas and opened in 1926, it had rapidly been 'disintegrating'. A small stream, over a period of 50 years, had turned into a 40ft deep ravine. 'Showbiz' stars have made the Riviera one of their 'clubs' and the Glen Campbell Los Angeles Open is annually held here. Ben Hogan won the US Open at Riviera in 1948 and in doing so set a record aggregate of 276 that remained for 19 years.

ROYAL GOLF CLUBS

England
Royal Ascot, Ascot, Berkshire.
Royal Ashdown Forest, Forest Row, Sussex.
Royal Birkdale, Southport, Lancashire.
Royal Blackheath, Eltham, London. SE9.
Royal Cinque Ports, Deal, Kent.
Royal Cromer, Cromer, Norfolk.
Royal Eastbourne, Eastbourne, Sussex.
Royal Epping Forest, Chingford, Essex.
Royal Guernsey, L'Ancresse, Guernsey.
Royal Jersey, Groubille, Jersey.
Royal Liverpool, Hoylake, Cheshire.
Royal Lytham & St Annes, St Annes on Sea, Lancashire.
Royal Mid-Surrey, Richmond, Surrey.
Royal North Devon, Westward Ho!, Devon.
Royal Norwich, Norwich, Norfolk.
Royal St George's, Sandwich, Kent.
Royal West Norfolk, Brancaster, Norfolk.
Royal Wimbledon, Wimbledon Common, London. SW19.
Royal Winchester, Winchester, Hampshire.
Royal Worlington, Worlington, Suffolk.

Ireland
Royal Belfast, Craigavad, Co Down.
Royal County Down, Newcastle, Co Down.
Royal Dublin, Dollymount, Dublin.
Royal Portrush, Co Antrim.

Scotland
Royal Aberdeen, Balgownie, Aberdeenshire.
Royal Albert, Montrose, Angus.
Royal & Ancient, St Andrews, Fife.
Royal Burgess Golfing Society, Barnton, Edinburgh.
Royal Cragaan, Braemar, Aberdeenshire.
Royal Dornoch, Dornoch, Sutherland.
Duff House Royal, Banff, Banffshire.
Royal Musselburgh, Prestonpans, Midlothian.
Royal Perth Golfing Society, Perth, Perthshire.
Royal Tarlair, Macduff, Banffshire.

Wales
Royal Porthcawl, Porthcawl, Glamorgan.
Royal St Davids, Harlech, Merioneth.

Africa
Royal Cape, Wynberg, Cape Province.
Royal Durban, Durban, Natal.

194

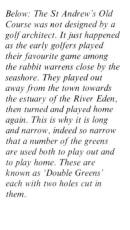

Below: The St Andrew's Old Course was not designed by a golf architect. It just happened as the early golfers played their favourite game among the rabbit warrens close by the seashore. They played out away from the town towards the estuary of the River Eden, then turned and played home again. This is why it is long and narrow, indeed so narrow that a number of the greens are used both to play out and to play home. These are known as 'Double Greens' each with two holes cut in them.

Royal Johannesburg, Transvaal.
Royal Port Alfred, Kowie West, Cape
  Province.
Royal Nairobi, Kenya.
Royal Salisbury, Rhodesia.

Australia
Royal Adelaide, Seaton, South Australia.
Royal Canberra, Canberra, Capital Territory.
Royal Fremantle, Fremantle, West Australia.
Royal Hobart, Hobart, Tasmania.
Royal Melbourne, Black Rock, Victoria.
Royal Perth, Perth, West Australia.
Royal Queensland, Brisbane, Queensland.
Royal Sydney, Sydney, New South Wales.

Canada
Royal Colwood, Victoria, British Columbia.
Royal Montreal, Montreal, Quebec.
Royal Ottawa, Quebec.
Royal Quebec, Boischâtel, Quebec.

India
Royal Bombay, Bombay Gymkhana,
  Bombay.
Royal Calcutta, Tollygunge, Calcutta.
Royal Western India, Nasik.

Other British-created 'Royal' clubs are: Royal
Colombo, Sri Lanka (Ceylon), Royal Hong
Kong, Royal Malta.

There are several 'Royal' clubs throughout the
world created by Royal Houses other than
British.

Royal and Ancient Golf Club of St Andrews, *Fife, Scotland*
6950yd, 6353m (Old Course)
There are those that claim St Andrews to be an unjust, unreal test of golf. Yet the same people will return day after day, month after month, year after year to test their skills against a course that is almost certainly the best known in the world. The fact is that nature more than architects provided this feast of golf and that is perhaps the reason why golfers of all classes sometimes believe St Andrews to be impossible. The Old Course gradually grew out of a narrow strip of land where in 1552 the community was permitted, by licence, to play at 'golf, futball, schuteing etc . . .'. It was not until 14 May 1754, that the Royal and Ancient Club was founded and it was ten years later that one of golf's first major decisions was made – a reduction of the number of holes on the Old Course from 22 to 18. Since then the Royal and Ancient has become the game's governing body throughout most of the world except in the United States. The course itself has developed in such a manner that it could be justly labelled the Mecca of golf. There are many remarkable holes and features. The 316yd 12th is short but full of danger. The 567yd 14th is suitably named 'Long' and for many, with its five Beardies bunkers on the left and greystone wall on the right, is the graveyard of championship hopes with Hell bunker (440yd from tee) and a steeply banked green still to contend with even after a successful drive. The Open Championship, staged at St Andrews for the 22nd time in 1978, has brought many wonderful moments to the Old Course, but

Below: The clubhouse of the Royal and Ancient Golf Club of St Andrews, Scotland.

there are the sadder stories such as the three-foot putt that Doug Sanders missed in 1970 which cost him the title.

St George's, Royal, *Sandwich, Kent*
6736yd, 6157m
The names J H Taylor, Walter Travis, Walter Hagen and Tony Jacklin all have one thing in common – all achieved historic 'firsts' over this supreme course. When the Open Championship first left Scotland in 1894 it was sited at Sandwich, founded in 1887, attracted a record entry of 94 and produced the first non-Scottish winner in Winchester's J H Taylor. Exactly ten years later in a keenly contested Amateur Championship Walter Travis – born in Australia but a resident of the US – became the first American citizen to win in Britain by defeating Ted Blackwell in the final. In 1922 it was the turn of Walter Hagen to boldly wave the stars and stripes when he became the first native-born American to win the Open Championship. Then, in 1967, Tony Jacklin, later to win both Opens in 11 months, earned himself immediate recognition by achieving the first hole in one captured live on British television when he aced the 165yd 16th en route to winning the Dunlop Masters. Since Sandwich was also the scene in 1930 of the first Walker Cup to be played this side of the Atlantic, it seems a shame to record that the last Open Championship to be played over this lovely links was in 1949 when South African Bobby Locke was the victor. However, with improved road communications completed or under construction, the club has again been placed on the Championship roster. It will host the Open Championship in 1981. The course has more memories than most and the record books still show that Henry Cotton's 67–65 start to the 1934 Open – the first of his three Championship successes – is the best in the history of the world's greatest golf event.

Saint-Nom-La-Breteche, *Versailles, Paris, France*
6821yd, 6235m
There are two courses and a unique situation where the championship circuit begins at the first on the Blue but then continues on the Red. Both courses were in fact designed by Fred Hawtree in 1959 and the course, which is sited 12 miles west of Paris, developed quickly enough for the World Cup to be staged there in 1963. The French Open was played there in 1965 and 1969 but the course is now the home of the annual Lancôme Trophy which was first played there in 1970.

Sawgrass, *Ponte Vedra, Florida, USA*
6758yd, 6177m
With the help of Gardner Dickinson, Sawgrass has become the permanent site for the US Tournament Players Championship. Originally designed in the late 1960s by Ed Seay, who cut the course from marshy wastelands, the course was ideally situated for a top tournament since its proximity to the ocean gave it a British seaside links look. But it needed a professional look and that is where Dickinson came in. He lengthened holes, re-designed bunkers and corrected green sizes in relation to the kind of shot required at a particular hole. The outcome was exactly what Dickinson was seeking – a course which tested each and every club in the pro bag, a course that penalized the wayward shot and a course which contained few, if any, blind shots. In March 1977, Sawgrass made its debut and Mark Hayes successfully carried off the title.

Scioto, *Columbus, Ohio*
6762yd, 6181m
Scioto was already famous through having staged the 1926 US Open (winner: Bobby Jones), the 1931 Ryder Cup and the 1950 US PGA (winner: Chandler Harper) before a youngster called Jack Nicklaus came along and developed his game over this superbly designed course which was built in 1912 under the guidance of supreme architect Donald Ross.

Sea Island G C, *St Simons Island, Georgia, USA*
6714yd, 6137m
Designed by English architects H S Colt and Charles Alison as two nine-holers, there are now 36 holes at Sea Island but the major course is still made up of those two original circuits. The front nine, known as the Seaside, is, as the name suggests, edged by the ocean and set among the dunes while the back nine, called the Plantation, is played through forests of oak and pine.

Seminole, *Palm Beach, Florida, USA*
6778yd, 6195m
Donald Ross, an architect whose work can be seen all along the East coast of America, and T Claiborn Watson, a Tennessee mountaineer, were responsible for designing and laying out Seminole in the '20s some 15–20 miles north of exclusive Palm Beach. In so doing they created a true linksland course. It was one of the South's first courses and although it passed through a period when it appeared golf might end, Seminole has remained as a supreme test with more than 200 dazzling white bunkers and large greens with subtle burrows.

Shinnecock Hills, *New York, USA*
6697yd, 6122m
On 22 December 1894 Shinnecock Hills was admitted to the USGA and therefore remains today as the oldest charter member of that organization. Three years earlier the 4423yd

course hacked out by William Dunn, a Scottish professional, had officially been opened for play and in 1896 both the US Amateur and Open Championships were staged there. Yet it was not until August 1977, that a major championship returned to Shinnecock Hills and on this occasion it was the turn of the bi-annual Walker Cup. The course today is much different. In 1931 it was virtually rebuilt by the golf course architect firm of Toomey and Flynn who managed to retain the existing old-fashioned beauty but at the same time instigate a modern-day look. Today Shinnecock, located in the resort of Southampton at the eastern end of Long Island, offers a stiff test to all golfers and indeed it stands out, because it is one of the few American courses that could be compared with the famous seaside links of Great Britain. It can be wild and windy, the greens are small although absolutely true and the holes have been given their own names ranging from Westward Ho (the first), Ben Nevis (the ninth), Eastward Ho (the tenth), and Home (the 18th). The ninth (441yd, par 4) is an absorbing test. The drive needs to be long enough to carry a steep-faced bunker mound in order to reach a valley beyond. Then another huge shot is required to reach the green which stands high above and where only the top of the flagstick can be seen.

Singapore Island, *Singapore*
Bukit Course: 6645yd, 6074m
Built in 1924 and later improved by English architect Frank Pennink for the 1969 World Cup (won by USA), the Bukit course is one of four centred around the Pierce and MacRitchie reservoirs. The others are the New (6874yd), the Island (6365yd) and the Sime (6314yd). The Bukit is a hilly course which offers a variety of shots and presents a difficult test of golf with greens that are hard and fast. It is a realistic championship course unlike the other three, the oldest of which is the Island, originally the Royal Island Club and which merged with the Royal Singapore Club in 1963 to form Singapore Island.

Sotogrande, *Cadiz, Spain*
6910yd, 6316m
Golf course architect-supremo Robert Trent Jones, a Lancashire-born American, was responsible for the old course, completed in 1965, and his influence can immediately be detected from the ten dog-leg holes, the excellent use of water, and the brilliant siting of bunkers and subtle greens. It was Jones's first effort in Europe. He 'imported' Bermuda grass, produced superb fairways and, indeed, did such a good job that the course was used less than a year after being opened for the Spanish Open.

Southern Hills, *Tulsa, Oklahoma, USA*
6962yd, 6364m
When Tommy Bolt won the 1958 US Open at Southern Hills – he finished four shots clear of Gary Player – he immediately pointed to his driver as the reason for his decisive victory. For Southern Hills is very much a driver's course – flat, unlike the name suggests, and long. There are 12 par 4s beginning with one of 459yd and a second hole of 450yd and two enormous par 5s – the monster 630yd fifth and the 552yd 16th. The course, designed by Oklahoma's Perry Maxwell and built in 1935 during the Depression, also possesses some of the hardest bunkers in the world for they are filled with a particular sand known as 'Number Six Wash'. This comes from the nearby Arkansas River and is so soft and fine that the ball will quite often bury itself. In 1977 the course staged the US Open again and became the news centre of the world on the fourth day when Hubert Green received a death threat en route to winning the title.

Spyglass Hill, *Pebble Beach, California, USA*
6810yd, 6225m
Robert Trent Jones designed this mammoth test of golf which was opened in 1966 and provides a series of searching questions from the 600yd first to the 405yd 18th. It is widely considered the hardest of the three courses on the Monterey Peninsula and on a windy day it can become a devil and almost impossible to play.

Above: The clubhouse of Shinnecock Hills, 1892, a year after the club was founded.

Sunningdale, *Berkshire, England*
Old Course: 6533yd, 5972m

A sum of £3800 – just £50 more than Arnold Palmer received for finishing seventh in the 1977 Open Championship – was paid to Willie Park, son of the first Open Championship, to create a golf course on heath land to the west of London. It was money wisely spent. The seeds were sown in the late summer of 1900 and just as a new century had began so too had a new look in golf-course design. Sunningdale had captured a pioneer, and Park's course, ready in 1901, has since developed into one of the best-known inland courses in the British Isles. Several outstanding tournaments have been staged at one time or another during their lives at Sunningdale where the 11th, only 325yd in length, can so often prove the downfall because the blind drive must be struck perfectly with bunkers on the left and trees on the right. Bobby Jones qualified over the Old Course in 1926 for the Open Championship and his card of 66 – 33 shots, 33 putts – is considered by many to be the perfect round of golf with nothing less than a three and nothing more than a four. Said Jones, 'I wish I could take this golf course home with me.' In 1922 Colt designed the New Course but it is to the Old Course, where James Braid won the first PGA Match Play in 1903, and to the ingenuity of Park that Sunningdale owes almost everything.

Sydney, Royal, *New South Wales, Australia*
6566yd, 6002m

Home of many Australian Opens, Royal Sydney is one of those rare marvels – a links course yet only ten minutes from the hub of the city. Formed in 1893, it was extended to a full 18 holes three years later and has grown into a rich and rewarding course where a knowledge of wind play is a necessity. The greens are small,

the bunkers, designed by Alister Mackenzie, are deep and filled with soft white sand and the majority of the holes run either north or south. Jack Nicklaus won his fourth Australian Open title when he collected the Championship over this course in 1975.

Tobago, *West Indies*
6498yd, 5942m

One of the best courses in the Caribbean, this was the brainchild of British businessman Patrick Coghlan. He came to this beautiful island a year after a hurricane had devastated the coconut plantations in 1963 and saw its possibilities as a golf course. He commissioned British architect John Harris to design a championship course, and the result is an outstanding example of the skill of Harris, who died in 1977. Its fairways sweep through coconut palms over undulating terrain, and while a test of the best golfers, it is always fair and offers interesting and spectacular holes. The course attracts many players from the USA and Canada, and twice yearly, in November and January, is the scene of well-patronized Mount Irvine Bay Pro-Am gatherings, organized by Leisuresports of London. The company formed to build the course later opened the luxury Mount Irvine Bay Hotel close by.

Troon, *Strathclyde, Scotland, Great Britain*
Old Course: 7064yd, 6457m

Until Tom Watson obliterated the Open Championship record with an aggregate of 268 at Turnberry, Troon had been the proud holder of

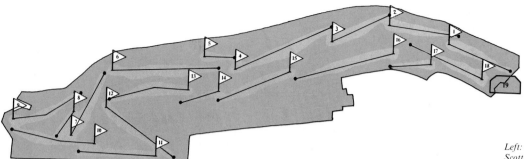

Left: The layout of the Scottish Troon Golf Course.

that record with a score of 276 achieved by Arnold Palmer in 1962 and equalled by Tom Weiskopf in 1973. Troon has staged four Open Championships – the first in 1923 which was 45 years after the birth of the course as a five-hole circuit. Gene Sarazen, who won the Open title in 1932, holed in one at the 8th hole – christened the Postage Stamp – during the Open of 1973.

Turnberry, *Turnberry, Strathclyde, Scotland*
Ailsa: 7060yd, 6453m
Beauty is in the eye of the beholder and there are few who would disagree that Turnberry's two majestic courses, the Arran and the Ailsa, are among the most picturesque in the world. The courses run parallel to one of the most enchanting strips of the southern Strathclyde coast offering breathtaking views of the lonely rock of Ailsa Craig, the Mull of Kintyre and the peaks of the Isle of Arran across the water. So it may

seem strange that the Ailsa course was deprived of a 'Major' championship until 1977 when Tom Watson won his second British Open by overcoming Jack Nicklaus after a dramatic final 36 holes. However, Turnberry's patient wait was a legacy of the two World Wars. Founded in 1903, Turnberry had two 13-hole courses by 1909, but World War I halted the club's progress when an airfield was established on the links. After the war ended Turnberry began to grow again. The Ailsa course, named by one of Turnberry's supremos, Arthur Tawle, was beginning to emerge from several years of reconstruction. Then came World War II and Turnberry became an airfield again with runways built across the courses. It was not until 1951 that Turnberry was reborn with a compelling new Ailsa course being unveiled and owing much to the skill of Scottish architect Mackenzie Ross. The British Match Play Championship was staged there in 1957, 1960 and 1963; the

Below: Always popular with golfers seeking sun in winter is the Mount Irvine Bay Course in Tobago.

Above: Turnberry's famous landmark, the lighthouse, is located by the 10th hole of the Ailsa Course.

Home Internationals were held there in 1960; the British Amateur in 1961; the Walker Cup in 1963; the John Player Classic in 1972 and 1973, and finally the Open Championship in 1977. The Ailsa course has several outstanding holes but the ninth and tenth are probably best known. 'For those in peril on the tee' was how one Scottish journalist described standing on the ninth tee which is sited on a pinnacle high above rocks. The hole is 475yd long – 15yd longer than the tenth which, like the previous hole, is landmarked by the white Turnberry lighthouse.

Vancouver, *Coquitlam, BC, Canada*
6661yd, 6089m
This course was largely inspired by Scottish emigrants and was laid out in 1910 in densely wooded, rolling coastal land. The back nine provide a particularly difficult test – finishing with five testing par 4s.

Wack Wack, *Manila, Philippines*
7078yd, 6470m
Originally built in 1933 but given a face lift in the early '60s when the greens were rebuilt and the

course lengthened, Wack Wack found real prominence in 1977 when it was the venue for the World Cup. It derives its name from the continual noise of crows that were constant pests when the course was first constructed by a group of expatriate American businessmen.

Wairakei, *North Island, New Zealand*
6903yd, 6310m
Born from a need for a course of championship length in New Zealand, Wairakei has grown, since its construction in the mid-50s into a superb test of golf with several scenic but demanding holes. The 608yd 14th has been named, like all the other holes, but its title, Rogue, is perhaps the most apt of all since it stands in the shadow of the bore hole by the same name and from the tee to the banana-shaped green presents a variety of problems. The course was designed by Commander John Harris, an English civil engineer and much-travelled, golf-course architect, and constructed under the guidance of another Englishman, Michael Wolveridge.

Walton Heath, *Tadworth, England*
Old Course: 6859yd, 6270m
Designed in 1904 by Herbert Fowler, the Old Course is one of England's proudest inland courses. It resembles in many respects a seaside course with huge bunkers and greens which remain as consistent as possible throughout all changes of weather.

Waterloo, Royal, *Ohain, Brussels, Belgium*
6813yd, 6228m
The original Royal Waterloo course was laid out in 1923. In 1960 a new 18 holes were designed by Fred Hawtree and the course, which features six successive holes that wind their way up and down through a beech wood, now provides a dramatic and interesting test of golf.

Waterville, *County Kerry, Republic of Ireland*
7074yd, 6469m
Lying on the south-west tip of Ireland, this course, exposed to the winds and gales blowing in from the Atlantic, presents as tough a challenge as any course in Europe. The back nine holes are as testing as it is possible to find, threading their way through sand dunes and hillocks, with the last three running by the side of the beach. The 206yd 17th ranks as one of the world's toughest short holes, with a wasteland of scrub and sand separating a pinnacle of a tee from an island green. Known as 'Mulcahy's Peak', the hole was designed by John A Mulcahy, former Irish emigrant, who made his fortune as a steel industrialist in the US. He returned to his homeland and built the course and the nearby famous Waterville Lake Hotel with its glorious views of lake, mountain and sea. The course has been the venue since 1974 for the Kerrygold Classic, a Pro-Am form of

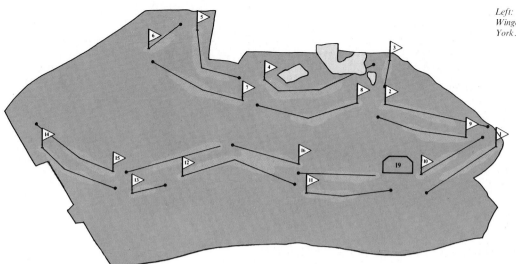

Left: The layout of the Winged Foot course in New York.

tournament, twice won by the course professional Liam Higgins, once by American George Burns and also by Tony Jacklin. The Classic was not held in 1978 as the course was selected for its most prestigious tournament, the World Cup. It has been the scene of several Irish championships, and also the final of a television knock-out event, won by Americans Raymond Floyd and Jane Blalock.

Wentworth, *Virginia Water, Surrey, England*
West Course: 6997yd, 6396m
This is the home of the World Match Play Championship and since the beginning of that tournament, in 1964, Wentworth has developed into one of England's most popular courses. However, the course has been respected ever since it was opened in the mid-'20s. In 1953 the Ryder Cup was staged over this rolling, woodland circuit and in 1956 the World Cup was played here. The course has a total of six par 5s and Arnold Palmer believes the 555yd 17th to be one of the finest long holes in Britain.

Winged Foot, *Mamaroneck, New York, USA*
West: 6980yd, 6380m
Bobby Jones won the third of his four US Opens over this course when he outpaced Al Espinosa by the embarrassing margin of 23 strokes in a play-off to the 1929 event, but it was victory by Hale Irwin in the same competition in 1974 that best illustrates Winged Foot. For this is an enormous course that calls for precision and power for the second shot with a total of 12 par 4s and ten of them measuring no less than 400yd. Irwin is renowned for his fairway woods and there can be little doubt that his ability in this department was a decisive factor and his winning margin of 287 – seven over par – belies his brilliance during that particular week in June. The West course, over which the Open was played, is generally considered to be better than the East but both are monuments to the exceptional talent of A W Tillinghast, the

architect who designed them in 1923. The West is certainly the more treacherous with those stiff par 4s to contend with and a total of 60 bunkers. The bunkers are considered to be some of the toughest in the world and certainly it requires a sound technique to successfully blast the ball from the deep traps that guard each and every green. In creating the course, Tillinghast instructed more than 7200 tons of rock to be moved and 7800 trees to be cut down but in doing so he produced a venue in which Westchester County can be proud.

Woodhall Spa, *Lincolnshire, England*
6831yd, 6244m
Originally constructed in 1905 under the guidance of Harry Vardon and altered seven years later by H S Colt, Woodhall Spa was totally redesigned during the twenties by the owner, Colonel S V Hotchkin, and since then has developed into one of Britain's most respected inland courses. It is an extremely attractive course, built on sandy soil and planted with silver birch, pine trees and an abundance of heather. The bunkers are regarded by many to be some of the toughest in Britain.

Yomiuri, *Tokyo, Japan*
6962yd, 6374m
The World Cup visited this course in 1966 when it was won by the US and that enabled the course to gain early praise from the professionals since it was designed only in 1964 by Japan's leading architect, Seichi Inoue. Since then it has gained a fine reputation. It is a course that offers a variety of interesting holes which are demanding but at the same time fair.

GOLF

or The Ancient Game of Goff
– and the Goffers!

BANNED BY DECREE OF JAMES IV IN 1491: "IT IS AGIN THE COMMON GOOD OF THE REALME AND DEFENCE THEREOF:"

It is a well knowne fact that Goffers are a tribe aparte.

Thru playing Goff unceasingly their very natures change, and they become tacurne, sullen, peevish and irritable!

They speake, eat, drink, sleepe and jabber Goff, forgetting their chattels and infants and spend monies only on balls, clubbs or a majic drink called wiski.

The clubb makers and wiski-sellers make enormous fortunes, while the Goffers families are in greate famine.

These Goffers have been knowne to rise with the lark to play Goff, and continue throughout the daylite hours only stopping for short tymes and wiski.

Such are the very odd ways of Goffers.

IRISH LINEN   by ULSTER Reg. No. 3176   MADE IN IRELAND

Ace American term for a Hole in One.

Address A player is said to have 'addressed the ball' when he has taken up his stance in order to play a shot, and has 'grounded his club'. The grounding of a club in a bunker is not allowed.

Advice In a competition or a match a player may take advice only from his partner, his caddie or his partner's caddie. If he takes advice from any other source he is penalized. This means that he either loses the hole or if it is a stroke play competition he must add two strokes to his score for the hole.

Air shot or fresh air shot is when a player in attempting a stroke completely misses the ball. The penalty is one stroke.

Albatross A score of three under par for a hole. Thus if the hole is par five and the player has holed out in two strokes he is said to have scored an Albatross. The terms relating to holes done in a score below par are all concerned with birds. Three under par is the largest under par score possible in normal conditions, and the Albatross (a large bird) is the term used to designate this.

All Flat (or all square). The term used in match play when a match is level at any stage, including the finish.

Alternate Replacements ready to make up the numbers in a stroke play championship or tournament when others withdraw. They would have been next to qualify and are placed in order according to their qualifying score. The term is also used in the United States for reserves in a team event.

Amateur According to the Rules of Golf an Amateur is a golfer who plays golf solely as a non-profit-making sport.

American Tournament A tournament in which every competitor plays all the other participants, also referred to as a 'Round Robin' tournament.

Apple Tree Gang The name given to the first pioneers of golf in the United States, so called because they played in an apple orchard. This was in 1892.

Apron of the Green The area of the fairway just short of the green. The grass within this area is normally cut shorter than the grass on the rest of the fairway.

Arc (of the swing) The groove or path in which the head of a golf club moves during the swing.

Artisan Artisan or, as they were originally defined, working men golfers, can play at many clubs in England within certain specified periods when the course is less busy. The Artisans are provided or provide themselves with their own club house. They run their own competitions and pay a subscription to the parent club, a subscription which is very much smaller than that paid by ordinary members. The oldest Artisan club in England is said to be the Bulwell Forest Artisans Club, Nottingham, which was formed in 1887. Many professionals in the early days came from the Artisan ranks.

As It Lies Unless a player is allowed special relief as governed by the Rules of Golf or by Local Rules or his ball is lost or unplayable, he is obliged to play it 'as it lies' once it has been struck from the tee.

Attend The flagstick is said to be attended when either the player's caddie, his partner or his partner's caddie pulls the flagstick out as the ball approaches the hole.

Away It is a rule of golf that a player takes his turn to play when his ball lies further from the hole. He is then said to be 'away'. On the putting green however, particularly in a stroke competition, a player who has already putted once may hole out before his partner, who may be further from the hole.

Back Door Sometimes called 'Tradesman's entrance'. Occasionally when a player putts, the ball rolls round the hole and enters it from the back. This is called 'going in the back door' or tradesman's entrance.

Back Nine An American expression but also used in other countries meaning the last nine holes on a golf course. Another term is second nine.

Backspin When a ball, having been played to the green, usually with a deep-faced iron, strikes the ground and spins backwards it is said to have backspin. Professionals and good amateurs are very good at this shot but less accomplished players find it harder to achieve. The art in playing this shot is in hitting the ball with a descending blow.

Backswing The movement by which the hands and arms take the club back to the top of the swing before bringing it down to make contact with the ball.

Baffy The old term for the wooden club which was, in many respects, similar to the modern No 3 or No 4 wood club. In the early days of the game this club was sometimes referred to as a 'baffing spoon', presumably because of its lofted shape.

Ball At Rest When the ball has stopped rolling it is said to be 'at rest'.

Ball Dropped In accordance with the rules, in certain circumstances it is permissable to drop a ball so that the game can continue. There is a correct procedure for dropping a ball. The player shall face the hole, stand erect and drop the ball behind him over his shoulder. (Rule 22 of the Rules of Golf.)

Ball Holed (or holed out) A ball is said to be 'holed' when it lies within the circumference of the hole and all of it is below the level of the lip of the hole.

Ball in Play A ball is in play as soon as it has been struck off the tee and until it rests in the hole, except when it is out of bounds, lost or lifted. The term 'keeping the ball in play' generally means that the striker keeps it out of HAZARDS or unplayable LIES and remains within the boundaries of the course.

Ball Lost The Rules of Golf allow five minutes search for a lost ball. The player or his side or their caddies are entitled to look for the ball and a sporting opponent will also help in the search.

Ball Mark The American term used for the mark made when the ball lands on the green. The player should repair any indentation so caused.

Ball Moved A ball is deemed to have moved if it leaves its original position. If the player accidentally moves the ball whether he has addressed it or not, he incurs a penalty of one stroke. A one-stroke penalty is also imposed if the ball is moved when a player clears away loose material lying close to it. The Rules of Golf also cover instances where a ball is moved by an opponent or by an opponent's ball.

Ball Played As It Lies That the ball should be played wherever it comes to rest is one of the earliest basic rules of the game. If there is a doubt whether or not the ball can be lifted it is best to play the ball 'as it lies'.

Bandit (hustler in US) A golfer who plays off a 'phoney' handicap in order to beat his opponents, often for side stakes.

Best Ball Competition A form of friendly match in which one plays the best ball of three others. Such matches are not common these days.

Better Ball Competition A form of stroke competition in which two partners play as a team, the better score of each player counting at each hole. The term is also used when one player plays against the better ball of two other players in a friendly game.

Birdie The term used when a player has holed out in one stroke less than the par score of a

hole.

Bisque The equivalent of a stroke in a game but which is little used now. It is a system of handicapping in which the player in receipt of a certain number of bisques or strokes can nominate the holes at which he takes them. He can say that he wishes to take a bisque after the hole has been played. Usually a player does so after he has halved a hole to run it into a win. This form of handicapping was once very popular.

Blaster The name given some years ago to the broadsoled deep-faced club used for recovery shots from bunkers or sandtraps. It is still in modern use to describe such clubs as the sand wedge, wedge etc.

Blind Hole Or Shot A blind hole is so-called when the green cannot be seen from the tee. A blind shot is played when some undulation of the ground or hazard prevents the player from seeing the green.

Bogey This is generally regarded as the score for each hole which should be taken by a scratch player in normal form making due allowances for average playing conditions. It is not the same as par, and indeed the Americans use the term 'bogey' for a score of one worse than par. In Britain the bogey score for the course is usually a stroke or two strokes higher than the 'standard scratch' or par. In a bogey competition the golfer plays against the bogey of each hole, taking handicap strokes as if in a match, with three-quarters of the difference between his handicap and the bogey score.

The term bogey has to a large extent been superseded by the term 'par' for each hole and by the standard scratch score for the course. However, a great number of clubs still use the term bogey. Bogey comes from a popular song of the 1890's 'Hush hush hush here comes the bogey man'. At a United Services Club in Hampshire bogey was described by one golfer as a tough opponent and was given the army rank of Colonel, hence the expression Colonel Bogey. The originator of the bogey score was Doctor Thomas Browne, Secretary of the Great Yarmouth Club.

Bold A term used usually in putting to describe a shot when the ball has been hit past the green or past the hole. It is also used to describe a putt which is too strong.

Bolt (a putt) When a player has despatched the ball into the hole at express speed. The expression comes from the description of a rabbit disappearing into its burrow.

Borrow The devious line of putting required to compensate for the natural slopes of a green. The aim is to counter or take advantage of the rise or fall of the green.

Boundary The perimeter of a golf course beyond which a ball landing is said to be 'Out of bounds'. A stroke is then penalized.

Bowf An old Scots term meaning bark (a dog's bark). In friendly games years ago players agreed that an opponent would have the right to utter a loud bark or grunt as another player was about to play. A player would be given the right to use a 'bowf' or 'woof' a limited number of times. A woof is sometimes used by Americans as a handicap in light-hearted games.

Brassie The old name for a No 2 wood. It derives its name from the fact that it had a brass plate on the sole to save wear while playing from the fairway.

Break Club An obstacle lying near the ball which might break the club. Rules now preserve golfers from most of these troubles. In any case modern courses do not have many such obstacles.

Buggy A mechanically driven vehicle which carries golfers as well as golf clubs around the golf course.

Bulger An early wooden club with a convex of the face – now obsolete.

Bunker (Sandtrap in USA) A hollow on the course filled with sand. Bunkers can be found at strategic positions on a fairway and around greens for the purpose of catching an inaccurate shot. Bunkers first came into being on seaside courses in a natural way, but are now man-made.

Burma Road The name used to describe the West Course of the Wentworth club. The name was coined by Major Rawlinson, then Secretary of the club who in the years following World War II was able to borrow some prisoners of war to rehabilitate the course which had become overgrown like a jungle. He said one day: 'Now they're working on our Burma Road'.

Bye The holes remaining to be played when the match has ended. On occasions players continue to play to see who can win on the remaining holes or 'on the bye'.

Caddie A person who carries a golfer's clubs, or on occasions, the person who pulls a competitor's trolley. The top professionals have their own personal caddie on whom they rely for much advice. The word 'caddie' is derived from the Old Scots noun 'cady' meaning carrier. The word 'cady' in turn may have derived from the French word 'cadet' meaning a young messenger.

Caddie Swing A none too complimentary phrase used to describe a natural golf swing as used by caddies in the earlier days of golf, or at least in the days towards the end of the last century and at the start of this century.

Calamity Jane The name given to the putter used by the famous Robert T Jones Jr. The original 'Calamity Jane' was a lady of the Wild West who was said to be able to sort out the problems of the men in her life. As Jones's putter was able to sort out many of his putting problems it was named after the legendary lady.

Callaway System The form of handicapping invented by Lionel Callaway, a British professional who emigrated to the United States and who became professional at the famous Pinehurst club. The system is meant mainly for golf meetings where competitors come from many areas, thus making for problems in traditional handicapping. In Callaway's system a player's handicap is determined after each round by deducting from his score after 18 holes the worst holes during the first 16. The number of 'worst' holes which can be deducted can vary from none for a competitor who has gone round in par to six holes. If for example a competitor's worst three holes up to the 16th are 7, 8, 7 his or her handicap would be 22.

Cambuta (Or chole, pall mall paganica) These were all names of ancient games in which a ball or some reasonably round object was hit by a roughly shaped club.

Card On which is recorded a player's score for the round.

Carry The distance between the time the golf ball is struck and when it lands. The word is mostly used in connection with the distance the ball has to be hit to clear some hazard, hence the expressions 'long carry' and 'difficult carry'.

Casual Water According to the Rules of Golf 'casual water' is 'Any temporary accumulation of water which is visible before or after a player takes his stance and which is not a hazard in itself or is not in a water hazard. Snow and ice are casual water or loose impediments, at the option of the player.

Centre-shafted putter A putter in which the shaft is joined to the centre of the clubhead in the centre. For many years this type of putter was banned in Britain but is now in universal use.

Character builder A phrase sometimes used in the United States to describe putts of an awkward length, which can be frequently missed although theoretically they should be holed. Such putts are said to be a test of the golfer's character.

Chip A short approach played with a lofted

club is the generally accepted meaning of the term, but the shot can be played with a variety of clubs in order to introduce a little run on the ball after it has landed.

Cheating In golf the penalties for cheating are most severe including expulsion from a club, or for a professional a heavy fine and suspension or expulsion from the particular organization to which he or she belongs.

Choke Holding the club further down the shaft than is customary to obtain more control. The term can also refer to an occasion when a player has failed to go through the ball and has left the stroke incomplete.

Cleek This club used by a Scots golfer for many years is now obsolete. It had a narrow face and about the same amount of loft as the modern No 2 iron. It was a particularly versatile club.

Closed Stance The position taken up by a golfer where the left foot is pushed further forward than the right foot in relation to the target. This stance may be adopted in order to play to the right of a hazard, or it may be used by a player who has a tendency to play to the left.

Club The place at which golf is played. Clubs derive their finances from membership fees and from fees gathered from visitors. Golf clubs

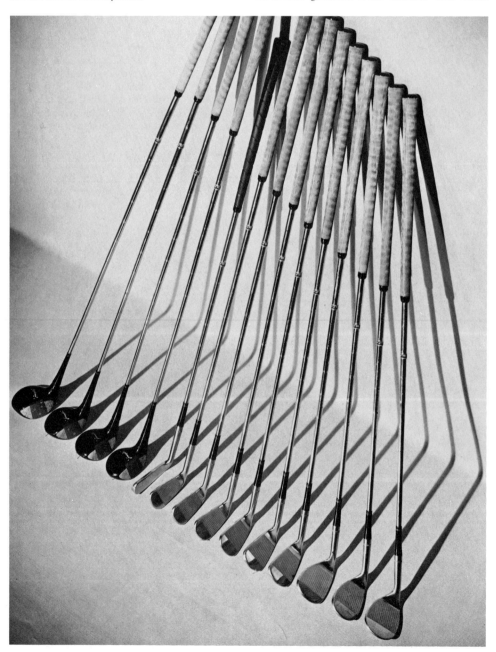

Right: A complete set of 14 golf clubs.

throughout the world vary in size and prestige and age.

Club (too much)   A term used to describe a shot which has gone further than intended. Conversely the term 'not enough club' is used to describe a shot which has fallen short of its target.

Clubhead   The part of the club with which the ball is struck.

Clubhead Cover   As the name suggests, these covers are put on the heads of wooden clubs in order to preserve them. The materials from which the clubs are made vary from man-made fibres to mink! Some golfers also have a club-head cover for their putter.

Clubs   The implements with which the ball is struck. Golfers are permitted to carry only fourteen clubs, a number which when first decided upon was purely arbitrary. These four-teen clubs can be made up of any combination of woods and irons but an average example would be four woods, nine irons and a putter.

Cocking the wrists   The bend or breaking of the wrists when the club is taken back towards the top of the swing. The cocking of the wrists is a completely natural reaction, and no golfer should attempt to do so deliberately.

Committee   A group of men and women in whose hands have been placed the responsibility of running a golf club or a section of a golf club. Most clubs have several committees, finance committee, house committee etc. Lady members of a golf club have their own committees.

Competitor   The Rules of Golf define a competitor as 'a player in a stroke competition. A fellow competitor is any player with whom the competitor plays . . .'.

Concede   To concede a hole is to award an opponent the hole before he or she has completed playing it. To concede a putt is the action taken when an opponent is so near the hole that theoretically it would be impossible to miss. The player who is thus conceded the putt then picks up the ball as if he had holed out.

Course   The Rules of Golf define a course thus: The whole area within which play is permitted. It is the duty of the authorities in charge to define its boundaries accurately. A course usually consists of eighteen holes but there are many of nine holes.

Course value   In Britain this may be taken into account when assessing the Standard Scratch Score of a course under the SSS system.

Crack   A word used to describe a first-class golfer. The word has become largely obsolete, but is still used occasionally especially by older devotees of the game.

Croquet putting   In the fifties and sixties many golfers with putting problems adopted what was called croquet style putting which consisted of having the legs astride the line of putt and hitting the ball in the manner used by croquet players. The putter used was of the centre shafted type. But the style was declared illegal in 1967, the authorities ruling that it was not a proper golf stroke. For some years the style was used with great success by the famous American professional, Sam Snead.

Cut   To hit the ball in such a manner as to send it curving to the right. The same as a slice.

Cut-up Shot   When golfers used to carry only a few clubs, they had to bring a certain amount of improvisation into their game and for instance had to try to get the ball into the air with a club which did not have a deeply lofted face. The cut-up shot was achieved by drawing the clubface across the ball from outside to inside.

Dead   The ball is said to be 'dead' when it lands so near the hole that it would be impossible (theoretically) to miss the putt. In such circumstances in match play an opponent can concede the putt. In stroke play competitions all putts must be holed.

Dimples   These are the indentations made on a golf ball so that it may fly through the air straight and true. Without such indentations a golf ball would fly no distance at all. There are said to be 333 indentations on every golf ball. In the early days, golf balls were smooth, but crafty golfers soon discovered that by hitting golf balls with a hammer it made the golf ball fly further.

Direction Posts   Posts erected to give golfers a correct line to a green which is hidden from view. These posts are usually sited on a fairway but may be placed at the back of a hidden green. In the latter instance there is occasionally a bell at the green to signal golfers playing behind that they may now proceed with their shot.

Divot   A word of Scottish origin meaning a piece of turf. A divot is said to be taken when turf is cut out by the club striking the ground with a descending blow. If a piece of turf has been removed it must be replaced and trampled on in order to restore that part of the course to its former state. Not to replace a divot is a cardinal sin as far as the playing of golf is concerned, because not only would the hole left by a divot damage the course but some player's ball might well land in the hole to his annoyance.

Dogfight   As the name implies a 'dogfight' is a

match where the fortunes of both players ebb and flow, making it a close encounter, with neither side giving much away.

Dog-leg Not all golf holes are straight and a hole which turns either to the right or left is termed a 'dog-leg'. If the hole veers to the left it is a 'left hand dog-leg', if it veers to the right it is a 'right hand dog-leg'. Invariably such holes call for great accuracy as there is almost always some trouble in the angle of the 'dog-leg'.

Dog-licence An out of date expression meaning that a match had been either won or lost by the margin of seven and six. Seven and sixpence was, at one time, the price of an annual licence for keeping a dog in Britain.

Dormie or Dormy A player is said to be 'dormie' when he is as many holes up/down as there are remaining to be played. A player is always 'dormie up', never 'dormie down'. The origin of the word is the latin word *dormire*, meaning to sleep. A golfer who is 'dormie' cannot be beaten even if he goes to sleep for the remainder of the round, and his opponent wins every remaining hole. He can, of course, win every remaining hole and halve the match, so being 'dormie' is not by any means the end of the game.

Double Bogey The American expression describing a hole at which someone's score has been two strokes above par for that hole.

Double Eagle A term used in America. It is three under par for a hole, in fact the same as Albatross.

Draw This word has two meanings in golf:
1. The order of play in a match-play competition. As well as the starting times the draw also gives the names of the opponents.
2. To draw a ball is to impart anti-clockwise spin to the ball intentionally so that it flies straight at the outset and then goes to the left, usually for the purpose of avoiding some hazard or hazards.

Drive The word 'drive' is, according to *Chamber's Twentieth Century Dictionary:* 'To play from the tee'.

Drive for show putt for dough An American term used to stress the value of putting and the fact that it is the holing of a putt which wins cash. However, not every modern golfer agrees with the sentiment of the expression.

Driver The wooden club with a straight face used to hit the ball from the tee. On rare occasions it is used by skilled golfers for a long shot from the fairway when the ball is lying well.

Drive the green or driving the green. When the ball has been hit from a tee landing on the intended green.

Driving Ranges A modern term. Driving ranges are to be found in many countries. They are for the purpose of practising golf, most of them having covered bays where golfers may practice in comfort and hit the golf balls supplied into the distance where they are picked up mainly by automatic means. In Japan where land is scarce and not all golfers are able to join golf clubs, driving ranges are elaborate and much used.

Duck hook When the ball flies away on a low trajectory, then turns violently to the left.

Duff (Fluff) To duff or fluff a shot is to hit the ground before the ball. The result of this misadventure is that the ball usually scuttles along the ground, but to vary the exercise the ball sometimes rises gently into the air and plops to the ground a few yards away.

Duffer The expression used to describe an extremely bad golfer, usually a novice.

Dyke A term peculiarly Irish. It means a hole done in one under par.

Eagle Describes a hole at which a player has holed out in two shots under par. The term originally came from the United States.

Eclectic (competition) The score worked out by taking the cards for two or more rounds and counting the best score at each hole.

Elysian Fields The narrow strip of ground at the famous 14th hole on the Old Course at St Andrews. The safe patch is surrounded by notorious bunkers such as Hell and the Beardies.

Etiquette The conduct expected of players on the course. The code of conduct is laid down in Section 1 of the Rules of Golf.

Face There are two meanings to this word: (a) the part of the clubhead with which the ball is struck; and (b) the part of a sandtrap or bunker usually facing the golfer as he or she plays the shot. Sometimes such faces or slopes are quite steep.

Fade (controlled fade) When an attempt is made to send the ball straight and then cause it to bend towards the right. Some considerable controversy surrounds this shot and the advisability of playing it.

Fairway The mown part of a golf course between tee and green, but not including the tee or green.

Fat of the Green An American term meaning

the largest area of ground between the flat and the edge of the green.

Featherie or Feathery The earliest golf ball. It was made from pieces of leather stitched together and filled with boiled feathers stuffed hard inside. This type of ball lasted until halfway through the last century.

Flagstick A thin movable post with a small flag or piece of bunting attached to indicate to those playing where the actual hole is.

Flat When the club is taken back low round the shoulders, the movement is described as a 'flat swing'. The term 'flat' is also used to describe the lie or set of the clubhead in relation to the shaft. The word is sometimes used to describe a match which is level or 'all square'.

Fluff A very bad shot caused by the club hitting the ground before making contact with the ball. The result is the ball goes only a short distance.

Follow-through This is the movement of the hands and arms after the ball has been struck by the club.

Fore The traditional shout from a golfer to warn another that he/she is in imminent danger of being hit by a ball which is travelling in his direction.

Forward Press An expression much used by golf teachers. It describes the position of the right knee and of the hands prior to taking the clubhead back on the first movement of the swing. The knees should be pressing inwards and the hands forward in the direction the ball is being hit.

Fourball A match in which each player plays his own ball, but the lower score of two partners is the side's score for the hole. The Rules of Golf describe a fourball thus: 'A match in which two play their better ball against the better ball of two other players'.

Foursome A match in which two golfers play against another two golfers, each side playing one ball which is hit by each partner in turn. In the United States this game is known as a 'Scotch Foursome' or a 'Two ball Foursome'.

Freeze When a golfer is in such a state of nervous tension that he or she is quite unable to complete the shot. 'Freezing' takes place usually on the greens when a player 'Freezes' on a putt and is either unable to lift the putter off the ground or is unable to play either backwards or forwards.

Front nine The term used in the US to refer to the first nine holes of a golf course.

Gamesmanship The word was first made famous by the author, Stephen Potter in his book *The Theory and Practice of Gamesmanship* the sub-title of which was 'How To Win Games Without Actually Cheating'. In point of fact it means dodges or manoeuvres all within the rules but calculated to upset one's opponent.

Gimmie Sometimes used in the US to indicate the ball is so near the hole that putt is conceded. What is sometimes claimed as a 'Gimmie' by the player whose ball is so near the hole is not always agreed to by the opponent!

Golden Bear The nickname by which Jack Nicklaus has been known since he came into prominence. The name comes from the colour of his hair.

Golf Here is the definition given by the *Chambers' Twentieth Century Dictionary*: Golf, sometimes golf or Scots gowf (origin uncertain, Dutch golf has been suggested). Other sources suggest the word comes from the old Scots word 'gouf' meaning to strike or cuff. A game played with a club or set of clubs over a prepared stretch of land, the aim being to propel the ball into a small series of holes.

Golf Bag A bag for carrying golf clubs.

Golf Buggy Universally used in many countries. As a rule golf buggies are electrically driven and seat two or even four players with their equipment.

Golf Course/Links The ground on which golf is played.

Golfing Societies Any number of golfers can form a society and hold competitions and matches. But for the purpose of having their members receive official handicaps, societies should be affiliated to the National body which deals with handicapping.

Golf Trolleys (sometimes called a caddie car) A piece of equipment which carries a golfer's equipment but which is pulled by hand. Much used in Britain.

Golf Widow Towards the end of the last century an artist named Harry Furniss drew a picture of a lady looking out of a window towards a golf course. He named it 'A Golf Widow'. Since then ladies whose husbands leave them frequently to play golf are 'Golf Widows'.

Grain An expression describing the way the grass of a green has been cut. Obviously, the grass lies differently when the mower is going one way than it does when the mower is going in the opposite direction. In the United States and other countries golfers refer to the nap on the green rather than grain.

Grass Bunkers Not common nowadays but they are still to be found on some British courses. In fact, Berkhamsted in Hertfordshire has no sand bunkers (sandtraps), only grass bunkers.

Great Triumvirate The first of the great professionals were two Englishmen – Vardon and Taylor and one Scotsman – Braid. Between them they dominated golf at around the turn of the century, Vardon winning six Open Championships and the other two five each.

Green Once the word 'Green' was used to describe the whole golf course but now the word refers to the surface used for putting.

Green Fee The amount payable by visitors when they play golf at a club of which they are not a member.

'Greenie' An American word referring to one of the several ways of gambling in golf in the United States. The 'Greenie' is won by the player who finishes nearest the pin at a short hole.

Greensome This popular game is not recognized in the Rules of Golf. It is a fourball play in which all the four players drive and then each side nominates which ball they wish to continue playing for the rest of the hole. Obviously, the ball chosen is almost invariably the longer or the best placed drive.

Green, through the A term used to describe a situation when the ball has landed in front of the putting surface and run over the green to the ground beyond.

Grip Used to describe the manner in which the golf club is held while playing. 'Grip' is hardly the correct expression, however, inasmuch as it suggests that the club should be held as in a vice. Grip can also mean that part of the shaft covered by some material around which the hands are placed.

Grips, types of There are three ways of gripping or holding a golf club: (1) the Vardon grip in which the little finger of the right hand overlaps the index finger of the left hand; (2) the interlocking grip in which the little finger of the right hand interlocks with the index finger of the left hand; (3) the two-handed grip in which both hands grip the club quite separately from each other. There is another very unusual grip in which the club is held with the left hand below the right. Such golfers are rare but they do exist.

Groove The arc in which the golf club should follow when a shot is being executed.

Ground the club The act of placing the clubhead on the ground hitting the ball.

Gutty or Gutta ball This type of golf ball was made of gutta-percha and was first made in 1848. The surface of the ball was smooth and golfers soon discovered that the ball flew better when it had been damaged so they soon began to score the covers with improved results. The Gutta ball remained in use for some 50 years.

Half A hole is said to be halved when each side holes out in the same number of strokes. A game is halved when each side has won the same number of holes. It could be, but it is very rare, that all the holes are halved.

Half Shot In the early days of the game when golfers carried few clubs they were forced to improvise shots. One of these improvised shots was the 'half shot', a shot played with a larger club than necessary but with not the same amount of force employed as would have been employed had a full shot been played.

Handicap No golfer can enter any competition unless he or she has a handicap. Handicaps are allocated in relation to the standard of the golfer concerned who has to hand in a number of cards to his or her club so that the officials can say what handicap the player is to have in relation to the scratch score of the course.

Handicap Allowance for Match Play In singles three-quarters of the difference between the handicaps is given; in foursomes three-eights. Half strokes are counted as one, fractions smaller than halves are not counted.

Hanging Lie When the ball is lying on a downward slope of the ground usually in lush grass.

Haskell The rubber cored ball invented by a Doctor Haskell which superseded the gutta ball at the turn of this century. The Haskell was the forerunner of the golf ball which we know today.

Hazards The Rules of Golf say: Any bunker or water hazard. Bare patches, scrapes, roads, tracks and paths are not hazards. The Rules then go on to define the various kinds of hazards, and to point out that it is up to officials in charge of a course to define accurately the extent of the hazards when there is any doubt. To have an intimate knowledge of the various kinds of hazards and indeed of everything pertaining to golf, all golfers should make themselves familiar with the rules.

Head The part of the club with which the ball is struck. The head is composed of a face, a sole, a toe and a heel.

Head Up A common fault with higher handicap golfers. It is the fault of lifting the head and taking the eye off the ball before the stroke has been completed.

Hickory Before the advent of steel shafts (legalised in Britain in 1929 but used in the United States before that) golf club shafts were for the most part made of hickory. The expression 'for the most part' is used because other materials such as cane were tried but not with any great success.

Hitting across the ball When the clubhead is thrown out at the top of the swing this causes the clubhead to go into an outside arc and forces the clubhead across the ball from outside to in. The result is almost certainly a slice.

Hitting down Bringing the clubhead down on the ball before the club strikes the ground.

Hitting early When the wrists are uncocked too early when the clubhead is being brought down into the ball.

Hitting late Uncocking the wrists at the very last moment, so that when the clubhead makes contact with the ball the hands are in front.

Hole The hole which is on every green is the ultimate destination of the ball, the hole is $4\frac{1}{4}$in (10.8cm) in diameter and at least 4in (10cm) deep. The lining is usually made of metal which should be sunk at least 1in (2.5cm) below the putting surface. Hole can also relate to the entire putting surface between the teeing ground and the green.

Hole high Same as Pin High. When the ball is level with the pin or hole.

Hole in One When a golfer strikes the ball from the tee and it eventually lands in the hole on the green which is the target, the golfer is said to have accomplished a 'hole in one'. In the United States the term for the feat is an 'ace'.

Hole Out To complete the playing of a hole of golf.

Holes Up The extent of a win by one opponent over another. But the term is not now used for matches which are not continued to the very last hole as they were in the earlier days of golf. Then two players went round the whole course and the match would end level or one player could end up one or more holes up. This was usually done in team matches when the totals of each individual game were added together at the end of play thus giving the aggregates of each side.

Home Green The final green of a course. If the course is a nine hole one then the Home Green will be the 9th, if an eighteen hole course the Home Green will be the 18th.

In Play The ball is in play as soon as the player has made contact with the ball on the teeing ground. It ceases to be in play when the ball has been holed out on the green, except when it is out of bounds, lifted or lost or another ball is substituted according to local rules which are in being.

Inside to Out This expression is used to describe a swing in which the club is taken back inside the line of flight and finishes with the club-face travelling to the right before righting itself. The result is that the ball flies from right to left of the intended line of flight.

Irons Those golf clubs which form the major part of a set and which have irons made from steel as opposed to wood. This refers to fairway irons, for putters are frequently made from other materials.

There are three grips (l–r) the two-handed grip, the interlocking, and the overlapping. The most popular is the latter. No matter which grip is used, the hands should be well on top of the club. Many golfers in order to attain the correct grip, start by placing the left hand on the club and then putting the right hand on top.

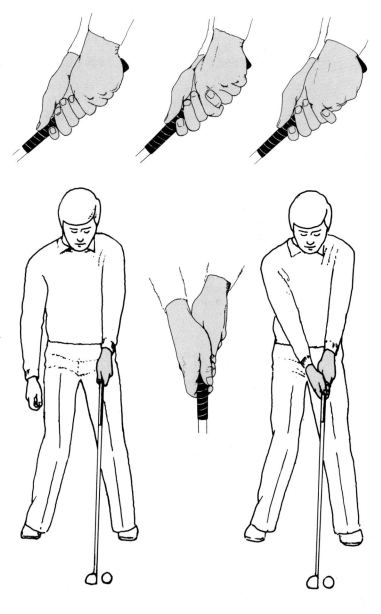

Jerk   A quick movement of the shoulders as a result of which the head moves. A bad shot invariably follows.

Jigger   This club at one time extensively used does not now form part of a golfer's armoury of clubs. It had a narrow face with a small amount of loft and could be used for a variety of shots such as recovery from the rough or little shots around the green.

Jitters   (or Yips) A player who has the 'jitters' or the 'yips' is one whose nerves have taken hold of him to such an extent that he is unable to perform a stroke satisfactorily. This state of affairs is usually most noticeable on the putting green.

Jungle   Very bad rough such as bushes or trees they are generally referred to as the 'jungle' or 'jungle country'.

Knock-out Competition   A term used to describe a Match Play competition.

Kolbe, Kolf or Kolven   All words originating in Germany or Holland (in old days known as the low countries). The words all mean 'club or game played with a club'. Their existence has been used as proof that golf originated in these countries. But golf as we know it was first played in Scotland according to most experts.

Ladies' Tee   The par of a golf course as far as ladies are concerned is measured from special tees which in most instances are placed forward of the mens' tees. The handicaps of ladies are calculated from these 'ladies' tees'.

Lag Up   Originating in the United States this term describes the action of a golfer who while trying to get the ball into the hole plays it in such a manner that he or she takes no risks of it going a long way past the hole. In other words it is playing safe.

Laminated   (wooden clubs). The heads of almost all wooden clubs are so constructed that layers of wood (usually beech and maple) are placed at right angles to the one before, thus giving a strength to the head which was not possible with materials previously used.

Lateral Water Hazard   According to the rules of golf a lateral water hazard is a water hazard or that part of a water hazard so situated that it is not possible or deemed by the Committee to be impracticable to drop a ball behind the water hazard and keep the spot at which the ball last crossed the margin of the hazard between the player and the hole.

Left Hand Below Right   (cack handed) A few self-taught golfers play with their left hand further down the shaft than the right. But such golfers are rare. However, a number of well-known players do use this method for putting, because they feel it gives them greater stability and thus greater accuracy.

Left-handed Golfers   There are large numbers throughout the world and several of them achieved great success such as the New Zealand professional, Bob Charles and the British amateur, P B Lucas. At present on the European professional circuit is a left-hander, Peter Dawson, who played for Britain in the 1977 Ryder Cup match against the United States.

Lie   (of the ball) The position of the ball when it has come to rest. The ball must be played from that lie or position unless relief is allowed under some particular rule, such as uphill lies, downhill lies, close lies etc. In no circumstances is it permitted for a golfer to improve the lie or position of the ball.

Lift and Drop   When a ball is unplayable, in other words when the player is unable to make a stroke, the ball can be lifted and dropped in accordance with the Rules of Golf. The method of dropping a ball is for the player to face the hole, stand erect and drop the ball behind him, over his shoulder. If the ball touches the player before it strikes the ground the player can redrop it without a penalty. If the ball touches the player after it has struck the ground or if it comes to rest against the player and moves when he moves there is no penalty and the ball can be played where it lies.

Like As We Lie   A term still used by club golfers indicating that the opposing sides have played the same number of strokes.

Line   The right direction the ball should travel on the putting green if it is to fall into the hole. The line to the hole might not always be the most direct one because of the various undulations which might be on the green. Such undulations must be taken into account when hitting the putt. The term 'line' can also be used for longer shots. Obviously, it would be unwise to choose a line for a shot if that line was a dangerous one. Better in such circumstances to take a 'line' which was safer.

Line of Flight   The direction in which it is intended to hit the ball.

Links   Originally golf was played in Scotland on land by the sea which was known as 'links'. The term has been used ever since, mostly to define a seaside course with its attendant sand dunes, etc., but also occasionally to describe an inland course which has, at least, some seaside characteristics. Some authorities maintain that the word 'links' was derived from an old English word meaning ridge of land. This is not generally accepted although there is some ground for thinking the word 'links' may have come from both English and Scottish sources.

Lip (of the hole) The extreme edge of the hole. When a ball stays on the edge of the hole, it is said to 'have lipped the hole'.

Local Knowledge Members of particular golf clubs who play the club's course regularly in time become familiar with the landmarks and problems of the course, and having done so put their past experiences to good use when playing. This is termed 'local knowledge'. At one time a visitor to a course claimed an extra stroke or two to counteract the local knowledge. The habit or custom has now been discontinued.

Local Rules These are supplementary to the rules of golf, and are made by the officials of a golf club to meet some special exigency present at their club and their club alone. Such rules are prominently displayed in the clubhouse.

Loft Used as a verb the word 'loft' means to hit the ball into the air usually for the purpose of overcoming a hazard. A lofted shot is also played when approaching the green even if there is no obstacle between ball and green. Used as a noun 'loft' means the angle or backward slope of the face of a golf club in relation to the shaft. The degree of loft increases with the number of the club. For instance a No 1 iron has very little loft whereas a No 9 iron has a considerable degree of loft.

Loop (in the swing) The term used to describe a swing which strays from the orthodox, but which executes a loop either inside or outside the line on either the backswing or the downswing or both. The American professionals, Gay Brewer and Miller Barber have won a great deal of prize-money even though both had a pronounced loop. Loop can also mean a number of holes which form what might be termed a circle, the player after playing the holes arriving back almost on his own tracks. The most famous 'loop' is formed by the 8th, 9th, 10th and 11th holes on the Old Course, St Andrews.

Loose Impediments These are natural objects which are not growing or which are not adhering to the ball. They include loose stones, but not stones embedded in the ground in any way. Leaves, twigs, insects or casts made by them all come under the description of 'loose impediments'. Such can be removed before playing a shot but in removing them the ball must not be disturbed. The Rules of Golf cover the subject under the heading, 'obstructions'.

Lost Ball A golf ball is deemed to have been lost if it is not found within five minutes of the player or player's caddie having started to look for it. After the five minutes have elapsed then the player whose ball has been lost has to play

another according to the Rules of Golf.

Make a Four Four golfers playing together in what is variously described as a Scotch Foursome (as in the US) or a Four Ball Foursome or Two Ball Foursome (a term sometimes used in Britain) is a popular form of golf. Sometimes at a club there may be three players, and as most consider a foursome in any form superior to a three ball game they invite someone else to 'make a four'.

Marker Can denote two entirely different facets of the game: (1) a small disc which is used to fix the spot on the green from which a ball has been lifted; and (2) a person who in important events walks round the course with competitors to register their scores. This used to be more prevalent than it is today, but markers are still used in events such as the Open Championship, at least in some countries.

Mashie Before golf clubs were numbered, they had names and the name 'mashie' was the club which corresponds to the No 5 iron of today. The name was first used because golfers on occasion cut or 'mashed' the ball. Some Scots maintain that this was not the origin of the word but that it is derived from the Scots word 'mashie', an implement used for pounding or mashing potatoes.

Mashie Niblick In the same way as the Mashie was the forerunner of the No 5 iron so does the mashie niblick correspond to the No 7 iron. In fact, it is a club between the mashie and the niblick which has a deeper face than the mashie but not so deep as the niblick.

Match The word used to describe any game of golf, but more particularly a game which is one of match play as against one in which scores are counted (medal play).

Matched Set A full set of golf clubs comprise fourteen clubs, and any player carrying more than that number is automatically disqualified. A matched set refers to a set which are all made by the same manufacturer and which are graded in relation to each other.

Matches (types of) According to the Rules of Golf recognised matches are as follows:
Single: A match in which one plays against another.
Threesome: A match in which one plays against two and each side plays one ball.
Foursome: A match in which two players play against another two players and each side plays one ball.
Three-ball: A match in which three players play against one another, each playing their own ball.
Best Ball: A match in which one player plays against the better ball of two or three others.

Match Play A form of golf in which the winner or in the case of foursomes, the winners, have won more holes than there are left to play, or if the game is level playing the 18th hole, wins or win the last hole. Another term sometimes used to describe a match-play event is a 'knockout'.

Medal Medal competitions have always been popular in golf clubs throughout the world. Usually, the medal competed for is or has been presented to the club and is held by the winner for a stated period.

Medal Play A competition which is decided by all the entrants recording their scores, the winner being the person who returns the lowest score. Medal Play competitions, (sometimes called stroke play competitions) can be over 18 holes, 36 holes or 72 holes. Medal play competitions have been a part of golf since 1744 when the Honourable Company of Edinburgh Golfers held a competition for the 'Silver Cup', the winner being the golfer who won the greatest number of holes. This is not quite the same as a medal competition but it was the first time golfers were not playing against each other in purely match play game. The St Andrews Club held a similar competition ten years later. But this type of competition was found to be complicated and unsatisfactory and in 1759 the St Andrews Club decided that in future the winner of the 'Silver Cup' would be the competitor who returned the lowest score. This is medal play as we know it today.

Medal Tee The tees on a golf course from which it is customary to play competitions. Such tees are normally further back than the ones generally used by club golfers when not playing competitions.

Merry When the ball lands on the green and runs over or when a putt goes well past the hole, some golfers describe the shot as being 'merry'

Mixed Foursome A competition in which a woman golfer and a man golfer play in partnership, each hitting the ball alternately.

Muff To duff or fluff a shot so that the result could only be described as very unsatisfactory.

Mulligan A reminder of the days when golf was less serious than it is today. In the United States a 'mulligan' is a second chance given to a player who on the first tee plays a bad shot. Naturally, such a friendly breach of the rules is allowed only in the 'friendliest' friendly games.

Municipal Course A course run by a municipality or some other public body on which anyone can play on payment of a fee. In Britain, St Andrews and Carnoustie are the best known courses of this type while in the United States

the Pebble Beach course, while not actually a public course, has no restrictions on those who can play there.

Nap Certain coarser types of grasses used on putting greens can affect the line or strength of a putt. Nap is most prominent in warm countries where there is a fast growth and the grass lies distinctly in the direction in which it has been mowed. In other words when the mower has been going from left to right the grass will lie in the opposite direction than it will when the mower has gone from right to left.

Nassau A three-in-one match popular in America. A point is awarded to the winner of the first nine holes, another on the second nine and one on the whole round of eighteen holes.

A dollar Nassau means there would be a dollar on the overall eighteen holes.

Net Score A player's score after the handicap has been deducted.

Never up, Never in One of the oldest clichés in golf. It means, as the expression suggests, that when putting if one does not hit the ball up to the hole it has no chance whatever of going in, whereas if the ball is hit boldly there is always the chance the ball will drop.

Niblick The deepest faced club which golfers carried until the time came when clubs were numbered. In the old days it was used chiefly for getting out of the rough tracks which characterised many golf courses in the early days of the game. The modern counterpart of a niblick would be one of the most lofted clubs, say the No 9 iron or the wedge.

Nine Hole Course Almost all golf courses are eighteen hole courses but there are throughout the world a number of nine hole courses, some of a high quality. Where land is at a premium it has been known to have a golf course composed of only six holes.

Nineteenth Hole (the) There are 18 holes in a round of golf and after completing them many golfers proceed to the bar, or as some will have it The Nineteenth!

Observer A person appointed to act in international matches and other important events. The duties of an 'observer' are to advise the referee if advice is needed and to note any breaches of the rules.

Old Man Par The par of the course. The great American golfer, Bobby Jones once wrote: 'I suppose that is the first round I ever played against an invisible opponent whose tangible form is the card and pencil; the toughest opponent of them all – Old Man Par'. In match play many golfers prefer not to try to match the game of their opponent but instead play against the par of the course. This for two reasons: (1) because they know that if they can equal or better par then they have a good chance of winning; and (2) that trying to forget the presence of the opponent is beneficial from a psychological point of view.

Open Stance   A player is in open stance when standing up preparatory to striking the ball the player has the left foot drawn back in relation to the line on which it is intended to hit the ball. Some golfers use the open stance for different reasons. Some consider it allows them a freer swing, others use it to counteract a tendency for them to hit the ball to the right. Other players (but only experienced ones) use it to fade the ball to the right.

Open to Shut   This fault in golf is caused by rolling the wrists to the right of the backward swing and then rolling them to the left on the downswing. The result of all this is to hit the ball along the ground to the left and usually into trouble.

Open Up the Hole   One of the great arts in golf is to make the journey from tee to green as safe as possible. It is desirable, therefore, to try to place the ball on a spot on the fairway from which there are no obstacles between the ball and the hole.

Out of Bounds   This does not mean the perimeter of the course in every instance as one might suppose. An artificial boundary or marking can be made by officials of a club or of a tournament beyond which a shot cannot be played. The player offending against the rule is penalised. It is possible in certain circumstances and on some courses such as links ones to play a shot outside the confines of the course, for example from a beach.

Out to In   The opposite to 'In to Out'. In the said situation the club is taken back outside the line of flight and as a consequence when the club is brought down to make contact with the ball it has to draw in. Such an action causes the clubhead to come across the ball causing it to veer away to the right of the intended line of flight.

Over the Green   When the ball has been hit too boldly and finishes in the ground at the back of the green causing the player to play yet another shot to get on to the putting surface.

Oxford and Cambridge Match   The annual golf match which is played between the two universities. The venues vary. The first match was played in 1887.

Pacing the Course   In important professional events the leading entrants make very careful notes of the distances of various land marks from the tee before the tournament starts. To obtain this information it is necessary for them to pace the course before the event commences.

Par   Par is the score which a first-class golfer would be expected to play to for a given hole. Par is based on yardage as recommended by various golfing bodies throughout the world. Par applies to each individual hole on a course and is based on the length of the hole only and not on the problems or difficulties of the hole. That is taken care of by the Standard Scratch Score in Britain and in other countries and by Course Rating in the United States.

Par Competition   This is a competition in which play is against a fixed score at each hole of the stipulated round or rounds. It is the same as a bogey or a Stableford competition.

Partner   A partner is a player associated with another player on the same side. The Rules of Golf's definition of the subject says: In a threesome, foursome or four-ball where the context so admits, the word 'player' shall be held to include his partner.

Penalty Stroke   A stroke which is added to a player's score for a breach of certain rules of the game of golf. A close study of the rules should be made for failure to implement them can only lead to greater penalties.

Persimmon   For a lengthy period the heads of all wooden clubs were made from this wood which came from the United States. But supplies became scarce and manufacturers were forced to find other means of making heads for the clubs. This they did by the use of laminated wood which is generally used today. During and following the days when persimmon was used other woods were experimented with but without success.

Piccolo Grip   This describes a very loose grip especially with the last two fingers of the left hand. It is a grip which was much used by the earlier British golf stars and was used presumably to give them greater flexibility at the top of the swing. On the downward swing users of the grip then tightened up their fingers. It is a grip neither to be encouraged nor made the subject of an experiment.

Pin   The same as flagstick. The pin or flagstick is placed in the hole on the putting greens to indicate to players where they must aim. According to the Rules of Golf the pin can be attended, i.e. is held or taken out of the hole when a player is putting.

Ping (putter)   A modern make of putter the head of which is so constructed as to make a 'ping' when the ball is hit.

Pin High   The ball is said to be 'pin high' when it finishes up on the green level with the hole. (The same as Hole High.)

Pipe   That part of the shaft nearest to the head of a golf club. The expression is not now generally used although some golfers who mishit the ball in such a way that it flies off that part of the club where the shaft and head are joined still exclaim: 'That's one off the pipe'.

Pitch   A shot to the green as a result of which the ball is lobbed into the air. Pitches can be played from various distances but generally are fairly short shots.

Pitch and Run   A shot much favoured by old-time golfers, but not so popular since the introduction of such clubs as the wedge. The intention of a pitch and run shot was to make the ball go up in the air a little way, land short and then run onto the pin. Such a shot required great judgement and skill.

Pitch mark   The indentation of the ground made by the ball as it lands. Pitch marks should be repaired with a knife or one of the small instruments marketed for the purpose. If such marks are not repaired then damage could be done to the greens and inconvenience caused to other golfers who might have to putt over a pitch mark.

Placing the Ball   In some countries such as Britain and some parts of the United States where temporarily during the winter some courses are wet or by reason of the weather have been damaged to some extent, golf club officials often allow players to lift the ball from a depression and place it on a good patch of grass. This is to save wear and tear on the course. This practice is of course rarely allowed in tournaments, although that has been known, as in the Colgate Women's World Championship at Sunningdale, England in 1977. This practice is also known as a 'preferred lie'.

Playing Safe   A shot made so as to avoid any hazards. It might not be a long shot but if the intention is properly carried out the ball will land in a position of safety. If more golfers played safe shots from time to time instead of trying to execute brilliant ones they would score better.

Playing Short   The instance when a golfer intentionally plays short so as to avoid some kind of hazard in order that he or she might have a less difficult next shot, and at the same time minimise the chances of being in some kind of trouble.

Playing the Like   An expression almost entirely peculiar to Britain; it indicates a stroke which for the hole will bring the score up to the level of the players' opponents.

Playing the Odd   Again an expression not universally used. It indicates that a player or his side will be playing a shot for the hole which is one more than the opponents' score. With the opponents' next score they will be playing the like, i.e. bringing the scores for the hole level once again.

Play-off   When in an important competition two or more players have tied on the same score for the first prize it is customary, in some instances at any rate, for the players to play further holes so that one outright winner can emerge. A play-off can be over a certain number of holes, usually from three upwards or it can be 'sudden death', i.e. the winner being the first to win the first hole outright. If there is no decision at the first hole then the contestants go on playing until there is an outright winner.

Play Through   By custom if a match fails to keep its place on the course and by so doing loses more than one clear hole it should allow the match following to pass through. Usually, 'playing through' is invited when some play or players in a match lose a ball and in looking for it are holding up the golfers playing behind.

Plugged Ball   A plugged ball is one which when it lands on wet or damp ground makes a small hole for itself on landing and does not move from that hole. The ball must be played where it lies except for certain exceptions which are provided for in the Rules of Golf.

Plus Handicap   A plus handicap is a handicap which is better than scratch. Instead of deducting his or her handicap from a gross score a plus golfer – of which there are few – adds his or her handicap on to the gross score.

Pot Bunker   A small round bunker or sand hazard to be found on some British seaside courses.

Practice Swing   A golfer is entitled if he or she so wishes to make a practice swing or practice swings for the purpose of 'loosening up' without having any intention of hitting the ball. Too many practice swings are, however, frowned upon because they waste time and by so doing can slow down the game, possibly causing delay to the players following behind.

Preferred Lies   This is the same as placing the ball. The manner in which the ball can be moved to a preferred lie is to lift the ball, clean it, put it down on the ground and then roll it with the clubhead to a piece of ground which will provide a reasonable lie. Preferred lies or placing the ball is allowed in countries such as Britain in winter only but on certain American courses preferred lies are in existence for the entire year.

Press There are two meanings to this golfing term. The first is to try to hit the ball much harder than is necessary. The aim of the golfer is that by trying to hit the ball harder it will go further. The reverse is very often the case. The other meaning of the term has its roots in the United States, where Nassau or wagers on a round and parts of a round are frequent. In this context press means the doubling of bets and various other connotations.

Pro-Ams Tournaments in which an amateur or amateurs form a partnership with a professional. Such tournaments are now popular in many parts of the world and often act as a pipe opener to a major event.

Professional A professional golfer is one who accepts prize-money in tournaments and who may also accept money for his services as an instructor or player or for the advertising of goods or golf equipment. There are two types of professionals: (a) those who spend their time playing in tournaments, in exhibition matches, TV matches etc; and (b) those who are based on golf clubs and whose role it is to attend to the needs of the club members by merchandising golf equipment and in teaching and playing.

Professional Golfers' Association Such associations exist in every country in which there is a sizeable number of golf professionals. The aim of such organizations is to look after the interests of professionals and to organize tournaments on their behalf. The oldest Association is the British which was formed in 1901. The Professional Golfers' Association of America was formed in 1916.

Public Golf Courses Such courses are numerous in golfing countries such as the United States and Britain. They are usually but not always controlled and owned by local authorities and are open for play to all who pay the required fee. Such courses are so popular that at some of them one is required to register for play at dawn or even before dawn.

Pull A pull is a shot which goes left of the intended line. It is not as vicious as a hook but can place those perpetrating it in just as much trouble.

Pull Cart American name for the vehicle on which clubs are placed and which is pulled round the course.

Push The opposite of pull. It is when the ball is struck to the right of the intended line of flight.

Putt The stroke used on the green, i.e. the putting surface of a golf course. However, there is nothing to debar a player using the stroke from the area surrounding the green if he so desires.

Putter The clubs used for putting. There are many varying makes and shapes of putters, but all of them have a straight face except a few which have a marginal loft. The shaft of a putter is shorter than any other club, and there are many different designs of heads. Generally the shaft is joined to one end of the putter's head or to the centre of the head. These days centre shafted putters, i.e. those which have the shaft joining the head in the centre, are the most popular.

Putting Green The closely cut area of a golf course on which the hole is situated. The expression is rarely used nowadays, instead the word 'green' is used and the term 'putting green' is used to describe the practice putting area.

Quail High This expression may have originated in Texas where there is very often a wind and it pays to keep the ball down. The great Ben Hogan writing on the subject of keeping the ball down said this: 'Quail High is the way we describe it in Texas. Keep the ball quail high and you find yourself scoring better than the player who has plenty of power but who is up in the clouds on every shot'. For the uninitiated, quails fly very low.

Quitting Quitting a shot means that the player has not played properly through the ball. This fault can manifest itself on any stroke whether played from the fairways or on the green. Without a proper follow-through only a poor stroke can result. The reason for not following through can be attributed to nervousness.

Rabbit A derogatory term used to describe a very poor golfer.

Record Score Another expression meaning the same thing as Course Record, the lowest score ever achieved on a golf course. A record score or new course record can only be made on a course in a competition. A low score made in a friendly match is disregarded for the purposes of a record.

Referee In important golf events such as a Championship or in international matches a referee accompanies all games to legislate on any questions on the Rules of Golf which arise.

Reverse Overlapping Grip This grip is used by some golfers for putting. It differs from an orthodox grip inasmuch as that instead of the little finger of the right hand overlapping the index finger of the left hand the index finger of the left hand overlaps the little finger of the right hand.

Rhythm The speed plus the smoothness which enables a player to swing the club in such a fashion that a good shot will result. In order to achieve good results a golf swing should be a one-piece affair, consequently a rhythmic, smooth swing must be employed.

Rim   The edge of the hole.

Ringer   In the United States the cumulative score based on a player's best ever score at each hole on one particular golf course over a given period of time is known as a 'Ringer Score'. In Britain it is known as an eclectic score.

Road Hole   The world famous 17th hole on the Old Course at St Andrews in Scotland which has destroyed many Championship hopes through the years.

Roll the Wrists   The act of rotating the wrists clockwise as the golf club is being taken back and anti-clockwise as the club is brought down and is following through the ball.

Rough   That part of a golf course which does not come under the heading of teeing ground, fairway, green or hazard. The grass of the rough is allowed to grow long.

Round (of golf)   A round of golf is officially played over 18 holes. If a course is a nine hole one, then another 9 should be played to complete 'the round'. To play a round means to play all the holes on the course.

Round Robin   A Round Robin tournament is one in which a number of competitors play each other, points being awarded for winning matches. Points are shared for halved matches. This form of competition is popular in the United States.

Royal & Ancient Golf Club of St Andrews   (R & A) The ruling body of the game as far as most countries of the world are concerned except the United States. The Royal & Ancient Club, which was founded in 1754, apart from being the ruling body also organises several championships including the Open Championship and the Amateur Championship (both British events).

Rubber Cored Ball   This ball, invented by Coburn Haskell from Cleveland, Ohio superseded the old solid gutta ball which had been in use for many years. Haskell's invention came into use in the United States in 1901 when the winner of the US Amateur Championship was successful with it. In the following years Sandy Herd won the Open Championship (British) at Hoylake playing the new ball which was manufactured by winding rubber yarn into a ball and covering it with gutta-percha.

Rub of the Green   Any interference with the ball when it is in play.

Rules of Amateur Status   These rules govern the activities of amateur golfers and set out certain acts which they must not indulge in if they wish to remain amateurs.

Rules of the Game of Golf   These rules drawn up by the Royal & Ancient Golf Club of St Andrews govern the game all over the world except for the United States. The first code of rules was not issued in the first instance by the R & A but by the Gentlemen Golfers of Leith in 1744. There were 13 such rules and they were adopted in 1954 by the St Andrews body and later by golfers elsewhere. Now there are many more than 13 rules but all golfers should be familiar with them.

Run   The distance the ball travels after it has landed on the ground and stopped bouncing. In dry conditions the run is likely to be considerable whereas in wet conditions the amount of distance the ball may run can be negligible.

Run Up   A shot to the green played in such a manner that the ball keeps low, being in the air only a short time before it runs along the ground towards its target. The shot is sometimes known as a pitch and run. It is the opposite of a pitch shot which has a high trajectory. For a run up shot a club with a little loft is used.

Sand Iron   An archaic term used to describe a club used for recovery shots from sand traps. Now the names given to the sand iron's successors are blaster and wedge.

Sandtrap   Bunkers in Britain but sandtraps in the United States and other countries. Bunkers in Britain were originally hollows, the grass of which had been removed by the constant playing of shots from them. In place of the grass there remained only sand, the courses being links ones. But sandtraps differ from those early bunkers because they are man-made.

Schenectady Putter   The original centre shafted putter. Such putters were in use in the United States from about 1903 onwards but were banned in Britain until 1952.

Sclaff   A Scots word meaning to slap. In golf, a stroke in which the sole of the club strikes the ground before making contact with the ball. The word is now almost entirely confined to Scottish golfers.

Score   The number of strokes a golfer has taken during a round of golf.

Score card   In a competition a player's score is required to be recorded, i.e. if the competition is by medal or stroke play. The means of recording such scores is by a score card. Score cards were first used in the Open Championship in Britain as long ago as 1865. Before the start of a round in a stroke play competition the players exchanged cards, each score being recorded by the opponent. At the end of the round the score is added up and signed by the players concerned, the marker who recorded the score and the person whose score it is. A player is responsible for ensuring that the score has been recorded correctly. Penalty for a wrongly marked card is disqualification.

Scotch Foursome   The term used in the United States to describe foursomes, presumably because the two ball game was first played by Scotsmen.

Scratch   A player who is scratch receives no handicap because of his ability to play round a course in a score which equals that set by the official body responsible. All handicapping in golf is related to a scratch score which in general terms may be said to be a perfect score or one which can be achieved by a first-class golfer. A scratch golfer gives strokes to all players with a higher handicap and receives strokes only from those with a plus handicap, of which there are few.

Secretary   The man/woman who in Britain and other countries is in charge of the day to day running of a golf club. In the United States this is generally done by a manager who is in full charge.

Seeding   Placing those who are likely winners of a match play event through the draw so that theoretically they will not meet until the later stages. But in practice seeded players are quite often beaten by unseeded players in early rounds.

Semi-rough   That part of the course lying between the fairways and the rough where the grass is cut back to some extent – hence the name 'semi-rough'.

Set (of clubs)   The full complement of clubs which are allowed to be carried during a round of golf, i.e. 14 clubs. A matched set indicates that the clubs are by the same maker and are of the same design. The rule setting the limit of golf clubs to 14 was published by the United States Golf Association in 1938 and by the Royal & Ancient Club of St Andrews some 18 months later. Previously golfers in the United States and Britain were allowed to carry any number of clubs and some of the leading professionals of the day did in fact use a great many, carried for them by their respective caddies.

Shanking   This, one of the worst faults in golf, is when the ball is hit with that part of the club at which the shaft joins the head. The result is that the ball flies off at a sharp angle to the right. Also known as socketing.

Short   When the ball falls short of the target.

Short Game   That part of the game played in the vicinity of the green. It includes pitching, chipping, playing from bunkers near the green and also putting.

Short Set   Some golf club manufacturers produce a matched set of perhaps seven clubs so that beginners can start the game without undue expense. Very often the set can be added to once the owner becomes more proficient in the game, until eventually there are 14 clubs. Other short sets are a complete range in themselves and cannot be matched up with other clubs at a later date.

Shutting the Face   Sometimes also described as 'hooding the face'. When the loft of the club is made less by having the ball much further back towards the right foot than it would be normally for a shot with that particular club. With the ball so far back the hands are then forced forward towards the intended line of flight. The shot is sometimes employed when playing from a difficult lie, i.e. when perhaps a high shot might well catch the branches of a tree.

Single   A match between two golfers.

Skying the Ball   To sky the ball is to send it straight up in the air. Such shots are almost always played with the wooden clubs.

Slice   According to *Chambers Twentieth Century Dictionary* the definition of a slice is as follows: 'To strike or play so as to send the ball curving to the right (left in left hand play)'.

Slow Play   To fail to keep one's proper place on a golf course is to indulge in slow play. If golfers for some reason or another are forcing the players behind to wait they should invite those behind to proceed through. Generally, falling one hole behind those playing in front constitutes slow play.

Socketing   The same as shanking, i.e. to hit the ball with that part of the club where the shaft joins the head. The result is that the ball veers off sharply to the right (left for left handed players).

Sole   The part of the clubhead which is on the ground when the ball is being addressed.

Spade Mashie   The old name for a deep faced club used for bunker play before the advent of more specialized clubs.

Spoon   The club which used to be known as a spoon is equivalent to a No 3 or No 4 wood. The club is generally used from a close lie on the fairway or for a long shot to the green.

Square   When a match is level either at any point during it or at the end of it. The same as 'all square'.

220

Square Stance When both feet are parallel to the intended flight of the ball.

Stableford A popular method of point scoring invented by a Dr Stableford, and much favoured in Britain. It is a form of scoring points against bogey at each hole instead of counting the holes up or down in relation to bogey. The method of scoring is as follows:

For a hole done in one over the fixed score   1 point
For a hole done in the fixed score   2 points
For a hole done in one under the fixed score   3 points
For a hole done in two under the fixed score   4 points
For a hole done in three under the fixed score   5 points

Stance The placing of the feet prior to making a stroke. Generally speaking there are three types of stance: Open, closed or square. The word 'stance' can also be used to describe the position the feet will have to take up when playing shots made unusual because of the undulations of the ground, i.e. uphill stance or downhill stance.

Standard Scratch Score A term used in Britain and in many other countries. It is in fact the score in which a scratch golfer is expected to go round a course playing from the medal or competition tees in summer conditions. It is the guideline of the course. Same as 'course value'.

Staying Down (on the ball) Keeping the head down during the playing of the shot thus enabling the hands to go through and upwards after the ball has been struck.

Steamy A colloquial word used sometimes in Britain to describe a shot which sends the ball past the target. It is used as a rule to describe a putt which is too bold.

Steel Shafts For very many years the shafts of golf clubs were made from hickory. Steel shafts were first used in the United States in 1924 but they were not legalised in Britain until 1929. Many years before iron and steel shafted clubs had been made in Britain but were immediately banned by the Royal & Ancient Golf Club of St Andrews.

Stroke This word has two different meanings in golf: (1) the act of hitting the ball; and (2) that which a player of a higher handicap receives from a player of a lower handicap at certain holes during the round. It may be that the difference in the players' handicaps is so slight that the higher handicap player receives only one stroke in the entire round.

Stroke Hole The hole or holes at which the higher handicap players receive a stroke from the lower handicap player.

Stroke Index The chart usually on the score cards issued by a club which indicates at which holes players receive a stroke if they are so entitled.

Stroke Play The form of golf in which the results of a competition or tournament are determined by the number of strokes taken

If a good shot is to be played, a golfer must have a comfortable and correct stance. Many advocate that for wooden clubs the ball should be opposite the left heel; for middle range shots it should be centrally placed between the two feet; and for short shots it should be located towards the right foot.

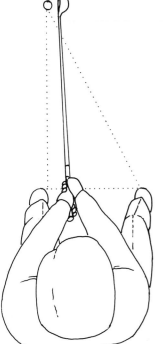
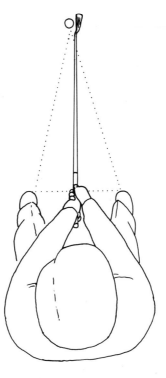
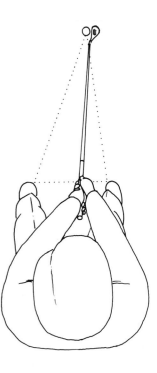

during the round. Same as medal play.

Strong When a shot is played too boldly and the ball finishes past the target. The expression is used in describing shots to the green and also for putts.

Style The way in which a golfer looks when playing. Although the ardent desire of all golfers is to repeat the same shot every time until it becomes purely mechanical, many golfers have a style which is individual and peculiar to themselves. A good style means that the golfer has more chance of repeating the stroke time and again and also will have less trouble in putting things right following any problems which may have arisen.

Stymie For many years golf was a game in which the keynote was playing the ball as it lay. This applied anywhere on the course, including the greens. This meant that on some occasions one ball lay directly between the hole and another ball. The ball further away from the hole had to be played first. Eventually this was thought to be unfair in match play competitions and it was abolished both in the United States and in Britain in 1951. The incident which had much bearing on making the decision happened at Hunstanton, England in 1951 when in the final of the English Amateur Championship the eventual winner laid his opponent a stymie at the 39th hole to take the title.

Sucker The description used when a ball has landed in wet ground and is embedded in the ground. 'Plugged ball' is also used to describe the same situation but more often describes the situation when a ball has landed in a bunker or sandtrap and is embedded in wet sand.

Sudden Death If a tournament has ended in one or more players tying a play-off is employed to find one outright winner. This often takes the form of a 'sudden death' play off. The first player to win a hole outright is declared the winner.

Sunningdale System (of handicapping) This system was first introduced at Sunningdale Golf Club in England and has never become popular with golfers. The method of scoring and handicapping employed is as follows: If a player becomes two holes down during a match his opponent gives him a stroke at the next hole; if the opponent wins the hole he or she receives another stroke; if the receiver of the stroke wins the hole they play the next one level; if the giver of the stroke wins he or she gives another stroke at the next hole etc. Perhaps it is because it sounds complicated that the system has had little or no recognition from golfers in general.

Sway The lateral movement of a golfer when playing a shot. It means that the head, shoulders or body have had to be moved back in a lateral movement because the weight has been moved to the right foot on the backswing. Having got into this position it is necessary for the golfer concerned to move back into the shot. The results of all this movement can often be disastrous.

Sweetspot Every golf club has a 'sweetspot' on its hitting surface. The sweetspot is almost always in the centre of the clubface because of the design of the clubhead and is in fact the spot where the strength of the clubhead is concentrated.

Swing The sweep of the golf club as the player takes it back to strike the ball and after doing so completes the arc by pushing the clubhead through and upwards. If that is done the result could be satisfactory, but a break in the swing, i.e. stopping the club immediately after striking the ball, would almost certainly result in a bad shot. Golfers are said to have either a 'good swing' or a 'bad swing'.

A great golf teacher, Ernest Jones once said, 'Golf is a simple game, its the people who play it who make it difficult.' The basic principle of the swing is to take the club as far back as possible and then push it upwards keeping the left arm straight. The swing should be in one movement with the aim being to bring the clubhead down at a speed which increases as the ball is struck. After impact, the hands should be pushed through and upwards.

During the swing there should be no swaying of the body; the power is generated by the hands and by the action of the legs, on both the upswing and the downswing.

Swing Weight In the old days of golf craftsmen made golf clubs by instinct and judged the result by 'feel'. Now manufacturers obtain the correct balance of a club by scientific means, and 'swing weight' is one of the tests applied to clubs when they are being manufactured to ensure the constancy of weight and balance of the clubs. The swing weight test also ensures that the shafts are related to all the heads which go to make up the complete set.

Takeaway Taking the club away from the ball at the commencement of the backswing. The takeaway refers to the first few inches of the backswing only.

Take Turf Good golfers, when they play an iron shot from the fairway, strike the ball first and then the club continues its downward movement momentarily and in so doing slices out a piece of turf. Not-so-good golfers rarely 'take turf' as they are not connecting with the ball correctly.

Tee The tee is the area from which a golfer strikes the ball at the start of a hole. It was originally known as the teeing ground, but through the years has been shortened to 'tee'. Markers denote from which point the drive can be made. It is not permissible to be in front of these markers or more than two club lengths behind them.

Teeing Up the Ball The act of placing the ball on the tee peg. Before tee pegs came into being golfers used a small quantity of damp sand from a box provided in order to make a small heap or pile on which to place the ball.

Tee Pegs These aids to golf were in general use by the '20s. Then they were made of wood,

having a small cup at one end to support the ball and the other end being pointed to enable it to be pushed into the ground without effort. Now most tee pegs are made of synthetic material. Tee pegs are not always used for short holes when iron clubs are employed, many golfers merely throwing the ball on the ground and allow for the loft of the club to get it away into the air.

Tempo No good golf swing can be achieved unless the club is swung at the proper tempo. If a proper tempo is maintained then the swing will have rhythm and also correct timing, i.e. hitting the ball when the clubhead is moving at maximum speed.

Texas Wedge An American term to describe a stroke with a putter made from off the putting surface or green. The name is said to have originated in Texas, but shots played with a putter have for long been in the repertoire of strokes made by golfers in Scotland and elsewhere. In fact in the early days of golf in Scotland it was known as the 'Musselburgh iron' being played by golfers who came from Musselburgh, a town which lies between Edinburgh and the golf courses of the Lothians such as Muirfield, North Berwick etc.

Thin A shot played with the bottom of the clubface. The result is the ball gains little height and as a rule flies past the target.

Threesome A term not much used. The more popular name is a Three Ball match.

Tie A match which has ended level after all the scheduled holes of the match have been completed.

Tiger A golfer of great ability; a scratch or low handicap player.

Tiger Country The name given to heavy rough. Presumably the name was given not because golfing tigers are prone to visit it but because it resembles jungle, the habitat of tigers. Certainly it is more likely that golfers less skilled than first-class players will tend to send their golf balls into 'Tiger Country'.

Timing No good golf shot can be played without good timing which entails bringing the clubhead into the ball at maximum possible speed. Timing is a combination of mental concentration and physical application working in harmony.

Top To hit the ball on the top or towards the top. The result is that it scurries along the ground.

Topspin When the ball is hit correctly by one of the wooden clubs it rotates forward during the course of its flight. When it lands it retains the forward rotating characteristic and so runs further along the ground than it would have done if it had not had topspin.

Torsion All golf clubs have a degree of torsion or bend during a stroke. Some golfers might describe torsion by saying the shafts are whippy. In fact, torsion is brought about by the shaft twisting or fighting against the clubhead.

Tradesman's Entrance An expression used in Britain mostly by older golfers when the ball runs round the hole and drops in from the back.

Trajectory (of the ball) The flight of the golf ball through the air. Different methods of playing the stroke decide whether or not the ball flies off on a high trajectory or a low trajectory.

Trap In Britain a bunker, in the US and in some other countries a trap or sandtrap.

Trolley In Britain known also as a caddie-car and in the United States a pull cart. A trolley has two wheels and is so constructed as to be able to carry a golfer's clubs. There are many different makes, the latest having wide wheels which do not damage a soft course in the winter. A trolley is pulled either by the player or by someone pulling it for him, sometimes a caddie, sometimes a friend. Trolleys were first used in the Twenties but took some time before becoming popular. They were the forerunner of the buggies now so popular in the United States and other countries. Buggies are power driven and usually carry two or four players and their clubs.

Twitch When a golfer has the twitch it means that he or she has become so affected by nerves that the hands cannot be controlled as they should be and the result is a quick jab at the ball which more often than not misses the hole.

Up A player is 'up' when in a match he has won more holes than his opponent. 'Up' can also be used to describe a putt which is level with or past the hole.

Upright A player has an 'upright stance' when he stands very erect when addressing the ball. It is sometimes said that he is 'upright'.

Upright Swing An upright swing is popular nowadays especially with some of the leading American golfers. The method they employ is to take the club back from the ball only a little way and then lift the clubhead up. Those who use such a method maintain that it is easier to generate speed on the downswing by taking the clubhead up quickly. Another school of thought, to which devotees of the wide arc method belong, say that only a wide arc can give a smooth swing. Generally an upright swing will bring better results to tall and strong golfers.

Waggle The backwards and forward movement of the hands and the clubhead before making a stroke. The purpose of the 'waggle' is to enable the player to get comfortably set before attempting to hit the ball. The movement also starts to generate power which is necessary, certainly for long shots.

Water Hazards According to the Rules of Golf a water hazard is any sea, lake, pond, river, ditch, surface draining ditch or other open water course (regardless of whether it contains water) and anything of a similar nature. All ground or water within the margin of a water hazard, whether or not it be covered with any growing substance, is part of the water hazard. The margin of a water hazard is deemed to extend vertically upwards. There is also such a thing as a lateral water hazard which is a water hazard or part of a water hazard running approximately to the line of play. Because of this there is a special rule concerning the dropping of the ball after it has been retrieved from the water. A water hazard or that part of the water hazard which is to be played as a lateral hazard should be distinctively marked.

Wedge The wedge was added to the battery of golf clubs in 1932. It is a deep faced club with a flanged sole the purpose of which is to remove the ball from sand traps and other hazards. Proficient golfers also use the wedge to play high shots to the green because its weight and its flanged sole enable the ball to stop immediately or almost immediately on landing. The wedge has a high degree of loft and is heavier than the most lofted club in the normal range of clubs, i.e. the No 9 iron.

Whipping The wax thread once universally used for binding a golf club at the point the shaft is joined to the head. Whipping is still used but not so frequently now as it was before the advent of synthetic materials now generally used to make what is called the hozel.

Whippy Used to describe a high degree of tension in a golf club shaft.

Winter Rules In countries in which it is necessary to protect golf courses from damage in wet weather, club officials bring into being what are called 'winter rules'. These rules permit golfers to lift from one spot on the course to another. Normally Winter Rules permit a player to lift the ball, clean it, and then roll it with the clubhead to a good piece of ground as near the original lie as possible. Apart from protecting the course and playing from a lie where the ball is lying in very soft ground, winter rules also enable a satisfactory golf shot to be played.

Yips A player suffering from nerves or nervous tension usually while putting is said to have 'the yips'.

facts and figures

HARRY VARDON

THE PROFESSIONAL GOLFERS' ASSOCIATION
'HARRY VARDON'
MEMORIAL TROPHY
·1937·

The Amateur International The Amateur international was first played in 1902, and was only an encounter between England and Scotland. Some thirty years later Ireland and Wales joined in to make it a four country competition.

Argentine Amateur Championship An old event, this Championship began in 1895, after British enthusiasts took the game to Argentina.

Argentine Ladies' Championship This Championship founded in 1894 is one year older than the country's Amateur Championship. British born players dominated the event for many years.

Australian Amateur Championship First played in 1906 this event was won by the famous British golfer, the Hon Michael Scott three times in the first five years.

Australian Ladies' Championship This Championship goes back to last century; it was first played in 1894.

Australian Open Championship The Hon Michael Scott was the first winner of the Australian Open Championship which was first played in 1904. It is now one of the world's major events with prize-money increasing year by year.

AUSTRALIAN OPEN CHAMPIONSHIP

Winners since 1946

	Winner	Club/Country	Venue	Score
1946	**H O Pickworth**	Manly	Royal Adelaide	289
1947	**H O Pickworth**	Victoria	Brisbane	285
1948	**H O Pickworth**	Royal Melbourne	Melbourne	289
1949	**E Cremin**	Unattached	Australian	287
1950	**N G Von Nida**	Sydney	Kooyonga	286
1951	**P W Thomson**	Riversdale	Metropolitan	283
1952	**N G Von Nida**	Royal Sidney	Lake Karrinyup	278
1953	**N G Von Nida**	New South Wales	Melbourne	278
1954	**H O Pickworth**	Royal Melbourne	Kooyonga	280
1955	**A D Locke**	South Africa	Gailes	290
1956	**B Crampton**	Sydney	Royal Sydney	289
1957	**F Phillips**	Sydney	Melbourne	287
1958	**Gary Player**	South Africa	Adelaide	271
1959	**K Nagle**	Unattached	Australian	284
1960	**Bruce Devlin**	The Lakes	Lake Karrinyup	282
1961	**F Phillips**	Pymble	Victoria	275
1962	**Gary Player**	South Africa	Royal Adelaide	281
1963	**Gary Player**	South Africa	Royal Melbourne	278
1964	**J Nicklaus**	USA	The Lakes	287
1965	**Gary Player**	South Africa	Kooyonga	264
1966	**Arnold Palmer**	USA	Royal Queensland	276
1967	**P W Thomson**	Australia	Commonwealth	281
1968	**J Nicklaus**	USA	Lake Karrinyup	270
1969	**Gary Player**	South Africa	Royal Sydney	288
1970	**Gary Player**	South Africa	Melbourne	280
1971	**J Nicklaus**	USA	Royal Hobart	269
1972	**P W Thomson**	Australia	Kooyonga	281
1973	**J C Snead**	USA	Royal Queensland	280
1974	**Gary Player**	South Africa	Lake Karrinyup	277
1975	**J Nicklaus**	USA	Australian	279
1976	**J Nicklaus**	USA	Australian	286
1977	**D Graham**	Australia	Australian	284

British Amateur Championship It was inaugurated by the Royal Liverpool Club in 1885 and played at Hoylake. Almost immediately it was taken over by the Royal & Ancient Golf Club and has been administered by that body ever since. It has always attracted a huge international field with a particularly strong entry from the US. Many of the world's greatest amateur golfers have won the event, including the legendary Robert Jones, Jr. The British amateur, John Ball won the Championship eight times. It has always been a match play event.

BRITISH AMATEUR CHAMPIONSHIP

Above: The British Amateur Championship Trophy.

	Winner	Runner-up	Venue	Score	No of Competitors
1885	**A F MacFie**	H G Hutchinson	Hoylake	7 and 6	44
1886	**H G Hutchinson**	Henry Lamb	St Andrews	7 and 6	42
1887	**H G Hutchinson**	John Ball	Hoylake	1 hole	33
1888	**John Ball**	J E Laidlay	Prestwick	5 and 4	38
1889	**J E Laidlay**	L M B Melville	St Andrews	2 and 1	40
1890	**John Ball**	J E Laidlay	Hoylake	4 and 3	44
1891	**J E Laidlay**	H H Hilton	St Andrews	20th hole	50
1892	**John Ball**	H H Hilton	Sandwich	3 and 1	45
1893	**Peter Anderson**	J E Laidlay	Prestwick	1 hole	44
1894	**John Ball**	S M Fergusson	Hoylake	1 hole	64
1895	**L M B Melville**	John Ball	St Andrews	19th hole	68
1896	**F G Tait**	H H Hilton	Sandwich	8 and 7	64
	(36 holes played on and after this date)				
1897	**A J T Allan**	James Robb	Muirfield	4 and 2	74
1898	**F G Tait**	S M Fergusson	Hoylake	7 and 5	77
1899	**John Ball**	F G Tait	Prestwick	37th hole	101
1900	**H H Hilton**	James Robb	Sandwich	8 and 7	68
1901	**H H Hilton**	J L Low	St Andrews	1 hole	116
1902	**C Hutchings**	S H Fry	Hoylake	1 hole	114
1903	**R Maxwell**	H G Hutchinson	Muirfield	7 and 5	142
1904	**W J Travis** (USA)	Ed Blackwell	Sandwich	4 and 3	104
1905	**A G Barry**	Hon O Scott	Prestwick	3 and 2	148
1906	**James Robb**	C C Lingen	Hoylake	4 and 3	166
1907	**John Ball**	C A Palmer	St Andrews	6 and 4	200
1908	**E A Lassen**	H E Taylor	Sandwich	7 and 6	197
1909	**R Maxwell**	Capt C K Hutchinson	Muirfield	1 hole	170
1910	**John Ball**	C Aylmer	Hoylake	10 and 9	160
1911	**H H Hilton**	E A Lassen	Prestwick	4 and 3	146
1912	**John Ball**	Abe Mitchell	Westward Ho!	38th hole	134
1913	**H H Hilton**	R Harris	St Andrews	6 and 5	198
1914	**J L C Jenkins**	C O Hezlet	Sandwich	3 and 2	232
1915–19	No Championship owing to the Great War				
1920	**C J H Tolley**	R A Gardner (USA)	Muirfield	37th hole	165
1921	**W I Hunter**	A J Graham	Hoylake	12 and 11	223
1922	**E W E Holderness**	J Craven	Prestwick	1 hole	252
1923	**R H Wethered**	R Harris	Deal	7 and 6	209
1924	**E W E Holderness**	E F Storey	St Andrews	3 and 2	201
1925	**Robert Harris**	K F Fradgley	Westward Ho!	13 and 12	151
1926	**Jesse Sweetser** (USA)	A F Simpson	Muirfield	6 and 5	216
1927	**Dr W Tweddell**	D E Landale	Hoylake	7 and 6	197
1928	**T P Perkins**	R H Wethered	Prestwick	6 and 4	220
1929	**C J H Tolley**	J N Smith	Sandwich	4 and 3	253
1930	**R T Jones** (USA)	R H Wethered	St Andrews	7 and 6	271
1931	**E Martin Smith**	J De Forest	Westward Ho!	1 hole	171
1932	**J De Forest**	E W Fiddian	Muirfield	3 and 1	235
1933	**Hon M Scott**	T A Bourn	Hoylake	4 and 3	269
1934	**W Lawson Little** (USA)	J Wallace	Prestwick	14 and 13	225
1935	**W Lawson Little** (USA)	Dr W Tweddell	Royal Lytham and St Annes	1 hole	232
1936	**H Thomson**	J Ferrier (AUS)	St Andrews	2 holes	283
1937	**R Sweeney, Jr** (USA)	L O Munn	Sandwich	3 and 2	223
1938	**C R Yates** (USA)	R C Ewing	Troon	3 and 2	241
1939	**A T Kyle**	A A Duncan	Hoylake	2 and 1	167
1940–45	Suspended during World War II				
1946	**J Bruen**	R Sweeney (USA)	Birkdale	4 and 3	263
1947	**W P Turnesa** (USA)	R D Chapman (USA)	Carnoustie	3 and 2	200
1948	**F R Stranahan** (USA)	C Stowe	Sandwich	5 and 4	168
1949	**S M McCready**	W P Turnesa (USA)	Portmarnock	2 and 1	204
1950	**F R Stranahan** (USA)	R D Chapman (USA)	St Andrews	8 and 6	324
1951	**R D Chapman** (USA)	C R Coe (USA)	Porthcawl	5 and 4	192
1952	**E H Ward** (USA)	F R Stranahan (USA)	Prestwick	6 and 5	286
1953	**J B Carr**	E Harvie Ward (USA)	Hoylake	2 holes	279
1954	**D W Bachli** (AUS)	W C Campbell (USA)	Muirfield	2 and 1	286

1955	**J W Conrad** (USA)	A Slater	Royal Lytham		
			and St Annes	3 and 2	240
1956	**J C Beharrel**	L G Taylor	Troon	5 and 4	200
1957	**R Reid Jack**	H B Ridgley (USA)	Formby	2 and 1	200

(In 1956 and 1957 the Quarter Finals, Semi Finals and Final were played over 36 holes)

| 1958 | **J B Carr** | A Thirlwell | St Andrews | 3 and 2 | 488 |

(In 1958, Semi-Finals and Final only were played over 36 holes)

1959	**D R Beman** (USA)	W Hyndman (USA)	Sandwich	3 and 2	362
1960	**J B Carr**	R Cochran (USA)	Portrush	8 and 7	183
1961	**M F Bonallack**	J Walker	Turnberry	6 and 4	250
1962	**R D Davies** (USA)	J Povall	Hoylake	1 hole	256
1963	**M S R Lunt**	J G Blackwell	St Andrews	2 and 1	256
1964	**Gordon J Clark**	M S R Lunt	Ganton	39th hole	220
1965	**M F Bonallack**	C A Clark	Porthcawl	2 and 1	176
1966	**R E Cole** (S Africa)	R D Shade	Carnoustie	3 and 2	206
1967	**R B Dickson** (USA)	R J Cerrudo (USA)	Formby	2 and 1	
1968	**M F Bonallack**	J B Carr	Troon	7 and 6	249
1969	**M F Bonallack**	W Hyndman (USA)	Hoylake	3 and 2	245
1970	**M F Bonallack**	W Hyndman (USA)	Newcastle Co		
			Down	8 and 7	256
1971	**S Melnyck** (USA)	J Simons (USA)	Carnoustie	3 and 2	256
1972	**T Homer**	A Thirlwell	Royal St George's	4 and 3	253
1973	**R Siderowf** (USA)	P H Moody	Royal Porthcawl	5 and 3	222
1974	**T Homer**	J Gabrielsen (USA)	Muirfield	2 holes	330
1975	**M M Giles** (USA)	M H James	Hoylake	8 and 7	206
1976	**R Siderowf** (USA)	J C Davies	St Andrews	37th hole	289
1977	**P McEvoy**	H M Campbell	Ganton	5 and 4	234

British Ladies' Championship This event was first played in 1893, the same year that the Ladies' Golf Union was formed. The venue was Lytham and 38 ladies were brave enough to enter. The winner was Lady Margaret Scott who beat the lady mostly responsible for starting the Championship, Miss Isette Pearson. Lady Margaret Scott won the Championship three years in succession. Only two other players have equalled Lady Margaret Scott's feat so far, Miss Cecil Leitch and Miss Enid Wilson. The greatest British woman player, Lady Heathcoat Amory (Miss J Wethered), won the title four times.

BRITISH LADIES' CHAMPIONSHIP

	Winner	*Runner-up*	*Venue*	*Score*
1893	**Lady Margaret Scott**	Miss Isette Pearson	St Annes	7 and 5
1894	**Lady Margaret Scott**	Miss Isette Pearson	Littlestone	3 and 2
1895	**Lady Margaret Scott**	Miss E Lythgoe	Portrush	5 and 4
1896	**Miss Pascoe**	Miss L Thomson	Hoylake	3 and 2
1897	**Miss E C Orr**	Miss Orr	Gullane	4 and 2
1898	**Miss L Thomson**	Miss E C Neville	Yarmouth	7 and 5
1899	**Miss M Hezlet**	Miss Magill	Newcastle Co	
			Down	2 and 1
1900	**Miss Adair**	Miss Neville	Westward Ho!	6 and 5
1901	**Miss Graham**	Miss Adair	Aberdovey	3 and 1
1902	**Miss M Hezlet**	Miss E Neville	Deal	19th hole
1903	**Miss Adair**	Miss F Walker-Leigh	Portrush	4 and 3
1904	**Miss L Dod**	Miss M Hezlet	Troon	1 hole
1905	**Miss B Thompson**	Miss M E Stuart	Cromer	3 and 2
1906	**Mrs Kennion**	Miss B Thompson	Burnham	4 and 3
1907	**Miss M Hezlet**	Miss F Hezlet	Newcastle Co	
			Down	2 and 1
1908	**Miss M Titterton**	Miss D Campbell	St Andrews	19th hole
1909	**Miss D Campbell**	Miss F Hezlet	Birkdale	4 and 3
1910	**Miss Grant Suttie**	Miss L Moore	Westward Ho!	6 and 4
1911	**Miss D Campbell**	Miss V Hezlet	Portrush	3 and 2
1912	**Miss G Ravenscroft**	Miss S Temple	Turnberry	3 and 2

(Final played over 36 holes after 1912)

| 1913 | **Miss M Dodd** | Miss Chubb | St Annes | 8 and 6 |
| 1914 | **Miss C Leitch** | Miss G Ravenscroft | Hunstanton | 2 and 1 |

1915–18 No Championship owing to Great War.
1919 Should have been played at Burnham in October, but abandoned owing to Railway Strike.

1920	**Miss C Leitch**	Miss M Griffiths	Newcastle Co Down	7 and 6
1921	**Miss C Leitch**	Miss J Wethered	Turnberry	4 and 3
1922	**Miss J Wethered**	Miss C Leitch	Princes	9 and 7
1923	**Miss D Chambers**	Miss A Macbeth	Burnham	2 holes
1924	**Miss J Wethered**	Mrs Cautley	Portrush	7 and 6
1925	**Miss J Wethered**	Miss C Leitch	Troon	37th hole
1926	**Miss C Leitch**	Mrs Garon	Harlech	8 and 7
1927	**Miss Thion de la Chaume** (France)	Miss Pearson	Newcastle Co Down	5 and 4
1928	**Miss Nanette Le Blan** (France)	Miss S Marshall	Hunstanton	3 and 2
1929	**Miss J Wethered**	Miss G Collett (USA)	St Andrews	3 and 1
1930	**Miss D Fishwick**	Miss G Collett (USA)	Formby	4 and 3
1931	**Miss E Wilson**	Miss W Morgan	Portmarnock	7 and 6
1932	**Miss E Wilson**	Miss C P R Montgomery	Saunton	7 and 6
1933	**Miss E Wilson**	Miss D Plumpton	Gleneagles	5 and 4
1934	**Mrs A M Holm**	Miss P Barton	Royal Porthcawl	6 and 5
1935	**Miss W Morgan**	Miss P Barton	Newcastle Co Down	3 and 2
1936	**Miss P Barton**	Miss B Newell	Southport	5 and 3
1937	**Miss J Anderson**	Miss D Park	Turnberry	6 and 4
1938	**Mrs A M Holm**	Miss E Corlett	Burnham	4 and 3
1939	**Miss P Barton**	Mrs T Marks	Portrush	2 and 1
1946	**Mrs G Hetherington**	Miss P Garvey	Hunstanton	1 hole
1947	**Mrs G Zaharias** (USA)	Miss J Gordon	Gullane	5 and 4
1948	**Miss Louise Suggs** (USA)	Miss J Donald	Royal Lytham	1 hole
1949	**Miss Frances Stephens**	Mrs Val Reddan	Harlech	5 and 4
1950	**Vicomtesse de Saint Sauveur** (France)	Mrs G Valentine	Newcastle Co Down	3 and 2
1951	**Mrs P G MacCann**	Miss Frances Stephens	Broadstone	4 and 3
1952	**Miss Moira Paterson**	Miss Frances Stephens	Troon	39th hole
1953	**Miss Marlene Stewart**	Miss P Garvey	Porthcawl	7 and 6
1954	**Miss Frances Stephens**	Miss E Price	Ganton	4 and 3
1955	**Mrs G Valentine**	Miss B Romack (USA)	Portrush	7 and 6
1956	**Miss Margaret Smith**	Miss M P Janssen	Sunningdale	8 and 7
1957	**Miss P Garvey**	Mrs G Valentine	Gleneagles	4 and 3
1958	**Mrs G Valentine**	Miss E Price	Hunstanton	1 hole
1959	**Miss E Price**	Miss B McCorkindale	Berkshire	37th hole
1960	**Miss B McIntyre**	Miss P Garvey	Harlech	4 and 2
1961	**Mrs A D Spearman**	Miss D J Robb	Carnoustie	7 and 6
1962	**Mrs A D Spearman**	Mrs M F Bonallack	Royal Birkdale	1 hole
1963	**Miss B Varangot** (France)	Miss P Garvey	Newcastle Co Down	3 and 1
1964	**Miss C Sorenson** (USA)	Miss B Jackson	Princes	37th hole
1965	**Miss B Varangot** (France)	Mrs I Robertson	St Andrews	4 and 3
1966	**Miss E Chadwick**	Miss V Saunders	Ganton	3 and 2
1967	**Miss E Chadwick**	Miss M Everard	Harlech	1 hole
1968	**Miss B Varangot** (France)	Mrs C Rubin (France)	Walton Heath	20th hole
1969	**Miss C Lacoste** (France)	Miss A Irvin	Portrush	1 hole
1970	**Miss D Oxley**	Mrs I Robertson	Gullane	1 hole
1971	**Miss Michelle Walker**	Miss B Huke	Alwoodley	3 and 1
1972	**Miss Michelle Walker**	Mrs C Rubin (France)	Hunstanton	2 holes
1973	**Miss A Irvin**	Miss Michelle Walker	Carnoustie	3 and 2
1974	**Miss C Semple** (USA)	Mrs A Bonallack	Royal Porthcawl	2 and 1
1975	**Mrs N Syms** (USA)	Miss S Cadden	St Andrews	3 and 2
1976	**Miss C Panton**	Miss A Sheard	Silloth	1 hole
1977	**Mrs A Uzielli**	Miss V Marvin	Hillside	6 and 5

BRITISH OPEN CHAMPIONSHIP

British Open Championship The Prestwick Club in Scotland had as its greenkeeper the famous St Andrews golfer, Tom Morris, and the club, proud of his success as a match player, decided in 1860 to hold an open competition for which it offered £5 in prize-money. Obviously the Club hoped that Morris would win and thus bring further fame to the Club. Their hopes were dashed, for the man to come out on top of the eight entrants was not Tom Morris but the Musselburgh golfer, Willie Park, who took the first prize – which as well as the cash included a Silver Belt, which the winner was to keep if he won it three years in succession. Park did not win the following year, for this time Tom Morris did win.

In 1868 and the two succeeding years Tom Morris, Jr, of St Andrews won and so the Belt became his own property. No competition was held in 1871, but that year discussions were held between the Prestwick Club, the Honourable Company of Edinburgh Golfers and the Royal & Ancient Club as to the possibility of putting up a silver trophy for competition, so that the Open Championship could be continued.

The clubs agreed on the matter and so the first competition for the Silver Trophy was held in 1972 again at Prestwick. The winner was again Tom Morris, Jr. It was to be his last victory for he died at the early age of 24 three years later.

By 1890 the entry had grown to 40. It included the name of John Ball who won the event and so became the first amateur golfer to do so and also the first Englishman. But the Championship came of age with the advent of The Great Triumvirate, Braid, Vardon and Taylor who dominated the event for some twenty years and won the title sixteen times between them, Vardon winning on six occasions, Braid and Taylor on five occasions. The only other man to win five times is the Australian, Peter Thomson.

British golfers were supreme until the end of World War I but then the Americans began to take over (St Andrews-born Jock Hutchison was the first man to take the trophy across the Atlantic). In the next decade Americans in the form of Hagen, Jones and others took over. Havers was the only home golfer to break the run which he did in 1924. But it was not until Cotton's first victory in 1934 that the American challenge started to fade. Then after a spell of home wins Locke and Thomson took over, their winning sequence being broken only by Max Faulkner at Portrush in 1951 and Ben Hogan at Carnoustie in 1953. Since then the Championship has been a truly international affair with winners from several countries, but mostly from the US.

There have been many memorable Championships and many exciting finishes. One of the greatest feats was that of the late Tony Lema at St Andrews in 1964 when without a full practice round he won the title. Hogan's win at Carnoustie in 1953 at the first attempt was also noteworthy.

The last amateur to win the Open Championship was Robert T Jones, Jr, who took the title three times. The last British golfer to win was Tony Jacklin at Royal Lytham in 1969. Jacklin might well have won the following year had not a thunderstorm broken over the course after he had played the first nine holes at St Andrews in 29 strokes. That Championship was eventually won by Jack Nicklaus after a play-off with fellow American, Doug Sanders, who missed a short putt on the last green to miss winning the title so enabling Nicklaus to tie.

The Belt

	Winner	*Score*	*Venue*	*Entrants*
1860	**W Park**, Musselburgh	174	Prestwick	8
1861	**Tom Morris, Sr**, Prestwick	163	Prestwick	8
1862	**Tom Morris, Sr**, Prestwick	163	Prestwick	8
1863	**W Park**, Musselburgh	168	Prestwick	14
1864	**Tom Morris, Sr**, Prestwick	167	Prestwick	16
1865	**A Strath**, St Andrews	162	Prestwick	10
1866	**W Park**, Musselburgh	169	Prestwick	10
1867	**Tom Morris, Sr**, St Andrews	170	Prestwick	10
1868	**Tom Morris, Jr**, St Andrews	157	Prestwick	10
1869	**Tom Morris, Jr**, St Andrews	154	Prestwick	14
1870	**Tom Morris, Jr**, St Andrews	149	Prestwick	17

The Cup

1872	**Tom Morris, Jr**, St Andrews	166	Prestwick	8
1873	**Tom Kidd**, St Andrews	179	St Andrews	26
1874	**Mungo Park**, Musselburgh	159	Musselburgh	32
1875	**W Park**, Musselburgh	166	Prestwick	18
1876	**Bob Martin**, St Andrews	176	St Andrews	34
	(David Strath tied but refused to play off)			
1877	**Jamie Anderson**, St Andrews	160	Musselburgh	24
1878	**Jamie Anderson**, St Andrews	157	Prestwick	26
1879	**Jamie Anderson**, St Andrews	169	St Andrews	46
1880	**Bob Ferguson**, Musselburgh	162	Musselburgh	30
1881	**Bob Ferguson**, Musselburgh	170	Prestwick	22
1882	**Bob Ferguson**, Musselburgh	171	St Andrews	40

1883	**W Fernie**, Dumfries	159	Musselburgh	41	
	(After a tie with Bob Ferguson, Musselburgh)				
1884	**Jack Simpson**, Carnoustie	160	Prestwick	30	
1885	**Bob Martin**, St Andrews	171	St Andrews	51	
1886	**D Brown**, Musselburgh	157	Musselburgh	46	
1887	**W Park, Jr**, Musselburgh	161	Prestwick	36	
1888	**Jack Burns**, Warwick	171	St Andrews	53	
1889	**W Park, Jr**, Musselburgh	155	Musselburgh	42	
	(After a tie with Andrew Kirkaldy)				
1890	**John Ball**, Royal Liverpool	164	Prestwick	40	
1891	**Hugh Kirkaldy**, St Andrews	166	St Andrews	82	

After 1891 the competition was extended to 72 holes and for the first time entry money was imposed.

1892	**H H Hilton**, Royal Liverpool	305	Muirfield	66	
1893	**W Auchterlonie**, St Andrews	322	Prestwick	72	
1894	**J H Taylor**, Winchester	326	Sandwich	94	
1895	**J H Taylor**, Winchester	322	St Andrews	73	
1896	**H Vardon**, Ganton	316	Muirfield	64	
	(After a tie with J H Taylor. Replay scores for 36 holes; Vardon, 157; Taylor, 161)				
1897	**H H Hilton**, Royal Liverpool	314	Hoylake	86	
1898	**H Vardon**, Ganton	307	Prestwick	78	
1899	**H Vardon**, Ganton	310	Sandwich	98	
1900	**J H Taylor**, Mid-Surrey	309	St Andrews	81	
1901	**James Braid**, Romford	309	Muirfield	101	
1902	**Alex Herd**, Huddersfield	307	Hoylake	112	
1903	**H Vardon**, Totteridge	300	Prestwick	127	
1904	**Jack White**, Sunningdale	296	Sandwich	144	
1905	**James Braid**, Walton Heath	318	St Andrews	152	
1906	**James Braid**, Walton Heath	300	Muirfield	183	
1907	**Arnaud Massy**, France	312	Hoylake	193	
1908	**James Braid**, Walton Heath	291	Prestwick	180	
1909	**J H Taylor**, Mid-Surrey	295	Deal	204	
1910	**James Braid**, Walton Heath	299	St Andrews	210	
1911	**H Vardon**, Totteridge	303	Sandwich	226	
	(After a tie with Arnaud Massy. The tie was over 36 holes, but Massy picked up at the 35th hole before holing out. He had taken 148 for 34 holes, and when Vardon holed out at the 35th hole his score was 143.)				
1912	**E Ray**, Oxhey	295	Muirfield	215	
1913	**J H Taylor**, Mid-Surrey	304	Hoylake	269	
1914	**H Vardon**, Totteridge	306	Prestwick	194	

1915–19	No Championship owing to the Great War			*Qual*	*Entrants*
1920	**George Duncan**, Hanger Hill	303	Deal	81	190
1921	**Jock Hutchison**, Glenview, Chicago	296	St Andrews	85	158
	(After a tie with R H Wethered, Royal and Ancient – Replay Scores Jock Hutchison 150, R H Wethered 159)				
1922	**Walter Hagen**, Detroit, USA	300	Sandwich	80	225
1923	**A G Havers**, Coombe Hill	295	Troon	88	222
1924	**Walter Hagen**, Detroit, USA	301	Hoylake	86	277
1925	**Jim Barnes**, USA	300	Prestwick	83	200
1926	**R T Jones** (USA)	291	Royal Lytham and St Annes	117	293
1927	**R T Jones** (USA)	285	St Andrews	108	207
1928	**Walter Hagen**, USA	292	Sandwich	113	271
1929	**Walter Hagen**, USA	292	Muirfield	109	242
1930	**R T Jones** (USA)	291	Hoylake	112	296
1931	**T D Armour**, USA	296	Carnoustie	109	215
1932	**G Sarazen**, USA	283	Prince's	110	224
1933	**D Shute**, USA	292	St Andrews	117	287
	(After a tie with Craig Wood, USA – Replay scores, D Shute 149, Craig Wood 154)				
1934	**T H Cotton**, Waterloo, Belgium	283	Sandwich	101	312
1935	**A Perry**, Leatherhead	283	Muirfield	109	264
1936	**A H Padgham**, Sundridge Park	287	Hoylake	107	286
1937	**T H Cotton**, Ashridge	290	Carnoustie	141	258
1938	**R A Whitcombe**, Parkstone	295	Sandwich	120	268
1939	**R Burton**, Sale	290	St Andrews	129	254

1940–45   No Championship owing to World War.

1946	**S Snead**, USA	290	St Andrews	100	225
1947	**Fred Daly**, Balmoral	293	Hoylake	100	263
1948	**T H Cotton**, Royal Mid-Surrey	284	Muirfield	97	272
1949	**A D Locke**, South Africa	283	Sandwich	96	224

(After a tie with Harry Bradshaw, Kilcroney – Replay Locke 135, Bradshaw 147)

1950	**A D Locke**, South Africa	279	Troon	93	262
1951	**Max Faulkner**, Unattached	285	Portrush	98	180
1952	**A D Locke**, South Africa	287	Royal Lytham	96	275
1953	**Ben Hogan**, USA	282	Carnoustie	91	196
1954	**P W Thomson**, Australia	283	Royal Birkdale	97	349
1955	**P W Thomson**, Australia	281	St Andrews	94	301
1956	**P W Thomson**, Australia	286	Hoylake	96	360
1957	**A D Locke**, South Africa	279	St Andrews	96	282
1958	**P W Thomson**, Australia	278	Royal Lytham and St Annes	96	362

(After a tie with D C Thomas, Sudbury – Replay scores, Thomson 139, Thomas 143)

1959	**Gary Player**, South Africa	284	Muirfield	90	285
1960	**K D G Nagle**, Australia	285	St Andrews	74	410
1961	**Arnold Palmer**, USA	284	Royal Birkdale	101	364
1962	**Arnold Palmer**, USA	276	Troon	119	379
1963	**R J Charles**, New Zealand	277	Royal Lytham and St Annes	119	261

(After a tie with Phil Rodgers, USA – Replay scores, Charles 140; Rodgers 148)

1964	**Tony Lema**, USA	279	St Andrews	119	327
1965	**P W Thomson**, Australia	285	Royal Birkdale	130	372
1966	**Jack Nicklaus**, USA	282	Muirfield	130	310
1967	**R de Vicenzo**, Argentina	278	Hoylake	130	326
1968	**Gary Player**, South Africa	289	Carnoustie	130	309
1969	**A Jacklin**, Potters Bar	280	Royal Lytham and St Annes	129	424
1970	**J Nicklaus**, USA	283	St Andrews	134	468

(After a tie with Doug Sanders, USA – Replay scores Nicklaus 72, Sanders 73)

1971	**L Trevino**, USA	278	Royal Birkdale	150	528
1972	**L Trevino**, USA	278	Muirfield	150	570
1973	**T Weiskopf**, USA	276	Troon	150	569
1974	**Gary Player**, South Africa	282	Royal Lytham and St Annes	150	679
1975	**T Watson**, USA	279	Carnoustie	150	629

(After a tie with J Newton, Australia – Replay scores Watson 71, Newton 72)

1976	**J Miller**, USA	279	Royal Birkdale	150	719
1977	**T Watson**, USA	268	Turnberry		
1978	**Jack Nicklaus**, USA	281	St Andrews		

British Professional Match Play Championship This old event – which began in 1903 – after being sponsored by the *News of the World* newspaper for many years, has since had a chequered career, but is now being successfully sponsored by the Sun Alliance Insurance Group.

British Women's Amateur Stroke Play Championship This is a comparatively new event which was started in 1969. It consists of two rounds qualifying, with the leading 32 competitors playing another 36 holes.

(From 1976 re-named Ladies' British Open Championship)

	Winner	*Club*	*Venue*	*Score*
1969	**Miss A Irvin**	Royal Lytham	Gosforth Park	295
1970	**Miss M Everard**	Hallamshire	Royal Birkdale	313
1971	**Mrs I C Robertson**	Dunaverty	Ayr Belleisle	302
1972	**Mrs I C Robertson**	Dunaverty	Silloth	296
1973	**Mrs A Stant**	Beau Desert	Purdis Heath	298
1974	**Miss J Greenhalgh**	Pleasington	Seaton Carew	302
1975	**Miss J Greenhalgh**	Pleasington	Gosforth Park	298
1976	**Miss J Lee Smith**	Gosforth	Fulford	299
1977	**Miss V Saunders**	Tyrrells Wood	Lindrick	306

(After a tie with Miss M Everard)

BRITISH WOMEN'S STROKE PLAY CHAMPIONSHIP

Canada Cup This competition between the professionals from the world's golfing countries is now known as the World Cup. The trophy was presented by a wealthy industrialist, John J Hopkins. It was first played for in 1953 at Montreal. The first winner was Argentina represented by Roberto de Vicenzo and Antonio Cerda.

Canadian Amateur Championship Golf was played in Canada before it was played in the US, consequently it is not surprising that the Canadian Amateur Championship is an old event. It was first played in 1894. It was a match play event until 1968 and the championship is now played over 72 holes.

Canadian Ladies' Championship This is another instance of a Ladies' Championship being instituted before the Men's Championship. The Canadian Ladies' Championship began in 1901. Like the national Amateur Championship it started as a match play event but is now stroke play.

CANADIAN OPEN CHAMPIONSHIP

Canadian Open Championship This old event (it started in 1904) is one of the world's major golf events attracting as it does a host of the leading golfers from the US and other countries. It offers substantial prize-money.

	Winner since 1945	*Club/Country*	*Venue*	*Score*
1945	**Byron Nelson**	Toledo	Toronto	280
1946	**G Fazio**	Los Angeles	Montreal	278
1947	**A D Locke**	South Africa	Toronto	268
1948	**C Congdon**	Tacoma, Washington	Vancouver	280
1949	**E J Harrison**	Little Rock	Toronto	271
1950	**J Ferrier**	San Francisco	Montreal	271
1951	**J Ferrier**	San Francisco	Toronto	273
1952	**J Palmer**	Badin, N C	Winnipeg	263
1953	**D Douglas**	Newark	Toronto	273
1954	**Pat Fletcher**	Saskatoon	Vancouver	280
1955	**Arnold Palmer**	Latrobe	Toronto	265
1956	**D Sanders**	Cedartown	Montreal	273
1957	**G Bayer**	California	Kitchener	271
1958	**Wes Ellis, Jr**	Ridgewood	Edmonton	267
1959	**D Ford**	Paradise	Montreal	276
1960	**Art Wall**	USA	Toronto	269
1961	**Jackie Cupit**	Texas	Winnipeg	270
1962	**Ted Kroll**	USA	Montreal	278
1963	**D Ford**	USA	Toronto	280
1964	**K D G Nagle**	Australia	Montreal	277
1965	**Gene Littler**	USA	Toronto	273
1966	**Don Massengale**	USA	Vancouver	280
1967	**W Casper**	USA	Montreal	279
1968	**R J Charles**	New Zealand	Toronto	274
1969	**T Aaron**	USA	Montreal	275
1970	**K Zarley**	USA	London, Ontario	279
1971	**L Trevino**	USA	Montreal	275
1972	**G Brewer**	USA	Ridgeway, Ontario	275
1973	**T Weiskopf**	USA	Quebec	278
1974	**B Nichols**	USA	Mississauga, Toronto	270
1975	**T Weiskopf**	USA	Royal Montreal	274
1976	**J Pate**	USA	Essex, Windsor	267
1977	**L Trevino**	USA	Glen Abbey C C	280

Commonwealth Tournament (Ladies) This tournament is played every four years between teams representing Great Britain, Australia, Canada and New Zealand. Other Commonwealth countries would be eligible to enter if they so wished. The tournament for which a trophy was presented by Viscountess Astor, was first played at St Andrews in 1959. Great Britain has won the event each time it has been played.

Commonwealth Tournament (Men) This tournament was inaugurated in 1954 and the first venue was St Andrews in Scotland when the Australian team won. The tournament is held every four years. So far competing teams have been Australia, Canada, Great Britain, New Zealand and South Africa.

Curtis Cup The Curtis Cup is contested every two years between the women amateur golfers of the British Isles and United States. It was presented by the Misses Harriot and Margaret Curtis, two famous American golfers who won four US Ladies' Championships between them. They first came to Britain to play in the British Ladies' Championship at Cromer, Norfolk in 1905. In that year there were sufficient Americans present to play a match against the British players, a match in which the Misses Curtis took part. Other unofficial matches took place in 1911, 1923 and 1930. The 1930 match, played at Sunningdale, England created much interest and as a result the Misses Curtis decided to present a trophy for biennial competition. The first match was played at Wentworth, England and it had a sensational ending: the Americans won by five matches to three with one halved, despite the fact the British team was a powerful one. Miss Margaret Curtis continued to play in championship golf until 1949 by which time she was 69 years of age.

CURTIS CUP

	Winners since 1932	*Venue*
1932	USA, $5\frac{1}{2}$ matches; Great Britain, $3\frac{1}{2}$ matches	Wentworth
1934	USA, $6\frac{1}{2}$ matches; Great Britain, $2\frac{1}{2}$ matches	Chevy Chase
1936	Great Britain, $4\frac{1}{2}$ matches; USA, $4\frac{1}{2}$ matches	Gleneagles
1938	USA, $5\frac{1}{2}$ matches; Great Britain, $3\frac{1}{2}$ matches	Essex County Club
1948	USA, $6\frac{1}{2}$ matches; Great Britain, $2\frac{1}{2}$ matches	Birkdale
1950	USA, $7\frac{1}{2}$ matches; Great Britain, $1\frac{1}{2}$ matches	Buffalo
1952	Great Britain, 5 matches; USA, 4 matches	Muirfield
1954	USA, 6 matches; Great Britain, 3 matches	Merion
1956	Great Britain, 5 matches; USA, 4 matches	Prince's, Sandwich
1958	Great Britain, $4\frac{1}{2}$ matches; USA, $4\frac{1}{2}$ matches	Brae Burn
1960	USA, $6\frac{1}{2}$ matches; Great Britain, $2\frac{1}{2}$ matches	Lindrick
1962	USA, 8 matches; Great Britain, 1 match	Colorado Springs
1964	USA, $10\frac{1}{2}$ matches; Great Britain, $7\frac{1}{2}$ matches	Porthcawl
1966	USA, 13 matches; Great Britain, 5 matches	Hot Springs, Virginia
1968	USA, $10\frac{1}{2}$ matches; Great Britain, $7\frac{1}{2}$ matches	Newcastle Co Down
1970	USA, $11\frac{1}{2}$ matches; Great Britain, $6\frac{1}{2}$ matches	Brae Burn.
1972	USA, 10 matches; Great Britain, 8 matches	Western Gailes
1974	USA, 13 matches; Great Britain, 5 matches	San Francisco
1976	USA, $11\frac{1}{2}$ matches; Great Britain, $6\frac{1}{2}$ matches	Royal Lytham & St Annes

Above: The Eisenhower Trophy.

Dutch Open Championship Although the Dutch claim to have started golf, the only Dutch Championship of any age is the Dutch Open. It attracts an international entry. The first Dutch Open was played in 1912.

Eisenhower Trophy This trophy was given by the Late President Dwight Eisenhower for competition between the world's amateur golfers. It is now called the World Amateur Team Championship.

English Amateur Championship This Championship was first played at Hoylake, the home of the Royal Liverpool Club in 1925. The event is controlled by the English Golf Union and entrants must be English-born or have one parent who is English and who was born in England. The Union can accept if it thinks fit a golfer with the necessary handicap qualification and who is a British subject, resident in England.

ENGLISH AMATEUR CHAMPIONSHIP

	Winner	*Runner-Up*	*Venue*	*Score*
1925	**T F Ellison**	S Robinson	Hoylake	1 hole
1926	**T F Ellison**	Sq Ldr C Hayward	Walton Heath	6 and 4
1927	**T P Perkins**	J B Beddard	Little Aston	2 and 1
1928	**J A Stout**	T P Perkins	Royal Lytham	3 and 2
1929	**W Sutton**	E B Tipping	Northumberland	3 and 2
1930	**T A Bourn**	C E Hardman	Burnham	3 and 2
1931	**L G Crawley**	W Sutton	Hunstanton	1 hole
1932	**E W Fiddian**	A S Bradshaw	Royal St George's	1 hole
1933	**J Woollam**	T A Bourn	Ganton	4 and 3
1934	**S Lunt**	L G Crawley	Formby	37th hole
1935	**J Woollam**	E W Fiddian	Hollinwell	2 and 1
1936	**H G Bentley**	J D A Langley	Deal	5 and 4
1937	**J J Pennink**	L G Crawley	Saunton	6 and 5
1938	**J J Pennink**	S E Banks	Moortown	2 and 1

1939	**A L Bentley**	W Sutton	Birkdale	5 and 4
1946	**I R Patey**	K Thom	Royal Mid-Surrey	5 and 4
1947	**G H Micklem**	C Stowe	Ganton	1 hole
1948	**A G B Helm**	H J R Roberts	Little Aston	2 and 1
1949	**R J White**	C Stowe	Formby	5 and 4
1950	**J D A Langley**	I R Patey	Deal	1 hole
1951	**G P Roberts**	H Bennett	Hunstanton	39th hole
1952	**E Millward**	T J Shorrock	Burnham & Berrow	2 holes
1953	**G H Micklem**	R J White	Royal Birkdale	2 and 1
1954	**A Thirlwell**	H G Bentley	Royal St George's	2 and 1
1955	**A Thirlwell**	M Burgess	Ganton	7 and 6
1956	**G B Wolstenholme**	H Bennett	Royal Lytham	1 hole
1957	**A Walker**	G Whitehead	Royal Liverpool	4 and 3
1958	**D Sewell**	D A Proctor	Walton Heath	8 and 7
1959	**G B Wolstenholme**	M F Bonallack	Formby	1 hole
1960	**D N Sewell**	M J Christmas	Hunstanton	41st hole
1961	**Ian Caldwell**	G Clark	Wentworth	37th hole
1962	**M F Bonallack**	M S R Lunt	Moortown	2 and 1
1963	**M F Bonallack**	A Thirlwell	Burnham & Berrow	4 and 3
1964	**Dr D Marsh**	R Foster	Hollinwell	1 hole
1965	**M F Bonallack**	Clive Clark	Berkshire	3 and 2
1966	**M S R Lunt**	D J Millensted	Royal Lytham	3 and 2
1967	**M F Bonallack**	G E Hyde	Woodhall Spa	4 and 2
1968	**M F Bonallack**	P D Kelley	Ganton	12 and 11
1969	**J Cook**	P Dawson	Royal St George's	6 and 4
1970	**Dr D Marsh**	S G Birtwell	Royal Birkdale	6 and 4
1971	**W Humphreys**	J Davies	Burnham & Berrow	9 and 8
1972	**H Ashby**	R Revell	Northumberland	5 and 4
1973	**H Ashby**	S C Mason	Formby	5 and 4
1974	**M James**	J A Watts	Woodhall Spa	6 and 5
1975	**N Faldo**	D Eccleston	Royal Lytham	6 and 4
1976	**P Deeble**	J Davies	Ganton	3 and 1
1977	**T Shingler**	J Mayell	Walton Heath	4 and 3

ENGLISH LADIES' CHAMPIONSHIP

English Ladies' Championship This event is not as old as many other Ladies' Championships, having been first played in 1912. It is open to women golfers who qualify under conditions laid down by the English Ladies' Golf Association which in itself is a comparatively new body. Previously the championship was run by the Ladies' Golf Union.

	Winner	*Runner-Up*	*Venue*	*Score*
1912	**Miss M Gardner**	Mrs Cautley	Princes	20th hole
1913	**Mrs F W Brown**	Mrs McNair	Nottingham	1 hole
1914	**Miss Cecil Leitch**	Miss Bastin	Walton Heath	2 and 1
1915–1918	No Championship owing to the Great War			
1919	**Miss Cecil Leitch**	Mrs Temple Dobell	St Annes	10 and 8
1920	**Miss J Wethered**	Miss Cecil Leitch	Sheringham	2 and 1
1921	**Miss J Wethered**	Mrs Mudford	St Annes	12 and 11
1922	**Miss J Wethered**	Miss J Stocker	Hunstanton	7 and 6
1923	**Miss J Wethered**	Mrs T A Lodge	Ganton	8 and 7
1924	**Miss J Wethered**	Miss D R Fowler	Cooden Beach	8 and 7
1925	**Miss D R Fowler**	Miss Joy Winn	Westward Ho!	9 and 7
1926	**Miss M Gourlay**	Miss E Corlett	Woodhall Spa	6 and 4
1927	**Mrs Guedalla**	Miss E Wilson	Pannal	1 hole
1928	**Miss E Wilson**	Miss D Pearson	Walton Heath	9 and 8
1929	**Miss M Gourlay**	Miss D Fishwick	Broadstone	6 and 5
1930	**Miss E Wilson**	Mrs R O Porter	Aldeburgh	12 and 11
1931	**Miss W Morgan**	Miss M Gourlay	Ganton	3 and 1
1932	**Miss D Fishwick**	Miss B Brown	Royal Ashdown	5 and 4
1933	**Miss D Pearson**	Miss M Johnson	Westward Ho!	5 and 3
1934	**Miss P Wade**	Miss M Johnson	Seacroft	4 and 3
1935	**Mrs M Garon**	Miss E Corlett	Birkdale	38th hole
1936	**Miss W Morgan**	Miss P Wade	Hayling	2 and 1
1937	**Miss W Morgan**	Miss M Fyshe	St Enodoc	4 and 2
1938	**Miss E Corlett**	Miss J Winn	Aldeburgh	2 and 1

Year	Winner		Venue	Score
1947	Miss M Wallis	Miss E Price	Ganton	3 and 1
1948	Miss Frances Stephens	Mrs Zara Bolton	Hayling	1 hole
1949	Mrs A C Critchley	Lady Katherine Cairns	Burnham	3 and 2
1950	Hon Mrs A Gee	Miss Pamela Davies	Sheringham	8 and 6
1951	Miss J Bisgood	Mrs A Keiller	St Annes Old Links	2 and 1
1952	Miss Pamela Davies	Miss J Gordon	Westward Ho!	6 and 5
1953	Miss J Bisgood	Miss J McIntyre	Prince's	6 and 5
1954	Miss Frances Stephens	Miss Elizabeth Price	Woodhall Spa	37th hole
1955	Mrs R Smith Stephens	Miss E Price	Moortown	4 and 3
1956	Miss Bridget Jackson	Mrs Ruth Ferguson	Hunstanton	2 and 1
1957	Miss J Bisgood	Miss M Nichol	Bournemouth	10 and 8
1958	Mrs M F Bonallack	Miss Bridget Jackson	Formby	3 and 2
1959	Miss R Porter	Mrs F Smith	Aldeburgh	5 and 4
1960	Miss M Nichol	Mrs M F Bonallack	Burnham	3 and 1
1961	Miss R Porter	Mrs P Reece	Littlestone	2 holes
1962	Miss J Roberts	Mrs M F Bonallack	Woodhall Spa	3 and 1
1963	Mrs M F Bonallack	Miss E Chadwick	Liphook	7 and 6
1964	Mrs A D Spearman	Miss M Everard	Royal Lytham	6 and 5
1965	Miss R Porter	Miss G Cheetham	Whittington Barracks	6 and 5
1966	Miss J Greenhalgh	Mrs J C Holmes	Hayling Island	3 and 1
1967	Miss A Irvin	Mrs A Pickard	Alwoodley	3 and 2
1968	Mrs S Barber	Miss D Oxley	Hunstanton	5 and 4
1969	Miss B Dixon	Miss M Wenyon	Burnham & Berrow	6 and 4
1970	Miss D Oxley	Mrs S Barber	Rye	3 and 2
1971	Miss D Oxley	Mrs S Barber	Royal Liverpool	5 and 4
1972	Miss M Everard	Mrs M F Bonallack	Woodhall Spa	2 and 1
1973	Miss M Walker	Miss C Le Feuvre	Broadstone	6 and 5
1974	Miss A Irvin	Mrs J Thornhill	Sunningdale	1 hole
1975	Miss B Huke	Miss L Harrold	Royal Birkdale	2 and 1
1976	Miss L Harrold	Mrs A Uzielli	Hollinwell	3 and 2
1977	Miss V Marvin	Miss M Everard	Burnham & Berrow	1 hole

Year	Winner	Club/Country	Venue	Score
1957	D Sewell	Hook Heath	Moortown	287
1958	A H Perowne	Royal Norwich	Royal Birkdale	289
1959	D Sewell	Hook Heath	Hollinwell	300
1960	G B Wolstenholme	Sunningdale	Ganton	286
1961	R D Shade	Duddingston	Hoylake	284
1962	A Slater	Wakefield	Woodhall Spa	209
1963	R D Shade	Duddingston	Royal Birkdale	306
1964	M F Bonallack	Thorpe Bay	Royal Cinque Ports	290
1965	C A Clark	Ganton ⎫		
	D J Millensted	Wentworth ⎬ tie	Formby	289
	M J Burgess	West Sussex ⎭		
1966	P M Townsend	Porters Park	Hunstanton	282
1967	R D Shade	Duddingston	Saunton	299
1968	M F Bonallack	Thorpe Hall	Walton Heath	210
1969	R Foster	Bradford ⎫ tie	Moortown	287
	M F Bonallack	Thorpe Hall ⎭		
1970	R Foster	Bradford	Little Aston	287
1971	M F Bonallack	Thorpe Hall	Hillside	294
1972	P H Moody	Notts	Royal Liverpool	296
1973	R Revell	Farnham	Hunstanton	294
1974	N Sundelson	South Africa	Moortown	291
1975	A W Lyle	Hawkstone Park	Hollinwell	298
1976	P Hedges	Langley Park	Saunton	294
1977	A W Lyle	Hawkstone Park	Royal Liverpool	293

ENGLISH OPEN STROKE PLAY CHAMPIONSHIP

Above: The Brabazon Trophy is awarded to the winner of the English Open Stroke Play Championship.

European Amateur Team Championship This is a comparatively new event which began in 1959. Teams of amateur golfers from various countries compete. The championship is played every two years and the venues alternate between the British Isles and the Continent of Europe.

French Amateur Championship France has several very old golf courses, including Pau which is the oldest; it is not surprising that French Championships are also old. The Amateur

Championship was first played in 1904 at La Boulie. It has always attracted a strong British entry.

French Ladies' Championship French Ladies' golf has always been strong and the country has produced many fine players. The event was started in 1909.

FRENCH OPEN CHAMPIONSHIP

French Open Championship It is fitting that the first French Open Championship which was played in 1906 at La Boulie was won by the great French professional, Arnaud Massy who went on to win the British Open Championship the next year. The winners include in addition to Massy, J H Taylor, James Braid, George Duncan, Walter Hagen, Henry Cotton, Roberto de Vicenzo, Byron Nelson, Bobby Locke, Kel Nagle, Bruce Devlin and Peter Oosterhuis.

	Winner	*Club/Country*	*Venue*	*Score*
1906	**A Massy**	La Boulie	La Boulie	292
1907	**A Massy**	La Boulie	La Boulie	298
1908	**J H Taylor**	Britain	La Boulie	300
1909	**J H Taylor**	Britain	La Boulie	293
1910	**James Braid**	Britain	La Boulie	298
1911	**A Massy**	Deauville	La Boulie	284
1912	**Jean Gassiat**	Chantilly	La Boulie	289
1913	**George Duncan**	Britain	Chantilly	304
1914	**J Douglas Edgar**	Britain	Le Touquet	288
1920	**Walter Hagen**	USA	La Boulie	298
1921	**A Boomer**	St Cloud	Le Touquet	284
1922	**A Boomer**	St Cloud	La Boulie	286
1923	**J Ockenden**	Britain	Dieppe	288
1924	**C J H Tolley**	Britain	La Boulie	290
1925	**A Massy**	La Nivelle	Chantilly	291
1926	**A Boomer**	St Cloud	St Cloud	280
1927	**George Duncan**	Britain	St Germain	299
1928	**C J H Tolley**	Britain	La Boulie	283
1929	**A Boomer**	St Cloud	Fourqueux	283
1930	**E R Whitcombe**	Britain	Dieppe	282
1931	**A Boomer**	St Cloud	Deauville	291
1932	**A J Lacey**	Britain	St Cloud	295
1933	**B Gadd**	Britain	Chantilly	283
1934	**S F Brews**	South Africa	Dieppe	284
1935	**S F Brews**	South Africa	Le Touquet	293
1936	**M Dallemagne**	St Germain	St Germain	277
1937	**M Dallemagne**	St Germain	St Cloud	278
1938	**M Dallemagne**	St Germain	Fourqueux	282
1939	**M Pose**	Argentina	Le Touquet	285
1946	**T H Cotton**	Britain	St Cloud	269
1947	**T H Cotton**	Britain	Chantilly	285
1948	**F Cavalo**	Fontainebleau	St Cloud	287
1949	**U Grappasonni**	Italy	St Germain	275
1950	**R de Vicenzo**	Argentina	Chantilly	279
1951	**H Hassanein**	Egypt	St Cloud	278
1952	**A D Locke**	South Africa	St Germain	268
1953	**A D Locke**	South Africa	La Boulie	276
1954	**F van Donck**	Belgium	St Cloud	275
1955	**Byron Nelson**	USA	La Boulie	271
1956	**A Miguel**	Spain	Deauville	277
1957	**F van Donck**	Belgium	St Cloud	266
1958	**F van Donck**	Belgium	St Germain	276
1959	**D C Thomas**	Sudbury	La Boulie	276
1960	**R de Vicenzo**	Argentina	St Cloud	275
1961	**K D G Nagle**	Australia	La Boulie	271
1962	**A Murray**	Australia	St Germain	274
1963	**B Devlin**	Australia	St Cloud	273
1964	**R de Vicenzo**	Argentina	Chantilly	272
1965	**R Sota**	Spain	St Nom-la-Breteche	268

1966	**D J Hutchinson**	South Africa	La Boulie	274
1967	**B J Hunt**	Britain	St Germain	271
1968	**P J Butler**	Britain	St Cloud	272
1969	**J Garaialde**	France	St Nom-la-Breteche	277
1970	**D Graham**	Australia	Chantaco	268
1971	**Liang Huan Lu**	Formosa	Biarritz	262
1972	**B Jaeckel**	USA	Biarritz & La Nivelle	265
1973	**P Oosterhuis**	Britain	La Boulie	280
1974	**P Oosterhuis**	Britain	Chantilly	284
1975	**B Barnes**	Britain	La Boulie	281
1976	**V Tshabalala**	South Africa	Le Touquet	272
1977	**S Ballesteros**	Spain	Le Touquet	282

German Open Championship This event has been going for over 60 years, and has been won by many famous golfers including Antonio Cerda, Bobby Locke, Roberto de Vicenzo, Henry Cotton and Peter Thomson. In recent years it has been popular with young American professionals.

Irish Amateur Championship First played in 1893, this event is open to all men amateur golfers of Irish birth or those who have one Irish parent. Players from both Eire and Northern Ireland are eligible to compete. It is controlled by the Golfing Union of Ireland.

**IRISH
AMATEUR
CHAMPIONSHIP**

Winners since 1946

	Winner	*Runner-up*	*Venue*	*Score*
1946	**J Burke**	R C Ewing	Dollymount	2 and 1
1947	**J Burke**	J Fitzsimmons	Lahinch	2 holes
1948	**R C Ewing**	B J Scannell	Royal Portrush	3 and 2
1949	**J Carroll**	Pat Murphy	Galway	4 and 3
1950	**B Herlihy**	B C McManus	Baltray	4 and 3
1951	**M Power**	J B Carr	Cork	3 and 2
1952	**T W Egan**	J C Brown	Royal Belfast	41st hole
1953	**J Malone**	M Power	Rosses Point	2 and 1
1954	**J B Carr**	J Forsythe	Carlow	4 and 3
1955	**Dr James Mahon**	George Crosbie	Lahinch	3 and 2
1956	**Garry Love**	George Crosbie	Malone	37th hole
1957	**J B Carr**	George Crosbie	Galway	2 holes
1958	**R C Ewing**	G A Young	Ballybunion	5 and 3
1959	**T Craddock**	J B Carr	Portmarnock	38th hole
1960	**M Edwards**	N Fogarty	Portstewart	6 and 5
1961	**D Sheahan**	J Brown	Rosses Point	3 and 2
1962	**M Edwards**	J Harrington	Baltray	42nd hole
1963	**J B Carr**	E C O'Brien	Kilarney	2 and 1
1964	**J B Carr**	A McDade	Royal Co Down	6 and 5
1965	**J B Carr**	T Craddock	Rosses Point	3 and 2
1966	**D Sheahan**	J Faith	Dollymount	3 and 2
1967	**J B Carr**	P D Flaherty	Lahinch	1 hole
1968	**M O'Brien**	F McCarroll	Royal Portrush	2 and 1
1969	**V Nevin**	J O'Leary	Co Sligo	1 hole
1970	**D B Sheahan**	M Bloom	Grange	2 holes
1971	**R Kane**	M O'Brien	Ballybunion	3 and 2
1972	**K Stevenson**	B Hoey	Royal Co Down	2 and 1
1973	**R K Pollin**	R M Staunton	Rosses Point	1 hole
1974	**R Kane**	M Gannon	Portmarnock	5 and 4
1975	**M D O'Brien**	J A Bryan	Cork	5 and 4
1976	**D Branigan**	D O'Sullivan	Royal Portrush	2 holes
1977	**M Gannon**	A Hayes	Westport	19th hole

Irish Ladies' Championship This very old championship was founded in 1894. It is open to women players with Irish qualifications as ordained by the Irish Ladies' Golf Union. Conditions of entry are liable to vary from time to time.

**IRISH
LADIES'
CHAMPIONSHIP**

Winners since 1946

	Winner	Runner-Up	Venue	Score
1946	**Miss P Garvey**	Mrs V Reddan	Lahinch	39th hole
1947	**Miss P Garvey**	Miss C Smye	Portrush	5 and 4
1948	**Miss P Garvey**	Mrs V Reddan	Rosslare	9 and 7
1949	**Miss C Smye**	Mrs J Beck	Baltray	9 and 7
1950	**Miss P Garvey**	Mrs T Marks	Rosses Point	6 and 4
1951	**Miss P Garvey**	Miss D Forster	Ballybunion	12 and 10
1952	**Miss D M Forster**	Mrs P G McCann	Newcastle	3 and 2
1953	**Miss P Garvey**	Mrs Hegarty	Rosslare	8 and 7
1954	**Miss P Garvey**	Mrs H V Glendinning	Portmarnock	13 and 12
1955	**Miss P Garvey**	Miss A O'Donohoe	Rosses Point	10 and 9
1956	**Miss P O'Sullivan**	Mrs J F Hegarty	Killarney	14 and 12
1957	**Miss P Garvey**	Mrs P G McCann	Portrush	3 and 2
1958	**Miss P Garvey**	Mrs Z Fallon	Carlow	7 and 6
1959	**Miss P Garvey**	Miss H Colhoun	Lahinch	12 and 10
1960	**Miss P Garvey**	Mrs P G McCann	Cork	5 and 3
1961	**Mrs P G McCann**	Miss A Sweeney	Newcastle	5 and 3
1962	**Miss P Garvey**	Mrs M Earner	Baltray	7 and 6
1963	**Miss P Garvey**	Miss E Barnett	Killarney	9 and 7
1964	**Mrs Z Fallon**	Miss P O'Sullivan	Portrush	37th hole
1965	**Miss E Purcell**	Miss P O'Sullivan	Mullingar	3 and 2
1966	**Miss E Bradshaw**	Miss P O'Sullivan	Rosslare	3 and 2
1967	**Mrs G Brandom**	Miss P O'Sullivan	Castlerock	3 and 2
1968	**Miss E Bradshaw**	Miss M McKenna	Lahinch	4 and 3
1969	**Miss M McKenna**	Mrs C Hickey	Ballybunion	3 and 2
1970	**Miss P Garvey**	Miss M Earner	Portrush	2 and 1
1971	**Miss E Bradshaw**	Miss M Mooney	Baltray	3 and 1
1972	**Miss M McKenna**	Mrs I Butler	Killarney	5 and 4
1973	**Miss M Mooney**	Miss M McKenna	Bundoran	2 and 1
1974	**Miss M McKenna**	Miss V Singleton	Lahinch	3 and 2
1975	**Miss M Gorry**	Miss E Bradshaw	Tramore	1 hole
1976	**Miss C Nesbitt**	Miss M McKenna	Co Sligo	20th hole
1977	**Miss M McKenna**	Miss R Hegarty	Ballybunion	2 holes

IRISH OPEN CHAMPIONSHIP

	Winner	Club/Country	Venue	Score
1927	**George Duncan**	Wentworth	Portmarnock	312
1928	**E R Whitcombe**	Meyrick Park	Newcastle	288
1929	**Abe Mitchell**	Unattached	Portmarnock	309
1930	**C A Whitcombe**	Crews Hill	Portrush	289
1931	**E W Kenyon**	West Lancs	Dollymount	291
1932	**A H Padgham**	Royal Ashdown Forest	Cork	283
1933	**E W Kenyon**	West Lancs	Malone	286
1934	**S Easterbrook**	Knowle	Portmarnock	284
1935	**E R Whitcombe**	Meyrick Park	Newcastle	292
1936	**R A Whitcombe**	Parkstone	Dollymount	281
1937	**B Gadd**	West Cheshire	Portrush	284
1938	**A D Locke**	South Africa	Portmarnock	292
1939	**A Lees**	Dore and Totley	Newcastle	287
1946	**F Daly**	Belfast	Portmarnock	288
1947	**H Bradshaw**	Kilcroney	Portrush	290
1948	**D J Rees**	South Herts	Portmarnock	295
1949	**H Bradshaw**	Kilcroney	Belvoir Park, Belfast	286
1950	**H O Pickworth**	Australia	Dollymount	287
1951–52	No Championship			
1953	**E C Brown**	Unattached	Belvoir Park, Belfast	272

Discontinued until 1975 when renewed with Carrolls sponsoring

CARROLLS IRISH OPEN

	Winner	Club/Country	Venue	Score
1975	**C O'Connor, Jr**	Carlow	Woodbrook	275
1976	**B Crenshaw**	USA	Portmarnock	284
1977	**H Green**	USA	Portmarnock	283

Winners since 1940

	Winner	*Club*	*Venue*	*Score*
1940	F Daly	City of Derry	Little Island	305
1941	H Bradshaw	Kilcroney	Rosses Point	293
1942	H Bradshaw	Kilcroney	Hermitage	285
1943	H Bradshaw	Kilcroney	Dun Laoghaire	277
1944	H Bradshaw	Kilcroney	Hermitage	291
1945	C McKendrick	Douglas	Kilkee	283
1946	F Daly	Balmoral	Clandeboye	285
1947	H Bradshaw	Kilcroney	Baltray	291
1948	J McKenna	Douglas	Galway	285
1949	Chris Kane	Royal Dublin	Portrush	301
1950	H Bradshaw	Portmarnock	Grange	277
1951	H Bradshaw	Portmarnock	Balmoral	280
1952	F Daly	Balmoral	West Meath	284
1953	H Bradshaw	Portmarnock	Dundalk	272
1954	H Bradshaw	Portmarnock	Newcastle	300
1955	E Jones	Carlow	Castletroy	276
1956	C Greene	Mill Town	Clandeboye	281
1957	H Bradshaw	Portmarnock	Ballybunion	286
1958	C O'Connor	Killarney	Belfast	279
1959	N V Drew	Knock	Mullingar	282
1960	C O'Connor	Royal Dublin	Warrenpoint	271
1961	C O'Connor	Royal Dublin	Lahinch	280
1962	C O'Connor	Royal Dublin	Bangor	264
1963	C O'Connor	Royal Dublin	Little Island	271
1964	E Jones	Bangor	Knock	279
1965	C O'Connor	Royal Dublin	Mullingar	283
1966	C O'Connor	Royal Dublin	Warrenpoint	269
1967	H Boyle	Jacobs Golf Centre	Tullamore (3 rounds)	214
1968	C Greene	Mill Town	Knock	282
1969	J Martin	Unattached	Dundalk	268
1970	H Jackson	Knockbracken	Massereene	283
1971	C O'Connor	Royal Dublin	Galway	278
1972	J Kinsella	Castle	Bundoran	289
1973	J Kinsella	Castle	Limerick	284
1974	E Polland	Balmoral	Portstewart	277
1975	C O'Connor	Royal Dublin	Carlow	275
1976	P McGuirk	C Louth	Waterville	291
1977	P Skerritt	St Annes	Woodbrook	281

Italian Open Championship Now an important event in the European Professional circuit this championship has always attracted good fields. In 1975, the American professional Bill Casper won the event. It has been in existence for over 50 years.

Japan Open Championship With the upsurge of golf in Japan this event is becoming more important. The Championship is over 50 years old but so good are the Japanese on their home ground that few overseas players have managed to win.

New Zealand Amateur Championship This event, established in 1893, is one of the oldest of Amateur Championships. It is an annual match play event with a different venue each year.

New Zealand Ladies' Open Championship Instituted in 1922.

New Zealand Open Championship This Championship dates back to 1907 when the first winner was an American, A D Duncan. The same man won it twice subsequently and there have also been other American winners. In recent years it has been dominated by Australians.

Winners since 1946

	Winner	*Club/Country*	*Venue*
1946	R H Glading	Hamilton	Manawatu
1947	R H Glading	Hamilton	New Plymouth
1948	A Murray	Titirangi	Otago

1949	**James Galloway**	Whangarei	Hastings
1950	**P W Thomson**	Riversdale, Australia	Christchurch
1951	**P W Thomson**	Riversdale, Australia	Titirangi
1952	**A Murray**	Unattached	Wanganui
1953	**P W Thomson**	Victoria, Australia	Otago
1954	**R J Charles**	Masterton	Wellington
1955	**P W Thomson**	Australia	Auckland
1956	**N W Berwick**	Australia	Christchurch
1957	**K Nagle**	Australia	Manawatu
1958	**K Nagle**	Australia	Hamilton
1959	**P W Thomson**	Australia	Paraparaumu
1960	**P W Thomson**	Australia	Invercargill
1961	**P W Thomson**	Australia	Wellington
1962	**K Nagle**	Australia	Titirangi
1963	**B Devlin**	Australia	Wanganui
1964	**K Nagle**	Australia	Christchurch
1965	**P W Thomson**	Australia	Auckland
1966	**R Charles**	New Zealand	Paraparaumu
1967	**K Nagle**	Australia	Hamilton
1968	**K Nagle**	Australia	Christchurch
1969	**K Nagle**	Australia	Wanganui
1970	**R J Charles**	New Zealand	Auckland
1971	**P W Thomson**	Australia	Dunedin
1972	**E W Dunk**	Australia	Paraparaumu
1973	**R J Charles**	New Zealand	Palmerston North
1974	**R Gilder**	USA	Christchurch
1975	**E W Dunk**	Australia	Hamilton
1976	**S Owen**	New Zealand	Wellington
1977	**Bob Byman**	USA	Auckland

RYDER CUP

Above: The Ryder Cup is awarded every two years by the US PGA and the British PGA.

Ryder Cup In 1926 a match was played between American professionals and British professionals at the Wentworth club in England. It ended in a sweeping victory for the home side but the match was voted a great success and it was decided that it should become a regular fixture in the golfing calendar. For such a match a trophy was necessary and the British Professional Golfers' Association approached a patron of the game, Mr Samuel Ryder, head of a large firm of seed merchants to give a trophy. This he willingly agreed to do at once purchasing a gold trophy for the sum of £750.

It was decided the match would be played every two years in the US and Britain alternately. The first match was played at Worcester, Massachusetts. Walter Hagen was Captain of the US team and Ted Ray captain of the British team. The Americans were the winners by nine matches to two with one halved.

	Winner	*Club/Country*
1927	USA, 9 matches; Great Britain, 2 matches; 1 match halved	Worcester, Mass
1929	Great Britain, 6 matches; USA, 4 matches; 2 matches halved	Moortown, Leeds
1931	USA, 9 matches; Great Britain, 3 matches	Scioto, Columbus
1933	Great Britain, 6 matches; USA, 5 matches; 1 match halved	Southport and Ainsdale
1935	USA, 8 matches; Great Britain, 2 matches; 2 matches halved	Ridgewood, New Jersey
1937	USA, 7 matches; Great Britain, 3 matches; 2 matches halved	Southport and Ainsdale
1939	Due to be played at Ponte Vedra, Jacksonville, but no contest owing to World War II	
1947	USA, 11 matches; Great Britain, 1 match	Portland, Oregon
1949	USA, 7 matches; Great Britain, 5 matches	Ganton, Scarborough
1951	USA, 9 matches; Great Britain, 2 matches; 1 match halved	Pinehurst, North Carolina
1953	USA, 6 matches; Great Britain, 5 matches; 1 match halved	Wentworth, Surrey
1955	USA, 8 matches; Great Britain, 4 matches	Palm Springs
1957	Great Britain, 7 matches; USA, 4 matches; 1 match halved	Lindrick, Sheffield

1959	USA, 7 matches; Great Britain, 2 matches; 3 matches halved	Palm Desert, California
1961	USA, 13 matches; Great Britain, 8 matches; 3 matches halved	Royal Lytham & St Annes
1963	USA, 10 matches; Great Britain, 4 matches; 2 matches halved	Atlanta, Georgia
1965	USA, 18 matches; Great Britain, 11 matches; 3 matches halved	Royal Birkdale
1967	USA, 21 matches; Great Britain, 6 matches; 5 matches halved	Houston, Texas
1969	Great Britain, 13 matches; USA, 13 matches; 6 matches halved	Royal Birkdale
1971	USA, 16 matches; Great Britain, 11 matches; 5 matches halved	St Louis, Missouri
1973	USA, 16 matches; Great Britain, 10 matches; 6 matches halved	Muirfield
1975	USA, 18 matches; Great Britain, 8 matches; 6 matches halved	Laurel Valley, Penn
1977	USA, 12 matches; Great Britain, 7 matches; 1 match halved	Royal Lytham & St Annes

Scottish Amateur Championship Golf has been played in Scotland for centuries yet the Scottish Amateur Championship was founded as recently as 1922. Golfers who are Scottish by birth or who have one parent who is Scottish are eligible to play. It is organized by the Scottish Golf Union.

SCOTTISH AMATEUR CHAMPIONSHIP

	Winner	Runner-up	Venue	Score
1922	J Wilson	E Blackwell	St Andrews	19th hole
1923	T M Burrell	Dr A R McCallum	Troon	1 hole
1924	W W Mackenzie	W Tulloch	Aberdeen	3 and 2
1925	J T Dobson	W W Mackenzie	Muirfield	3 and 2
1926	W J Guild	S O Shepherd	Leven	2 and 1
1927	A Jamieson Jr	Rev D S Rutherford	Gailes	22nd hole
1928	W W Mackenzie	W E Dodds	Muirfield	5 and 3
1929	J T Bookless	J E Dawson	Aberdeen	5 and 4
1930	K Greig	T Wallace	Carnoustie	9 and 8
1931	J Wilson	A Jamieson Jr	Prestwick	2 and 1
1932	J McLean	K Greig	Dunbar	5 and 4
1933	J McLean	K C Forbes	Aberdeen	6 and 4
1934	J McLean	W Campbell	Western Gailes	3 and 1
1935	H Thomson	J McLean	St Andrews	2 and 1
1936	E D Hamilton	R Neill	Carnoustie	1 hole
1937	H McInally	K G Patrick	Barassie	6 and 5
1938	E D Hamilton	R Rutherford	Muirfield	4 and 2
1939	H McInally	H Thomson	Prestwick	6 and 5
1946	E C Brown	R Rutherford	Carnoustie	3 and 2
1947	H McInally	J Pressley	Glasgow Gailes	10 and 8
1948	A S Flockhard	G N Taylor	Royal Aberdeen	7 and 6
1949	R Wight	H McInally	Muirfield	1 hole
1950	W C Gibson	D A Blair	Prestwick	2 and 1
1951	J M Dykes	J C Wilson	St Andrews	4 and 2
1952	F G Dewar	J C Wilson	Carnoustie	4 and 3
1953	D A Blair	J W McKay	Western Gailes	3 and 1
1954	J W Draper	W G H Gray	Nairn	4 and 3
1955	R R Jack	A C Miller	Muirfield	2 and 1
1956	Dr F W G Deighton	A MacGregor	Old Troon	8 and 7
1957	J S Mongomerie	J Burnside	Balgownie	2 and 1
1958	W D Smith	I R Harris	Prestwick	6 and 5
1959	Dr F W G Deighton	R M K Murray	St Andrews	6 and 5
1960	J R Young	S Saddler	Carnoustie	5 and 3
1961	J Walker	S W T Murray	Western Gailes	4 and 3
1962	S W T Murray	R D B M Shade	Muirfield	2 and 1
1963	R D Shade	N Henderson	Troon	4 and 3
1964	R D Shade	J McBeath	Nairn	8 and 7
1965	R D Shade	G B Cosh	St Andrews	4 and 2

1966	R D Shade	C J L Strachan	Western Gailes	9 and 8
1967	R D Shade	A Murphy	Carnoustie	5 and 4
1968	G B Cosh	R L Renfrew	Muirfield	4 and 3
1969	J M Cannon	A H Hall	Troon	6 and 4
1970	C W Green	H B Stuart	Balgownie	1 hole
1971	S Stephen	C W Green	St Andrews	3 and 2
1972	H B Stuart	A K Pirie	Prestwick	3 and 1
1973	I Hutcheon	Allan Brodie	Carnoustie	3 and 1
1974	G H Murray	A K Pirie	Western Gailes	2 and 1
1975	D Greig	G H Murray	Montrose	7 and 6
1976	G H Murray	H B Stuart	St Andrews	6 and 5
1977	Allan Brodie	P McKellar	Troon	1 hole

SCOTTISH LADIES' CHAMPIONSHIP

Winners since 1947

	Winner	Runner-Up	Venue	Score
1947	Miss J Donald	Miss J Kerr	Elie	5 and 3
1948	Mrs A M Holm	Mrs Falconer	Gleneagles	5 and 4
1949	Miss J Donald	Mrs A M Holm	Troon	6 and 4
1950	Mrs A M Holm	Mrs E C Bedows	St Andrews	6 and 5
1951	Mrs G Valentine	Miss M C Paterson	Nairn	3 and 2
1952	Miss J Donald	Mrs R T Peel	Gullane	13 and 11
1953	Mrs G Valentine	Miss J Donald	Carnoustie	8 and 7
1954	Mrs R T Peel	Mrs G Valentine	Turnberry	7 and 6
1955	Mrs G Valentine	Miss N Couper	North Berwick	8 and 6
1956	Mrs G Valentine	Mrs A M Holm	Dornoch	8 and 7
1957	Miss M Speir	Mrs A M Holm	Troon	7 and 5
1958	Miss D T Sommerville	Miss J S Robertson	Elie	1 hole
1959	Miss J S Robertson	Miss B McCorkindale	Nairn	6 and 5
1960	Miss J S Robertson	Miss D T Sommerville	Turnberry	2 and 1
1961	Mrs I Wright (Miss Robertson)	Miss A M Lurie	St Andrews	1 hole
1962	Miss J B Lawrence	Mrs C Draper	Dornoch	5 and 4
1963	Miss J B Lawrence	Mrs I C Robertson	Troon	2 and 1
1964	Miss J B Lawrence	Mrs S M Reid	Gullane	5 and 3
1965	Mrs I C Robertson	Miss J B Lawrence	Nairn	5 and 4
1966	Mrs I C Robertson	Miss M Fowler	Machrihanish	2 and 1
1967	Miss J Hastings	Miss A Laing	North Berwick	5 and 3
1968	Miss J Smith	Mrs J Rennie	Carnoustie	10 and 9
1969	Mrs J H Anderson	Miss K Lackie	West Kilbride	5 and 4
1970	Miss A Laing	Mrs I C Robertson	Dunbar	1 hole
1971	Mrs I C Robertson	Mrs A Ferguson	Royal Dornoch	3 and 2
1972	Mrs I C Robertson	Miss C J Lugton	Machrihanish	5 and 3
1973	Mrs I Wright	Dr A J Wilson	St Andrews	2 holes
1974	Dr A J Wilson	Miss K Lackie	Nairn	22nd hole
1975	Miss L A Hope	Miss J W Smith	Elie	1 hole
1976	Miss S Needham	Miss T Walker	Machrihanish	3 and 2
1977	Miss C Lugton	Miss M Thomson	Royal Dornoch	1 hole

SCOTTISH OPEN AMATEUR STROKE PLAY CHAMPIONSHIP

	Winner	Club	Venue	Score
1967	B J Gallacher	Bathgate	Muirfield	291
1968	R D Shade	Duddingston	Prestwick	282
1969	J S Macdonald	Dalmahoy	Carnoustie	288
1970	D Hayes	South Africa	Glasgow Gailes and Barassie	275
1971	I Hutcheon	Montifieth	Leven & Lundin Links	277
1972	B N Nicholson	Nairn	Dalmahoy & Ratho Park	290
1973	D M Robertson / G J Clark	Dunbar / Whitley Bay } tie	Dunbar	284
1974	I Hutcheon	Monifieth	Blairgowrie	283
1975	C W Green	Dumbarton	Nairn & Nairn Dunbar	295
1976	S Martin	Downfield	Monifieth & Carnoustie	283
1977	P McKellar	East Renfrewshire	Muirfield	299

Winners since 1946

	Winner	*Club*	*Venue*	*Score*
1946	**W Anderson**	Murcar	Nairn	296
1947	**J McCondichie**	Hilton Park	Luffness	287
1948	**J Panton**	Glenbervie	Prestwick	299
1949	**J Panton**	Glenbervie	Nairn	282
1950	**J Panton**	Glenbervie	Longniddry	276
1951	**J Panton**	Glenbervie	Ayr, Belleisle	290
1952	**J Campbell**	Royal Aberdeen	Lossiemouth	292
1953	**H Thomson**	Unattached	Gullane	283
1954	**J Panton**	Glenbervie	Turnberry	283
1955	**J Panton**	Glenbervie	Elie	272
1956	**E C Brown**	Buchanan Castle	Nairn	281
1957	**E C Brown**	Buchanan Castle	Barassie	284
1958	**E C Brown**	Buchanan Castle	Royal Dornoch	286
1959	**J Panton**	Glenbervie	Turnberry	282
1960	**E C Brown**	Buchanan Castle	West Kilbride	278
1961	**R T Walker**	Downfield	Forres	271
1962	**E C Brown**	Unattached	Dunbar	283
1963	**W Miller**	Cardross	Crieff	284
1964	**R T Walker**	Downfield	Machrihanish	277
1965	**E C Brown**	Cruden Bay	Forfar	271
1966	**E C Brown** **J Panton**	Cruden Bay Glenbervie } tie	Cruden Bay (36)	137
1967	**H Bannerman**	Royal Aberdeen	Montrose	279
1968	**E C Brown**	Cruden Bay	Monktonhall	286
1969	**G Cunningham**	Troon Municipal	Machrihanish	284
1970	**R D Shade**	Duddingston	Montrose	276
1971	**B J Gallacher**	Wentworth	Lundin	282
1972	**H Bannerman**	Banchory	Strathaven	268
1973	**B J Gallacher**	Wentworth	Kings Links	275
1974	**B J Gallacher**	Wentworth	Drumpellier	276
1975	**D Huish**	North Berwick	Duddingston	279
1976	**J Chillas**	Crow Wood	Haggs Castle	286
1977	**B J Gallacher**	Wentworth	Barnton	282

Spanish Open Championship With Spain becoming one of the leading golfing countries, the Spanish Open Championship is becoming more important each year. In point of fact this is an old event which was first played in 1912. Arnold Palmer (1975) and Jerry Heard (1974) are two notable overseas winners of the title.

South African Amateur Championship South Africa, one of the leading golf countries for a number of years has produced many good professionals several of whom have come to fame via the South African Amateur Championship. It is and always has been a match play event. It is controlled by the South African Golf Union.

South African Ladies' Championship This match play event is held annually and organized by the South African Ladies' Golf Association.

South African Open Championship Gary Player when he won the title in 1977 had achieved 11 victories in the event. The other great South African golfer, Bobby Locke, has won the Championship nine times, twice as an amateur.

	Winner	*Club/Country*	*Venue*	*Score*
1930	**S F Brews**	Durban	East London	297
1931	**S F Brews**	Durban	Port Elizabeth	302
1932	**C McIlvenny**	Port Elizabeth	Mowbray	304
1933	**S F Brews**	Durban	Maccauvlei	297
1934	**S F Brews**	Durban	Port Elizabeth	319
1935	**A D Locke**	State Mines	Johannesburg	296
1936	**C E Olander**	East London	Royal Cape	297
1937	**A D Locke**	State Mines	East London	288
1938	**A D Locke**	State Mines	Maccauvlei	279

1939	**A D Locke**	State Mines	Royal Durban	279
1940	**A D Locke**	Maccauvlei	Port Elizabeth	293
1946	**A D Locke**	Unattached	Royal Johannesburg	285
1947	**R W Glennie**	Rondebosch	Mowbray, Cape Town	293
1948	**M Janks**	Houghton	East London	298
1949	**S F Brews**	Houghton	Maccauvlei	291
1950	**A D Locke**	Ohenimuri	Durban	287
1951	**A D Locke**	Ohenimuri	Houghton	275
1952	**S F Brews**	Houghton	Humewood	300
1953	**J R Boyd**	East Rand	Royal Cape	302
1954	**R C Taylor**	Kensington	East London	289
1955	**A D Locke**	Unattached	Zwartkop	283
1956	**Gary Player**	Killarney	Durban	286
1957	**H Henning**	Johannesburg	Humewood	289
1958	**A A Stewart**	Randfontein Estates	Bloemfontein	278
1959	**D Hutchinson**	E Rand Prop Mines	Johannesburg	282
1960	**Gary Player**	Killarney	Mowbray	288
1961	**R Waltman**	Springs C C	East London	289
1962	**H R Henning**	South Africa	Johannesburg	285
1963	**R Waltman**	Springs C C	Durban	281
1964	**A Henning**	South Africa	Bloemfontein	278
1965	**Gary Player**	South Africa	Cape Town	273
1966	**Gary Player**	South Africa	Johannesburg	274
1967	**Gary Player**	South Africa	East London	279
1968	**Gary Player**	South Africa	Houghton	278
1969	**Gary Player**	South Africa	Durban	273
1970	**T Horton**	Britain	Royal Durban	285
1971	**S Hobday**	Rhodesia	Mowbray, Cape Town	276
1972	**Gary Player**	South Africa	Royal Johannesburg	274
1973	**R J Charles**	New Zealand	Durban	282
1974	**R Cole**	South Africa	Royal Johannesburg	272
1975	**Gary Player**	South Africa	Mowbray, Cape Town	278
1976	**D Hayes**	South Africa	Houghton	287
	(with alteration in timing played twice in 1976)			
1976	**Gary Player**	South Africa	Durban	280
1977	**Gary Player**	South Africa	Johannesburg	273

UNITED STATES AMATEUR CHAMPIONSHIP

United States Amateur Championship After two unofficial championships the US Amateur Championship was first played officially in 1895. The first venue was Newport, Rhode Island and the first winner, Charles Blair Macdonald. Macdonald's father-in-law, J H Whigham followed him as champion for the next two years. The first non-American to win the title was an Australian, Walter Travis in 1900, and the only British golfer to win it was Harold Hilton in 1911. For most of its life it was contested by match play. In 1965 it changed to stroke play but in 1973 it reverted to match play. The Championship is run by the US Golf Association.

	Winner	*Runner-Up*	*Venue*	*Score*
1893	**W G Lawrence**	C B Macdonald	Newport R I	4 and 3
1894	**L B Stoddart**	C B Macdonald	St Andrews	5 and 4
1895	**C B Macdonald**	C Sands	Newport R I	12 and 11
1896	**H J Whigham**	J G Thorp	Shinnecock	8 and 7
1897	**H J Whigham**	W R Betts	Wheaton, Ill	8 and 6
1898	**Finlay S Douglas**	W B Smith	Morris County	5 and 3
1899	**H M Harriman**	F S Douglas	Onwentsia	3 and 2
1900	**W J Travis**	F S Douglas	Garden City	2 holes
1901	**W J Travis**	W E Egan	Atlantic City	5 and 4
1902	**Louis N James**	E M Byers	Glen View	4 and 3
1903	**W J Travis**	E M Byers	Nassau	4 and 3
1904	**H Chandler Egan**	F Herreschoff	Baltusrol	8 and 6
1905	**H Chandler Egan**	D E Sawyer	Wheaton, Ill	6 and 5
1906	**E M Byers**	Geo S Lyon	Englewood	2 holes
1907	**Jerome D Travers**	Arch. Graham	Cleveland	6 and 5
1908	**Jerome D Travers**	Max H Behr	Midlothian	8 and 7
1909	**R Gardner**	H C Egan	Wheaton, Ill	4 and 3
1910	**W C Fownes, jun**	W K Wood	Brookline	4 and 3
1911	**H H Hilton**	F Herreschoff	Apawamis	37th hole

1912	**Jerome D Travers**	Charles Evans	Wheaton, Ill	7 and 6
1913	**Jerome D Travers**	G Anderson	Garden City	5 and 4
1914	**F Ouimet**	Jerome D Travers	Ekwanok	6 and 5
1915	**R A Gardner**	J G Anderson	Detroit	5 and 4
1916	**Chas Evans**	R A Gardner	Merion	4 and 3
1919	**D Heron**	R T Jones	Oakmount	5 and 4
1920	**C Evans**	F Ouimet	Engineers Club	5 and 4
1921	**J Guildford**	Robert Gardner	St Louis, Clayton	7 and 6
1922	**J Sweetser**	Chas Evans	Brookline	3 and 2
1923	**Max Marston**	J Sweetser	Flossmoor	38th hole
1924	**R T Jones, Jr**	G von Elm	Merion	9 and 8
1925	**R T Jones, Jr**	W Gunn	Oakmont	8 and 7
1926	**G von Elm**	R T Jones	Baltusrol	2 and 1
1927	**R T Jones, Jr**	C Evans	Minikahda	8 and 7
1928	**R T Jones, Jr**	T P Perkins	Brae Burn	10 and 0
1929	**H R Johnston**	Dr O F Willing	Del Monte	4 and 3
1930	**R T Jones, Jr**	E V Homans	Merion	8 and 7

(On and after 1931 Sectional Qualifying Competitions over 36 holes medal play were inaugurated)

1931	**F Ouimet**	J Westland	Beverley	6 and 5
1932	**C R Somerville**	J Goodman	Baltimore	2 and 1
1933	**G T Dunlap**	M R Marston	Kenwood	6 and 5
1934	**W Lawson Little**	D Goldman	Brookline	8 and 7
1935	**W Lawson Little**	W Emery	Cleveland	4 and 2
1936	**J Fischer**	J McLean	Garden City	37 holes
1937	**J Goodman**	R Billows	Portland	2 holes
1938	**W P Turnesa**	B P Abbott	Oakmont	8 and 7
1939	**M H Ward**	R Billows	Glenview	7 and 5
1940	**R D Chapman**	W B McCullough	Winged Foot	11 and 9
1941	**M H Ward**	B P Abbott	Omaha	4 and 3
1942–45	No Championship			
1946	**S E Bishop**	S Quick	Baltusrol	37th hole
1947	**R H Riegel**	J Dawson	Pebble Beach	2 and 1
1948	**W P Turnesa**	R Billows	Memphis	2 and 1
1949	**C R Coe**	Rufus King	Rochester	11 and 10
1950	**S Urzetta**	F R Stranahan	Minneapolis	39th hole
1951	**W J Maxwell**	J Cagliardi	Saucon Valley	4 and 4
1952	**J Westland**	A Mengert	Seattle	3 and 2
1953	**G Littler**	D Morey	Oklahoma City	1 hole
1954	**Arnold Palmer**	R Sweeney	Detroit	1 hole
1955	**E Harvie Ward**	W Hyndman	Richmond	9 and 8
1956	**E Harvie Ward**	C Krocsis	Lake Forest, Ill	5 and 4
1957	**H Robbins**	Dr F Taylor	Brookline	5 and 4
1958	**C Coe**	T Aaron	San Francisco	5 and 4
1959	**J W Nicklaus**	C R Coe	Broadmoor	1 hole
1960	**D R Beman**	R Gardner	St Louis, Miss	6 and 4
1961	**J W Nicklaus**	D Wysong	Pebble Beach	8 and 6
1962	**L E Harris, Jr**	D Gray	Pinehurst	1 hole
1963	**D R Beman**	D Sikes	Des Moines	2 and 1
1964	**W Campbell**	E Tutwiler	Canterbury, Ohio	1 hole
	(Changed to stroke play)			
1965	**R Murphy**	USA	Tulsa, Okla	291
1966	**G Cowan**	Canada	Ardmore, Penn	285
1967	**R Dickson**	USA	Colorado	285
1968	**B Fleisher**	USA	Columbus	284
1969	**S Melnyk**	USA	Oakmont	286
1970	**L Wadkins**	USA	Portland	280
1971	**G Cowan**	Canada	Wilmington	280
1972	**M Giles**	USA	Charlotte, N C	285
	(Reverted to match-play)			
1973	**C Stadler**	D Strawn	Inverness	6 and 5
1974	**J Pate**	J Grace	Ridgewood	2 and 1
1975	**F Ridley**	K Fergus	Richmond	2 holes
1976	**B Sander**	P Moore	Bel-Air	8 and 6
1977	**J Fought**	D Fischesser	Aronimink	9 and 8

UNITED STATES LADIES' CHAMPIONSHIP

Finalists since 1930

	Winner	Runner-Up	Venue	Score
1930	**Miss Glenda Collett**	Miss V Van Wie	Los Angeles	2 and 1
1931	**Miss H Hicks**	Mrs G C Vare	Buffalo	2 and 1
1932	**Miss V Van Wie**	Mrs G C Vare	Peabody	10 and 8
1933	**Miss V Van Wie**	Miss H Hicks	Exmoor	4 and 3
1934	**Miss V Van Wie**	Miss T Traung	Whitemarsh Valley	2 and 1
1935	**Mrs G C Vare**	Miss P Berg	Interlachen	3 and 2
1936	**Miss Pam Barton**	Mrs M O Crews	Canoe Brook	4 and 3
1937	**Mrs J A Page**	Miss P Berg	Memphis City	7 and 6
1938	**Miss P Berg**	Mrs J A Page	Westmoreland	6 and 5
1939	**Miss B Jameson**	Miss D Kirby	Wee Burn	3 and 2
1940	**Miss B Jameson**	Miss J Cochran	Pebble Beach	6 and 5
1941	**Mrs H Newell**	Miss H Sigel	Brookline	5 and 3
1942–1945 No Championship				
1946	**Mrs G Zaharias**	Mrs C Sherman	Southern Hills	11 and 9
1947	**Miss L Suggs**	Miss D Kirby	Detroit	2 holes
1948	**Miss Grace Lenczyk**	Miss H Sigel	Pebble Beach	4 and 3
1949	**Mrs M A Porter**	Miss D Kielty	Merion	3 and 2
1950	**Miss Beverley Hanson**	Miss Mae Murray	Atlanta	6 and 4
1951	**Miss D Kirby**	Miss Claire Doran	St Paul, Minn	2 and 1
1952	**Mrs J Pung**	Miss S McFedters	Long Beach	2 and 1
1953	**Miss M L Faulk**	Miss P Riley	Rhode Island	3 and 2
1954	**Miss B Romack**	Miss M Wright	Pittsburgh	4 and 2
1955	**Miss Pat Lesser**	Miss J Nelson	Charlotte	7 and 6
1956	**Miss Marlene Stewart**	Miss J Gunderson	Indianapolis	2 and 1
1957	**Miss J Gunderson**	Mrs A C Johnstone	Del Paso	8 and 6
1958	**Miss A Quast**	Miss B Romack	Wee Burn, Darien	3 and 2
1959	**Miss B McIntire**	Miss J Goodwin	Washington	4 and 3
1960	**Miss J Gunderson**	Miss J Ashley	Tulsa	6 and 5
1961	**Mrs A Decker**	Miss P Preuss	Tacoma	14 and 13
1962	**Miss J Gunderson**	Miss A Baker	Rochester	9 and 8
1963	**Mrs Anne Welts**	Miss P Conley	Williamstown	2 and 1
1964	**Miss B McIntire**	Miss J Gunderson	Prairie Dunes	3 and 2
1965	**Miss J Ashley**	Mrs Anne Welts	Denver	5 and 4
1966	**Mrs D Carner**	Mrs J D Streit	Pittsburgh	41st hole
1967	**Miss L Dill**	Miss J Ashley	Annandale	5 and 4
1968	**Mrs J A Carner**	Mrs A Welts	Birmingham	5 and 4
1969	**Miss C Lacoste**	Miss S Hamlin	Las Colinas	3 and 2
1970	**Miss M Wilkinson**	Miss C Hill	Darien	3 and 2
1971	**Miss L Baugh**	Miss B Barry	Atlanta	1 hole
1972	**Miss M Budke**	Miss C Hill	St Louis	5 and 4
1973	**Miss C Semple**	Mrs A Sander	Montclair	1 hole
1974	**Miss C Hill**	Miss C Semple	Broadmoor	5 and 4
1975	**Miss Beth Daniel**	Miss D Horton	Brae Burn	3 and 2
1976	**Miss D Horton**	Mrs M Bretton	Del Paso	2 and 1
1977	**Miss Beth Daniel**	Miss Cathy Sherk	Cincinnati	3 and 2

UNITED STATES MASTERS' TOURNAMENT

United States Masters' Tournament One of the most famous events on the golfing calendar, this Championship was originally the brainchild of the famous American amateur, Robert T Jones, and is played each year at the Augusta National Club. It was first played in 1934 and is an invitation event.

Venue – Augusta National Golf Course, Augusta, Georgia

	Winner	Score
1934	**Horton Smith**	284
1935	**Gene Sarazen**	282
1936	**Horton Smith**	285
1937	**Byron Nelson**	283
1938	**Henry Pickard**	285
1939	**Ralph Guldahl**	279
1940	**Jimmy Demaret**	280
1941	**Craig Wood**	280
1942	**Byron Nelson**	280

1946	Herman Keiser	282
1947	Jimmy Demaret	281
1948	Claude Harmon	279
1949	Sam Snead	283
1950	Jimmy Demaret	282
1951	Ben Hogan	280
1952	Sam Snead	286
1953	Ben Hogan	274
1954	Sam Snead	289
1955	Cary Middlecoff	279
1956	Jackie Burke	289
1957	Doug Ford	283
1958	Arnold Palmer	284
1959	A Wall	284
1960	Arnold Palmer	282
1961	Gary Player (South Africa)	280
1962	Arnold Palmer	280
1963	Jack Nicklaus	286
1964	Arnold Palmer	276
1965	Jack Nicklaus	271
1966	Jack Nicklaus	288
1967	G Brewer	280
1968	R Goalby	277
1969	G Archer	281
1970	W Casper	279
1971	C Coody	279
1972	Jack Nicklaus	286
1973	T Aaron	283
1974	Gary Player (South Africa)	278
1975	Jack Nicklaus	276
1976	Ray Floyd	271
1977	Tom Watson	276
1978	Gary Player (South Africa)	277

United States Open Championship Like many other championships this great event followed one or two unofficial events which were, in effect, championships. Officially the US Open Championship did not begin until 1895, the same year as its amateur counterpart. The venue for both was Rhode Island. As British professionals dominated the American golf scene at its outset it is not surprising that the first championship was won by a British player, the Englishman, Horace Rawlings. The first American to win was John McDermott, who was successful in 1911. McDermott also won the following year. Perhaps the most famous and most successful Championship of all was that of 1913 when a young American boy, an amateur by the name of Francis Ouimet beat the great British professionals Harry Vardon and Ted Ray after a play-off. Ouimet was later honoured by being elected Captain of the Royal and Ancient Golf Club of St Andrews, and became one of the best loved figures in golf.

UNITED STATES OPEN CHAMPIONSHIP

	Winner	*Club/Country*	*Venue*	*Score*
1894	**Willie Dunn**	W Campbell	St Andrews, NY	2 holes
	(After 1874 decided by Medal Play)			
1895	**H J Rawlins**	USA	Newport	173
1896	**J Foulis**	USA	Southampton	152
1897	**J Lloyd**	USA	Wheaton, Ill	162
1898	**F Herd**	USA	Shinnecock Hills	328
	(72 holes played from 1898)			
1899	**W Smith**	USA	Baltimore	315
1900	**H Vardon**	England	Wheaton, Ill	313
1901	**W Anderson**	USA	Myopia, Mass	315
1902	**L Aucherlonie**	USA	Garden City	305
1903	**W Anderson**	USA	Baltusrol	307
1904	**W Anderson**	USA	Glenview	304
1905	**W Anderson**	USA	Myopia	335
1906	**A Smith**	USA	Onwentsia	291
1907	**A Ross**	USA	Chestnut Hill, Pa	302
1908	**F McLeod**	USA	Myopia	322
1909	**G Sargent**	USA	Englewood, N J	290

1910	A Smith	USA	Philadelphia	289
1911	J J McDermott	USA	Wheaton, Ill	307
1912	J J McDermott	USA	Buffalo, N Y	294
1913	F Ouimet	USA	Brookline, Mass	304

(After a tie with H Vardon and E Ray)

1914	W Hagen	USA	Midlothian	297
1915	J D Travers	USA	Baltusrol	290
1916	C Evans	USA	Minneapolis	286
1919	W Hagen	USA	Braeburn	301
1920	E Ray	England	Inverness	295
1921	J Barnes	USA	Washington	289
1922	G Sarazen	USA	Glencoe	288
1923	R T Jones	USA	Inwood, Long Island, NY	295

(After a tie with R A Cruikshank. Play-off – Jones 76, Cruikshank 78)

1924	C Walker	USA	Oakland Hills	297
1925	W MacFarlane	USA	Worcester	291
1926	R T Jones	USA	Scioto	293
1927	T D Armour	USA	Oakmont	301
1928	J Farrell	USA	Olympia Fields	294

(After a tie with R T Jones. Play-off – Farrell 143, Jones 144)

1929	R T Jones	USA	Winged Foot, NY	294

(After a tie with A Espinosa. Play-off – Jones 141, Espinosa 164)

1930	R T Jones	USA	Interlachen	287
1931	B Burke	USA	Inverness	292

(After a tie with G von Elm. Play-off – Burke 149, 148; von Elm 149, 149)

1932	G Sarazen	USA	Fresh Meadow	286
1933	J Goodman	USA	North Shore	287
1934	O Dutra	USA	Merion	293
1935	S Parks	USA	Oakmont	299
1936	T Manero	USA	Springfield	282
1937	R Guldahl	USA	Oakland Hills	281
1938	R Guldahl	USA	Cherry Hills	284
1939	Byron Nelson	USA	Philadelphia	284

(After a tie with G Sarazen; Play-off – Nelson 70, Sarazen 73)

1940	W Lawson Little	USA	Canterbury Ohio	287

(After a tie with G Sarazen; Play-off – Little 70, Sarazen 73)

1941	Craig Wood	USA	Fort Worth, Texas	284
1946	Lloyd Mangrum	USA	Canterbury	284

(After a tie with Byron Nelson and Vic Ghezzie)

1947	Lew Worsham	USA	St Louis	282

(After a tie with Sam Snead. Replay scores Worsham 69, Snead 70)

1948	Ben Hogan	USA	Los Angeles	276
1949	Cary Middlecoff	USA	Medinah, Ill	286
1950	Ben Hogan	USA	Merion, Pa	287

(After a tie with Lloyd Mangrum and George Fazio, Replay scores Hogan 69, Mangrum 73, Fazio 75)

1951	Ben Hogan	USA	Oakland Hills	287
1952	Julius Boros	USA	Dallas, Texas	281
1953	Ben Hogan	USA	Oakmont	283
1954	Ed Furgol	USA	Baltusrol	284
1955	J Fleck	USA	San Francisco	287

(After a tie with Ben Hogan; Replay scores Fleck 69, Hogan 72)

1956	Cary Middlecoff	USA	Rochester	281
1957	Dick Mayer	USA	Inverness	282

(After a tie with Cary Middlecoff; Tie scores, Mayer 72, Middlecoff 79)

1958	Tommy Bolt	USA	Tolsa, Okla	283
1959	W Casper	USA	Mamaroneck	282
1960	Arnold Palmer	USA	Denver	280
1961	Gene Littler	USA	Birmingham	281
1962	J W Nicklaus	USA	Oakmont	283

(After a tie with Arnold Palmer; Nicklaus 71, Palmer 74)

1963	Julius Boros	USA	Brookline	293

(After a tie, play-off J Boros 70, Jack Cupit 73, Arnold Palmer 76)

1964	Ken Venturi	USA	Washington	278

1965	**Gary Player**	South Africa	St Louis	282
	(After tie with K Nagle (AUS); Replay Scores, Player 71, Nagle 74)			
1966	**W Casper**	USA	San Francisco	278
	(After tie with Arnold Palmer. Replay scores, Casper 69, Palmer 73)			
1967	**J W Nicklaus**	USA	Baltusrol	275
1968	**Lee Trevino**	USA	Rochester	275
1969	**Orville Moody**	USA	Houston	281
1970	**A Jacklin**	England	Chaska	281
1971	**Lee Trevino**	USA	Merion	280
	(After a tie with J Nicklaus. Play-off – Trevino 68, Nicklaus 71)			
1972	**J W Nicklaus**	USA	Pebble Beach	290
1973	**J Miller**	USA	Oakmont	279
1974	**H Irwin**	USA	Winged Foot	287
1975	**L Graham**	USA	Medinah	287
	(After a tie with J Mahaffey – Play-off Graham 71, Mahaffey 73)			
1976	**J Pate**	USA	Atlanta, Georgia	277
1977	**H Green**	USA	Southern Hills	278

	Winner	*Runner-Up*	*Club/Country*	*Score*
1916	**Jim Barnes**	Jock Hutchison	Siwanoy	1 hole
1919	**Jim Barnes**	Fred McLeod	Engineers' Club	6 and 5
1920	**Jock Hutchison**	Douglas Edgar	Flossmoor	1 hole
1921	**Walter Hagen**	Jim Barnes	Inwood Club	3 and 2
1922	**Gene Sarazen**	Emmet French	Oakmont	4 and 3
1923	**Gene Sarazen**	Walter Hagen	Palham	38th hole
1924	**Walter Hagen**	Jim Barnes	French Lick	2 holes
1925	**Walter Hagen**	W E Mehihorn	Olympic Fields	6 and 4
1926	**Walter Hagen**	Leo Diegel	Salisbury	4 and 3
1927	**Walter Hagen**	Joe Turnesa	Dallas, Texas	1 hole
1928	**Leo Diegel**	Al Espinosa	Five Farms	6 and 5
1929	**Leo Diegel**	J Farrell	Hill Crest	6 and 4
1930	**Tommy Armour**	G Sarazen	Fresh Meadow	1 hole
1931	**T Creavy**	D Shute	Wannamoisett	2 and 1
1932	**O Dutra**	F Walsh	St Paul's	4 and 3
1933	**G Sarazen**	W Goggin	Milwaukee	5 and 4
1934	**P Runyan**	Craig Wood	Buffalo	38th hole
1935	**J Revolta**	T D Armour	Oklahoma	5 and 4
1936	**D Shute**	J Thomson	Pinehurst	3 and 2
1937	**D Shute**	H McSpaden	Pittsburgh	37th hole
1938	**P Runyan**	S Snead	Shawnee	8 and 7
1939	**H Picard**	B Nelson	Pomonok	37th hole
1940	**Byron Nelson**	S Snead	Hershey, Pa	1 hole
1941	**Vic Ghezzi**	Byron Nelson	Denver	38th hole
1942	**S Snead**	Jim Turnesa	Atlantic City	2 and 1
1943	No Championship			
1944	**Bob Hamilton**	B Nelson	Spokane, Wash	1 hole
1945	**Byron Nelson**	Sam Byrd	Dayton, Ohio	4 and 3
1946	**Ben Hogan**	Ed Oliver	Portland	6 and 4
1947	**Jim Ferrier**	Chick Harbert	Detroit	2 and 1
1948	**Ben Hogan**	Mike Turnesa	Norwood Hills	7 and 6
1949	**S Snead**	Johnny Palmer	Richmond, Va	3 and 2
1950	**Chandler Harper**	Henry Williams	Scioto, Ohio	4 and 3
1951	**S Snead**	Walter Burkemo	Oakmont, Pa	7 and 6
1952	**Jim Turnesa**	Chick Harbert	Big Spring, Louis	1 hole
1953	**Walter Burkemo**	Felice Lorza	Birmingham, Mich	2 and 1
1954	**Chick Harbert**	Walter Burkemo	St Paul, Minn	4 and 3
1955	**D Ford**	C Middlecoff	Detroit	4 and 3
1956	**J Burke**	T Kroll	Boston	3 and 2
1957	**L Hebert**	D Finsterwald	Miami Valley, Dayton	3 and 1
	Changed to Stroke Play			
1958	**D Finsterwald**	USA	Havertown, Penn	276
1959	**Bob Rosburg**	USA	Minneapolis	277
1960	**Jay Hebert**	USA	Akron, Ohio	281
1961	**Jerry Barber**	USA	Olympia Fields	277
	(After a tie)			

UNITED STATES PGA CHAMPIONSHIP

Above: The PGA Cup.

1962	**Gary Player**	South Africa	Newtown Square	278
1963	**J W Nicklaus**	USA	Dallas, Texas	279
1964	**Bobby Nichols**	USA	Columbus, Ohio	271
1965	**D Marr**	USA	Ligonier, Penn	280
1966	**A Geiberger**	USA	Akron, Ohio	280
1967	**Don January**	USA	Denver	281
	(After a tie)			
1968	**Julius Boros**	USA	San Antonio, Texas	281
1969	**Ray Floyd**	USA	Dayton, Ohio	276
1970	**Dave Stockton**	USA	Tulsa, Okla	279
1971	**J W Nicklaus**	USA	Palm Beach, Fla	281
1972	**Gary Player**	South Africa	Birmingham, Mich	281
1973	**J W Nicklaus**	USA	Cleveland	277
1974	**L Trevino**	USA	Clemmons, N C	276
1975	**J W Nicklaus**	USA	Akron, Ohio	276
1976	**D Stockton**	USA	Congressional, Wash	281
1977	**L Wadkins**	USA	Pebble Beach	282

(After a sudden death play-off at the third extra hole with G Littler)

United States Public Links Championship This event was founded by the US Golf Association in 1922. The entries for the Championship total many thousands. Competitors must be bona fide public course golfers. Members of private clubs are excluded. The trophy was given by one of the founders of the event, Mr James D Standish.

United States Seniors' Amateur Championship This event is comparatively new: it began in 1955. Those eligible must be more than 55 years of age. Whereas the Seniors' Golf Association Championship is contested by stroke play, this Championship is decided by match play.

United States Seniors' Golf Association Tournament This event is sponsored by the Association whose name it bears and which goes back to 1905. The minimum age is 55. The Association also plays many international matches against Senior golfers of other countries.

United States Seniors' Women's Amateur Championship Amateur lady golfers whose age exceeds 50 and whose handicaps are 15 or less can compete in this event. The first two finalists were two famous players, Miss Orcutt and Mrs Glenna Collett Vare.

United States Ladies' Championship This championship was founded by the US Golf Association in 1895 and was held at Meadowbrook, New York. There were 13 competitors and 13 proved lucky for Mrs Charles Brown who won with an aggregate of 132 over 18 holes. That was the only time the Championship was a stroke play event. Since then it has always been match play.

UNITED STATES WOMEN'S OPEN CHAMPIONSHIP

United States Women's Open Championship With the upsurge of women professionals this Championship was instituted in 1946. Outstanding winner in 1947 was the French amateur, Catherine Lacoste.

	Winner	*Club*	*Venue*	*Score*
1946	**Miss P Berg**	Minneapolis	Spokane	5 and 4
	(After 1946 changed to medal play)			
1947	**Miss B Jameson**	San Antonio	Greensboro	300
1948	**Mrs G Zaharias**	Detroit	Atlantic City	300
1949	**Miss Louise Suggs**	Carrolton	Maryland	291
1950	**Mrs G Zaharias**	Skycrest	Wichita	291
1951	**Miss B Rawls**	Austin	Atlanta	294
1952	**Miss Louise Suggs**	Carrolton	Bala	284
1953	**Miss B Rawls**	Austin	Rochester	302
	(After a tie with Mrs J Pung)			
1954	**Mrs G Zaharias**	Salem C C	Peabody	291
1955	**Miss F Crocker**	Witchita C C	Wichita	299
1956	**Mrs K Cornelius**	Northland C C	Duluth	302
	(After a tie with Miss B McIntire)			
1957	**Miss B Rawls**	Winged Foot C C	Mamaroneck	299
1958	**Miss M Wright**	Forest Lake C C	Bloomfield Hills	290
1959	**Miss M Wright**	Churchill Valley C C	Pittsburgh	287
1960	**Miss B Rawls**	Worcester C C	Worcester	292
1961	**Miss M Wright**	Dallas, Texas	Springfield	293

1962	**Mrs M Lindstrom**	Missouri	Myrtle Beach	301
1963	**Miss M Mills**	Mississippi	Kenwood	289
1964	**Miss M Wright**	Dallas, Texas	San Diego	290
	(After a tie with Miss Ruth Jessen, Seattle)			
1965	**Miss C Mann**		Northfield	290
1966	**Miss S Spuzich**	Indianapolis	Hazeltine National	297
1967	**Miss C Lacoste**	France	Hot Springs	294
1968	**Mrs S M Berning**	Oklahoma	Moselem Springs	289
1969	**Miss Donna Caponi**	California	Scenic-Hills	294
1970	**Miss Donna Caponi**	California	Muskogee	287
1971	**Mrs J Gunderson-Carner**	Florida	Erie	288
1972	**Mrs S M Berning**	Oklahoma	Mamaroneck	299
1973	**Mrs S M Berning**	Oklahoma	Rochester	290
1974	**Miss S Haynie**	Texas	La Grange	295
1975	**Miss S Palmer**	Texas	Northfield	295
1976	**Mrs J Carner**	Florida	Springfield	292
	(After a tie with Miss S Palmer)			
1977	**Miss H Stacy**	USA	Hazeltine National	292

Walker Cup Match Mr George Walker, a former President of the US Golf Association presented the famous trophy for which this match is played. Like most other international matches, this one started as an unofficial match; in 1921 a match between American and British amateur golfers was played on the links of the Royal Liverpool Club in England (won incidentally by the US). It was decided to have an annual official match and it was then that Mr Walker donated the trophy. The match was in fact held in 1922, 1923 and 1924 but it was decided to hold it every two years. The US teams have dominated the match; Britain has won only twice, both times at St Andrews.

WALKER CUP

	Winner	*Venue*
1922	USA, 8 matches; Great Britain, 4 matches	National Links
1923	USA, 6½ matches; Great Britain, 5½ matches	St Andrews
1924	USA, 9 matches; Great Britain, 3 matches	Garden City
1926	USA, 6½ matches; Great Britain, 5½ matches	St Andrews
1928	USA, 11 matches; Great Britain, 1 match	Chicago
1930	USA, 10 matches; Great Britain, 2 matches	Royal St George's
1932	USA, 9½ matches; Great Britain, 2½ matches	Brooklyn
1934	USA, 9½ matches; Great Britain, 2½ matches	St Andrews
1936	USA, 10½ matches; Great Britain, 1½ matches	Pine Valley
1938	Great Britain, 7½ matches; USA, 4½ matches	St Andrews
1947	USA, 8 matches; Great Britain, 4 matches	St Andrews
1949	USA, 10 matches; Great Britain, 2 matches	Winged Foot
1951	USA, 7½ matches; Great Britain, 4½ matches	Birkdale
1953	USA, 9 matches; Great Britain, 3 matches	Merion
1955	USA, 10 matches; Great Britain, 2 matches	St Andrews
1957	USA, 8½ matches; Great Britain, 3½ matches	Minikahda
1959	USA, 9 matches; Great Britain, 3 matches	Muirfield
1961	USA, 11 matches; Great Britain, 1 match	Seattle
1963	USA, 14 matches; Great Britain, 10 matches	Turnberry
1965	Great Britain, 12 matches; USA, 12 matches	Baltimore
1967	USA, 15 matches; Great Britain, 9 matches	Royal St George's
1969	USA, 13 matches; Great Britain, 11 matches	Milwaukee
1971	Great Britain, 13 matches; USA, 11 matches	St Andrews
1973	USA, 14 matches; Great Britain, 10 matches	Brookline
1975	USA, 15½ matches; Great Britain, 8½ matches	St Andrews
1977	USA, 16 matches; Great Britain, 8 matches	Shinnecock Hills

Welsh Amateur Championship This Championship was instituted in 1895. Competitors must have at least one parent who is Welsh. It is contested by match play and is held annually.

WELSH AMATEUR CHAMPIONSHIP

Winners since 1946

	Winner	*Runner-Up*	*Venue*	*Score*
1946	**J V Moody**	A Marshman	Porthcawl	9 and 8
1947	**S B Roberts**	A Breen Turner	Harlech	8 and 7
1948	**A A Duncan**	S B Roberts	Porthcawl	2 and 1

1949	**A D Evans**	Mervyn A Jones	Aberdovey	2 and 1
1950	**J L Morgan**	D J Bonnell	Southerndown	9 and 7
1951	**J L Morgan**	W I Tucker	Harlech	3 and 2
1952	**A A Duncan**	J L Morgan	Ashburnham	4 and 3
1953	**S B Roberts**	D Pearson	Prestatyn	5 and 3
1954	**A A Duncan**	K Thomas	Tenby	6 and 5
1955	**T J Davies**	P Dunn	Harlech	at 38th
1956	**A Lockley**	W I Tucker	Southerndown	2 and 1
1957	**E S Mills**	H Griffiths	Harlech	2 and 1
1958	**H C Squirrell**	A D Lake	Conway	4 and 3
1959	**H C Squirrell**	N Rees	Porthcawl	8 and 7
1960	**H C Squirrell**	P Richards	Aberdovey	2 and 1
1961	**A D Evans**	J Toye	Ashburnham	3 and 2
1962	**J Povall**	H C Squirrell	Royal St David's	3 and 2
1963	**W I Tucker**	J Povall	Southerndown	4 and 3
1964	**H C Squirrell**	W I Tucker	Royal St David's	1 hole
1965	**H C Squirrell**	G Clay	Royal Porthcawl	6 and 4
1966	**W I Tucker**	E N Davies	Aberdovey	6 and 5
1967	**J K Povall**	W I Tucker	Ashburnham	3 and 2
1968	**J Buckley**	J Povall	Conway	8 and 7
1969	**J L Toye**	E N Davies	Royal Porthcawl	1 hole
1970	**E N Davies**	J Povall	Royal St David's	1 hole
1971	**C Brown**	H C Squirrell	Southerndown	6 and 5
1972	**E N Davies**	J L Toye	Prestatyn	40th hole
1973	**D McLean**	T Holder	Ashburnham	6 and 4
1974	**S Cox**	E N Davies	Caernarvonshire	3 and 2
1975	**J L Toye**	W I Tucker	Royal Porthcawl	5 and 4
1976	**M P D Adams**	W I Tucker	Royal St David's	6 and 5
1977	**D Stevens**	J Povall	Southerndown	3 and 2

WELSH LADIES' CHAMPIONSHIP

Welsh Ladies' Championship Instituted in 1905. The Championship is for women amateur golfers with the necessary qualifications of birth and parentage. It is played annually every summer and in 1935, at Tenby, the event had to be abandoned owing to a snowstorm.

Winners from 1947

	Winner	*Runner-Up*	*Venue*	*Score*
1947	**Miss M Barron**	Miss E Jones	Prestatyn	1 hole
1948	**Mrs N Seely**	Miss M Barron	Prestatyn	12 and 11
1949	**Miss S Bryan-Smith**	Mrs E D Brown	Newport	3 and 2
1950	**Dr Garfield Evans**	Miss N Cook	Porthcawl	2 and 1
1951	**Mrs E Bromley-Davenport**	Miss N Cook	Royal St Davids	1 hole
1952	**Miss E Lever**	Miss P Roberts	Southerndown	6 and 5
1953	**Miss Nancy Cook**	Miss E Lever	Llandudno	3 and 2
1954	**Miss Nancy Cook**	Mrs E D Brown	Tenby	1 hole
1955	**Miss Nancy Cook**	Miss P Roberts	Holyhead	2 holes
1956	**Miss P Roberts**	Miss Barron	Royal Porthcawl	2 and 1
1957	**Miss M Barron**	Miss P Roberts	Royal St David's	6 and 4
1958	**Mrs M Wright**	Miss P Roberts	Newport	1 hole
1959	**Miss P Roberts**	Miss A Gwyther	Conway	6 and 4
1960	**Miss M Barron**	Mrs E Brown	Tenby	8 and 6
1961	**Mrs M Oliver**	Miss N Seddon	Aberdovey	5 and 4
1962	**Mrs M Oliver**	Miss P Roberts	Radyr	4 and 2
1963	**Miss P Roberts**	Miss N Seddon	Royal St David's	7 and 5
1964	**Mrs M Oliver**	Mrs M Wright	Southerndown	1 hole
1965	**Mrs M Wright**	Mrs E Brown	Prestatyn	3 and 2
1966	**Miss A Hughes**	Miss P Roberts	Ashburnham	5 and 4
1967	**Mrs M Wright**	Miss C Phipps	Royal St David's	21st hole
1968	**Miss S Hales**	Mrs M Wright	Royal Porthcawl	3 and 2
1969	**Miss P Roberts**	Miss A Hughes	Caernarvonshire	3 and 2
1970	**Mrs A Briggs**	Miss J Morris	Newport	19th hole
1971	**Mrs A Briggs**	Mrs E N Davies	Royal St David's	2 and 1
1972	**Miss A Hughes**	Miss J Rogers	Tenby	3 and 2
1973	**Mrs A Briggs**	Mrs J John	Holyhead	3 and 2
1974	**Mrs A Briggs**	Dr H Lyall	Ashburnham	3 and 2

1975	**Mrs A Johnson**	Miss K Rawlings	Prestatyn	1 hole
1976	**Miss T Perkins**	Mrs A Johnson	Royal Porthcawl	4 and 2
1977	**Miss T Perkins**	Miss P Whitley	Aberdovey	5 and 4

Winners since 1946

WELSH PROFESSIONAL CHAMPIONSHIP (INSTITUTED 1904)

	Winner	*Club*	*Venue*	*Score*
1946	**H Gould**	Royal Porthcawl	Porthcawl	308
1947	**K Williams**	Radyr	Llandrindod	280
1948	**H Gould**	Royal Porthcawl	Aberdovey	291
1949	**H Gould**	Royal Porthcawl	Radyr	275
1950	**G James**	Newport	Newport	303
1951	**H Gould**	Southerndown	Llandudno	305
1952	**W S Collins**	North Wales	Southerndown	301
1956	**D Smalldon**	Cardiff	Royal Porthcawl	300
1957	**J Black**	Royal St David's	Llandudno (36 holes)	144
1958	**R H Kemp, Jr**	Glamorganshire	Radyr	275
1959	**D Smalldon**	Cardiff	Newport	288
1960	**R H Kemp, Jr**	Unattached	Llandudno	288
1961	**S Mouland**	Glamorganshire	Southerndown	286
1962	**S Mouland**	Glamorganshire	Royal Porthcawl	302
1963	**H Gould**	Southerndown	Wrexham	291
1964	**B Bielby**	Portmadoc	Tenby	297
1965	**S Mouland**	Glamorganshire	Penarth	281
1966	**S Mouland**	Glamorganshire	Conway	279
1967	**S Mouland**	Glamorganshire	Pyle and Kenfig (54 holes)	219
1968	**R J Davies**	South Herts	Southerndown	292
1969	**S Mouland**	Glamorganshire	Llandudno	277
1970	**W Evans**	Pennard	Tredegar Park	289
1971	**J Buckley**	North Wales	St Pierre	291
1972	**J Buckley**	Rhos-on-Sea	Royal Porthcawl	298
1973	**A Griffiths**	Wrexham	Newport	289
1974	**M Hughes**	Aberystwyth	Cardiff	284
1975	**C DeFoy**	Bryn Meadows	Whitchurch	285
1976	**S Cox**	Wenvoe Castle	Radyr	284
1977	**C DeFoy**	Calcot Park	Glamorganshire (36 holes)	135

World Amateur Team Championship This famous event was first known as the Eisenhower Trophy because the trophy was presented by the famous World War II leader and President of the United States. The event is held every four years, in a different country each year. Teams are composed of four players, the best three four round scores counting. The event was played for the first time in St Andrews, Scotland in 1958.

World Cup This event is for professional teams from any country. Teams are composed of two players; all four rounds from each member of the team count. There is also an individual prize. The trophy formerly known as the Canada Cup was presented by Mr John J Hopkins, a Canadian businessman, for the fostering of goodwill between the golfing nations of the world. It is held annually and the venue is located in a different country each year.

WORLD CUP Until 1966 called Canada Cup

	Winner	*Runner-Up*	*Venue*	*Score*
1953	**Argentina** (A Cerda and R de Vicenzo) (Individual, A Cerda, Argentina, 140)	Canada (S Leonard and B Kerr)	Montreal	287
1954	**Australia** (P Thomson and K Nagle) (Individual, S Leonard, Canada, 275)	Argentina (A Cerda and R de Vicenzo)	Laval-sur-Lac	556
1955	**United States** (C Harbert and Ed Furgol) (Individual, E Furgol, US after play-off with P Thomson, F van Donck, 279)	Australia (P Thomson and K Nagle)	Washington	560
1956	**United States** (Ben Hogan and Sam Snead) (Individual, B Hogan, US, 277)	South Africa (A D Locke and Gary Player)	Wentworth	567
1957	**Japan** (Torakichi Nakamura and Koichi Ono)	United States (Sam Snead and Jimmy Demaret)	Tokyo	557

Canada Cup

(Individual, T Nakamura, Japan, 274)

1958	**Ireland** (H Bradshaw and C O'Connor)	Spain (A Miguel and S Miguel)	Mexico City	579

(Individual, A Miguel, Spain after play-off with C O'Connor, 286)

1959	**Australia** (P Thomson and K Nagle)	United States (Sam Snead and C Middlecoff)	Melbourne	563

(Individual, S Leonard, Canada, 275 after tie with P Thomson)

1960	**United States** (Arnold Palmer and Sam Snead)	England (H Weetman and B J Hunt)	Portmarnock	565

(Individual, Flory van Donck, Belgium, 279)

1961	**United States** (Sam Snead and J Demaret)	Australia (P Thomson and K Nagle)	Puerto Rico	560

(Individual, Sam Snead, USA, 272)

1962	**United States** (Sam Snead and Arnold Palmer)	Argentina (F de Luca and R de Vicenzo)	Buenos Aires	557

(Individual, R de Vicenzo, Argentina, 276)

1963	**United States** (Arnold Palmer and Jack Nicklaus)	Spain (S Miguel and R Sota)	St Nom-La Breteche	482

(Individual, Jack Nicklaus, USA, 237 (63 holes))

1964	**United States** (Arnold Palmer and Jack Nicklaus)	Argentina (R de Vicenzo and L Ruiz)	Maui, Hawaii	554

(Individual, Jack Nicklaus, USA, 276)

1965	**South Africa** (Gary Player and H Henning)	Spain (A Miguel and R Sota)	Madrid	571

(Individual, Gary Player, 281)

1966	**United States** (Arnold Palmer and Jack Nicklaus)	South Africa (Gary Player and H Henning)	Tokyo	548

(Individual, G Knudson, Canada, H Sugimoto, Japan – 272 Knudson won play-off)

1967	**United States** (Arnold Palmer and Jack Nicklaus)	New Zealand (R J Charles and W Godfrey)	Mexico City	557

(Individual, Arnold Palmer, USA, 276)

1968	**Canada** (Al Balding and G Kudson)	United States (J Boros and Lee Trevino)	Olgiata, Rome	569

(Individual Al Balding, Canada, 274)

1969	**United States** (O Moody and Lee Trevino)	Japan (T Kono and H Yasuda)	Singapore	552

(Individual, Lee Trevino, USA, 275)

1970	**Australia** (B Devlin and David Graham)	Argentina (R de Vicenzo and V Fernandez)	Buenos Aires	545

(Individual R de Vicenzo, Argentina, 269)

1971	**United States** (J Nicklaus and Lee Trevino)	South Africa (H Henning and Gary Player)	Palm Beach Florida	555

(Individual, J Nicklaus, USA, 271)

1972	**Taiwan** (Hsieh Min Nan and Lu Liang Huan)	Japan (Takaaki Kono and Takashi Murakami)	Melbourne	438

(Individual, Hsieh Min Nan, Taiwan, 217 (3 rounds only))

1973	**United States** (J Miller and J Nicklaus)	South Africa (Gary Player and H Baiocchi)	Marbella	558

(Individual, J Miller, USA, 277)

1974	**South Africa** (R Cole and Dale Hayes)	Japan (I Aoki and M Ozaki)	Caracas	554

(Individual, R Cole, South Africa, 271)

1975	**United States** (J Miller and Lou Graham)	Taiwan (Hsieh Min Nan and Kuo Chie Hsiung)	Bangkok	554

(Individual, J Miller, USA, 275)

1976	**Spain** (S Ballesteros and M Pinero)	United States (J Pate and D Stockton)	Palm Springs, USA	574

(Individual, E Acosta, Mexico, 282)

1977	**Spain** (S Ballesteros and A Garrid)	Philippines (R Lavares and B Ardo)	Manila	591

(Individual, Gary Player, 289)

World Series One of the world's most important professional events, this competition is played each year at Akron, Ohio. Competitors may compete only if invited to do so and only the world's leading golfers receive invitations to tee up.

Championships
Highest score: Walter Danecki, an American, in 1965 in a qualifying test at Hillside, Southport scored 108 in the first round and 113 in the second round.
Most putts: Dave Hill took six putts on the 5th green of the Oakmont course during the US Open in 1962.

Championship Winners
Gary Player	South African Open	11 times
Peter Thomson	New Zealand Open	9 times
Gary Player	Australian Open	7 times
Harry Vardon	British Open	6 times
Ben Hogan	US Open	4 times

Competitions – Highest Rounds
Von Cittern at Biarritz in 1888 316 strokes .
John Murphy in US 298 strokes for 18 holes.

Courses, Most Played On
Ralph Kennedy, an American, claims to have played on 3615 different courses.

Fewest Putts in a Game
Collen-Smith – 14 putts at Betchworth Park, Surrey in 1947.
Chatten – 16 putts at Elkhart, Indiana.

Highest Golf Course in the World
Tuctu, Peru is 14,335ft above sea level.

Highest Score at One Hole
Tommy Armour scored 26 at the 17th hole in the Shawnee Tournament in 1927.

Highest Score at a Short Hole
German amateur Herman Tissies took 15 at the 8th hole at Troon in the British Open in 1950.

Hole in One
First Recorded: Tom Morris Jr at the 8th at Prestwick during the British Open in 1868.
Greatest Number: American Art Wall has 37 registered holes-in-one. British professional Charles Chevalier scored 30 in his career.
Longest: Bob Mitera on the 444yd (406m) 10th hole at the Miracle Hill Club in Omaha in 1965. David Hulley on the 380yd (347m) 5th hole at Tankersley Park, Yorkshire in 1961.
More than One: Eric Fiddian in the Irish Open scored two holes in one in 1933. John Hudson holed out on the 12th and 11th in the Martini Professional Tournament in 1971.
Most in One Year: J O Boydstone of California holed out 11 times in 1.
Longest By a Woman: Marie Robie, 393yd, 1st hole at Furnace Brook, Massachusetts, 1940.
Oldest Player: Charles Youngman, 93 years old at the Tam O'Shanter Club in Toronto, Canada. George Millar, 93, at the Anaheim Club in California, T South, 91, at Highcliffe Castle, Hampshire. Mary Kent at 90 at the Forest Hill Club, Florida.
Youngest Player: Coby Orr, age 5, at Riverside Club in Texas in 1975. In Britain, Harry Pratt, age 7½ at Thurlestone, Devon.

Longest Championship Course
For the 1968 British Open, Carnoustie was stretched to 7252yd (6531m).

Longest Championship Matches
T Egan beat J C Brown at the 41st hole in the 1952 Irish Amateur Championship at Royal Belfast. D Sewell beat M Christmas at the 41st hole in the English Amateur Championship at Hunstanton. Jo Anne Carner beat Marlene Streit at the 41st hole in the 1966 US Ladies' Championship.

Longest Championship Drives
In the 1933 British Open Craig Wood, the American professional, drove the ball at the 5th hole a distance of 430yd. There was a following wind. In the same event at the same venue in 1970 Jack Nicklaus at the 18th hole drove the ball a distance estimated at 300yd. There were no favourable conditions.

Longest Drives
American professional George Bayer is credited with a drive of 'over 500yd' and another American professional is credited with a drive of 515yd. Both drives were under distinctly favourable conditions as was that of T H Haydon at Budleigh Salterton in England when he drove the ball 450yd. The longest drive with no favourable conditions would seem to be that of Irish golfer Tommie Campbell, of the Portmarnock Club, who is credited with a drive of 392yd.

Lowest Championship Round
Baldovino Dassu of Italy in the 1971 Swiss Open Championship played a round of 60. The course measured 6885yd (6295m).

Oldest Champions
Oldest winner of the British Open Championship: Roberto de Vicenzo aged 44 years 93 days, beating Harry Vardon by 51 days.
Oldest winner of the US Open Championship: Ted Ray aged 43 years.
Oldest winner of the US Masters Tournament: Sam Snead aged 41 years.
Oldest winner of the US PGA Championship: Julius Boros aged 48 years.
Jack Cannon won the Scottish Amateur Championship when he was 53 years old.

Youngest Champions
Youngest winner of the British Open Championship: Tom Morris Jr aged 18 years.
Youngest winner of the US Open Championship: Horace Rawlings aged 19 years.
Youngest winner of the British Ladies' Championship: Miss May Hezlet aged 17 years.
Youngest winner of the US Ladies' Championship: Miss Beatrice Hoyt aged 16 years.

Picture Credits:

Colorsports: 37, 116 (bottom right)
Irish Linen Guild: 202
Cordel Wilson: 90
Morgan Wells: 206
H W Neale: 2/3, 4/5, 7, 9 (bottom left), 11, 16, 17, 22 (bottom), 24, 26, 27, 29, 30, 31, 32, 33 (bottom), 34, 39 (centre), 42 (top), 45, 46, 47 (bottom right and top), 48, 49, 52/53, 54/55, 58 (both), 61 (both), 64 (both), 65, 66, 68, 70, 76/77, 82 (bottom), 83, 84 (centre), 85, 86 (bottom), 89, 91, 95 (bottom), 104, 105, 108 (both), 109, 110, 111, 112, 114, 115, 118 (both), 120, 122/123, 126/127, 129 (both), 131 (top and bottom), 132 (both), 133, 134 (top), 135 (both), 136, 137 (top), 153, 154, 155, 156, 172, 182/183, 224 (repeat of 134 top), 226, 235, 240.
Peter Dazeley: front and back covers, 8 (centre), 14, 19 (top), 22 (top), 35, 57 (top), 69, 71 (inset), 96, 97, 101, 102/103, 117 (top), 121, 138 (bottom), 139 (top), 141, 143, 161 (both), 162/163 (both), 174, 178, 181, 191, 195, 198, 199 (bottom), 200.
Douglas Caird: 13, 124
Planet News Ltd: 60 (top), 88
Central Press Photos Limited: 8 (bottom), 62, 84 (left), 119, 137 (bottom)
New York Times Photos: 116 (bottom left), 134 (bottom).
K R Hailey: 9 (centre), 26 (top left), 38 (centre), 43, 57 (bottom), 78
John G Hemmer: 189
G M Cowie, St Andrews: 6, 8, 67 (top), 94 (repeat of 6), 233
Sport and General Press Agency: 10, 21 (top), 94 (repeat of 6), 233
Sport and General Press Agency: 10, 21 (top), 23 (centre), 36, 63 (top), 82 (top).
World Wide Photos: 107 (top)
Tom Scott Library: 67 (bottom), 113, 126, 139, 253
MacGregor Golf Advisory Staff: 130 (centre)
Essex Sport Picture Services: 106

Peter Ayres: 12, 107 (bottom)
Ken Lewis: 63 (centre)
British Transport Films: 183 (top)
Wilson Sporting Goods Co: 15
Sportapics Ltd: 117 (bottom)
The Topical Press Agency Ltd: 18, 92, 93, 131 (centre)
Associated Press Photo: 19 (bottom), 33 (top), 39 (top), 60 (bottom)
J A Hopper: 175
United Press Associations: 20 (top)
International News Photos: 20 (centre)
U P International: 40, 42 (bottom), 87 (right)
Press Association Ltd: 21 (centre), 38 (top)
J D Forbes: 23 (top)
P A Reuter Photos Ltd: 41, 95 (top)
U S Golf Association: 47 (centre), 72, 86 (both), 197
Angus Young: 25, 28 (both), 50/51 (both), 56 (both), 74 (top), 75 (all 5), 79, 98 (top), 122 (inset), 125, 128 (both).
Fox Photos: 71, 130 (bottom)
Jack Nowland: 73
P Chapman: 80, 98/99, 100
Acme Newspictures Inc: 95 (centre)
British Tourist Authority: 165
D R Stuart: 138 (top)
Sidney Harris Ltd: 140
Information Services, Canada House, London: 149
Corfu Golf Club: 151
Ganton Golf Club: 160
Portuguese Tourist Board: 164 (top)
Irish Tourist Board: 164 (bottom), 170/171
Laurel Valley Golf Club: 173
Thailand Tourist Board: 185

Acknowledgements
The author wishes to thank Roy Williams who designed this book and Peter Seddon who drew the diagrams of the courses and the line illustrations.